Alaska Atlas & Gazetteer™

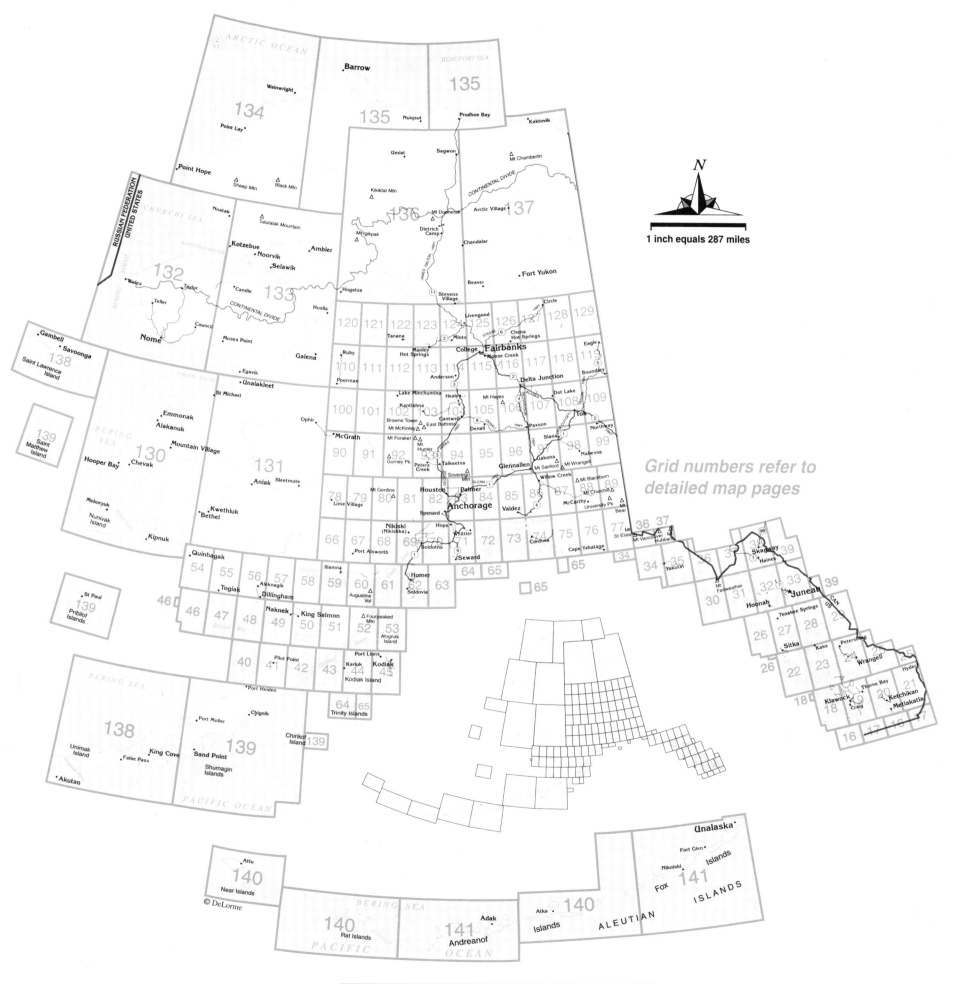

1 inch equals 287 miles

Grid numbers refer to detailed map pages

© DeLorme

Important Notices

DeLorme has made reasonable efforts to provide you with accurate maps and related information, but we cannot exclude the possibility of errors or omissions in sources or of changes in actual conditions. DELORME MAKES NO WARRANTIES OF ANY KIND, EITHER EXPRESS OR IMPLIED, INCLUDING THE WARRANTIES OF MERCHANTABILITY AND FITNESS FOR A PARTICULAR PURPOSE. DELORME SHALL NOT BE LIABLE TO ANY PERSON UNDER ANY LEGAL OR EQUITABLE THEORY FOR DAMAGES ARISING OUT OF THE USE OF THIS PUBLICATION, INCLUDING, WITHOUT LIMITATION, FOR DIRECT, CONSEQUENTIAL OR INCIDENTAL DAMAGES.

Nothing in this publication implies the right to use private property. There may be private inholdings within the boundaries of public reservations. You should respect all landowner restrictions.

Some listings may be seasonal or may have admission fees. Please be sure to confirm this information when making plans.

Safety Information

To avoid accidents, always pay attention to actual road, traffic and weather conditions and do not attempt to read these maps while you are operating a vehicle. Please consult local authorities for the most current information on road and other travel-related conditions.

Do not use this publication for marine or aeronautical navigation, as it does not depict navigation aids, depths, obstacles, landing approaches and other information necessary to performing these functions safely.

FOURTH EDITION. Copyright © 2001 DeLorme. All rights reserved.
P.O. Box 298, Yarmouth, Maine 04096   (207) 846-7000   www.delorme.com

FOLD OUT

ALASKA
PERSPECTIVES

PUBLIC LAND STATUS

Barrow
Kotzebue
Fort Yukon
Nome
Fairbanks
DENALI NATIONAL PARK
Anchorage
Juneau
Attu Island

© DeLorme

LEGEND

- National Forests, Parks or Wildlife Refuges
- BLM Lands
- State Lands
- Native Lands
- Major Military Lands

(Less than 1% of the land in Alaska is privately owned.)

EARLY NATIVE DISTRIBUTION

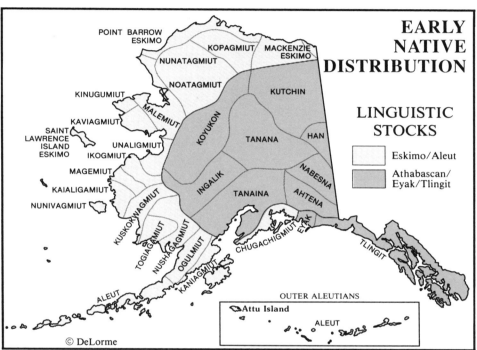

POINT BARROW ESKIMO
KOPAGMIUT
MACKENZIE ESKIMO
NUNATAGMIUT
NOATAGMIUT
KUTCHIN
KINUGUMIUT
MALEMIUT
KAVIAGMIUT
SAINT LAWRENCE ISLAND ESKIMO
UNALIGMIUT
IKOGMIUT
KOYUKON
TANANA
HAN
MAGEMIUT
KAIALIGAMIUT
INGALIK
NABESNA
NUNIVAGMIUT
TANAINA
AHTENA
KUSKOKWAGMIUT
TOGIAGAMIUT
NUSHAGAGMIUT
OGULMIUT
KANIAGMIUT
CHUGACHIGMIUT
EYAK
TLINGIT
ALEUT

LINGUISTIC STOCKS

- Eskimo/Aleut
- Athabascan/Eyak/Tlingit

OUTER ALEUTIANS
Attu Island
ALEUT

© DeLorme

PERMAFROST REGIONS

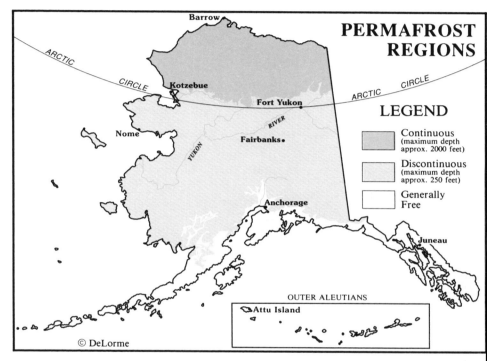

Barrow
ARCTIC CIRCLE
Kotzebue
Fort Yukon
ARCTIC CIRCLE
Nome
YUKON RIVER
Fairbanks
Anchorage
Juneau
OUTER ALEUTIANS
Attu Island

LEGEND

- Continuous (maximum depth approx. 2000 feet)
- Discontinuous (maximum depth approx. 250 feet)
- Generally Free

© DeLorme

TEMPERATURE/PRECIPITATION/DAYLIGHT HOURS
average minimum/maximum temperatures (Fahrenheit); precipitation in inches

		Anchorage	Barrow	Bethel	Fairbanks	Juneau	Ketchikan	Kodiak	Nome	
January	Temperature	8/25	−20/−14	−5/13	−17/−1	22/29	26/38	24/33	−4/13	Temperature
	Precipitation	0.80	0.20	0.81	0.55	3.98	14.01	0.88	0.88	Precipitation
	Daylight Hours	6:25	0	6:31	5:07	7:07	7:43	7:16	5:16	Daylight Hours
February	Temperature	13/27	−24/−20	−2/20	−17/7	25/36	30/40	24/37	−8/10	Temperature
	Precipitation	0.86	0.18	0.71	0.41	3.66	12.36	5.67	0.56	Precipitation
	Daylight Hours	9:04	6:58	9:07	8:31	9:23	9:41	9:28	8:34	Daylight Hours
March	Temperature	12/35	−30/−15	4/26	−5/23	30/40	31/44	27/39	−4/14	Temperature
	Precipitation	0.65	0.15	0.80	0.37	3.24	12.22	5.16	0.63	Precipitation
	Daylight Hours	11:44	11:32	11:41	11:41	11:46	11:48	11:46	11:41	Daylight Hours
April	Temperature	26/45	−8/3	14/36	18/41	37/49	36/49	30/40	7/25	Temperature
	Precipitation	0.63	0.20	0.65	0.28	2.83	11.93	4.47	0.67	Precipitation
	Daylight Hours	14:42	16:31	14:39	15:10	14:24	14:08	14:21	15:08	Daylight Hours
May	Temperature	36/55	14/24	32/51	35/60	38/55	40/59	36/52	26/40	Temperature
	Precipitation	0.63	0.16	0.83	0.57	3.46	9.06	6.65	0.58	Precipitation
	Daylight Hours	17:27	24:00	17:21	18:39	16:47	16:12	16:39	18:29	Daylight Hours
June	Temperature	46/62	28/39	42/61	46/68	43/63	46/63	41/56	38/54	Temperature
	Precipitation	1.02	0.36	1.29	1.29	3.02	7.36	5.72	1.14	Precipitation
	Daylight Hours	19:18	24:00	19:07	21:39	18:15	17:26	18:04	21:21	Daylight Hours
July	Temperature	51/65	34/45	45/66	50/72	48/65	50/64	48/60	45/57	Temperature
	Precipitation	1.96	0.87	2.18	1.84	4.09	7.80	3.80	2.18	Precipitation
	Daylight Hours	18:27	24:00	18:21	20:11	17:36	16:54	17:26	20:00	Daylight Hours
August	Temperature	45/64	34/44	46/61	45/67	48/65	51/66	49/60	45/56	Temperature
	Precipitation	2.31	0.97	3.65	1.82	5.10	10.60	4.03	3.20	Precipitation
	Daylight Hours	15:51	19:03	15:47	16:35	15:25	15:02	15:20	16:31	Daylight Hours
September	Temperature	40/55	28/35	38/53	35/55	44/58	45/59	45/55	35/47	Temperature
	Precipitation	2.51	0.64	2.58	1.02	6.25	13.61	7.18	2.59	Precipitation
	Daylight Hours	12:57	13:31	12:56	13:06	12:51	12:46	12:50	13:05	Daylight Hours
October	Temperature	26/42	9/19	24/38	16/31	38/49	41/51	35/49	23/33	Temperature
	Precipitation	1.86	0.51	1.48	0.81	7.64	22.55	7.85	1.38	Precipitation
	Daylight Hours	10:07	8:51	10:09	9:47	11:15	11:31	10:22	9:48	Daylight Hours
November	Temperature	15/28	−7/4	11/30	−7/11	30/38	35/45	30/43	10/20	Temperature
	Precipitation	1.08	0.27	0.98	0.67	5.13	17.90	6.89	1.02	Precipitation
	Daylight Hours	7:18	2:37	7:23	6:19	7:52	8:22	7:59	6:25	Daylight Hours
December	Temperature	6/21	−19/−12	−2/19	−15/0	25/33	31/39	25/35	−4/11	Temperature
	Precipitation	1.06	0.17	0.95	0.73	4.48	15.82	7.39	0.82	Precipitation
	Daylight Hours	5:32	0	5:41	3:49	6:25	7:08	6:35	4:00	Daylight Hours

SIZE COMPARISON

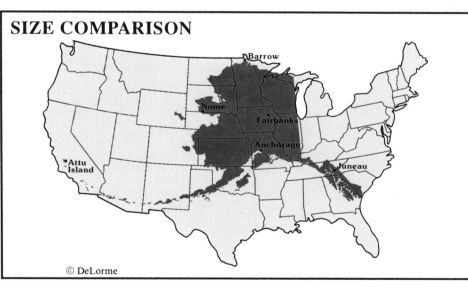

Barrow
Nome
Fairbanks
Anchorage
Attu Island
Juneau

© DeLorme

POLAR VIEW
(air distances in miles)

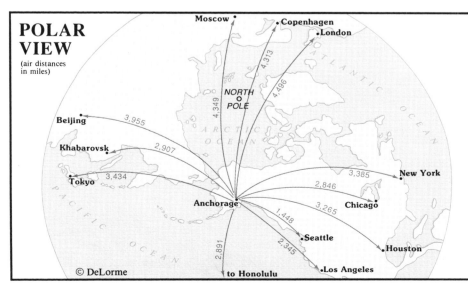

Moscow
Copenhagen
London
4,313
Beijing 3,955
4,349 NORTH POLE
4,490
Khabarovsk 2,907
3,385
Tokyo 3,434
New York
2,846
Anchorage
3,265 Chicago
1,448
2,891 Seattle
Houston
2,345
to Honolulu
Los Angeles

© DeLorme

ALASKA
PHYSICAL RELIEF

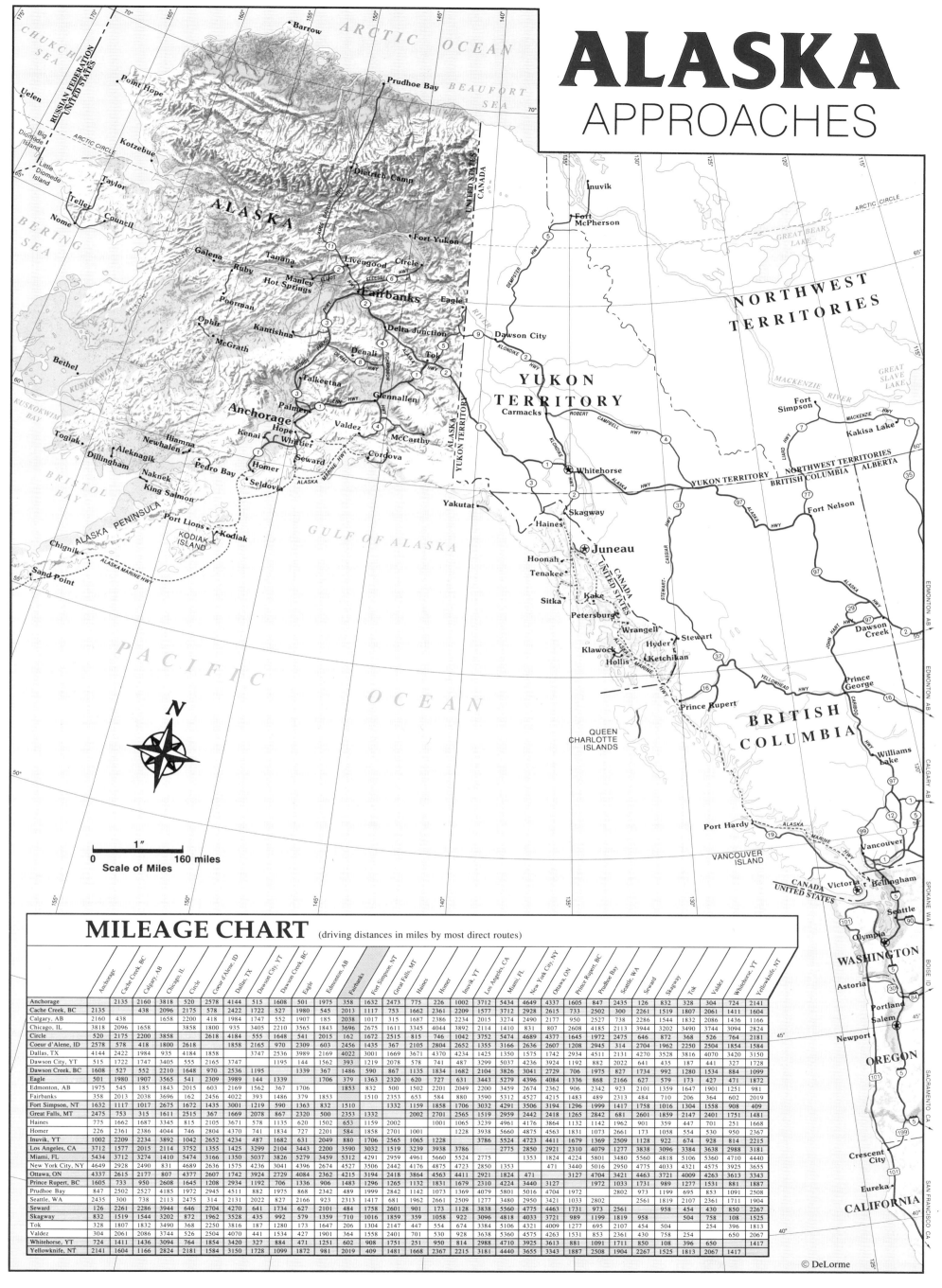

ALASKA
APPROACHES

MILEAGE CHART (driving distances in miles by most direct routes)

	Anchorage	Cache Creek, BC	Calgary, AB	Chicago, IL	Circle	Coeur d'Alene, ID	Dallas, TX	Dawson City, YT	Dawson Creek, BC	Eagle	Edmonton, AB	Fairbanks	Fort Simpson, NT	Great Falls, MT	Haines	Homer	Inuvik, YT	Los Angeles, CA	Miami, FL	New York City, NY	Ottawa, ON	Prince Rupert, BC	Prudhoe Bay	Seattle, WA	Seward	Skagway	Tok	Valdez	Whitehorse, YT	Yellowknife, NT
Anchorage		2135	2160	3818	520	2578	4144	515	1608	501	1975	358	1632	2473	775	226	1002	3712	5434	4649	4337	1605	847	2435	126	832	328	304	724	2141
Cache Creek, BC	2135		438	2096	2175	578	2422	1722	527	1980	545	2013	1117	753	1662	2361	2209	1577	3712	2928	2615	733	2502	300	2261	1519	1807	2061	1411	1604
Calgary, AB	2160	438		1658	2200	418	1984	1747	552	1907	185	2038	1017	315	1687	2386	2234	2015	3274	2490	2177	950	2527	738	2286	1544	1832	2086	1436	1166
Chicago, IL	3818	2096	1658		3858	1800	935	3405	2210	3565	1843	3696	2675	1611	3345	4044	3892	2114	1410	831	807	2608	4185	2113	3944	3202	3490	3744	3094	2824
Circle	520	2175	2200	3858		2618	4184	555	1648	541	2015	162	1672	2515	815	746	1042	3752	5474	4689	4377	1645	1972	2475	646	872	368	526	764	2181
Coeur d'Alene, ID	2578	578	418	1800	2618		1858	2165	970	2309	603	2456	1435	367	2105	2804	2652	1355	3166	2636	2607	1208	2945	314	2704	1962	2250	2504	1854	1584
Dallas, TX	4144	2422	1984	935	4184	1858		3747	2536	3989	2169	4022	3001	1669	3671	4370	4234	1425	1350	1575	1742	2934	4511	2131	4270	3528	3816	4070	3420	3150
Dawson City, YT	515	1722	1747	3405	555	2165	3747		1195	144	1562	393	1219	2078	578	741	487	3299	5037	4236	4084	1192	882	2022	641	435	187	441	327	1728
Dawson Creek, BC	1608	527	552	2210	1648	970	2536	1195		1339	367	1486	590	867	1135	1834	1682	2104	3826	3041	2729	706	1975	827	1734	992	1280	1534	884	1099
Eagle	501	1980	1907	3565	541	2309	3989	144	1339		1706	379	1363	2320	620	727	631	3443	5279	4236	4084	1336	868	2166	627	579	173	427	471	1872
Edmonton, AB	1975	545	185	1843	2015	603	2169	1562	367	1706		1853	832	500	1502	2201	2049	2200	3459	2674	2362	906	2342	923	2101	1359	1647	1901	1251	981
Fairbanks	358	2013	2038	3696	162	2456	4022	393	1486	379	1853		1510	2353	653	584	880	3590	5312	4527	4215	1483	489	2313	484	710	206	364	602	2019
Fort Simpson, NT	1632	1117	1017	2675	1672	1435	3001	1219	590	1363	832	1510		1332	1159	1858	1706	3032	4291	3506	3194	1296	1999	1417	1758	1016	1304	1558	908	409
Great Falls, MT	2475	753	315	1611	2515	367	1669	2078	867	2320	500	2353	1332		2002	2701	2515	1519	2959	2442	2418	1265	2842	681	2601	1859	2147	2401	1751	1481
Haines	775	1662	1687	3345	815	2105	3671	578	1135	620	1502	653	1159	2002		1001	1065	3239	4961	4176	3864	1132	1142	1962	359	447	701	530	251	2002
Homer	226	2361	2386	4044	746	2804	4370	741	1834	727	2201	584	1858	2701	1001		1228	3938	5660	4875	4563	1831	1073	2661	173	1058	554	530	950	2367
Inuvik, YT	1002	2209	2234	3892	1042	2652	4234	487	1682	631	2049	880	1706	2515	1065	1228		3786	5524	4723	4411	1369	1228	2509	1128	922	674	928	814	2215
Los Angeles, CA	3712	1577	2015	2114	3752	1355	1425	3299	2104	3443	2200	3590	3032	1519	3239	3938	3786		2775	2850	2921	2310	4079	1277	3838	3096	3384	3638	2988	3181
Miami, FL	5434	3712	3274	1410	5474	3166	1350	5037	3826	5279	3459	5312	4291	2959	4961	5660	5524	2775		1353	1208	2945	5801	3480	5560	4818	5106	5360	4710	4440
New York City, NY	4649	2928	2490	831	4689	2636	1575	4236	3041	4396	2674	4527	3506	2442	4176	4875	4723	2850	1353		471	3440	5016	2950	4775	4033	4321	4575	3925	3655
Ottawa, ON	4337	2615	2177	807	4377	2607	1742	3924	2706	4084	2362	4215	3194	2418	3864	4563	4411	2921	1208	471		3127	4704	3421	4463	3721	4009	4263	3613	3343
Prince Rupert, BC	1605	733	950	2608	1645	1208	2934	1192	706	1336	906	1483	1296	1265	1132	1831	1369	2310	2945	3440	3127		1972	1033	1731	989	1277	1531	881	1887
Prudhoe Bay	847	2502	2527	4185	1972	2945	4511	882	1975	868	2342	489	1999	2842	1142	1073	1228	4079	5801	5016	4704	1972		2802	973	1199	695	853	1091	2508
Seattle, WA	2435	300	738	2113	2475	314	2131	2022	827	2166	923	2313	1417	681	1962	2661	2509	1277	3480	2950	3421	1033	2802		2561	1819	2107	2361	1711	1904
Seward	126	2261	2286	3944	646	2704	4270	641	1734	627	2101	484	1758	2601	359	173	1128	3838	5560	4775	4463	1731	973	2561		958	454	430	850	2267
Skagway	832	1519	1544	3202	872	1962	3528	435	992	579	1359	710	1016	1859	447	1058	922	3096	4818	4033	3721	989	1199	1819	958		504	758	108	1525
Tok	328	1807	1832	3490	368	2250	3816	187	1280	173	1647	206	1304	2147	701	554	674	3384	5106	4321	4009	1277	695	2107	454	504		254	396	1813
Valdez	304	2061	2086	3744	526	2504	4070	441	1534	427	1901	364	1558	2401	530	530	928	3638	5360	4575	4263	1531	853	2361	430	758	254		650	2067
Whitehorse, YT	724	1411	1436	3094	764	1854	3420	327	884	471	1251	602	908	1751	251	950	814	2988	4710	3925	3613	881	1091	1711	850	108	396	650		1417
Yellowknife, NT	2141	1604	1166	2824	2181	1584	3150	1728	1099	1872	981	2019	409	1481	1668	2367	2215	3181	4440	3655	3343	1887	2508	1904	2267	1525	1813	2067	1417	

© DeLorme

Visitor Information Centers

There are numerous local, regional and state visitor information centers throughout Alaska, found in most major cities and towns and along principal highways. To locate these in the Atlas, look on the maps for the appropriate symbol.

General information is available from the Alaska Division of Tourism, Ninth Floor, State Office Building, Juneau, AK 99811, (907) 465-2010.

For information on all matters relating to public lands, including parks, forests and wildlife refuges, contact one of the Public Lands Information Centers listed here. These offices represent all federal and state land managing agencies, including Alaska Department of Fish and Game, Alaska Department of Natural Resources, National Park Service, US Fish & Wildlife Service, USDA Forest Service, Bureau of Land Management and US Geological Survey.

PUBLIC LANDS INFORMATION CENTERS

605 West Fourth Avenue, Suite 105, Anchorage, AK 99501, (907) 271-2737 .... Page 82 D3
250 Cushman Street, Suite 1A, Fairbanks, AK 99701, (907) 456-0527 .... Page 115 A5
P.O. Box 359, Tok, AK 99780, (907) 883-5667 .... Page 108 C3

Campgrounds

This chart includes a selected list of private campgrounds in Alaska. To locate these campgrounds in the Atlas, look on the appropriate map for the campground symbol and corresponding four-digit number. For more information contact the Alaska Campground Owners Association, P.O. Box 84884, Fairbanks, AK 99708, (907) 883-5877 or the Alaska Division of Tourism, Ninth Floor, State Office Building, Juneau, AK 99811, (907) 465-2010.

Public campgrounds, shelters and cabins, located on state and federal land, can be identified by the symbols indicated in the Legend. Undeveloped or primitive camping is permitted on many public tracts. Contact the proper land managing agency for more information.

	NAME, LOCATION	TENT SITES	RV SITES	PAGE & GRID
1000	Auke Bay RV Park, Auke Bay		50	33 C3
1005	Best View RV Park, Wasilla	20	64	83 B4
1010	Bing Brown's, Sterling	15	30	70 B1
1020	The Bull Shooter RV Park, Tok	6	49	108 C3
1030	Centennial Park Campgrounds, Soldotna	160	160	69 C5
1040	Chandalar RV Park, Willow	25	58	93 D6
1050	Clover Pass Resort, Ketchikan		32	20 C1
1060	Cripple Creek Resort, Ester		16	115 A4
1070	Crooked Creek RV Park, Kasilof	21	41	69 C5
1080	Crow Creek Gold Mine, Girdwood	10	20	71 A4
1090	Denali Grizzly Bear Campground, McKinley Village	30	30	104 B3
1100	Eagle Claw RV, Valdez	20	175	85 D5
1110	Funny River Fish Camp, Soldotna	6	5	70 C1
1120	Green Ridge Camper Park, Wasilla	50	37	83 B4
1130	H & H Lakeview Campground, Sunshine	40	20	93 D6
1140	Haines Hitch-Up RV Park, Haines		92	38 D2
1150	Harris River Wilderness Cabins, Hollis	10	3	19 C4
1160	Hillside Motel & RV Park, Anchorage		60	82 D3
1170	The Homestead RV Park, Palmer	7	60	83 B4
1180	Hylen's Camper Park, Ninilchik		75	69 D4
1190	Kenai Princess RV Park, Cooper Landing		37	70 C3
1200	Kenai Riverbend Campground, Soldotna	50	250	69 B5
1210	Kyllonen's RV Park, Anchor Point	20	30	62 A1
1220	Last Resort, Nenana	4	8	114 B2
1230	Log Cabin Resort & RV Park, Klawock	8	12	19 B3
1240	Lynx Creek Campground, McKinley Park	15	20	104 A3
1250	McKinley KOA, Healy	12	78	104 A2
1260	Mountain Point RV Park, Ketchikan		20	20 C1
1270	Nancy Lake Marina Resort, Willow	20	50	82 B3
1280	Norlite, Fairbanks	75	175	115 A5
1290	Oceanside RV Park, Haines		22	38 D2
1300	Oceanview RV Park, Homer	5	85	62 B1
1320	Port Chilkoot Camper Park, Haines	20	50	38 D2
1330	Rita's Campground, Tok	12	20	108 C2
1340	Sheep Mountain Lodge, Palmer	6	10	84 A3
1350	Sourdough Campground & RV Park, Tok	15	60	108 C2
1360	Sunrise Inn, Cooper Landing	12	12	71 C3
1370	Swiftwater Park Campground, Soldotna	50	50	69 C5
1380	Tanana Valley Campgrounds, Fairbanks	15	20	115 A5
1290	Tatlanika Trading Co. & Museum, Clear	15	11	114 D2
1400	Tok RV Village, Tok	11	84	108 C3
1410	Tolsona Wilderness Campground, Glennallen	30	26	96 D3
1415	Trapper Creek Inn and General Store, Trapper Creek	10	15	93 C6
1420	Twin Creek RV Park, Petersburg		30	24 B1
1440	Willow Island Resort, Willow	50	50	82 A2

National Lands

The federally owned lands listed in this chart cover almost 81 million acres. Most of this land is managed by the Bureau of Land Management, National Park Service or USDA Forest Service. Undeveloped or primitive camping and backcountry hiking are possible in most areas. Check with the proper authorities for hunting and fishing rules, regulations and restrictions.

For more information on any area, contact one of the Public Lands Information Centers listed in Visitor Information Centers *above.*

ACCESS ABBREVIATIONS
A – air   L – land   W – water

NAME, LOCATION	ACCESS	ACREAGE	CAMPSITES	CABINS/SHELTERS	BOATING	HIKING	FISHING	HUNTING	COMMENTS	PAGE & GRID
Admiralty Island National Monument – Kootznoowoo Wilderness, Tongass National Forest	AW	955,921		●	●		●	●	Called Kootznoowoo ("Fortress of the Bears") by Tlingit Indians because of large brown bear population. Largest concentration of nesting bald eagles in world.	27 B4
Aniakchak National Monument and Preserve, King Salmon	A	600,000		●	●		●	●	Very remote, extensive volcanic area. Central feature, Aniakchak Caldera *(see Float Trips and Unique Natural Features).*	139 B5
Bering Land Bridge National Preserve, Nome	A	2,700,000			●		●		Remnant of land bridge that connected Asia and North America. Neighboring Eskimo villages. Hot springs.	132 B3
Cape Krusenstern National Monument, Kotzebue	AW	660,000			●		●		114 beach ridges along arctic coastal plain record changing shorelines of Chukchi Sea and 6,000 years of prehistoric human use *(see Historic Sites/Museums).*	132 A4
Chena River Lakes Project, Fairbanks	L	19,710	●		●	●	●		Northernmost US flood control project. Multiuse recreation area including 250-acre lake with swimming beach.	115 A6
Chuck River Wilderness, Tongass National Forest	AW	74,298			●		●	●	Steep terrain. Fiords popular for kayaking.	28 B3
Chugach National Forest, Anchorage	ALW	5,469,226	●	●	●	●	●	●	Second largest forest in US. Portage and Columbia Glaciers and Copper River Delta *(see Unique Natural Features and Wildlife Refuges).* 200 miles of hiking trails *(see Hiking).*	71 A4
Coronation Island Wilderness, Tongass National Forest	AW	19,232			●		●	●	Undeveloped island with windswept beaches, cliffs and rocky shoreline. Peaks rising to nearly 2,000 feet. Access difficult.	18 A1
Denali National Park and Preserve, McKinley Park	AL	6,000,000	●			●	●	●	Spectacular subarctic wilderness with massive Mt. McKinley as towering centerpiece. Short loop trails and backcountry hiking. Mountaineering. 91-mile Denali Park Road. Barren-ground caribou, grizzly bears, moose, wolves and Dall sheep. Includes 1.9-million-acre Wilderness.	104 B2
Endicott River Wilderness, Tongass National Forest	AW	98,729			●		●	●	Endicott River flows through glacially carved canyon. Terrain from spruce – hemlock rainforest, brush and small trees to glacial alpine areas over 5,000 feet high.	32 A2
Gates of the Arctic National Park and Preserve, Anaktuvuk Pass	A	8,400,000			●		●	●	Vast arctic tundra and scenic headland of Brooks Range. Inhabited by Nunamiut Eskimo and Athabascan peoples. Major barren-ground caribou range. Includes 7-million-acre Wilderness.	136 C3
Glacier Bay National Park and Preserve, Gustavus	AW	3,300,000	●		●	●	●	●	16 tidewater glaciers. Humpback, minke and orca whales; porpoises and seals. Peaks over 10,000 feet, including Mt. Fairweather (15,300 feet). Glacier tour boats. Includes 2.8-million-acre Wilderness. *(See Unique Natural Features.)*	32 C1
Karta River Wilderness, Tongass National Forest	AW	39,889		●	●	●	●	●	Located on eastern side of Prince of Wales Island. Karta River, Salmon and Karta Lakes. Five-mile hiking trail along river. Four cabins.	19 B4
Katmai National Park and Preserve, King Salmon	AW	4,000,000	●		●	●	●	●	Rich volcanic history with 15 active volcanoes. Critical brown bear habitat. Valley of 10,000 Smokes *(see Unique Natural Features).* Backcountry hiking. Includes 3.5-million-acre Wilderness. *(See Unique Natural Features.)*	50 B3
Kenai Fjords National Park, Seward	ALW	669,000	●	●	●	●	●		Glacially carved coastal mountain fiords. Exit Glacier *(see Unique Natural Features).* Mountain goats, moose, bald eagles, sea lions and seals.	71 D3
Klondike Gold Rush National Historical Park, Skagway	ALW	13,000		●		●	●		Historic center of Klondike Gold Rush surrounded by spectacular wilderness. Chilkoot and White Pass Trails. Visitor center. Museum. *(See Hiking and Historic Sites/Museums.)*	38 C2
Kobuk Valley National Park, Kotzebue	AW	1,700,000			●		●		Arctic area surrounded by Baird and Waring Mountains. Great Kobuk Sand Dunes *(see Unique Natural Features).* Caribou herds. Includes 190,000-acre Wilderness.	133 A6
Kuiu Wilderness, Tongass National Forest	AW	60,581			●	●	●	●	On southern part of Kuiu Island, encompasses many bays and islands. Scenic portage trail from Affleck Canal to Petrof Bay.	23 C3
Lake Clark National Park and Preserve, Anchorage	A	4,000,000			●		●	●	"Alaskan Alps" where Alaska and Aleutian Ranges meet. Iliamna and Redoubt Volcanoes *(see Unique Natural Features).* 50-mile-long Lake Clark. River running. Includes 2.5-million-acre Wilderness.	67 D4
Maurelle Islands Wilderness, Tongass National Forest	AW	4,937			●		●	●	Group of nearly 30 islands rising to 400 feet above sea level. Rocky shoals and windformed trees.	18 B2
Misty Fiords National Monument Wilderness, Tongass National Forest	AW	2,142,243		●	●	●	●	●	Steep-walled canyons, glaciers and long, narrow fiords. Diverse wildlife. Annual precipitation 150 inches.	21 B3
Noatak National Preserve, Kotzebue	A	6,500,000			●		●	●	Large arctic river basin ringed by mountains of Brooks Range. Excellent canoeing and kayaking on gentle, slow-moving Noatak River *(see Float Trips).* Includes 5.8-million-acre Wilderness.	133 A4
Petersburg Creek – Duncan Salt Chuck Wilderness, Tongass National Forest	AW	46,777		●	●	●	●	●	Popular recreation area located on Kupreanof Island.	24 A1
Pleasant – Lemesurier – Inian Islands Wilderness, Tongass National Forest	W	23,096			●			●	Several islands in Icy Strait near Gustavus. Wildlife includes whales, sea otters and cliff-nesting shorebirds.	32 C1
Russell Fiord Wilderness, Tongass National Forest	ALW	348,701		●	●	●	●	●	Russell and Nunatak Fiords, tidewater glaciers, icebergs. Snow-capped mountain peaks to 8,460 feet.	35 B4
Sitka National Historical Park, Sitka	AW	106				●			Park commemorates 1804 Battle of Sitka. Town important hub of 19th-century Russian America. *(See Historic Sites/Museums.)*	27 D3
South Baranof Wilderness, Tongass National Forest	AW	319,568		●	●	●	●	●	Dense coastal rainforest on southern Baranof Island. Annual precipitation over 200 inches. 4,000-foot mountains and numerous glaciers.	22 B2
South Etolin Island Wilderness, Tongass National Forest	W	83,371			●		●	●	Located on south end of Etolin Island. Numerous passages and small islands.	24 D2
South Prince of Wales Wilderness, Tongass National Forest	AW	90,996		●	●		●	●	Southern tip of Prince of Wales Island. Low tidal wetlands to 2,000-foot rock walls. Klinkwan, 19th-century deserted Indian village. Includes 75 smaller islands.	17 A4
Steese National Conservation Area, Chena Hot Springs	L	1,200,000			●	●	●	●	Primary attractions Birch Creek National Wild River *(see Float Trips)* and Pinnell Mountain National Recreation Trail *(see Hiking).*	126 C3
Stikine – LeConte Wilderness, Tongass National Forest	AW	448,841		●	●		●	●	Stikine River surrounded by rugged, glaciated peaks. LeConte Glacier *(see Unique Natural Features).* Popular recreation area. Hot springs.	24 B2
Tebenkof Bay Wilderness, Tongass National Forest	AW	66,839			●	●	●	●	Located on west side of Kuiu Island. Dense rainforest, small islands, coves; alpine terrain above 2,000 feet. Kayaking in Tebenkof Bay.	23 B3
Tongass National Forest, Juneau	AW	16,500,000	●	●	●	●	●	●	Largest US national forest. 19 wilderness areas *(see this section).* Islands, glaciers, rainforest, fiords. Mendenhall Glacier *(see Unique Natural Features).* Over 400 miles of trails *(see Hiking).*	32 B3
Tracy Arm – Fords Terror Wilderness, Tongass National Forest	AW	653,179			●		●	●	Two long, narrow fiords with tidewater glaciers continually calving icebergs. Rugged mountains, valleys and high waterfalls.	28 B3
Trans-Alaska Pipeline Utility Corridor, Fairbanks	LW	2,780,000			●		●	●	Scenic terrain paralleling pipeline from Yukon River to Prudhoe Bay. Fully traversed by Dalton Highway *(see Scenic Drives).*	124 A1
Warren Island Wilderness, Tongass National Forest	AW	11,181			●		●	●	Windswept beaches, cliffs, rocky shoreline. Peaks over 2,000 feet, including Warren Peak at 2,329 feet. Access very difficult.	18 A2
West Chichagof – Yakobi Wilderness, Tongass National Forest	AW	264,747		●	●	●	●	●	Rugged mountain terrain on two islands. 65 miles of Pacific Ocean coastline.	26 C2
White Mountains National Recreation Area, Fairbanks	L	1,000,000		●	●	●	●	●	Unusual limestone cliffs. Beaver Creek National Wild River. Summer hiking and extensive winter trails. *(See Float Trips, Hiking and Unique Natural Features.)*	125 D4
Wrangell – St. Elias National Park and Preserve, Glennallen	AL	13,000,000			●		●	●	Largest US national park. Massive mountains, canyons, glaciers and icefields. Three mountain ranges. Mt. St. Elias and Malaspina Glacier *(see Unique Natural Features).* Includes 8.7-million-acre Wilderness.	97 D4
Yukon – Charley Rivers National Preserve, Eagle	AL	2,500,000			●		●	●	130 miles of Yukon River *(see Unique Natural Features)* and entire 106-mile Charley River *(see Float Trips).* Area untouched by glaciers. Remnants of gold mining era. Prime habitat for endangered peregrine falcon.	129 D6

State Lands

For more information on state parklands, contact one of the Public Lands Information Centers listed in Visitor Information Centers *on page 6.*

ACCESS ABBREVIATIONS
A–air L–land W–water

NAME, NEAREST COMMUNITY	ACCESS	ACREAGE	CAMPSITES	PICNIC AREA	TOILETS	WATER	HIKING	BOAT LAUNCH	FISHING	COMMENTS	PAGE & GRID
Anchor River State Recreation Area, Homer	L	213	38		●	●			●	Located at most westerly point of US highway system. Popular fishing and camping area.	62 A1
Anchor River State Recreation Site, Homer	L	53	9		●	●			●	Campsites among large spruce trees bordering river. Fishing for Dolly Varden.	62 B1
Beecher Pass State Marine Park, Wrangell	AW	660							●	Located on Mitkof Island. Undeveloped.	24 B1
Bernice Lake State Recreation Site, Kenai	L	152	11	●	●	●		●		Quiet, peaceful wayside on small lake.	69 B5
Bettles Bay State Marine Park, Whittier	AW	680							●	Well-protected boat anchorage. Views of Bettles Glacier. Undeveloped.	72 A1
Big Bear/Baby Bear Bays State Marine Park, Sitka	AW	1,023							●	Located in Peril Strait. Undeveloped.	27 B2
Big Delta State Historical Park, Delta Junction	L	10			●	●	●			Historic crossroad. Rika's Roadhouse. Museum. *(See Historic Sites/Museums.)*	116 D3
Big Lake North State Recreation Site, Big Lake	L	19	60	●	●	●		●	●	Swimming, boating, waterskiing and sailing. Ice fishing and skating.	82 B3
Big Lake South State Recreation Site, Big Lake	L	16	20	●	●	●		●	●	Same recreational activities as northern unit *(see above)*.	82 B3
Birch Lake State Recreation Site, Delta Junction	L	191	10		●			●	●	Lake stocked with rainbow trout and silver salmon.	116 C1
Blueberry Lake State Recreation Site, Valdez	L	192	15	●	●		●		●	Panoramic views of Chugach Range, glaciers and Keystone Canyon area.	86 D1
Bonnie Lake State Recreation Site, Palmer	L	129	8		●			●	●	One-mile-long lake. Boating and canoeing. Fishing for trout, salmon and grayling.	84 A1
Boswell Bay State Marine Park, Cordova	AW	799							●	Located on Hinchinbrook Island. Beachcombing and hunting. Undeveloped.	73 C5
Buskin River State Recreation Site, Kodiak	ALW	196	18	●	●	●	●		●	Popular fishing spot. Sandy ocean beach. WWII military remnants.	45 A5
Caines Head State Recreation Area, Seward	LW	5,961	4	●	●		●		●	Beaches, alpine meadows, jagged peaks. Sweeping ocean views. Abandoned WWII fort. Coastal Trail *(see Hiking)*.	71 D4
Canoe Passage State Marine Park, Cordova	AW	2,735							●	Located on Hawkins Island. Undeveloped.	73 B5
Captain Cook State Recreation Area, Kenai	L	3,466	65	●	●	●	●	●	●	Forests, lakes, streams, saltwater beaches on Cook Inlet. Swimming. Remains of Tanaina Indian barabaras (housepits).	69 A5
Chena River State Recreation Area, Fairbanks	L	254,080	61	●	●	●	●		●	Multiuse area along winding stretch of Chena River. Ten separate recreation sites. Three hiking trails. Cross-country ski trails.	116 A1
Chena River State Recreation Site, Fairbanks	L	27	59	●	●	●		●	●	Located along river in Fairbanks.	115 A5
Chilkat Islands State Marine Park, Haines	AW	6,560							●	Located in Lynn Canal. Undeveloped.	38 D2
Chilkat State Park, Haines	LW	6,045	15	●	●	●	●	●	●	Spectacular glacier views across Chilkat Inlet. Coastline trail.	38 D2
Chilkoot Lake State Recreation Site, Haines	L	80	32	●	●	●		●	●	Campsites along scenic lakeshore.	38 C1
Chugach State Park, Anchorage	ALW	495,204	125	●	●	●	●		●	Accessible, pristine wilderness in Anchorage backyard. Spectacular alpine scenery. Tidal bore *(see Unique Natural Features)*.	83 D4
Clam Gulch State Recreation Area, Soldotna	L	129	116	●	●	●			●	Panoramic views of Aleutian Mountain Range. Popular razor clamming area.	69 D5
Clearwater State Recreation Site, Delta Junction	L	27	18		●	●		●	●	Grayling fishing. Access to Tanana and Goodpaster Rivers. Migrating sandhill cranes.	117 D4
Crooked Creek State Recreation Site, Soldotna	L	49	75	●	●	●	●		●	Bank fishing for king and silver salmon and steelhead.	69 C5
Dall Bay State Marine Park, Ketchikan	AW	585							●	Located on Gravina Island. Undeveloped.	20 D1
Decision Point State Marine Park, Whittier	AW	460	2						●	Good for kayaks and small boats. Camping beaches. Located in Passage Canal. Undeveloped.	72 A1
Deep Creek State Recreation Area, Ninilchik	L	155	300		●	●		●	●	Fishing for halibut and king salmon. Razor clamming and beachcombing. Bald eagles.	69 D4
Delta State Recreation Site, Delta Junction	AL	7	22	●	●	●				Stopping point for camping between Tok and Fairbanks.	116 D3
Denali State Park, Talkeetna	L	324,240	86	●	●	●	●	●	●	Outstanding views of Mt. McKinley *(see Unique Natural Features)* from highway and Kesugi Ridge.	93 B6
Donnelly Creek State Recreation Site, Delta Junction	L	42	12		●	●				Scenic campground with views of Alaska Range. Delta Junction Bison Range *(see Wildlife Refuges)*.	106 B3
Driftwood Bay State Marine Park, Seward	AW	1,480							●	Located in Day Harbor. Popular boat anchorage. Mountain views. Undeveloped.	64 A1
Dry Creek State Recreation Site, Glennallen	L	372	58	●	●	●	●		●	Area heavily timbered with birch and spruce.	97 D4
Eagle Trail State Recreation Site, Tok	L	640	40	●	●	●	●			Scenic setting against Alaska Range. Alpine hiking and wildlife viewing. Dall sheep. Valdez-to-Eagle Trail.	108 D2
Entry Cove State Marine Park, Whittier	AW	370	1						●	Boat anchorage. Views of Tebenkof Glacier. Located at Point Pigot. Undeveloped.	72 A1
Fielding Lake State Recreation Site, Delta Junction	L	300	7		●			●	●	Scenic campground at 2,973-foot elevation in Alaska Range.	106 D3
Finger Lake State Recreation Site, Palmer	L	47	41	●	●	●	●	●	●	Water recreation area. Swimming, boating, canoeing and sailing.	83 B4
Ft. Abercrombie State Historical Park, Kodiak	ALW	183	14	●	●	●	●		●	Remains of WWII fort *(see Historic Sites/Museums)*. Trails through stands of Sitka spruce. Whale/puffin watching. Tide pools.	45 A5
Funter Bay State Marine Park, Juneau	AW	162							●	Located on Admiralty Island. Boat dock. Undeveloped.	32 C3
Granite Bay State Marine Park, Whittier	AW	2,105							●	Anchorages in two bays. Located on Esther Island. Undeveloped.	72 A1
Gruening State Historical Park, Juneau	AW	12							●	Home and grounds of last Alaska territorial governor and first US Senator, Ernest Gruening. Good fishing access.	32 C3
Haines State Forest and Resource Mgmt Area, Haines	LW	250,600					●		●	Undeveloped, multiple-use forest with diverse terrain and habitats. 35 miles of logging roads for recreational use. Hunting.	38 C1
Halibut Point State Recreation Site, Sitka	AW	22		●	●	●	●		●	Day-use area. Forest trails. Salmon stream. Rain shelters.	27 D3
Harding Lake State Recreation Area, Delta Junction	L	169	89	●	●	●	●	●	●	One of few road-accessible recreation lakes in interior Alaska.	116 C1
Horseshoe Bay State Marine Park, Seward	AW	970							●	Located on Latouche Island. Boat anchorage. Undeveloped.	72 D2
Independence Mine State Historical Park, Palmer	L	761			●	●	●			Historic gold mine located in rugged Talkeetna Mountains *(see Historic Sites/Museums)*.	83 A4
Jack Bay State Marine Park, Valdez	AW	811	5						●	Located in Valdez Arm. Fair-weather anchorage. Undeveloped.	85 D4
Joe Mace Island State Marine Park, Wrangell	AW	62							●	Located in Sumner Strait. Undeveloped.	23 C4
Johnson Creek State Recreation Site, Juneau	AW	65								Undeveloped area.	33 C3
Johnson Lake State Recreation Area, Soldotna	L	324	50	●	●	●		●	●	Campground with lake views. Swimming and canoeing. Year-round rainbow trout and kokanee fishing.	69 C5
Juneau Trail System State Trail, Juneau	LW	15					●		●	Five trails totaling 14.7 miles, including Mt. Juneau and Perseverance *(see Hiking)*.	33 C4
Kachemak Bay State Park and Wilderness Park, Homer	AW	368,290	8	●	●		●		●	Scenic, high mountain terrain. Fiords, coves and vast glacier fields. Beachcombing. Numerous hiking trails.	62 B2
Kasilof River State Recreation Site, Soldotna	L	50	16		●	●	●		●	Campground located on Kasilof River.	69 C5
Kayak Island State Marine Park, Cordova	AW	1,437							●	Island located in Gulf of Alaska. Landing site of 1741 Bering Expedition. Undeveloped.	65 B5
Kenai River Special Management Area, Sterling	LW	2,170	138	●	●	●	●	●	●	More than 105 miles of rivers and lakes. Prime area for fishing, boating, camping and wildlife viewing.	70 C2
Kepler–Bradley Lakes State Recreation Area, Palmer	L	344		●	●	●	●	●	●	Day-use area. Seven lakes stocked with grayling, rainbow trout and silver salmon. Equestrian trails.	83 B4
King Mountain State Recreation Site, Palmer	L	20	22	●	●	●				Views of King Mountain and glacier-fed Matanuska River.	84 A1
Lake Louise State Recreation Area, Glennallen	L	90	36	●	●	●		●	●	20-mile-long chain of lakes. Fishing for lake trout and grayling. Berry picking.	96 C1
Liberty Falls State Recreation Site, Chitina	L	10	8		●		●			Scenic waterfalls.	87 B3
Little Nelchina State Recreation Site, Glennallen	L	22	11		●		●	●	●	Convenient rest area and overnight stop for travelers. Access point for hunters.	85 A4
Little Susitna River Public Use Facility, Wasilla	L	38	145	●	●	●	●	●	●	Located within Susitna Flats State Game Refuge *(see Wildlife Refuges)*.	82 C2
Little Tonsina State Recreation Site, Copper Center	L	103	8		●	●			●	Overnight stop near Trans-Alaska Pipeline. Fishing for grayling.	86 C2
Long Lake State Recreation Site, Palmer	L	480	9		●	●		●	●	Located in valley at edge of Talkeetna Mountains. Deep, mile-long lake. Fishing for grayling.	84 A1
Lower Chatanika State Recreation Area, Fairbanks	L	570	65	●	●	●		●	●	Large pond for swimming, non-motorized boating and fishing.	125 D5
Magoun Islands State Marine Park, Sitka	AW	1,130							●	Located in Krestof Sound. Undeveloped.	27 D2
Matanuska Glacier State Recreation Site, Palmer	L	229	12		●	●	●			Panoramic views of Matanuska Glacier *(see Unique Natural Features)* and Chugach Mountains.	84 A2
Montana Creek State Recreation Site, Talkeetna	L	82	89	●	●	●	●		●	Salmon fishing.	93 D6
Moon Lake State Recreation Site, Tok	L	22	15		●	●		●		Scenic location between Tanana River and Alaska Range.	108 C1
Moose Creek State Recreation Site, Palmer	L	40	12	●	●	●	●		●	Convenient base camp while touring Matanuska Valley.	83 B4
Mosquito Lake State Recreation Site, Haines	L	5	10		●	●		●	●	Small, quiet lake with fishing for cutthroat trout and Dolly Varden.	37 C5
Nancy Lake State Recreation Area, Willow	L	22,685	98	●	●	●	●	●	●	Extensive lake-studded area. Canoe trail system *(see Float Trips)*. 12 public-use cabins.	82 B2
Nancy Lake State Recreation Site, Willow	L	36	30	●	●	●		●	●	Swimming, waterskiing and sailing. Fishing for red salmon and rainbow trout.	82 B2
Ninilchik State Recreation Area, Ninilchik	L	97	165	●	●	●			●	Popular beach for razor clamming. Forest and beach campgrounds.	69 D4
Old Sitka State Historical Park, Sitka	AW	51			●		●	●	●	Historic settlement *(see Historic Sites/Museums)*. Fish migration observation area.	27 D3
Oliver Inlet State Marine Park, Juneau	AW	560			●		●	●	●	Located on Admiralty Island. Public-use cabin.	33 D4
Pasagshak State Recreation Site, Kodiak	ALW	20	10		●	●			●	Scenic Pasagshak Bay. Reversing river. King and silver salmon.	45 C5
Pioneer Park State Recreation Site, Sitka	LW	3		●	●	●	●			Day-use picnic area. Short trail along ocean.	27 D3
Point Bridget State Park, Juneau	AW	2,850					●		●	Forested mountains. Wildflower meadows. Rocky ocean beach. Spectacular views. Marine mammals.	32 B3
Porcupine Creek State Recreation Site, Tok	L	240	12		●	●	●		●	Rest area and overnight stop. Fishing for grayling.	98 B1
Portage Cove State Recreation Site, Haines	ALW	7	9	●	●	●			●	Located on bluff with panoramic views of Chilkoot Inlet and mountain ranges.	38 D2
Quartz Lake State Recreation Area, Delta Junction	L	600	16	●	●	●	●	●	●	Fishing for rainbow trout and silver salmon. Trans-Alaska Pipeline *(see Historic Sites/Museums)*.	116 D3
Refuge Cove State Recreation Site, Ketchikan	AW	13		●	●				●	Day-use picnic area located along Tongass Narrows.	20 C1
Rocky Lake State Recreation Site, Big Lake	L	48	10		●	●		●	●	Boating and waterskiing.	82 B3
Safety Cove State Marine Park, Seward	AW	960							●	Located in Day Harbor. Boat anchorage. Beach camping. Views of Ellsworth Glacier. Undeveloped.	64 A1
Salcha River State Recreation Site, Delta Junction	L	61	25	●	●	●		●	●	Fishing for grayling and king and chum salmon. Moose and bear hunting.	116 C1
Sandspit Point State Marine Park, Seward	AW	600							●	Spectacular views of Resurrection Bay and Eldorado Narrows. Beach camping. Tide pools. Undeveloped.	64 A1
Sawmill Bay State Marine Park, Valdez	AW	2,320							●	Located in Valdez Arm. Popular anchorage surrounded by 4,000-foot peaks. Undeveloped.	85 D4
Security Bay State Marine Park, Petersburg	AW	500							●	Located in Chatham Strait. Undeveloped.	23 A3
Settlers Cove State Recreation Site, Ketchikan	AW	38	12	●	●	●	●		●	Scenic swimming beach. Scuba diving. Heavily used picnic area.	20 B1
Shelter Island State Marine Park, Juneau	AW	3,560	1	●	●		●		●	Located in Lynn Canal.	32 C3
Shoup Bay State Marine Park, Valdez	AW	4,560	3						●	Located in Valdez Arm. Boat anchorage. Shoup Glacier. Kittiwake rookery. Undeveloped.	85 D4
Shuyak Island State Park, Kodiak	AW	11,000			●		●		●	Remote, rugged coastal wilderness. Popular hunting and fishing spot. Four public-use cabins.	53 B4
South Esther Island State Marine Park, Whittier	AW	3,360							●	Protected anchorage. Scenic overlooks. Fish hatchery. Located on Esther Island. Undeveloped.	72 A1
Squirrel Creek State Recreation Site, Copper Center	L	350	14		●	●			●	Convenient rest area or overnight stop. Fishing for grayling.	86 B2
St. James Bay State Marine Park, Juneau	AW	10,220					●		●	Located off Lynn Canal. Undeveloped.	32 B2
Stariski State Recreation Site, Homer	L	30	13	●	●	●				Located on high bluff overlooking Cook Inlet with views of Aleutian Chain. Whale whatching.	62 A1
Sullivan Island State Marine Park, Juneau	AW	2,163							●	Located in Lynn Canal. Undeveloped.	32 A2
Summit Lake State Recreation Site, Palmer	L	360					●			Berry picking. Located in Hatcher Pass.	83 A4
Sunny Cove State Marine Park, Seward	AW	960							●	Vertical rock cliffs. Located on Fox Island in Resurrection Bay. Undeveloped.	64 A1
Surprise Cove State Marine Park, Whittier	AW	2,280	7				●		●	Popular anchorage. Short trail. Tide pools. Located in Cochrane Bay. Undeveloped.	72 A1
Taku Harbor State Marine Park, Juneau	AW	700							●	Located in Stephens Passage. Boat dock. Undeveloped.	33 D4
Tanana Valley State Forest, Fairbanks	L	1,786,330	1				●	●	●	Extensive, undeveloped area within Tanana River Basin. Hunting.	115 A4
Thom's Place State Marine Park, Wrangell	AW	1,198							●	Located on Wrangell Island. Undeveloped.	24 D2
Thumb Cove State Marine Park, Seward	AW	720							●	Views of Porcupine Glacier. Located in Resurrection Bay. Undeveloped.	71 D4
Tok River State Recreation Site, Tok	L	38	50	●	●	●	●			Very popular overnight rest area. Canoeing on Tok and Tanana Rivers.	108 C3
Tolsona Creek State Recreation Site, Glennallen	L	600	10		●		●		●	Rest area and overnight stop.	96 D3
Totem Bight State Historical Park, Ketchikan	W	11			●		●			Model coastal Indian village dedicated to southeastern Alaska Native cultures *(see Historic Sites/Museums)*.	20 C1
Upper Chatanika River State Recreation Site, Fairbanks	L	73	15		●	●			●	Access point for river trips *(see Float Trips)*.	125 D6
Willow Creek State Recreation Area, Willow	L	3,583	7	●	●	●			●	Fishing for grayling, rainbow trout; king, chum, silver and pink salmon.	82 A2
Wolf Lake State Recreation Site, Palmer	L	23	4	●	●		●		●	Swimming beach.	83 B4
Wood–Tikchik State Park, Dillingham	AW	1,555,200	3		●				●	Largest US state park. Remote, undeveloped wilderness. Rugged mountains to open tundra. Excellent fishing and boating.	56 B2
Worthington Glacier State Recreation Site, Valdez	L	113		●	●		●			High alpine tundra and many hanging glaciers. Trail leads to glacier *(see Unique Natural Features)*. Visitor center.	86 D1
Zeigler Cove State Marine Park, Whittier	AW	720	1						●	Protected anchorage. Located in Port Wells. Undeveloped.	72 A1

Historic Sites/Museums

For more information on historic sites and museums contact the Alaska Division of Tourism, Ninth Floor, State Office Building, Juneau, AK 99811, (907) 465-2010.

ALASKA HIGHWAY – Delta Junction – Page 116 D3 1,422-mile highway from Dawson Creek, British Columbia, to Delta Junction. Built 1942 in eight months by US Army Corps of Engineers for WWII military transport; originally called Alaska–Canada Military Highway (Alcan). Considered one of 20th century's great engineering achievements. Opened to public 1948.

ALASKA STATE MUSEUM – Juneau – Page 33 C4 Human and natural history. Native culture and art of Alaska. Over 150 wildlife and historical displays, including exhibits on Russian-American history, gold mining, Alaska purchase and Trans-Alaska Pipeline. Full-sized bald eagle nesting tree. Extensive archival photograph collection.

ALASKALAND – Fairbanks – Page 115 A5 44-acre pioneer theme park established 1967 by city to commemorate centennial of Alaska's purchase from Russia. Gold Rush Town features relocated historic buildings, including Wickersham House and Pioneer Museum; Mining Valley depicts Fairbanks gold mining; drydocked Yukon River sternwheeler S.S. *Nenana*, on National Register of Historic Places; Native Village.

ANCHORAGE MUSEUM OF HISTORY AND ART – Anchorage – Page 82 D3 Collections emphasize art, history and Native cultures of Alaska. Sculpture, paintings, works on paper, and traditional and contemporary crafts. Alaska Gallery includes exhibits on archaeology, exploration, Russian settlement, US purchase, gold rush era, WWII and statehood. Full-scale and miniature dioramas illustrate Native culture.

ATTU BATTLEFIELD – Attu Island – Page 140 A1 Site of only WWII battle on North American continent. Island captured by Japan in June 1942, then recaptured by US in three-week bloody and costly battle in May 1943. Loss caused Japan to secretly evacuate other occupied Aleutian island, Kiska, two months later. National Historic Landmark.

BARANOF MUSEUM – Kodiak – Page 45 A5 Collection of Russian, Aleut and Koniag objects from Kodiak and Aleutian Islands. Located in Erskine House, one of oldest Russian buildings in Alaska, built in 1790s as storehouse for sea otter pelts. National Historic Landmark.

BIG DELTA STATE HISTORICAL PARK – Delta Junction – Page 116 D3 Located along Tanana River and Valdez-to-Fairbanks Trail, important crossroad for travelers, traders, gold miners and military in early 1900s. Centerpiece, restored Rika's Roadhouse, functioned as gathering place, post office, fur exchange, restaurant and lodging house from 1909 to 1947. Museum in restored sod-roof log cabin, with displays of pioneer and Athabascan artifacts. *(See State Parklands.)*

CAPE KRUSENSTERN NATIONAL MONUMENT – Kotzebue – Page 132 A4 114 beach ridges record in time sequence estimated 6,000 years of prehistoric human use of coastline. Some archaeological findings older than well-known remains of ancient Greek civilizations on Mediterranean Sea. *(See National Parklands.)*

CARRIE McLAIN MEMORIAL MUSEUM – Nome – Page 132 D3 Displays and artifacts concentrating on Eskimo life and Nome gold rush *(see this section—Gold Rush Days)*. Other exhibits include Bering Land Bridge, Seward Peninsula minerals and history of dog mushing. Extensive photography collection.

CASTLE HILL STATE HISTORIC SITE – Sitka – Page 27 D3 Location of Tlingit Indian village until early 1800s, then site of various headquarters of Russian-American Company during Alaska's Russian occupation. Buildings included impressive Baranof's Castle (burned in 1894), named after first chief Russian manager Alexander Baranof. Site of official transfer of Alaska from Russia to America in 1867 and where first American flag flew. Also first place flag with 49 stars was raised when Alaska achieved statehood in 1959. Interpretive plaques. Panoramic views of Sitka Sound.

CLAUSEN MEMORIAL MUSEUM – Petersburg – Page 24 A1 Concentrates on area's ties to sea. Tlingit Indian and Norwegian pioneer artifacts. Displays of past and current fishing techniques. World record king salmon (126.5 pounds) and chum salmon (36 pounds). Re-created cannery owner's office.

CORDOVA MUSEUM AND HISTORICAL SOCIETY – Cordova – Page 74 B1 Exhibits of area Native and pioneer history. Displays on Copper River and Northwestern Railroad. Original Fresnel lens from Cape St. Elias Lighthouse. Eyak Indian and Chugach Eskimo artifacts.

CORRINGTON MUSEUM OF ALASKAN HISTORY – Skagway – Page 38 C2 History of Alaska from prehistoric times to present, using scrimshawed walrus tusks and original art.

DOG MUSHING MUSEUM – Fairbanks – Page 115 A5 Headquarters of Alaskan Dog Mushers' Association and North American championship race. Exhibit on dog mushing history. Live dog sled demonstrations; slides and videos of dog racing.

EAGLE HISTORIC DISTRICT – Eagle – Page 119 A6 Military, judicial, transportation and communications hub of turn-of-century interior Alaska. Closest American settlement to Klondike Gold Rush *(see this section)*. High point 1905 when polar explorer Roald Amundsen trekked from ice-locked ship in Arctic Ocean to telegraph discovery of Northwest Passage. More than 100 historic buildings remain, including federal courthouse, customs house and Ft. Egbert *(see this section)*. Walking tours conducted by Eagle Historical Society.

FOREST SERVICE INFORMATION CENTER – Juneau – Page 33 C4 Exhibits and films on southeast Alaska history and natural resources. Located in Centennial Hall.

FT. ABERCROMBIE STATE HISTORICAL PARK – Kodiak – Page 45 A5 Fort established in 1941 as part of North Pacific Coastal Defense to protect Kodiak Naval Air Station and Ft. Greely Garrison during WWII Aleutian Campaign. Closed 1945, abandoned 1947, state park established 1969. Remnants of guns and gun carriages, ammunition bunkers, observation platform and other structures. Self-guided walking tour. National Register of Historic Places.

FT. EGBERT – Eagle – Page 119 A6 Established 1899 to help prevent problems among miners during gold rush. High point 1903 under Lieutenant William "Billy" Mitchell as base for construction of 2,000-mile Washington–Alaska Military Cable and Telegraph System (WAMCATS), which provided first direct communication between Alaska and outside world. Restored and partially reconstructed buildings include water wagon shed, granary, quartermaster storehouse, NCO quarters and mule barn. Tours.

GOVERNOR'S MANSION – Juneau – Page 33 C4 Designed 1911 by James Knox Taylor, example of early 20th-century American architecture, with significant design features used to blend structure with site. First occupied 1913 by Territorial Governor Walter E. Clark.

IDITAROD NATIONAL HISTORIC TRAIL – Nome – Page 132 D3 Network of more than 2,300 miles of trails from Nome to Seward, first used by ancient hunters and then by early-20th-century gold seekers. Mail route, "Seward to Nome Mail Trail," until 1924. Named for Athabascan Indian village on Iditarod River near site of 1908 gold discovery. Most famous historic event 1925 when 20 dog mushers carried diptheria serum 674 miles over trail from Nenana to Nome in 127.5 hours. Annual 1,049-mile Iditarod Trail Sled Dog Race, "The Last Great Race," started 1967, commemorates 1925 event, runs from Anchorage to Nome every March. (Note: Length of historic trail and race checkpoints marked in Atlas; *see Legend*. For clarity, maps show trail parallel to railroad tracks, where they actually coincide.)

ISABEL MILLER MUSEUM – Sitka – Page 27 D3 Exhibits highlight local history and people. Eight-foot-square scale model of 1860s Sitka. Photographs, furniture, paintings and Russian tools. In Centennial Building.

JUNEAU–DOUGLAS CITY MUSEUM – Juneau – Page 33 C4 Exhibits and audiovisual presentations on area, featuring gold mining and cultural history. Tools and artifacts. Native art. Children's Discovery Room.

KENAI VISITOR AND CULTURAL CENTER – Kenai – Page 69 B5 Former Ft. Kenay Museum located in Bicentennial Building. Local and natural history of area. Native and Russian artifacts, including tools, photographs and church icons.

MUSEUM OF ALASKA TRANSPORTATION AND HISTORY – Palmer – Page 83 B4 Alaska history depicted through industrial and transportation development. Trains, planes, cars, trucks, farming equipment and watercraft. Several displays inside Alaska Railroad cars and diesel engine. Outdoor exhibits.

NANA MUSEUM OF THE ARCTIC – Kotzebue – Page 133 B4 "Living culture" museum. Demonstrations of Eskimo crafts including animal skin sewing and ivory carving. Traditional Native dancers. Diorama of arctic wildlife. Jade Mountain factory where jade products are made.

NATIONAL BANK OF ALASKA HERITAGE LIBRARY AND MUSEUM – Anchorage – Page 82 D3 Alaskan, Native and Russian art. Prehistoric artifacts and gold rush period displays. Book collection includes volumes on history, exploration and Native culture.

OLD SITKA STATE HISTORICAL PARK – Sitka – Page 27 D3 First settlement in southeast Alaska, established 1799 by Russian-American Company manager, Alexander Baranof. Burned by Tlingit Indians in 1802 and relocated to present-day location in 1804. Site marked by Russian Orthodox cross and interpretive plaque. Short trail and visitor center.

OSCAR ANDERSON HOUSE – Anchorage – Page 82 D3 Built 1915, believed to be first permanent residence built in newly established town. Constructed by civic and business leader Oscar Anderson. Occupied by Anderson family until 1974. Restored, with period furnishings. National Register of Historic Places.

POTTER SECTION HOUSE STATE HISTORIC SITE – Anchorage – Page 82 D3 Restored railroad service building along Alaska Railroad. Served as living quarters for track workers. Displays of Alaska railroad history. Outside exhibits feature railcar, personnel transport car and massive snowblower. Tours. Located at Mile 115 Seward Highway.

PRATT MUSEUM – Homer – Page 62 B1 Natural and cultural history of Kenai Peninsula and Kachemak Bay. Marine aquariums, botanical garden, Alaskan mammals, whale skeletons, Native tools and marine vessels.

SAMUEL K. FOX MUSEUM – Dillingham – Page 56 D3 Display of Yup'ik Eskimo arts and crafts. Traveling exhibits from other Alaska regions.

SHELDON JACKSON MUSEUM – Sitka – Page 27 D3 Excellent collection of artifacts, art and historical items representing Alaska's main ethnic groups, mostly obtained in late 1800s by missionary Sheldon Jackson. Native vehicles, hunting and fishing equipment, clothing, baskets and totem poles. Housed in first concrete building in territory, built 1895. Located on Sheldon Jackson College campus.

SHELDON MUSEUM & CULTURAL CENTER – Haines – Page 38 D1 Interpretation of Tlingit Indian culture and pioneer history of upper Lynn Canal. Gold rush memorabilia. Slide show and video. Guided tours.

SITKA NATIONAL HISTORICAL PARK – Sitka – Page 27 D3 Commemorates Battle of Sitka, last major conflict between Europeans and Alaskan Natives. Fought 1804 between Tlingits and Russian fur traders, battle signified end of Tlingit independence and establishment of Russian stronghold in North America. Two park units include site of Tlingit fort and battleground, Russian Bishop's House and collection of 28 totem poles exhibited along park's wooded pathways *(see Hiking)*. Visitor center. Access by boat and plane.

ST. MICHAEL'S CATHEDRAL – Sitka – Page 27 D3 Exact replica of 1840s structure destroyed by fire in 1966, rebuilt 1967–1976. Constructed with logs and handhewn planks in shape of cross. Original furnishings and icons, including Our Lady of Sitka, known as "Sitka Madonna."

STATE CAPITOL – Juneau – Page 33 C4 Six-story structure, built 1930 as Federal and Territorial Building, now houses governor's offices, state legislature and government agencies. Large pillars at front of building made of native marble from southeast Alaska quarry. Upper floors display photographs of early Juneau. Tours.

TANGLE LAKES ARCHEOLOGICAL DISTRICT – Paxon – Page 106 D2 With 400 recorded sites, 455,000-acre area contains one of highest concentrations of archaeological sites in Alaska. District may have supported human occupation 12,000–15,000 years ago. Evidence of Siberian cultures supports theory of migration across Bering Land Bridge. Located between Miles 15 and 45 Denali Highway. Popular recreation area. National Register of Historic Places.

TONGASS HISTORICAL MUSEUM – Ketchikan – Page 20 C1 More than 40 exhibits of area history and culture. Native culture and art, copper and gold mining, logging and fishing. Located in Centennial Building, commemorating 1867 purchase of Alaska from Russia.

TOTEM BIGHT STATE HISTORICAL PARK – Ketchikan – Page 20 C1 Replicas of 19th-century southeast Alaska Native community house and totem art providing 20th-century interpretation of Tlingit and Haida social customs, technology and art. Constructed 1938–1941 as joint US Forest Service–Civilian Conservation Corps project. Trail through rainforest to Clan House and 14 totem poles. National Register of Historic Places.

TOTEM HERITAGE CENTER – Ketchikan – Page 20 C1 Collection of 33 original, unrestored totem poles and fragments retrieved from original locations in Tlingit and Haida villages between Yakutat and British Columbia. Among last examples of art form flourishing between 18th and 20th centuries, now exhibited in specially constructed building. Guided tours and demonstrations. National Register of Historic Places.

TRANS-ALASKA PIPELINE – Fairbanks – Page 115 A5 800-mile-long, 48-inch-diameter oil pipeline from Prudhoe Bay oilfields to terminal in Valdez. Built 1974–1977 with participation by 70,000 people. Transports almost two million barrels of oil per day. Northern half of pipeline runs above ground to protect sensitive arctic permafrost and parallels Dalton Highway. Southern half parallels Richardson Highway. Elevated pipeline can be viewed from turnout north of Fairbanks at Mile 7 Steese Highway, or along Dalton Highway *(see Scenic Drives)*. Visitor information office at Alyeska Pipeline Terminal in Valdez offers interpretive displays and brochures. Tours of Valdez terminal and Prudhoe Bay pumping/production facilities available.

UNIVERSITY OF ALASKA MUSEUM – Fairbanks – Page 115 A5 Natural history of Alaska. Exhibits include wildlife, geology, and art, tools and clothing of Native and pioneer Alaskans. State's largest gold collection. Guided tours.

VALDEZ HERITAGE CENTER MUSEUM – Valdez – Page 85 D5 History of Valdez and surrounding area. Photographs of 1964 earthquake. Scale model of oil pipeline terminal in Valdez. Exhibit on 1989 Exxon *Valdez* oil spill. Replica of miner's cabin. Firefighting equipment.

WICKERSHAM STATE HISTORIC SITE – Juneau – Page 33 C4 Large Victorian house purchased in 1928 by James V. Wickersham, one of first judges and representatives to Congress for Territory of Alaska. Displays include Wickersham's Alaska collection of early histories, diaries and documents; historical photographs; period furnishings; and Native, Russian and pioneer artifacts. Located on Chicken Ridge, considered Juneau's "Nob Hill." National Register of Historic Places.

GOLD RUSH DAYS

When an 1897 issue of a Seattle newspaper reported a steamer from Alaska with prospectors and a "a ton of gold" on board from the Klondike River, it set off the last of the great gold rushes in America. Thousands of prospectors were attracted from all over, hoping to strike it rich. This section includes some of the state's many sites relating to gold, starting with that very intense period near the turn of the century.

CHILKOOT TRAIL – Dyea – Page 38 C2 Arduous 33-mile trail from Dyea over Chilkoot Pass to Bennett Lake in British Columbia. One of only three glacier-free corridors through Coast Range. Vital link first in Native trading during pre-gold rush period and then during Klondike Gold Rush of 1897–1898. Shortest and best-known route for thousands of gold-seeking "stampeders" on first leg of journey to goldfields. Prospectors finished rest of 600-mile trip to Klondike by boat on Yukon River. Trail abandoned 1899 with establishment of White Pass & Yukon Route Railroad *(see this section)*. Historic ruins, settlements and artifacts along way. National Register of Historic Places. *(See Hiking.)*

COLDFOOT GOLD CAMP – Coldfoot – Page 136 C3 Located in southern portion of Brooks Range, 58 miles north of Arctic Circle. One of northernmost gold mining camps, established about 1899 and deserted 1912 when miners rushed northward to new strike at nearby Wiseman. Standing and collapsed structures can be seen from dirt road off highway, as well as small cemetery for inhabitants of once-thriving camp. Interpretive center with photographs of Coldfoot and adjacent areas. Located at Mile 173.6 Dalton Highway.

CROW CREEK MINE – Girdwood – Page 71 A4 Example of turn-of-century gold mine. Eight original buildings include bunkhouse, mess hall and blacksmith's shop. Panning for gold. National Register of Historic Places.

DYEA – Dyea – Page 38 C2 Gateway to Chilkoot Pass, once rivaled Skagway as largest town in Alaska. Settlement rapidly declined after opening of White Pass & Yukon Route Railroad *(see this section)* in 1898, leaving hotels, banks and stores vacant. Remains include scattered foundation ruins, rotting stubs of once extensive wharfs and Slide Cemetery, where 60 victims of 1898 avalanche on Chilkoot Trail *(see this section)* lie buried. National Register of Historic Places.

GOLD DREDGE NO. 8 – Fairbanks – Page 115 A5 Five-deck 250-foot-long ship representative of large-scale gold mining in Fairbanks area. Built 1928, in use until 1959. Displaced 1,065 tons of rock and gravel as it plied rich goldfields of Pedro, Engineer and Goldstream Creeks. Located at Mile 9 Old Steese Highway. Tours.

GOLD RUSH CEMETERY – Skagway – Page 38 C2 Resting place for early Skagway residents including notorious con-man Jefferson Randolph "Soapy" Smith, killed 1898 in shootout with surveyor Frank Reid, also killed and buried here.

INDEPENDENCE MINE STATE HISTORICAL PARK – Palmer – Page 83 A4 Largest hard-rock or lode gold mine in southcentral Alaska. Produced over 150,000 ounces of gold by 1942, from claims covering almost 3,000 acres, employing over 300 people. Closed 1951, 801-acre park established 1970s. Walking tour includes bunkhouses, warehouses, commissary, manager's home, mess hall, assay office and tunnel entrance. Interpretive signs. Tours. Visitor center. Simulated mining tunnel with hard-rock display. National Register of Historic Places. *(See State Parklands.)*

KLONDIKE GOLD RUSH NATIONAL HISTORICAL PARK – Skagway – Page 38 C2 Preserved historic buildings and portions of Chilkoot and White Pass Trails *(see this section)* from period of Klondike Gold Rush. Skagway Historic District *(see this section)*. *(See National Parklands.)*

NOME GOLD – Nome – Page 132 D3 Discovery of gold at Anvil and Snow Creeks in 1898 resulted in Alaska's greatest gold rush—in yield and number of people involved. Estimated 20,000 gold-seekers attracted to area previously inhabited by only handful of settlers, mined more than $60 million of gold by 1911 from area creeks and beaches. Miners still camp on beaches every summer and pan for gold. As many as 100 gold dredges, many currently in use, scattered throughout Seward Peninsula, with over 40 around Nome, some just north of airport.

SKAGWAY HISTORIC DISTRICT – Skagway – Page 38 C2 Heart of downtown Skagway designated part of Klondike Gold Rush National Historical Park *(see this section)*. Boardwalks, false-fronted buildings and horse-drawn wagons evoke gold-rush-era atmosphere. About 100 buildings remain including Pantheon Saloon, Lynch & Kennedy Dry Goods Store, Verbauwhede Confectionary, Captain William Moore Cabin and White Pass & Yukon Route Railroad Depot. Walking tours and interpretive programs. Visitor center. National Register of Historic Places.

TRAIL OF '98 MUSEUM – Skagway – Page 38 C2 Collection of Klondike Gold Rush and Native artifacts from period 1897–1899. Miners' tools, sleds, scrapbooks and photographs, clothing and gambling paraphernalia. Original Baldwin steam locomotive displayed outside. Located in Skagway City Hall, Alaska's oldest granite building.

WHITE PASS & YUKON ROUTE RAILROAD – Skagway – Page 38 C2 Narrow-gauge railway built 1898–1900 at peak of Klondike Gold Rush. First railroad in Alaska and northernmost in North America at time. Considered one of world's great engineering feats, climbs to 2,865 feet above sea level, with grades as steep as 3.9 percent. Served mining industry until 1980s, then switched to excursion service. 21-mile narrated trip to White Pass summit. Spectacular views include trestles, gorges and waterfalls.

WHITE PASS TRAIL – Skagway – Page 38 C2 Second most popular route during Klondike Gold Rush. 40-mile route from Skagway to Bennett Lake in British Columbia, less steep than Chilkoot Trail *(see this section)*, allowing use of pack horses to carry supplies. Also called Dead Horse Trail for more than 3,000 horses that died from starvation and overwork, many at Dead Horse Gulch along way. Wagon toll road to White Pass City improved travel, but White Pass & Yukon Route Railroad *(see this section)* replaced trail in 1898. Presently not accessible on foot, visible from turnouts along Klondike Highway and from WP&YR Railroad paralleling trail. National Register of Historic Places.

Hiking

This section includes a sampling of developed hiking trails in Alaska. These trails range from short, easy routes to long and extremely difficult climbs through remote mountain wilderness. Many trails are accessible only by boat or plane. Backcountry hiking (no marked trails) is also very popular and, in fact, the only way to access the majority of the state's parklands.

Be sure to make adequate preparations before any hike and always check trail conditions with the appropriate land managing agency. For more information, contact one of the Public Lands Information Centers as listed in Visitor Information Centers *on page 6.*

For additional trail listings, see National Parklands and State Parklands.

Note: *All distances are one-way unless they are otherwise indicated.*

CHILKOOT TRAIL – Klondike Gold Rush National Historical Park – 33-mile route – Page 38 B2 Trail extends from Dyea to Bennett, British Columbia. Long used by Chilkoot Indians as trading route, then by thousands during Klondike Gold Rush *(see Historic Sites/Museums—Gold Rush Days)*. Difficult but popular historic trail with extremely intimidating steep section at pass. Allow 3–5 days to complete. Many reminders of gold rush activity along route. Elevation Gain: 3,700 feet.

CIRCLE–FAIRBANKS HISTORIC TRAIL – Fairbanks – 58-mile route – Page 125 D6 Part of original transportation route used by Athabascan Indians, which ran between Circle City and Fairbanks. Traverses series of high ridgetops. Trailheads located at both ends: Fairbanks Creek Road four miles from Cleary Summit and Twelvemile Summit at Mile 86 Steese Highway. Not actively maintained. Elevation Gain: 1,700 feet.

COASTAL TRAIL – Caines Head State Recreation Area – 4.5-mile route – Page 71 D4 Leaves from parking area at Lowell Point. Important to time trip around tides: three-mile stretch between Tonsina Point and North Beach can only be hiked during low tide. Leave Seward at least two hours before low tide to avoid becoming stranded along route. Stay on designated trail. Camping shelter at end of trail in North Beach.

FULLER LAKES TRAIL – Kenai National Wildlife Refuge – 2.3-mile route – Page 70 C2 Begins 1.5 miles east of east end of Skilak Lake Road and 2.5 miles west of Russian River Ferry parking area. Trail provides access to Mystery Creek Unit of Kenai Wilderness. Fairly steep climb to Lower Fuller Lake with little elevation gain beyond. Several areas may be wet or muddy. Excellent views of Kenai Range along trail. Fishing. Elevation Gain: 1,400 feet.

GRANITE TORS TRAIL – Chena River Recreation Area – 15-mile loop – Page 116 A2 Trailhead at campground, Mile 39.5 Chena Hot Springs Road. Leads to Granite Tors *(see Unique Natural Features)*. Spectacular view from top. Part of trail rocky.

GREWINGK GLACIER – Kachemak Bay State Park – 3.2-mile route – Page 62 B2 Trailhead accessible from Kachemak Bay. Easy hike over flat terrain, through stands of spruce and cottonwood and across outwash of Grewingk Glacier. Superb views of glacier and surrounding area. Rock cairns mark trail across outwash. Caution: Access to glacial ice is difficult and hazardous.

HALIBUT POINT STATE RECREATION SITE – Halibut Point State Recreation Site – 0.5-mile loop – Page 27 D3 Begins at footbridge crossing Granite Creek. Two spur trails to beach and picnic shelter. Easy trail follows beach, then winds back into forest. Elevation Gain: 30 feet.

HARDING ICEFIELD TRAIL – Kenai Fjords National Park – 3.5-mile route – Page 71 D3 Trailhead at Ranger station. Hike provides spectacular views of Exit Glacier and Harding Icefield *(see Unique Natural Features)* as well as valley below. Steep and sometimes slippery terrain.

HISTORIC IDITAROD/CROW PASS TRAIL – Chugach State Park – 26-mile route – Page 83 D4 Leaves from Eagle River Visitor Center in Chugach State Park. Section of historic trail *(see Historic Sites/Museums)* formerly used as transportation and mail route between villages of Portage and Knik. Abandoned 1919 when railway was completed; reopened for hiking in 1971. Short day hikes available at both ends of trail. Trail ends at Crow Creek trailhead. Elevation Gain: 2,600 feet.

LAZY MOUNTAIN – Palmer – 4-mile route – Page 83 B4 Trail used in early 1940s as horsepacking trail for hunters. Entire Matanuska Valley from Sutton to Anchorage can be viewed from peak. Picnic area and rest rooms at trailhead. Elevation Gain: 3,520 feet.

LITTLE COAL CREEK TRAIL – Denali State Park – 4.5-mile route – Page 94 A1 Trailhead at parking lot, Mile 163.8 Parks Highway. Easy access to alpine country. Outstanding views from top of Indian Mountain. Option of continuing on trail along Kesugi Ridge route to Byers Lake Campground (27.4 miles, rated difficult). Elevation Gain: 3,300 feet.

MT. JUNEAU TRAIL – Juneau – 3-mile route – Page 33 C4 Begins one mile from beginning of Perseverance Trail *(see this section)*, at end of Basin Road. Danger of avalanche may persist until late spring. Extremely steep climb near end to summit; ice ax useful until early summer. Spectacular views of Juneau. Caution: Do not leave trail! Elevation Gain: 2,876 feet.

PERSEVERANCE TRAIL – Juneau – 3-mile route – Page 33 C4 Trailhead at end of Basin Road. Trail starts in cul-de-sac, follows gentle grade around horn of Mt. Juneau. Trail ends in clearing next to Gold Creek. Views of Ebner Falls *(see Unique Natural Features)*. Old mining ruins scattered throughout clearing. Use caution while exploring historic area. Great danger of avalanche in winter and early spring. Elevation Gain: 700 feet.

PINNELL MOUNTAIN – Steese National Conservation Area – 27.3-mile route – Page 126 C3 Clearly marked trail traverses series of alpine ridgetops entirely above timberline. Spectacular views. Steep and rugged in many areas. Allow at least three days. Accessible from two trailheads: Mile 85.6 or 107.3 Steese Highway. Small log emergency shelters located along trail. National Recreation Trail.

POINT BRIDGET TRAIL – Point Bridget State Park – 3.5-mile route – Page 32 B3 Trailhead at Mile 39 Glacier Highway, one mile north of North Bridget Cove sign. Trail passes through rainforest muskeg, meadows, old-growth rainforest and beach. Ends at Point Bridget. Panoramic view of Lynn Canal, Chilkat Range and mountains north and east of Berner's Bay.

SEDUCTION POINT – Chilkat State Park – 6.75-mile route – Page 38 D2 Scenic beach and forest walk. Outstanding views of Davidson Glacier with prolific bird and sea life along way. Allow 9–10 hours; plan to do last beach stretch at low or mid tide. Camping on cove east of Seduction Point.

SITKA NATIONAL HISTORICAL PARK TRAIL – Sitka National Historical Park – 1.5-mile route – Page 27 D3 Begins at visitor center. Two easy, maintained loops. Totem poles along loop to battleground and fort. Prime area to view fish spawning in Indian River during late summer and early fall. *(See Historic Sites/Museums.)*

SKI LOOP TRAIL – White Mountains National Recreation Area – 5-mile route – Page 125 D4 Begins at Mile 28 Elliott Highway. Follow Summit Trail for first two miles, then trail on right for 1.5 miles, then Wickersham Creek Trail for remaining 1.5 miles. Trail ascends for one mile, then descends for last four miles. Views of Alaska Range at overlook at mile 1. Year-round trail with some wet and muddy sections. Elevation Gain: 460 feet.

SKILAK LOOKOUT TRAIL – Kenai National Wildlife Refuge – 2.5-mile route – Page 70 C2 Begins three miles east of Upper Skilak Campground and two miles west of Hidden Lake Campground. Passes through spruce–cottonwood forest. Ends on knob overlooking Skilak Lake. Several steep sections. Spectacular views. No fishing. Elevation Gain: 750 feet.

SUMMIT TRAIL – White Mountains National Recreation Area – 20-mile route – Page 125 D4 Developed trail with boardwalk over wetter areas. Follows ridgeline northward and passes through treeless alpine tundra, then drops into spruce forests. Borealis–LeFevre Cabin located across Beaver Creek (reservations necessary). Use caution crossing creek. Elevation Gain: 900 feet.

TURNAGAIN ARM TRAIL – Chugach State Park – 9.4-mile route – Page 82 D3 Trailhead at Potter Section House State Historic Site *(see Historic Sites/Museums)* and park headquarters. Parallels coastline and Seward Highway, ends at Windy Corner. Scenic overlooks provide views of Chugach and Kenai Mountains. Favorite "first hike of the year" for many because snow clears in early spring. Well-developed and fairly easy to hike.

TWIN PEAKS TRAIL – Chugach State Park – 3.5-mile route – Page 83 C4 Trailhead at Eklutna Lake Campground. Popular well-maintained trail provides panoramic views of entire Eklutna Valley. Difficult hike with steep sections follows west side of Twin Peaks Mountain. Sheep often seen grazing in Goat Mountain bowl. Hikers can choose own route across tundra. Good berry picking.

CHUGACH NATIONAL FOREST TRAILS

BYRON GLACIER TRAIL – 0.8-mile route – Page 71 A5 Begins six miles down Portage Glacier Road (past Begich–Boggs Visitor Center). First half of trail flat, wide and well-maintained; second half rocky with small stream crossings. Close-up views of glacier with rugged mountains in all directions. Trail ends at snowfields below glacier. Good family outing. High avalanche hazard in winter. Elevation Gain: 100 feet.

LOST LAKE TRAIL – 7-mile route – Page 71 D4 Begins at gravel pits at Mile 5 Seward Highway. Good family trail with spectacular views. Provides access to alpine country where hike can be extended in almost any direction. Trail ends at Lost Lake, two miles above timberline. Elevation Gain: 1,820 feet.

McKINLEY LAKE TRAIL – 2.1-mile route – Page 74 C2 Begins at Mile 21 Copper River Highway. Easy and wide trail through lush, moss-covered mature spruce and hemlock forest. Tent camping near lake, and cabins at each end of trail (reservations required). Trail ends at McKinley Lake Recreation Cabin. Expect rain. Bear country. Good hunting and fishing. Elevation Gain: 25 feet.

PIPELINE LAKES TRAIL – 1.8-mile route – Page 74 C2 Begins at Mile 20.8 Copper River Highway. Short, easy hike through wet muskeg follows old water pipeline occasionally visible. Excellent trout and grayling fishing in numerous lakes along trail. Ends at junction with McKinley Lake Trail. Expect rain. Elevation Gain: 75 feet.

POWER CREEK TRAIL – 2.5-mile route – Page 74 B1 Trailhead located at end of Power Creek Road. Magnificent scenery. First 0.5 mile excellent for family outings—thereafter, hazards require caution. Potential side trips to view glaciers. Trail follows whitewater of Power Creek through narrow valley, ends at Power Creek Basin. Numerous side streams and waterfalls. Expect rain. Elevation Gain: 350 feet.

PTARMIGAN CREEK TRAIL – 3.5-mile route – Page 71 C4 Begins at Ptarmigan Creek Campground at Mile 23 Seward Highway. Fairly easy hike with good chance of seeing goats and sheep on mountain peaks and slopes. Ends at Ptarmigan Lake. Good fishing in lake and stream one mile below outlet. Avalanche hazard in winter. Elevation Gain: 255 feet.

RESURRECTION PASS TRAIL SYSTEM – 35.2-mile route – Page 71 A3 Begins five miles south of Hope. Popular trail offers beautiful scenery, good lake fishing and six public-use cabins (reservations required). Trail splits at mile 20.5: one direction leads to Schooner Bend ending at Mile 52.3 Sterling Highway; other leads across Devils Pass, ending at Mile 39 Seward Highway. Brown bear country. Elevation Gain: 2,400 feet.

RUSSIAN LAKES TRAIL – 21-mile route – Page 70 C3 Begins at Russian Lake Campground, Mile 52 Sterling Highway. First three miles to Lower Russian Lake good family trail. Trail continues to Upper Russian Lake and Cooper Lake. Public-use cabin on Upper Russian Lake (reservations required). Brown bear country. Good fishing in lakes. Elevation Gain: 768 feet.

TONGASS NATIONAL FOREST TRAILS

AMALGA (EAGLE GLACIER) TRAIL – 5.5-mile route – Page 32 B3 Trailhead at Mile 28.4 Glacier Highway, just past Eagle River. Begins at parking lot and passes under bridge leading toward Eagle Glacier. Several beaver ponds along way. Impressive views of glacier. Easy hike. Elevation Gain: 200 feet.

ANAN CREEK TRAIL (#448) – 1-mile route – Page 25 D3 Access by boat or floatplane. Begins in Anan Bay at recreation cabin. Easy trail parallels shore, offering good views of Anan Lagoon, ends at Anan Bear Observatory. (Note: Bears also use trail—make your presence known!) Elevation Gain: 100 feet.

CASCADE CREEK TRAIL – 4.5-mile route – Page 29 D4 Access by boat or plane. Begins at Cascade Creek Cabin, follows Cascade Creek and ends at Swan Lake. Difficult trail. Access to fishing and outstanding scenery. Elevation Gain: 1,514 feet.

DAN MOLLER TRAIL – 3-mile route – Page 33 C4 Small parking area with marked trailhead off Pioneer Avenue. Old road serves as first part of trail. Most of trail consists of elevated planks over muskegs, very slippery when wet or frosty. Popular for cross-country skiing. Avalanche-prone area. Trail ends at Dan Moller Cabin (reservations required). Elevation Gain: 1,600 feet.

DEER MOUNTAIN/JOHN MOUNTAIN TRAIL – 9.9-mile route – Page 20 C1 Begins at junction of Granite Basin and Ketchikan Dump Roads. Steep climb to summit with many switchbacks. Spectacular scenic overlooks to Ketchikan and Tongass Narrows. Trail continues past Deer Peak to John Mountain, ending at Lower Silvis Lake. Elevation Gain: 3,001 feet.

ELLA LAKE TRAIL – Misty Fiords National Monument – 2.5-mile route – Page 21 C3 Access by boat or floatplane. Begins in Ella Bay. Beach marker sign at trailhead visible from bay. Difficult trail runs through old second-growth forest, muskeg and marsh. Ends at Lower Ella Lake. Excellent trout and salmon fishing in Ella Creek. Elevation Gain: 254 feet.

HARVEY LAKE TRAIL – 0.5-mile route – Page 24 B1 Access by boat or plane. Begins at Duncan Canal and passes through old-growth Sitka spruce and western hemlock. Flat terrain. Remnants of mining activity near trailhead. Trail ends at Harvey Lake Cabin. Elevation Gain: 105 feet.

INDIAN RIVER TRAIL – 5.5-mile route – Page 27 D3 Begins at pumphouse/dam at end of Indian River Road and ends at base of Indian River Falls. Within walking distance of downtown Sitka. Trail follows Indian River, meandering through rainforest. Easy trail; elevation gain gradual. Elevation Gain: 700 feet.

PERSEVERANCE LAKE TRAIL – 2-mile route – Page 20 C1 Begins on Harriet Hunt Lake Road at parking lot. Easy trail crosses muskeg and old-growth forest. Good hiking surface on boardwalk tread. Swinging bridge crosses Ward Creek. Fishing in Perserverance Lake at trail's end. Elevation Gain: 450 feet.

PETERSBURG MOUNTAIN – 2.5-mile route – Page 24 A1 Access by boat to state dock. Begins across narrows from Petersburg. Difficult hike offers outstanding views of Petersburg and Coast Range Mountains, ending atop Narrows Peak. Elevation Gain: 2,750 feet.

PUNCHBOWL LAKE TRAIL – Misty Fiords National Monument – 0.75-mile route – Page 21 B3 Access by boat or floatplane. Begins at south end of Punchbowl Cove *(see Unique Natural Features)*. Steep trail with several switchbacks, very narrow with deep drops in places. Considered Misty Fiords' most scenic trail with views of cove and Punchbowl Creek waterfall. Trail ends at beginning of logjam on lake. Elevation Gain: 600 feet.

SALT CHUCK TRAIL – 1-mile route – Page 19 B4 Begins at south end of Lake No. 3 in old clearcut at edge of gravel. Historic sites of Salt Chuck and Rush and Brown Mines along trail. Trail follows banks of Ellen Creek for most of way, with spur trail crossing creek and looping around Ellen Lake. Ends at Salt Chuck ruins. Elevation Gain: 75 feet.

SHAKES HOT SPRINGS TRAIL (#625) – 0.3-mile route – Page 24 B2 Access by boat via Hot Springs Slough. Trail follows easy grade to Shakes Hot Springs Recreation Site containing two hot tub structures with changing rooms. Gravel surface part of way. Elevation Gain: 25 feet.

TWENTY-MILE SPUR TRAIL – 3-mile route – Page 19 C4 Begins off Craig–Klawock–Hollis Road, 0.25 miles east of Harris River bridge. Trail follows former logging road, in second-growth forest. Parallels Harris River to headwaters, ending at box canyon in Klawock Mountains. Also used by mountain-bikers and cross-country skiers. Elevation Gain: 100 feet.

WEST GLACIER TRAIL – 3.4-mile route – Page 33 C3 Begins on north side of parking lot. Most of trail below glacier trimline. Last section difficult to follow—look for cairns marking route. Ends at top of rock outcrop. Used for access to Mendenhall Glacier *(see Unique Natural Features)* by experienced ice climbers. Not recommended for inexperienced hikers. Elevation Gain: 1,300 feet.

Downhill Ski Areas

For more information on skiing contact the Alaska Division of Tourism, Ninth Floor, State Office Building, Juneau, AK 99811, (907) 465-2010.

NAME	LOCATION	PAGE & GRID	VERTICAL DROP	NUMBER OF RUNS	LIFTS	CROSS-COUNTRY TRAILS
Alpenglow	5 miles East of Anchorage	83 D3	1,500 feet	3	2 D-Chairs, 1 T-Bar	no
Alyeska Resort and Ski Area	35 miles South of Anchorage	71 A4	3,125 feet	60	4 D-Chairs, 1 Quad, 2 Rope Tows	yes
Cleary Summit	22 miles North of Fairbanks	125 D6	1,300 feet	21	2 T-Bars, 1 Platter	no
Eaglecrest Ski Area	Juneau	33 C3	1,400 feet	30	2 D-Chairs, 1 Platter	yes
Hilltop Ski Area	8 miles East of Anchorage	83 D3	294 feet	9	1 D-Chair, 1 Rope Tow	yes
Skiland	21 miles North of Fairbanks	125 D6	1,057 feet	26	1 D-Chair	no

Freshwater Fishing

To locate freshwater fishing spots in this Atlas, look on the appropriate page for the freshwater fishing symbol and corresponding four-digit number. This chart has been compiled with the assistance of the Alaska Department of Fish and Game. It is most important to be thoroughly familiar with all rules, regulations and restrictions before fishing in any area. For a copy of the current Alaska Sport Fishing Regulations Summary booklet or more information contact the department at Capital Office Park, 1255 West 8th Street, P.O. Box 3-2000, Juneau, AK 99802, (907) 465-4112.
Note: Symbols on the maps mark only the bodies of water; location does not necessarily indicate public access or the best fishing area.

ACCESS ABBREVIATIONS
B – boat   H – hike
F – fly   R – road

FISH SPECIES SYMBOLS
○ – wild   □ – hatchery   ☆ – wild/hatchery
● – most significant wild   ■ – most significant hatchery   ★ – most significant wild/hatchery

Body of Water	Access	Page & Grid
4000 Aaron Creek	B/F	25 C3
4004 Admiralty Creek	B/F	33 D3
4008 Afognak Lake	F/B	53 D3
4012 Alagnak (Branch) R	F	58 D1
4016 Alexander Creek	F/B	82 B1
4020 Alexander, Lake	F/H	28 B1
4024 American River	R/H	45 B4
4028 Anan/Boulder Lakes	B/F	25 D3
4032 Anchor River	R	62 B1
4036 Anchorage Bowl Lks	R	82 D3
4040 Andreafsky River	B/F	130 B3
4044 Andrew Creek	B/F	24 B2
4048 Ankau Lagoon	R/B	34 B3
4052 Anvik River	B/F	131 A4
4056 Avoss Lake	BH/F	22 B2
4060 Ayakulik (Red) River	F	44 D1
4064 Baranof Lake	BH/F	27 D4
4066 Bear Creek	R	24 B1
4068 Berry Creek	R	107 B6
4076 Big Goat Creek	F	21 B3
4080 Big Lake	R	82 B3
4088 Birch Creek	R	127 A6
4092 Birch Lake	R	116 C1
4096 Bird Creek	R/H	83 D4
4100 Blossom/Wilson R	B/F	21 C3, 4
4104 Blue Lake	R/H	27 D3
4108 Bluff Cabin Lake	H	116 D3
4110 Bob Johnson Lake	R/H	136 C4
4112 Boulder Lake	H	106 D1
4116 Brooks River	F/B	50 B3
4120 Brushkana Creek	R	105 C4
4124 Buskin River	R	45 A4
4128 Butte Creek	H	105 D5
4132 Campbell Creek	R/H	82 D3
4136 Carroll Creek	B	20 B2
4140 Castle River	B/F	23 B4
4144 Caswell Creek	R	82 A3
4148 Chandler Lake	F	136 B2
4152 Chatanika River	R	125 D5
4156 Chatanika River	R	125 D6
4160 Chena Lake	R	115 A6
4164 Chena River	R	115 A6
4168 Chilkat Lake	B/F	38 C1
4172 Chilkat River System	R	38 C1
4176 Chilkoot Lake	R/B	38 C1
4180 Chilkoot River System	R	38 C1
4184 Chuitna River	F	81 D4
4188 Clarence Lake	F	95 B5
4192 Clark Area, Lake	F/B	67 D4
4196 Clear Creek	R	74 B3
4198 Clearwater Creek	R	116 D3
4200 Coal Mine Road Lakes	R/H	106 B3
4204 Coghill Lake	F	84 D2
4208 Connell/Talbot Lakes	R/H	20 C1
4212 Copper Lake	F	98 C1
4216 Cottonwood Creek	R/H	83 B3
4220 Cowee Creek	R	32 B3
4224 Craig Lake	H	107 B5
4228 Crescent Creek	R/H	71 C3
4232 Crooked Creek	R	69 D5
4236 Crooked Creek	R	106 D1
4240 Crosswind Lake	F	96 C2
4244 Dall River	F	136 D4
4248 Deep Creek	R	69 D4
4252 Deep Lake	F	96 C2
4260 Denali–Clearwater Cr	R	106 D1
4264 Deshka River	F/B/R	82 A2
4268 Dewey Lakes	H	38 C2
4272 Distin Lake	F/H	28 B1
4276 Donna Lake	H	107 A5
4280 Donna Lake, Little	H	107 A5
4284 Donnelly Lake	H	106 A3
4288 Duncan Saltchuck Cr	B/F	23 A4
4292 Dune Lake	F	114 C1
4296 Eagle River	R/H	83 D4
4300 Eagle River/Lake	B/F	25 D3, 4
4304 Eklutna Tail Race	R	83 C4
4308 Elusive Lake	R/H	136 B4
4312 Eshamy Lake/Creek	F/B	72 C1
4316 Essowah Lake	F	17 A3
4320 Eva, Lake	BH/F	27 C3
4324 Exchange Creek	F	24 D1
4328 Eyak River	R	74 C1
4332 Falls Creek	R	24 B1
4336 Fielding Lake	R	106 D3
4340 Filmore Lake System	F/B	17 C3
4344 Fish Creek	R	33 C3
4348 Fish Creek	R	82 C3
4352 Fish Creek (Hyder)	R	21 A4
4356 Fish Cr (Thorne Arm)	B	20 C2
4360 Florence, Lake	F	27 A4
4364 Four Mile Lake	H	108 C3
4368 Frazer Lake/River	F	44 C1
4372 Galbraith Lake	R	136 B4
4376 George, Lake	B/F	107 A6
4380 Geskakmina Lake	F	113 B6
4384 Glacier Lake	R	106 D2
4388 Goodnews River	F	54 D2
4392 Goodpaster River	B	117 D4
4396 Goose Creek	R/H	93 D6
4400 Goulding Lakes	F	26 A1
4404 Gulkana River	B/R	96 B3
4408 Hamilton Creek	B/F	23 A4
4412 Harding Lake	R	116 C1
4416 Harding River	B/F	25 C3
4420 Harriet Hunt, Lake	R	20 C1
4424 Harris River	R	19 C4
4428 Hasselborg Lake	F/H	28 B1
4432 Herman Lake	H	37 C5

Body of Water	Access	Page & Grid
4436 Hess Creek	R	124 B1
4440 High Lake	F	85 A5
4444 Hoktaheen Lake	F	31 D4
4448 Holitna River	B/F	131 C6
4452 Hugh Smith Lake	B	21 D3
4456 Humpback Lake Syst	F	21 D3
4460 Iliamna Lk/Tributaries	F/B	59 B4
4464 Ingram Creek	R	71 A4
4468 Iniakuk Lake	F	136 C2
4472 Innoko River	B/F	131 B5
4476 Italio River	F	35 C4
4480 Itkillik Lake	R/H	136 B4
4484 Jan Lake	R	108 B1
4488 Jim Creek	R/H	83 B5
4492 Jim River	R	136 D3
4496 Jims Lake	F	28 B1
4500 Kadake Creek	B/F	23 A3
4504 Kah Sheets River Syst	B/F	24 B1
4508 Kanektok River	F	54 A1
4512 Kanuti River	R	136 D2
4516 Karluk River	F	44 B1
4520 Karta River System	B/F	19 B4
4524 Kasilof River	R/B	69 C5
4528 Katalla River	F	75 C4
4532 Kathleen, Lake	F	27 A4
4536 Kegan River System	F	20 D1
4540 Kenai Lake	F/R	71 C3
4544 Kenai River	B/F/R	70 C1
4548 Kepler–Bradley SRA	R/H	83 B4
4552 Ketchikan Creek	R	20 C1
4556 Klawock River System	F	19 B3
4560 Klutina Lake	R	86 B1
4564 Klutina River	R	86 A1
4568 Kobuk River	F	133 B6
4572 Kodiak I Roadside Lks	R/H	45 A4
4576 Kook Lake	F	27 B4
4580 Koole Lake	F/H	116 B1
4584 Koyukuk R, Mid Fk	R	136 C4
4588 Koyukok River, S Fk	R	136 C3
4592 Kurupa Lake	F	136 B1
4596 Kustatan River	F	69 A4
4598 Kuzitrin River	R	132 C4
4600 Kvichak River	F/B	58 D2
4604 Lake Creek	F/B	82 A1
4608 Lake Louise Road Lks	R	96 D1
4612 Landmark Gap Lake	H	106 D2
4616 Lewis River	F	82 C1
4620 Lisa Lake	H	107 B5
4624 Little Harding Lake	R	116 C1
4628 Lost Lake	R	116 C1
4632 Lost River	R/H	35 C3
4636 Louise, Lake	R	96 C1
4640 Manzanita Lake Syst	B/F	21 B2
4644 Manzoni, Lake	F	21 B3
4648 Marten Lake System	B/F	25 C3
4652 Martin Lake	F	75 C3
4656 Martin River	F	75 C3
4660 McDonald Syst, Lake	B/F	20 A1
4664 McKinley Lake	F	74 C2
4668 Meadows Road Lakes	R/H	106 A3
4672 Mendeltna Creek	R	96 B1
4676 Minto Flats	R/B	124 D2
4680 Montana Creek	R	93 D6
4684 Montana Creek	R	33 C3
4688 Moose Creek	R	96 D3
4692 Moose River	B/F/R	70 B1
4696 Mulchatna River	F/B	58 A1
4700 Naha River System	B/F	20 B2
4704 Nakat Lake System	F	17 C3
4708 Naknek Lk/Bay of Is	F/B	51 B3
4712 Naknek River	B/F	50 B1
4716 Nakwasina River	B/F	27 C3
4720 Nancy Lake Rec Area	R/H	82 B2
4724 Newhalen River	F	59 A5
4728 Ninilchik River	R	69 D4
4732 Niukluk River	R	132 C3
4736 Noatak River	F	134 D4
4740 Nome River	R	132 D3
4744 Nowitna River	B/F	111 A4
4748 Nushagak River	F/B	57 D4
4752 Nuyakuk River	F	57 A4
4756 Ohmer Creek	R	24 B1
4760 Olds River	R/H	45 B4
4764 Orchard Lake	F/B	20 A2
4768 Pasagshak River	R	45 C5
4772 Pat's Lake System	R	24 C2
4776 Paxson Lake	R	96 A3
4780 Perseverance Lake	R/H	20 C1
4784 Peters Creek	R	93 D5
4788 Peters River	F	137 A6
4792 Petersburg Creek/Lake	B/F	24 A1
4796 Peterson Creek	R	33 C3
4800 Piledriver Slough	R	115 B6
4804 Pilgrim River	R	132 C3
4808 Plotnikof Lake	F	22 B2
4812 Polly Creek	F	68 C2
4816 Poplar Grove Creek	R	97 C4
4820 Power Creek	R	74 B1
4824 Prudhoe Bay	R	135 D7
4828 Pullen Creek	R	38 C2
4832 Quartz Lake	R	116 D3
4836 Rainbow Lake	F/H	116 D2
4840 Rainbow Lake	R	20 B1
4844 Ravine/Bonnie Lakes	R	84 A1
4848 Ray River	R	124 A1
4852 Red Lake System	R	23 D4
4856 Reflection Lake	F/B	25 D3
4860 Rezanof Lake	F	22 B2
4864 Robertson #2 Lake	H	108 B1

FRESHWATER FISHING, *continued*

Column groups: **SALMON** (Chum, Coho, King, Pink, Sockeye) · **TROUT** (Brook, Cutthroat, Dolly Varden/Char, Lake, Rainbow, Steelhead) · **OTHER** (Burbot, Grayling, Northern Pike, Sheefish, Smelt, Whitefish, Razor Clams) · **FACILITIES** (Dock/Boat Ramp, Fuel/Water, Campground/Toilet, Public Cabin, Commercial Lodging)

#	Body of Water	Access	Page & Grid
4868	Rock Creek	R	106 D2
4872	Roslyn Creek	R/H	45 B5
4876	Russian River	R/H	70 C3
4880	Sagavanirktok River	R	136 A4
4884	Salcha River	R	116 B2
4888	Salmon Bay System	F	24 C1
4892	Salmon Lake	R	132 D3
4896	Salonie Creek	R/H	45 B4
4900	Saltery Creek	F/H	45 B4
4904	Sarkar River System	R/F	19 A3
4908	Schrader, Lake	F	137 A6
4912	Scottie Creek	R	99 B6
4916	Sculpin Lake	R	87 B4
4920	Selawik River	F	133 B6
4924	Sevenmile Lake	R	106 C3
4928	Shaw Creek	R	116 C3
4932	Sheep Creek	R/B	93 D6
4936	Ship Creek	R	83 D3
4940	Silver Salmon Creek	F	68 D2
4944	Sinuk River	R	132 D3
4948	Sitkoh Creek/Lake	BH/F	27 B3
4952	Situk River	R	35 C3
4956	Skilak Lake	R/B/F	70 C2
4960	Sourdough Creek	R	97 B4
4964	Staney Creek	R	19 A3
4968	Summit Lake	R	106 D3
4972	Surge Lake	BH/F	31 D4
4976	Susitna Lake	B/F	96 C1
4980	Susitna River	F/B	82 B2
4984	Susitna River, Little	R/HB	83 B3
4988	Susitna River, Upper	F/B	93 C6
4992	Swan Lake	F/B	20 B2
4996	Swanson River	R/B	70 B1
5000	Swanson River Lakes	R/H	70 A2
5004	Swede Lake	H	96 A3
5008	Swede Lake, Little	H	106 D3
5012	Sweetwater System	R/F	19 A4
5016	Taiya/Dyea Rivers	R	38 B2
5020	Talachulitna River	F/B	81 A5
5024	Talarik Creek, Lower	F	59 B4
5028	Talkeetna River	B/F/R	94 C1
5032	Tanada Lake	F	98 C2
5036	Tangle Lakes	R	96 A2
5040	Tebay River Drainage	F	87 C4
5044	Ten Mile Lake	R	106 D3
5048	Theodore River	F	82 C1
5052	Thoms Lake/Creek	B/F	24 D2
5056	Thorne River	R	19 A4
5060	Tikchik/Nuyakuk Lks	F	56 A2
5064	Togiak River	F/B	55 C4
5068	Tokun, Lake	F	75 C4
5072	Tolsona/Moose Lake	R	96 D2
5076	Triangle Lake	F	113 B6
5080	Tsiu River	F	76 D1
5084	Tulsona Creek	R	97 C4
5088	Turner Lake	F	33 C5
5092	Tustumena Lake	B/FH	69 D5
5096	Twentymile River	R/H	71 A5
5100	Twin Lake, East	F	113 C5
5104	Twin Lake, West	F	113 C5
5108	Twin Lakes	R/H	136 C4
5112	Tyee Lake	F	25 D4
5116	Tyone Lake	B/F	96 B1
5120	Uganik Lake System	F/B	44 B3
5124	Ugashik Lakes	F	42 B1
5128	Unalakleet River	F	131 A4
5132	Van Lake	R	87 C4
5136	Virginia Lake	B/F	24 C2
5140	Walker Lake	F	136 C1
5144	Walker Lake	F	37 C5
5148	Walker Lake System	B/F	21 A3
5152	Ward Lake System	R	20 C1
5156	Wasilla Cr/Rabbit Sl	R/H	83 B4
5160	Whipple Creek	R	20 C1
5164	Willow Creek	R/HB	82 A3
5168	Willow Creek, Little	R/B	82 A3
5172	Windfall Lake	R/H	33 B3
5176	Wood River Lakes	F/B	56 C2
5180	Wulik River	F	132 A4
5184	Yentna Drainage Lks	F/B	82 A1
5188	Yentna River	F/B	82 A1
5192	Young Lake	F	33 D4

Saltwater Fishing

To locate saltwater fishing spots in this Atlas, look on the appropriate page for the saltwater fishing symbol and corresponding four-digit number. This chart has been compiled with the assistance of the Alaska Department of Fish and Game. It is most important to be thoroughly familiar with all rules, regulations and restrictions before fishing in any area. For a copy of the current Alaska Sport Fishing Regulations Summary booklet or more information contact the department at Capital Office Park, 1255 West 8th Street, P.O. Box 3-2000, Juneau, AK 99802, (907) 465-4112. Note: Symbols on the maps mark only the bodies of water; location does not necessarily indicate public access or the best fishing area.

Column groups: **BOAT** (Chum Salmon, Coho Salmon, King Salmon, Pink Salmon, Sockeye Salmon, Halibut, Rockfish, Dolly Varden, Flounder/Sole/Other, Shellfish) · **SHORELINE** (Chum Salmon, Coho Salmon, King Salmon, Pink Salmon, Sockeye Salmon, Halibut, Rockfish, Cutthroat Trout, Dolly Varden, Flounder/Sole/Other) · **FACILITIES** (Dock/Boat Ramp, Fuel/Water, Campground/Toilet, Public Cabin, Commercial Lodging)

#	Body of Water	Access	Page & Grid
6000	Auke Bay	R	33 C3
6004	Bell I/Yes Bay	F/B	20 A1, 2
6008	Billys Hole	B/F	72 A3
6012	Blind Slough	R/B	24 B1
6016	Caamano Point	B	20 C1
6020	Cape Strait	B	24 A1
6024	Carroll Inlet	B	20 C2
6028	Carroll Point	B	20 C2
6032	Chatham Strait	B/F	27 B4
6036	Chilkat Inlet	B/R	38 D2
6040	Chilkoot Inlet	B/R	38 D2
6044	Chiniak Bay	B/R	45 B5
6048	Clover Passage	B/R	20 C1
6052	Cochrane Bay	B/F	72 B1
6056	Coghill Lagoon	B/F	84 D2
6060	Cook Inlet	B/F/R	69 C4
6064	Cross Sound	B/F	31 D4
6068	Culross Passage	B/F	72 B1
6072	Eastern Passage	B	24 C2
6076	Elfin Cove	B/F	31 D5
6080	Eshamy Bay/Lagn	B/F	72 C2
6084	Esther Passage	B/F	72 A2
6088	Frederick Sound	B/F	28 D2
6092	Frederick Sound	B	24 A1
6096	Galena Bay	B/F	73 A4
6100	Gambier Bay	B/F	28 C2
6104	Gastineau Channel	B/R	33 D4
6108	Glacier Bay	B/F	31 A5
6112	Grindall Island	F/B	20 C1
6116	Hell's Hole	B/F	73 B5
6120	Herring Bay	B/F	20 C2
6124	Hinchinbrook I (N)	B/F	73 C4
6128	Hinchinbrook I (S)	B/F	73 C4
6132	Hoonah Sound	B/F	27 B3
6136	Icy Strait	B/F	32 C1
6140	Jackpot Bay	B/F	72 C1
6144	Kachemak Bay	S/F/R	62 B2
6148	Kalsin Bay	B/R	45 B5
6152	Kelp Bay	B/F	27 C4
6156	Khaz Bay	B/F	26 B1
6160	Knight Island	B/F	72 C2
6164	Long Bay	B/F	72 B1
6168	Lutak Inlet	B/R	38 C1
6172	Lynn Canal	B	32 B2
6176	Main Bay	B/F	72 B1
6180	Middle Bay	B/R	45 B5
6184	Monashka Bay	B/R	45 A5
6192	Mountain Point	B/R	20 C1
6196	Neets Bay	B	20 A1
6200	Noyes Island	B	18 B2
6204	Passage Canal	B/F	71 A5
6206	Patton Bay	B/F	65 A5
6208	Peril Strait	B/F	27 C2
6212	Pigot Bay	B/F	72 A1
6216	Point Alava	B	20 B3
6220	Point Ellis	B	23 B3
6224	Port Banks	B/F	22 A1
6228	Port Chalmers	B/F	72 D3
6232	Port Frederick	B/F	32 D1
6236	Port Snettisham	B/F	28 A2
6240	Portage Cove	B/F	38 D2
6244	Pybus Bay	B/F	28 C1
6248	Redoubt Bay	B/F	22 A1
6252	Resurrection Bay	S/F/R	71 D4
6256	Salisbury Sound	B/F	26 C2
6260	San Alberto Bay	B	19 C3
6264	Shelter Island	B	32 C3
6268	Simpson Bay	B/F	74 B1
6272	Sitka Sound	B/F	27 D3
6276	Sitkoh Bay	B/F	27 B4
6280	Stephens Passage	B	28 B2
6284	Taiya Inlet	B/F	38 C2
6288	Taku Inlet	B	33 C4
6292	Tee Harbor	B	32 C3
6296	Thorne Bay	B	19 B4
6300	20 Fathom Bank	B	20 C1
6304	Unakwik Inlet	B/F	72 A2
6308	Ushk Bay	B/F	26 B2
6312	Valdez Arm	BF/R	85 D4
6316	Vallenar Point	B	20 C1
6320	Warm Springs Bay	B/F	27 D4
6324	Whale Bay	B/F	22 A1
6328	Women's Bay	B/F	45 B5
6332	Wrangell Narrows	R/B	24 B1
6336	Yakutat Bay	B/F	34 B3

Float Trips

The listings in this chart provide a sampling of the many float trips Alaska has to offer. Detailed descriptions, including all hazards, portages, current water conditions and land ownership must be obtained before starting out. For more information contact one of the Public Lands Information Centers listed in Visitor Information Centers on page 6.
Nine of Alaska's 25 National Wild and Scenic Rivers (NW&SR) are included here. The remaining 16 are identified along the riverways in the Atlas. These rivers have been federally designated because of outstanding natural, cultural and/or recreational features.

ABBREVIATIONS

Type of Craft	Access	Skill Level	
C–canoe	A–air	B–beginner	A–advanced
K–kayak	L–land	I–intermediate	E–expert
R–raft	W–water		

NAME	PAGE & GRID	LENGTH (miles)	TYPE OF CRAFT	ACCESS	SKILL LEVEL	WHITEWATER CLASS	PUT-IN	TAKE-OUT	COMMENTS
Aniakchak River	139 B4	32	R	A	B/A	I–IV	Surprise Lake	Aniakchak Bay	Spectacular trip from lake inside volcano, along boulder-lined river to saltwater bay. NW&SR.
Beaver Creek	126 C1	127	CKR	AL	B/I	I	Nome Cr, Mi 57 Steese Highway	via plane, Victoria Creek	Rolling hills, jagged White Mountains peaks, Yukon Flats marshes. NW&SR.
Birch Creek	126 C3	126	CKR	L	B/A	I–III	Mile 94.5 Steese Highway	Mile 147 Steese Highway	Upland plateaus, forested valleys and rolling hills. Class III rapids. NW&SR.
Chatanika River Trail	126 C1	60	CKR	L	B/I	I	Mile 66 Steese Highway	Mile 11 Elliot Highway	Clear-water stream paralleling highway. No major obstacles.
Chitina River	88 C2	62	KR	L	I	II–III	Kennicott River near McCarthy	O'Brien Creek near Chitina	Includes Kennicott and Nizina Rivers. Spectacular views of Wrangell Mountains.
Copper River	98 B1	244	CKR	ALW	I/A	II–IV	Slana River Bridge	Cordova Road at Flag Point	Wrangell Mountains, canyons, glaciers, Copper River Delta. Shorter trips possible.
Cross Admiralty Canoe Route	28 B1	32	CK	AW	B/A	—	Mole Harbor	Angoon	Scenic route across Admiralty Island linking eight lakes and Mitchell Bay. Several portages.
Delta River	106 D3	29	CKR	L	B/A	I–III	Tangle Lks, Mile 22 Denali Hwy	Mile 212.5 Richardson Hwy	Tundra-covered hills, steep slopes, rock cliffs. Alaska Range. NW&SR.
Eagle River, Upper	83 C4	13	CKR	L	I/A	I–III	Mile 7.5 or 9 Eagle River Road	Eagle River Campground	Glacial stream through Chugach Mountains. Easy access from Anchorage.
Fortymile River, Middle Fork	118 C2	90	CKR	AL	B/E	I–V	via plane, Joseph	O'Brien Creek Bridge	Deep, winding canyons. Forests. Mining ruins. Portage Class III–V rapids. Add 182 miles to Eagle. NW&SR.
Fortymile River, South Fork	109 A4	72	CKR	L	B/I	I–III	Mile 49 Taylor Highway	O'Brien Creek Bridge	Active gold mining area. Add 92 miles for trip to Eagle. NW&SR.
Gulkana River, Main Fork	96 A3	45	CKR	L	B/I	I–III	Paxson Lake Campground	Sourdough Campground	Wild but subdued scenery. Abundant wildlife. Highlight Canyon Rapids. Popular route. NW&SR.
Honker Divide Canoe Route	19 A4	30	CK	LW	A	—	Hatchery Creek Bridge	Public dock, Thorne Bay	Traverses series of lakes and Thorne River across Prince of Wales Island. Primitive. Very difficult.
Kobuk River	136 C1	125	CKR	A	I/A	II–IV	via plane, Walker Lake	via plane, Kobuk	Popular trip through wide valley and two scenic canyons. NW&SR.
Nancy Lake Canoe Trail System	82 B2	8	C	L	B/I	—	Mile 4.5 Nancy Lake Parkway	same as put-in	Chain of lakes in Link Lake Loop. Well-marked portages. Good weekend trip; longer trip possible.
Nenana River	105 C4	130	CKR	L	I/E	I–V	Mile 18 Denali Highway	Tenana River at Nenana	Scenic glacial river with sections of Class V whitewater. No canoes, upper and lower sections.
Noatak River	136 C1	396	CKR	A	B/I	I–II	via plane, headwaters Noatak River	via plane, Noatak	Wilderness trip through canyon, tundra and forest above Arctic Circle. NW&SR.
Nowitna River	100 A3	250	CKR	AW	B/I	I	via plane, Meadow Cr confluence	via plane, Yukon River	Trip through Nowitna NWR (*see Wildlife Refuges*). Camping beaches. Rockhounding. NW&SR.
Squirrel River	133 A5	53	CKR	A	B	I	via plane, North Fork confluence	via plane, Kiana	Broad valley, tundra, 2,000-foot Kiana Hills. Good family trip. Above Arctic Circle.
Stikine River, North Arm Route	24 B1	18	CK	ALW	I/A	—	Mile 35.5 Mitkof Highway	Kakwan Point	Upriver paddling through spectacular steep-walled, glaciated valley. LeConte Glacier (*see Unique Natural Features*).
Swan Lake Route	70 B1	60	CK	L	B/I	I	Swan Lake Road, E/W entrances	Moose River Bridge	30 lakes and forks of Moose River in Kenai NWR (*see Wildlife Refuges*). Varied wildlife.
Swanson River Route	70 A2	80	CK	L	B/I	I–II	Paddle Lake	North Kenai Road Bridge	40 lakes and 46 miles of Swanson River in Kenai NWR (*see Wildlife Refuges*). National Recreation Trail.
Tazlina River System	85 A4	74	KR	L	I/A	II–III	Mile 138 Glenn Highway	Mile 110 Richardson Hwy	Trip on Nelchina, Little Nelchina and Tazlina Rivers and Tazlina Lake. Wildlife.
Unalakleet River	133 D6	76	CKR	A	B	I	via plane, Tenmile Cr confluence	Unalakleet	Remote scenic area. Oxbows, marshes, gravel bars. Fishing for salmon, grayling and arctic char.
Upper Tangle Lake/Gulkana River, Mid Fk	106 D2	77	KR	L	B/I	I–III	Tangle River Campground	Sourdough Campground	Through tundra and forest of Alaska Range to Main Fork, Gulkana River. NW&SR.
Yukon River	119 A6	155	CKR	L	B/I	I	Taylor Highway, Eagle	Steese Highway, Circle	Scenic, traversable section of one of North America's longest rivers. Through Yukon–Charley Rivers Nat Preserve.

Boat Ramps

To locate boat ramps in this Atlas, look on the appropriate map for the boat ramp symbol and corresponding four-digit number. This chart was compiled with the assistance of the Alaska Department of Fish and Game, Division of Sport Fish. For more information on boat ramps contact this agency at 1255 West 8th Street, P.O. Box 3-2000, Juneau, AK 99802, (907) 465-4180.

SURFACE ABBREVIATIONS

A–asphalt	G–gravel	S–sand
C–concrete	L–landing mat	W–wood planks

FACILITY	LOCATION	SURFACE	LANES	BOARDING DOCK	FEE	RESTROOMS	PICNIC AREA	CAMPGROUND	BOAT RENTAL	SMALL BOAT HARBOR	PARKING	PAGE & GRID
3000 Alaganik Slough	Mile 17 Copper River Highway	C	1			●		●				74 C2
3004 Aleknegik Boat Launch	Wood–Tikchik State Park	G	1			●					●	56 C2
3008 Amalga Harbor	Juneau	C	2	●	●	●					●	32 C3
3012 Anton Larsen Bay	Kodiak Island	C	1								●	45 A4
3016 Auke Bay	Juneau	C	2	●	●	●				●	●	33 C3
3020 Bar Harbor	Ketchikan	C	1	●		●				●		20 C1
3024 Beach Lake	Birchwood	G	1			●	●				●	83 C3
3028 Bernice Lake	Mile 10 North Kenai Road	G	1			●		●			●	69 B5
3032 Big Eddy Jetty	Kenai River, Mile 14	G	1			●		●				69 B5
3036 Big Lake East	Mile 52 Parks Highway	C	2			●	●	●				82 B3
3040 Big Lake Lodge	Big Lake	G	1			●						82 B3
3044 Bing Brown's Landing	Kenai River, Mile 39.5	G	1			●	●	●			●	70 B1
3048 Birch Lake	Mile 308 Richardson Highway	S	1			●						116 C1
3052 Bluffs on Susitna	Mile 86 Parks Highway	G	2		●	●					●	82 A2
3056 Boat Harbor	Dillingham	C	1		●					●	●	56 D3
3060 Bonnie Lake	Mile 83 Glenn Highway	G	1			●		●			●	84 A1
3064 Burkeshore Marina	Big Lake	C	2			●					●	82 B3
3068 Byers Lake Campground	Mile 147 Parks Highway	G	1			●	●	●			●	93 B6
3072 Centennial Park	Kenai River, Soldotna	C	1			●	●	●	●	●	●	69 C5
3076 Chatanika	Mile 39 Steese Highway	G	1			●						125 D6
3080 Chatanika River	Mile 11.4 Elliott Highway	G	1			●						125 D5
3084 Chena River State Recreation Site	University Avenue, Fairbanks	C	1			●	●	●			●	115 A5
3088 Chilkat State Park	Haines	C	1	●		●	●	●				38 D2
3092 Chitina River	Edgerton Highway	G	1									87 B4
3096 Christiansen Lake	Talkeetna	G	1	●		●	●				●	93 C6
3100 Clearwater Lake	Mile 269 Richardson Highway	C	1									116 D3
3104 Clearwater Creek	Mile 1415 Alaska Highway	C	1			●						117 D4
3108 Cordova Boat Harbor	Cordova	C	2	●		●				●	●	74 B1
3112 Crescent Harbor	Sitka	C	1			●				●	●	27 D3
3116 Cunningham Park	Lower Kenai River	L	1			●	●	●				69 B5
3120 Deep Creek	Ninilchik	C	2			●	●	●			●	69 D4
3124 Deshka Landing	Mile 67 Parks Highway	G	1		●						●	82 B2
3128 Dog Bay	Kodiak	C	1	●		●				●	●	45 A5
3132 Dot Brown's Fish Camp	Kenai River, Mile 43.3	G	1			●					●	70 C1
3136 Douglas Harbor	Douglas	C	1		●	●	●			●	●	33 C4
3140 Eagle Rock	Kenai River	G	1			●	●	●			●	69 B5
3144 Echo Cove	Juneau	C	1		●	●	●				●	32 B3
3148 Eyak River	Cordova	G	1			●						74 B1
3152 Fielding Lake State Recreation Site	Mile 200.5 Richardson Highway	C	1			●	●	●				106 D3
3156 Finger Lake	Wasilla	G	2	●		●	●	●			●	83 B4
3160 Fish Creek Marina	Big Lake	G	1				●	●	●		●	82 B3
3164 George Lake Lodge	Mile 1385 Alaska Highway	G	1									107 A5
3168 Goodpaster	Big Delta	C	1									116 D3
3172 Haines Harbor	Haines	C	1		●	●				●	●	38 D2
3176 Harding Lake	Mile 322 Richardson Highway	C	1			●	●	●			●	116 C1
3180 Harris Harbor	Juneau	C	1		●					●	●	33 C4
3184 Hidden Lake	Kenai Peninsula	G	1			●	●	●				70 C2
3188 Hollis	Prince of Wales Island	C	1									19 C4
3192 Homer Boat Harbor	Homer Spit	C	4	●		●		●		●	●	62 B2
3196 Hoonah Harbor	Hoonah	C	1	●						●		32 D2
3200 Hyder Harbor	Hyder	C	1	●						●		21 A4
3204 Iliamna Lake	Newhalen	G	1									59 B5
3208 Izaak Walton Campground	Moose/Kenai River	A	1			●	●	●	●			70 B1
3212 Jan Lake	Mile 1353.5 Alaska Highway	G	1			●						108 B1
3216 Jim's Landing	Kenai River, Mile 70	G	1			●	●	●			●	70 C2
3220 Johnson Lake	Mile 110 Sterling Highway	G	1			●	●	●			●	69 C5
3224 Kasilof Harbor	Lower Kasilof River	C	1	●		●					●	69 C5
3228 Kasilof River	Sterling Highway Bridge	C	1			●	●	●			●	69 C5
3232 Kasilof River, Upper	Tustumena Lake Outlet	G	1			●	●	●			●	69 D5
3236 Kenai Keys	Kenai River, Mile 43.5	G	1									70 C1
3240 Kenai Lake	Mile 41 Sterling Highway	G	1			●	●	●			●	71 C3
3244 Kenai Lake	Mile 104 Seward Highway	G	1			●					●	71 C4
3248 Kenai Lake Outlet	Cooper Landing	G	1									70 C3
3250 Kenai Riverbend Campground	Kenai River, Mile 13.8	G	1			●	●	●	●			69 B5
3252 Kenai, City Ramp	Lower Kenai River	C	2			●						69 B5
3256 Kepler Lake	Mile 37 Glenn Highway	G	1			●	●	●	●		●	83 B4
3260 King Run	Kenai River, Mile 15.3	G	1			●	●	●	●	●		69 B5
3264 Klawock River	Klawock	G	1							●		19 B3
3268 Klondike Inn	Big Lake	G	1			●	●		●		●	82 B3
3272 Knudson Cove	Ketchikan	C	2	●					●	●	●	20 C1
3276 Kodiak Boat Harbor	Kodiak	C	2	●						●	●	45 A5
3280 Lake Camp Access	Katmai National Park	G	1	●		●	●				●	50 B2
3284 Letnikof Cove	Haines	C	1							●		38 D2
3288 Little Susitna River	Wasilla	C	2	●	●	●	●	●			●	82 C2
3292 Long Lake	Mile 85 Glenn Highway	G	1			●		●			●	84 A1
3296 Longmare Lake	Kenai Peninsula	C	1								●	70 B1
3300 Lucile Lake	Mile 41 Parks Highway	G	1			●	●	●			●	83 B4
3304 Lutak Inlet	Haines	C	1		●						●	38 C2
3308 Manley Hot Springs	Manley Hot Springs	C	1			●	●				●	113 A5
3312 Matanuska Lake	Mile 35 Glenn Highway	G	1	●		●	●	●			●	83 B4
3316 Metlakatla	Metlakatla	C	1	●						●		20 D1
3320 Miller's Landing	Mile 57 Parks Highway	G	1			●	●	●			●	82 B3
3324 Mirror Lake	Mile 23 Glenn Highway	G	2			●	●				●	83 C4
3328 Mitkof Point	Petersburg	C	1								●	24 B1
3332 Mountain Point	Ketchikan	C	2									20 C1
3336 Naknek City Dock	Naknek	C	1									49 B5
3340 Naknek River	King Salmon	G	1						●		●	50 B1
3344 Nancy Lake	Mile 67 Parks Highway	C	1			●	●	●				82 B2
3348 Nenana	Nenana	C	1								●	114 B2
3352 Ninilchik Village	Lower Ninilchik River	C	1			●	●	●	●	●	●	69 D4
3356 Nordale	Chena River	G	1									115 A6
3360 North Cove	Craig	C	1							●	●	19 C3
3364 North Douglas	Juneau	C	1		●							33 C3
3368 Papkes Landing	Petersburg	C	1							●	●	24 B1
3372 Paxson Lake	Mile 173 Richardson Highway	C	1			●		●				96 A3
3376 Pelican Boat Launch	Pelican	G	1							●		26 A1
3380 Petersburg, North Harbor	Petersburg	W	1			●				●		24 A1
3384 Petersburg, South Harbor	Petersburg	C	1	●						●	●	24 A1
3388 Placer River	Portage	G	1								●	71 A5
3392 Poachers Cove	Kenai River, Mile 17.1	G	1			●	●	●	●	●		69 C5
3396 Port Valdez Harbor	Valdez	C	1			●				●		85 D5
3400 Portage Cove	Kake	C	1	●						●		23 A4
3404 Porters	Kenai River, Mile 15.2	G	1			●						69 B5
3408 Quartz Lake	Mile 277.8 Richardson Highway	C	1			●	●	●	●			116 D3
3416 Riverside Campground	Kenai River, Mile 17	G	1			●	●	●				69 B5
3420 Rocky Lake	Mile 52 Parks Highway	G	1			●	●	●			●	82 B3
3424 Salamatof, Lower	Kenai River, Mile 26.9	G	1								●	70 C1
3428 Salamatof, Upper	Kenai River, Mile 28.6	G	1									70 C1
3432 Salcha	Mile 325.3 Richardson Highway	C	1			●	●	●				116 C1
3436 Scout Lake Road	Kenai River, Mile 34.6	G	1								●	70 B1
3440 Sealing Cove	Sitka	C	1	●		●				●	●	27 D3
3444 Seventeenmile Lake	Jonesville	G	2				●				●	83 B5
3448 Seward Public Ramp	Seward	C	2	●		●	●	●		●	●	71 D4
3452 Shaw Creek	Mile 288.7 Richardson Highway	C	1		●							116 C2
3456 Ship Creek	Anchorage	G	1								●	82 D3
3460 Shoemaker Harbor	Wrangell	C	1	●			●	●		●	●	24 C2
3464 Situk River (Lower Landing)	Situk	G	1				●	●			●	35 C3
3468 Situk River/Nine Mile Bridge	Yakutat	G	1				●				●	35 B4
3472 Skagway Harbor	Skagway	C	2			●				●		38 C2
3476 Skilak Lake, Lower	Kenai Peninsula	L	1			●	●	●			●	70 C2
3480 Skilak Lake, Upper	Kenai Peninsula	L	1			●	●	●			●	70 C2
3484 Soldotna	Kenai River, Mile 16	G	1			●				●		69 B5
3488 Sourdough	Mile 148 Richardson Highway	G	2			●		●			●	96 B3
3492 South Rolly Lake	Mile 67 Parks Highway	G	1			●	●	●			●	82 B2
3496 Starrigavan	Old Sitka	C	1	●		●	●				●	27 D3
3500 Stormy Lake	North Kenai	C	1			●	●	●			●	69 A5
3504 Summit Lake	Mile 194 Richardson Highway	G	1			●					●	106 D3
3508 Susitna Landing	Mile 82 Parks Highway	G	5		●	●	●				●	82 A2
3512 Swiftwater Park and Ramp	Kenai River, Mile 23	C	1			●	●	●	●		●	69 C5
3516 Talkeetna	Mile 14 Talkeetna Spur	G	2			●					●	93 C6
3520 Tee Harbor	Juneau	G	1							●		32 C3
3524 Thorne Bay	Prince of Wales Island	C	1	●						●		19 B4
3528 Twentymile River	Portage	S	1								●	71 A5
3532 Upper Trail Lake	Mile 30 Seward Highway	G	1									71 B4
3536 Wasilla Lake	Mile 40 Parks Highway	G	1	●		●	●		●		●	83 B4
3540 Whittier Boat Harbor	Whittier	C	2	●		●				●	●	71 A5
3544 Willow Creek	Mile 72 Parks Highway	G	1			●	●	●			●	82 A2
3548 Wood River	Dillingham	C	1								●	56 D3
3552 Wrangell Harbor	Wrangell	A	1	●						●		24 C2
3556 Yakutat Harbor	Yakutat	C	1	●						●	●	35 B3
3560 Yukon River	Mile 56 Dalton Highway	C	1			●						124 A1

Unique Natural Features

Many of the features listed in this category are found within Alaska parks and forests. For more information on these areas see National Parklands and State Parklands.

ANIAKCHAK CALDERA – Aniakchak National Monument and Preserve – Page 139 B4 Six-mile-diameter, 2,000-foot-deep, explosive volcanic crater, one of world's largest. Resulted from collapse of huge volcano thousands of years ago, when 15.4 cubic miles of debris were hurled from its core and scattered for 20 miles on surrounding countryside. Caldera contains 2,200-foot cone, Vent Mountain, and Surprise Lake, headwaters of Aniakchak River *(see Float Trips)*. Caldera floor dotted with cinder cones, lava and ash flows, and explosion pits. Last volcanic eruption in 1931. National Natural Landmark.

BAILEY BAY HOT SPRINGS – Tongass National Forest – Page 20 A1 Highest surface temperature of any known springs in southeast Alaska. Not altered significantly for recreation use; good opportunity for study of hot springs flora. Access on 2.2-mile trail. Shelter.

BLUE RIVER LAVA FLOW GEOLOGICAL AREA – Misty Fiords National Monument – Page 25 C4 9,500-acre area includes remains of lava flow which moved down Lava Fork and Blue River Valleys from Canada, creating Blue Lake and temporarily damming Unuk River which then carved channel through lava. Youngest-known lava flow in southeast Alaska.

CHITISTONE FALLS – Wrangell–St. Elias National Park and Preserve – Page 89 B3 Formed by Chitistone River dropping 300 feet over sheer wall. Located in Upper Chitistone Canyon.

COLUMBIA GLACIER – Chugach National Forest – Page 85 D4 One of largest tidewater glaciers in North America, 42 miles long and four miles wide at terminus. Actively retreating, last of 52 Alaskan tidewater glaciers to still fill length of its fiord. Cliffs of ice towering as high as 300 feet above water calve translucent, house-sized icebergs into Columbia Bay. Access by state ferry, charter boat or plane.

EBNER FALLS – Juneau – Page 33 C4 Scenic falls cascading down 3,576-foot Mt. Juneau to Gold Creek. Access on Perseverance Trail *(see Hiking)*.

EXIT GLACIER – Kenai Fjords National Park – Page 71 D3 Retreating remnant of larger glacier which once extended to Resurrection Bay. Descends 2,500 feet over three miles. From ranger station easy loop trails lead to base of glacier and rough-cut three-mile trail following glacier flank to Harding Icefield *(see this section and Hiking)*.

GLACIER BAY – Glacier Bay National Park and Preserve – Page 31 B5 16 tidewater glaciers, 12 actively calving icebergs into bay. Remnants of Little Ice Age which began 4,000 years ago. Mountains rise up to three vertical miles directly from bay. Access by boat or plane.

GRAND CANYON OF THE NOATAK – Noatak National Preserve – Page 133 A5 Strikingly scenic 65-mile-long canyon carved out by Noatak River *(see Float Trips)*. Migration route for plants and animals between subarctic and arctic environments.

GRANITE TORS – Chena River State Recreation Area – Page 116 A2 Grouping of tall granite spires rising from tundra. Some as high as 200 feet. Reached on Granite Tors Trail *(see Hiking)*.

GREAT KOBUK SAND DUNES – Kobuk Valley National Park – Page 133 A6 Sand created by grinding action of ancient glaciers, then carried to Kobuk Valley by wind and water, creating 25-square-mile dune area. Summer temperatures can exceed 90° Fahrenheit. Also Little Kobuk and Hunt River Dunes.

HARDING ICEFIELD – Kenai Fjords National Park – Page 70 D3 300-square-mile icefield most dominant park feature, one of four major icecaps in US. Discovered early 20th century when mapping team realized several coastal glaciers originated from same massive system. Snowclad surface interrupted only by isolated mountain peaks called nunataks, Eskimo word for "lonely peaks."

HUBBARD GLACIER – Wrangell–St. Elias National Park and Preserve – Page 37 B4 At 80 miles, one of North America's longest glaciers, beginning in Canada and terminating in Disenchantment Bay. Movement threatens to close off adjacent Russell Fiord, as temporarily happened in mid-1980s. Access by charter boat or plane.

ILIAMNA LAKE – Newhalen – Page 59 B5 Largest lake in state at 75 miles long, 20 miles across and 1,000 square miles. Freshwater harbor seals. Supports one of world's largest sockeye salmon runs. Located near Katmai National Park and Preserve.

ILIAMNA VOLCANO – Lake Clark National Park and Preserve – Page 68 D1 10,016-foot, active, cone-shaped stratovolcano, composed of layers of lava flows and pyroclastic rocks. Vented steam to more than 10,000 feet in 1978. Visible from eastern side of park. National Natural Landmark.

JUNEAU ICEFIELD – Juneau – Page 33 B4 1,500-square-mile icefield located in Coast Mountain Range. Supplies 39 glaciers, including Mendenhall *(see this section)*. Annual snowfall exceeds 100 feet.

LECONTE GLACIER – Stikine–LeConte Wilderness – Page 24 A2 Originating from Stikine Icefield, southernmost tidewater glacier in North America. High volume of icebergs produced ice for refrigeration in 19th and early 20th centuries. Access by charter boat or plane.

MALASPINA GLACIER – Wrangell–St. Elias National Park and Preserve – Page 34 A2 North America's largest piedmont glacier, formed by other glaciers converging to form broad ice mass. Flows out of St. Elias Range between Icy and Yakutat Bays and covers 1,500-square-mile area, larger than state of Rhode Island. Carries so much glacial silt that plants and trees take hold on extremities, grow to maturity and topple over edge as glacier retreats. National Natural Landmark.

MATANUSKA GLACIER – Palmer – Page 84 B2 27 miles long, four miles wide at terminus and 1,000 feet thick. Stable enough to walk on. Access on private road. Good views from Matanuska Glacier State Recreation Site.

MENDENHALL GLACIER – Juneau – Page 33 C3 One of state's most accessible glaciers. 12 miles long, 1.5 miles wide, extending from Juneau Icefield *(see this section)* to Mendenhall Lake. Forward movement two feet per day, but retreating 25–30 feet annually due to melting. Six trails offer various viewpoints. Visitor center. Located in Mendenhall Glacier Recreation Area.

MT. EDGECUMBE – Kruzof Island – Page 26 D2 3,201-foot extinct volcano dominates island near Sitka. Activity since last ice age spanned several thousand years, leaving island with many unique volcanic formations. Inactive for last 200 years.

MT. McKINLEY – Denali National Park and Preserve – Page 103 D4 Highest point in North America. Mountain includes two separate peaks: South Peak, its true summit at 20,320 feet; North Peak, 19,470 feet. 18,000 feet above surrounding area, greater than Mt. Everest. Officially named for 25th US president, but called Denali, "High One," by Athabascan Native people. Part of Alaska Range. Permanent snowfields cover more than 50 percent of mountain. Often difficult to see; cloud-hidden as much as 75 percent of summer.

MT. ST. ELIAS – Wrangell–St. Elias National Park and Preserve – Page 36 A1 Second highest peak in US at 18,008 feet. Sited and recorded during 1741 Bering Expedition, first climbed in 1897. Part of St. Elias Range, one of world's highest coastal mountain ranges.

MT. WRANGELL – Wrangell–St. Elias National Park and Preserve – Page 97 D6 At 14,163 feet, highest active volcano in state and northernmost on Pacific Rim. Last erupted 1930. Viewed from nearby highways, plume of steam and ash-covered snow near summit visible on clear days.

MULDROW GLACIER – Denali National Park and Preserve – Page 103 C6 At 32 miles, longest glacier on north side of Alaska Range. Terminus covered with rock, soil and shrub growth. Experienced powerful surges in 1956, advancing more than four miles before slowing down by 1957. Descends from Mt. McKinley to within one mile from McKinley Park Road, between Eielson Visitor Center and Wonder Lake.

NEW EDDYSTONE ROCK – Misty Fiords National Monument – Page 21 B3 237-foot-high volcanic plug projecting from depths of Behm Canal. Made of basalt, part of volcanic vent where magma rose to surface repeatedly from bottom of canal.

NOGAHABARA DUNES – Koyukuk National Wildlife Refuge – Page 133 C7 10,000-acre active sand dune. Formed from wind-blown deposits about 10,000 years ago.

POLYCHROME PASS – Denali National Park and Preserve – Page 104 B1 Spectacular, multicolored landscape with shades of red, orange and purple. Created during the Ice Age by wind and water erosion. Located at Mile 45.9 McKinley Park Road.

PORTAGE GLACIER – Chugach National Forest – Page 71 B5 Six miles long, one mile wide at terminus, creating Portage Lake *(see this section)*. Spectacular views from Begich–Boggs Visitor Center, with picture windows, observation deck, simulated ice cave, interpretive displays and movie. Easy access from Seward Highway. One of state's most visited sites. Located in 8,600-acre Portage Glacier Recreation Area. Also Explorer, Middle and Byron Glaciers *(see Hiking)*.

PORTAGE LAKE – Chugach National Forest – Page 71 A5 Aquamarine, iceberg-filled lake, only decades old, formed by retreating Portage Glacier *(see this section)*. 1.7 miles long, approximately 600 feet deep. Dramatic views from Begich–Boggs Visitor Center. Warning: Climbing on unstable icebergs dangerous.

PUNCHBOWL COVE – Misty Fiords National Monument – Page 21 B3 Located in Rudyerd Bay. Spectacular cove and surrounding high cliffs formed by large glaciers. 3,150-foot vertical cliff on east side.

REDOUBT VOLCANO – Lake Clark National Park and Preserve – Page 68 C2 Active, cone-shaped stratovolcano. At 10,197 feet, second highest of 76 major volcanoes of Alaska Peninsula and Aleutian Islands. Numerous eruptions recorded from late 1700s to 1989, when steam and ash were blown to 35,000 feet. View from eastern side of park. Visible from Anchorage. National Natural Landmark.

TIDAL BORE – Anchorage – Page 71 A4 Steep-fronted tide crest, from one to six feet high, caused by tides flowing into constricted inlets at speeds up to 12 miles per hour; also called bore tide. 40-foot tide range of Cook Inlet increases effect as tides surge into both Turnagain and Knik Arms. Viewpoints in Turnagain Arm along Seward Highway about 30 miles south of Anchorage.

TOGIAK TUYA – Togiak National Wildlife Refuge – Page 55 D4 Two-mile-long, flat-topped volcano, formed when lava erupted under glacier and spread sideways. Rare geologic feature, located in Togiak Valley.

VALLEY OF 10,000 SMOKES – Katmai National Park and Preserve – Page 51 C4 Major eruption of Novarupta Volcano in 1912 left 40-square-mile area buried beneath volcanic ash deposits as deep as 700 feet. Deep, narrow gorges cut through ash by turbulent Ukak River. Valley named in 1916 by Robert Griggs of National Geographic Society upon seeing steam rising as high as 1,000 feet from thousands of fumaroles or small holes and cracks in ash. Only a few active vents remain today.

WHITE MOUNTAINS – White Mountains National Recreation Area – Page 125 B5 Unusual limestone peaks, pinnacles and cliffs, distinctly different from terrain of rest of state's interior.

WORTHINGTON GLACIER – Worthington Glacier State Recreation Site – Page 86 D1 3.8-mile-long, 1.5-mile-wide, three-fingered glacier originating from Girls Mountain. One-mile trail along edge of glacier. Access from Richardson Highway. One of state's most accessible glaciers. National Natural Landmark.

YUKON RIVER – Eagle – Page 119 B6 One of longest North American rivers, running 2,300 miles from Atlin Lake in British Columbia. Enters Alaska near Eagle, crosses state, empties into Bering Sea. 1,400 river miles in Alaska. Drainage basin 320,000 square miles, 193,000 in Alaska. *(See Float Trips.)*

ALSO IN ALASKA...

ARCTIC CIRCLE Line of latitude approximately 66°33' north of equator circumscribing northern frigid zone. Southernmost point at which sun does not set at summer solstice or rise at winter solstice. (Shown in Atlas from page 132 in western part of state to page 137 in the east. *See also Physical Relief map, pages 2–3 and Alaska Perspectives, page 4.*)

AURORA BOREALIS (NORTHERN LIGHTS) Charged particles produced by sunspot activity collide with gases in earth's upper atmosphere in northern latitudes, causing spectacular multicolored drapery- and arc-like patterns of light in night sky. Colors include red, yellow, violet and green and vary with intensity of interaction. Visible in varying degrees all around state; interior and far north considered best places for viewing, from August to May.

CONTINENTAL DIVIDE Imaginary dividing line from Seward Peninsula in west *(see page 132)*, through Brooks Range, to Canadian border in east *(see page 137)*, between watersheds of Arctic Ocean and Bering Sea. Separates Atlantic and Pacific Ocean drainage in lower 48 states. *(See also Physical Relief map, pages 2–3.)*

MIDNIGHT SUN Summer daylight hours increase with proximity to North Pole, because of earth's tilting on axis toward sun. Barrow most extreme location: no sunset for approximately 84 days (May–August) as sun circles just above horizon. However, no sunrise from mid-November to mid-January, as sun stays just below horizon, when earth is tilted in opposite direction.

MUSKEG Openings found between forest stands consisting of bog plant communities growing on deep peat and dominated by sphagnum moss, sedges, rushes and shrubs. Sparse tree growth consists of hemlock and lodgepole pine in scrub form. Habitat for many plants; provides streamflow and home for wildlife. Found over much of state.

PERMAFROST Ground remaining frozen for two or more years. Continuous permafrost occurs primarily north of Arctic Circle *(see this section)* and in alpine regions, extending to depths of approximately 2,000 feet. Discontinuous permafrost in southern sections (including interior and southcentral regions) starts one to ten feet below surface, to depths of approximately 250 feet. Also extends many miles offshore beneath Beaufort Sea. *(See also Alaska Perspectives, page 4.)*

TAIGA Russian term meaning "land of little sticks," applied to areas of scant tree growth near Arctic Circle *(see this section)*. White and black spruce most common trees. Woods carpeted with mosses and lichens. Open areas filled with shrubs including dwarf birch, blueberry and willow. Found in southcentral and interior parts of state.

TUNDRA Treeless areas consisting of dwarfed shrubs and miniature wildflowers adapted to short growing season. Subsoils permanently frozen. Two types: moist and dry, with numerous gradations in between. Moist tundra may contain sedges, cottongrass and dwarfed shrubs. Dry tundra plants live scattered among barren rocks at higher elevations, growing close to ground in own microclimate. Wildflowers provide stunning summer displays; plants provide important food for wildlife. Found in arctic and subarctic regions.

Mountain Ranges

NAME	HIGHEST ELEVATION	PAGE & GRID
Ahklun Mountains	3,000 feet	55 C3
Alaska Range	20,320 feet	103 D4
Alatna Hills	3,020 feet	136 D2
Aleutian Range	7,585 feet	68 B2
Askinuk Mountains	2,342 feet	130 C2
Baird Mountains	4,300 feet	133 A5
Bendeleben Mountains	3,730 feet	132 C4
Brabazon Range	5,700 feet	35 C5
Brooks Range	8,025 feet	136 B2
Chigmit Mountains	5,000 feet	68 C1
Chugach Mountains	13,176 feet	84 C2
Coast Mountains	10,290 feet	33 B4
Darby Mountains	3,273 feet	133 D4
Davidson Mountains	6,210 feet	137 B5
De Long Mountains	4,915 feet	134 D3
Endicott Mountains	7,000 feet	136 C1
Fairweather Range	15,300 feet	30 B3
Igichuk Hills	2,010 feet	132 A4
Kaiyuh Mountains	2,844 feet	133 D7
Kenai Mountains	6,612 feet	62 C2
Kiglapak Mountains	1,070 feet	54 D1
Kigluaik Mountains	4,714 feet	132 D3
Kilbuck Mountains	3,600 feet	131 D4
Kokrines Hills	4,978 feet	121 D4
Kuskokwim Mountains	4,508 feet	101 C3
Lookout Ridge	2,344 feet	134 C4
Mentasta Mountains	8,235 feet	98 A1
Moore Mountains	3,000 feet	27 B2
Mulgrave Hills	2,285 feet	132 A4
Nulato Hills	3,411 feet	131 A4
Nutzotin Mountains	8,560 feet	99 C4
Philip Smith Mountains	8,048 feet	136 C3
Purcell Mountains	3,831 feet	133 B7
Ray Mountains	5,500 feet	122 A3
Robinson Mountains	9,603 feet	76 C2
Romanzof Mountains	9,060 feet	137 B4
Schwatka Mountains	6,500 feet	136 C1
Selawik Hills	3,307 feet	133 B5
Sheklukshuk Range	2,100 feet	133 B7
Shublik Mountains	5,685 feet	137 A4
Sischu Mountains	3,510 feet	111 D6
St. Elias Mountains	18,000 feet	36 C2
Talkeetna Mountains	8,800 feet	94 B2
Taylor Mountains	3,583 feet	131 D6
Waring Mountains	1,800 feet	133 B6
Waxell Ridge	10,000 feet	76 B1
White Mountains	5,000 feet	125 B5
Wrangell Mountains	16,390 feet	88 A1
York Mountains	2,349 feet	132 C2
Zane Hills	4,053 feet	133 B7

HIGHEST PEAKS

17 of the 20 highest peaks in the US are found in Alaska. These, plus two additional peaks over 14,000 feet, are listed here.

NAME	ELEVATION	PAGE & GRID
Mt. McKinley	20,320 feet	103 D4
Mt. St. Elias	18,008 feet	36 A1
Mt. Foraker	17,400 feet	93 A4
Mt. Bona	16,421 feet	89 C4
Mt. Blackburn	16,390 feet	88 B1
Mt. Sanford	16,237 feet	97 D6
South Buttress	15,885 feet	103 D4
Mt. Vancouver	15,700 feet	37 A4
Mt. Churchill	15,638 feet	89 C4
Mt. Fairweather	15,300 feet	30 A2
Mt. Hubbard	14,950 feet	37 A5
Mt. Bear	14,831 feet	89 C5
East Buttress	14,730 feet	103 D5
Mt. Hunter	14,573 feet	93 A4
Browne Tower	14,530 feet	103 D5
Mt. Alverstone	14,500 feet	37 A5
University Peak	14,470 feet	89 C4
Mt. Wrangell	14,163 feet	97 D6
Mt. Augusta	14,070 feet	36 A2

Wildlife Refuges

More than 80 million acres of Alaska public land have been set aside as wildlife refuges, under both federal and state management. These areas have been established for various purposes; among them, the protection of wildlife and habitats, the fulfillment of international migratory bird treaty obligations, the allowance of continued subsistence by local residents and to provide opportunities for interpretation, environmental education and recreation.

For more information on any of the areas listed in this section, contact one of the Public Lands Information Centers listed in Visitor Information Centers *on Page 6.*

NOTES ON WILDLIFE WATCHING

In General

Keep your distance: Observe animals from a safe distance. Use binoculars, spotting scope or telephoto lens for a closer look.

Don't hurry: Approach animals slowly and quietly. Avoid sudden movements.

Blend in: Wear muted colors. Avoid using scented soaps or perfumes.

Avoid disturbing animals: Especially females with their young.

Don't feed animals: Besides being dangerous, it's also against Alaska state law.

Never litter: Properly dispose of garbage. Wildlife can be endangered by discarded plastic and other refuse.

On Bear Watching

Avoid surprising bears: Look for signs of bears and make plenty of noise.

Avoid crowding bears: Respect their personal space.

Avoid attracting bears: This can inadvertently happen through improper handling of food or garbage.

Identify yourself: Talk to the bear in a normal voice. Wave your arms.

Don't run: You can't outrun a bear. Talk and raise your arms as mentioned above. Raise your voice and become more aggressive if the bear comes closer. Bang pots and pans.

Surrender: If a brown bear actually touches you, fall down and play dead. Lie flat on your stomach or curl up in a ball with your hands behind your neck. A brown bear will usually break off its attack when it feels the threat has been eliminated. If a black bear attacks you, fight back vigorously.

[Source: Alaska Department of Fish and Game pamphlets, "The Bears and You" and "Bear Facts." For copies or more information contact one of the Public Lands Information Centers on Page 6.]

ALASKA CHILKAT BALD EAGLE PRESERVE – Klukwan – 49,320 acres – Page 38 C1 Critical habitat for world's largest concentration of bald eagles. As many as 4,000 eagles attracted to area between late September and early December to feed on spawned-out salmon in ice-free waters of Chilkat River. Known as "Bald Eagle Council Grounds" due to eagles' habit of perching in trees in groups. Main viewing area between Miles 18 and 24 Haines Highway.

ALASKA PENINSULA NATIONAL WILDLIFE REFUGE – Chignik – 3,500,000 acres – Page 139 B4 Located on Pacific side of Alaska Peninsula. Varied landscape including active volcanoes, lakes, rivers, tundra and rugged coastline dominated by Aleutian Range. Showcase of animal and plant adaptation in arctic marine environment. Moose, caribou, wolves, brown bears and wolverines. Sea lions, seals, otters and whales. Ducks, geese and shorebirds. Renowned caribou and brown bear hunting. Outstanding fishing for king and silver salmon, arctic char, lake trout, northern pike and grayling. Hiking, boating and camping.

ANCHOR RIVER AND FRITZ CREEK STATE CRITICAL HABITAT AREA – Homer – 19,000 acres – Page 62 B1 Floodplains and lower hillside slopes of two river drainage systems. Habitats range from bog to spruce forest. One of only major moose overwintering areas on southern Kenai Peninsula, providing good willow browse for 20 percent of area population. Popular for year-round recreation including wildlife viewing, hunting, fishing, trapping and photography. Access from North Fork Road or trails from Ohlson Mountain Road.

ANCHORAGE COASTAL WILDLIFE REFUGE – Anchorage – 32,476 acres – Page 82 D3 16-mile area along coast encompassing tidal flats, marsh and alder–bog forest. Greatest number and diversity of birds in Anchorage area. Best viewing at Potter Marsh. Peak concentrations during spring migration. Nesting Canada geese during summer. Waterfowl hunting. Elevated boardwalk and interpretive signs. Access along Seward Highway.

ARCTIC NATIONAL WILDLIFE REFUGE – Oksrukuyik – 19,049,236 acres – Page 136 B4 Northernmost unit of National Wildlife Refuge System. Refuge encompasses spectacular assemblage of arctic plants, wildlife and landforms. Designed to cover range of 110,000-member Porcupine caribou herd. Musk-ox, Dall sheep, wolves, wolverines, polar and grizzly bears. Long severe winters; brief, intense summers. Snow-covered at least nine months of year. Annual plant and tree growth very slight. Rugged Brooks Range. Float trips, hiking, backpacking, hunting and fishing. Access by plane. Includes 8-million-acre Wilderness.

BECHAROF NATIONAL WILDLIFE REFUGE – King Salmon – 1,200,000 acres – Page 50 B2 Dominated by Becharof Lake, second largest lake in Alaska, surrounded by rolling hills, tundra wetlands and volcanic peaks. Lake produces one of world's largest salmon runs, attracting large brown bear population. Moose, caribou, wolves and wolverines. Sea lions, sea otters, seals and whales. Hunting for bear and caribou. Fishing for salmon, arctic char and grayling. Access by plane. Refuge includes 400,000-acre Wilderness.

CAPE NEWENHAM STATE GAME REFUGE – Platinum – 13,952 acres – Page 46 A1 Primary feature Chagvan Bay with vast eelgrass beds. Spring and fall stopovers by hundreds of thousands of ducks, geese and shorebirds. Area critical for black brant. No developed access.

CHILKAT RIVER STATE CRITICAL HABITAT AREA – Klukwan – 4,800 acres – Page 38 C1 Wide floodplain filled with braided stream channels, gravel bars and islands, located at confluence of Tsirku and Chilkat Rivers. Gathering spot for largest concentration of bald eagles in world *(see this section—Alaska Chilkat Bald Eagle Preserve)*. Also winter moose habitat. No visitor facilities. Access from Haines Highway.

CINDER RIVER STATE CRITICAL HABITAT AREA – Pilot Point – 25,856 acres – Page 41 C3 Large expanse of wetlands, tideflats and estuarine waters at mouth of Ugashik River on north shore of Alaska Peninsula. Large flocks of migrating waterbirds. Important area for cackling Canada geese. No public-use facilities. Access by small plane or boat.

CLAM GULCH STATE CRITICAL HABITAT AREA – Kasilof – 2,560 acres – Page 69 C5 Intertidal area consisting of long, narrow, sandy belt extending over 30 miles along lower Cook Inlet. Popular razor clamming area. Salmon fishing in Deep Creek from May to July. Access from numerous points along Sterling Highway. Public campground nearby.

COPPER RIVER DELTA STATE CRITICAL HABITAT AREA – Cordova – 597,120 acres – Page 74 B1 Vast 35-mile-wide complex of wetlands and tidelands bisected by Copper River. Largest contiguous Pacific coast wetlands. Resting and feeding area for over 20 million migrating shorebirds, including the entire Pacific coast population of dunlins and western sandpipers. Also entire population of dusky Canada geese and large number of trumpeter swans. Greatest species diversity found in May. Waterfowl, moose and bear hunting; trapping, salmon fishing and clamming. Access by plane, boat or from Copper River Highway.

CREAMER'S FIELD MIGRATORY WATERFOWL REFUGE – Fairbanks – 1,664 acres – Page 115 A5 Variety of habitats including fields, bog, lake, forest and former dairy farm. Best known for spring and fall concentrations of migrating ducks, geese and cranes. Two-mile, self-guided nature path with moose-viewing tower. Access from College and Farmer's Loop Roads in Fairbanks.

DELTA JUNCTION BISON RANGE – Delta Junction – Page 106 B3 72,000-acre tract established to protect American bison brought to area from Montana in 1920s. Herd currently numbers about 350. Bison can be seen with binoculars from viewpoint at Mile 241.3 Richardson Highway. Interpretive display.

DUDE CREEK STATE CRITICAL HABITAT AREA – Gustavus – 4,083 acres – Page 32 C1 Open, wet meadow habitat, bisected by forest-fringed Dude Creek. Key resting area for migrating lesser sandhill cranes, especially during September. Popular year-round recreation area. No public-use facilites. Access from Good River Road.

EGEGIK STATE CRITICAL HABITAT AREA – Egegik – 8,064 acres – Page 49 D4 Extensive tideflats and wetlands at mouth of Egegik River in Egegik Bay. Large flocks of migrating waterbirds, including sea and dabbling ducks and geese, and shorebirds in spring and fall. No public-use facilities. Access by small plane or boat.

FOX RIVER FLATS STATE CRITICAL HABITAT AREA – Homer – 7,104 acres – Page 62 A3 Low-lying marshlands and tidal flats extending from head of Kachemak Bay. Primary value as staging area for thousands of migrating waterfowl and shorebirds in spring and fall. Popular for waterfowl hunting. No public-use facilities. Access on steep switchback trail from Homer East End Road out of Homer.

GOOSE BAY STATE GAME REFUGE – Anchorage – 10,880 acres – Page 82 C3 Wetlands drained by Goose Creek. Important spring and fall stopover for migrating waterfowl. Good area for fall hunting. Inland access points along Knik–Goose Bay Road.

INNOKO NATIONAL WILDLIFE REFUGE – McGrath – 3,850,000 acres – Page 131 A6 Two separate sections encompassing most of Innoko River basin. Extensive wetlands provide nesting habitat for more than 250,000 waterfowl. Wolves, black and grizzly bears, caribou and furbearers, including large beaver population. Hunting for moose and black bear. Fishing for northern pike. Float trips. Access by plane or boat. Includes 1.2-million-acre Wilderness.

IZEMBEK NATIONAL WILDLIFE REFUGE – Cold Bay – 320,893 acres – Page 138 C2 Located on tip of Alaska Peninsula facing Bering Sea. Landscape of glacier-capped volcanoes, valleys and tundra uplands. Large eelgrass bed in Izembek Lagoon haven for migratory birds, including emperor geese and world population of black brant. Wintering Steller's eider and sea ducks. Brown bear, caribou, ptarmigan and furbearers. Hunting for waterfowl, ptarmigan and caribou. Access by boat or on foot, with very limited access by road from Cold Bay. Includes 300,000-acre Wilderness.

IZEMBEK STATE GAME REFUGE – Cold Bay – 181,440 acres – Page 138 C2 Izembek Lagoon, with one of world's largest eelgrass beds, provides important feeding and staging habitat for millions of migrating waterfowl and other birds from North America, Asia and Pacific. Primary species: black brant, emperor geese and Steller's eiders. Road access from Cold Bay.

KACHEMAK BAY STATE CRITICAL HABITAT AREA - Homer - 222,080 acres - Page 62 B2 Includes all of Kachemak Bay, a large, highly productive, ice-free estuarine environment with diverse and abundant marine life. Tens of thousands of feeding waterfowl, shorebirds and seabirds in spring, summer and fall. Marine mammals year-round. Popular location for halibut and salmon fishing. Easy access along Homer Spit.

KALGIN ISLAND STATE CRITICAL HABITAT AREA – Kalgin Island – 3,520 acres – Page 69 C4 Remote area located on Kalgin Island in Cook Inlet. Spring and fall resting and feeding habitat for waterfowl and shorebirds. No public-use facilities. Access by boat or chartered plane.

KANUTI NATIONAL WILDLIFE REFUGE – Allakaket – 1,430,000 acres – Page 136 D2 Vast, remote wetland basin straddling Arctic Circle, composed of Kanuti Flats and rolling plains of Kanuti and Koyukuk Rivers. Nesting habitat for waterfowl, primarily Canada and white-fronted geese and ducks. Critical refuge during times of drought in traditional breeding areas. Moose, black and grizzly bears, wolves and wolverines. Fishing for northern pike and grayling. Access by plane from Fairbanks.

KENAI NATIONAL WILDLIFE REFUGE – Soldotna – 1,970,000 acres – Page 69 C5 Western slopes of Kenai Mountains and forested lowlands bordering Cook Inlet. Includes all Alaska habitat types—tundra, mountains, wetlands and forests. Originally established to preserve large moose population. Also Dall sheep, mountain goat, caribou, coyotes, wolves, grizzly and black bears, lynx and wolverines. Excellent fishing for numerous species. Over 200 miles of trails and routes including Swanson River Route *(see Float Trips)*. Access from Sterling Highway. Includes 1.4-million acre Wilderness.

KODIAK NATIONAL WILDLIFE REFUGE – Kodiak – 1,865,000 acres – Page 45 A3 Area covers two-thirds of Kodiak Island and portion of Afognak Island, including mountains, bays, inlets and wetlands. Originally established to protect brown bear habitat. Two million seabirds. Large numbers of bald eagles year-round. Rafting and camping. Cabins. Fishing for all five Pacific salmon species. Renowned for brown bear hunting. Access by boat or plane.

KOYUKUK NATIONAL WILDLIFE REFUGE – Galena – 3,550,000 acres – Page 133 D7 Extensive floodplain including 14 rivers, hundreds of creeks and 15,000 lakes. Refuge provides habitat for salmon, beaver and waterfowl. 400,000 migrating ducks and geese in fall. Black and grizzly bears, moose, wolves, caribou and furbearers. Nogahabara Dunes *(see Unique Natural Features)*. Hunting for moose. Fishing for northern pike and grayling. Access by plane. Includes 400,000-acre Wilderness.

McNEIL RIVER STATE GAME SANCTUARY – 80 mi. W of Homer – 83,840 acres – Page 60 D1 Rolling shrub and grasslands extending from coast upstream to above McNeil River Falls. Renowned for unique concentration of brown bears. Each summer, as many as 100 bears come from as far as 30 miles to feed on migrating salmon attempting to navigate falls. Access by small plane or boat. Permit required. National Natural Landmark.

MENDENHALL WETLANDS STATE GAME REFUGE – Juneau – 3,789 acres – Page 33 C4 Wetlands, tidelands and submerged lands along Gastineau Channel. Best known for Canada geese, ducks and bald eagles seen feeding along shoreline year-round. Popular for wildlife viewing, boating, fishing, hunting and horseback riding. Scenic turnout, viewing platform and interpretive signs. Access from several points along Egan Drive.

MINTO FLATS STATE GAME REFUGE – Nenana – 500,000 acres – Page 114 B2 Large expanse of lowlying wetlands dotted with numerous lakes, oxbows and potholes. Spring and fall migratory bird stop. High density duck and swan nesting. Also fish, furbearer and big game populations. Popular for fishing, hunting and trapping. Access from Murphy Dome Road and Parks Highway or by boat on Tanana River.

NOWITNA NATIONAL WILDLIFE REFUGE – Ruby – 1,560,000 acres – Page 110 B2 Forested lowlands, hills, lakes, marshes, ponds and streams in central Yukon River Valley. Dominant feature Nowitna River, designated National Wild and Scenic River *(see Float Trips)*. Waterfowl protection primary purpose. Black bears, moose and furbearers. Popular for moose and bear hunting. Fishing for northern pike and sheefish. Access by plane.

PALMER HAY FLATS STATE GAME REFUGE – Matanuska – 26,048 acres – Page 83 B4 45-square-mile complex of forest, wetlands, tidal sloughs, lakes and tideflats. Hay flats major stopover for migrating waterfowl. Popular waterfowl hunting and fishing area. Access by boat from Glenn Highway at Knik River Bridge.

PILOT POINT STATE CRITICAL HABITAT AREA – Pilot Point – 46,016 acres – Page 41 B4 Estuarine wetlands environment at mouth of several rivers in Ugashik Bay. Stopover for large flocks of migrating waterbirds, including ducks, geese and shorebirds. Important fall feeding and staging habitat for cackling Canada geese. No public-use facilities. Access by small boat or plane.

PORT HEIDEN STATE CRITICAL HABITAT AREA – Port Heiden – 72,128 acres – Page 139 B4 Extensive estuarine environment of tideflats and wetlands along shores of large bay, Port Heiden. Large flocks of migrating waterbirds, including ducks, geese and shorebirds in spring and fall. No developed access.

PORT MOLLER STATE CRITICAL HABITAT AREA – Port Moller – 127,296 acres – Page 138 C3 Located along shores of Port Moller, large bay on north shore of Alaska Peninsula. Stopover for hundreds of thousands of migrating ducks (eiders and other seaducks), geese (emperors) and shorebirds in spring and fall. Access by plane or boat.

REDOUBT BAY STATE CRITICAL HABITAT AREA – 40 mi. SW of Anchorage – 183,640 acres – Page 69 A4 268-square-mile, low-lying expanse of wetlands on west side of Cook Inlet. Resting and feeding area for hundreds of thousands of migrating waterfowl and summer nesting area for ducks, geese and swans. Best known as nesting ground for Tule white-fronted geese. Brown bears during salmon spawning season. Winter moose habitat. Very popular waterfowl hunting area. Access by plane or boat.

SELAWIK NATIONAL WILDLIFE REFUGE – Kotzebue – 2,150,000 acres – Page 133 B6 Estuaries, lakes, river deltas and tundra slopes straddling Arctic Circle. Prominent feature tundra wetlands between Waring Mountains and Selawik Hills, supporting abundance of waterbirds, waterfowl and mammals. Hundreds of thousands of nesting ducks. Moose, grizzly bear, furbearers and wintering caribou. Sheefish, whitefish, grayling and northern pike. Portions of Selawik River designated Wild and Scenic River. River rafting. Evidence of human, animal and plant migration still exists where Bering Land Bridge once crossed from Asia. Access by boat or plane. Includes 240,000-acre Wilderness.

STAN PRICE STATE WILDLIFE SANCTUARY – Admiralty Island – 613 acres – Page 28 A1 Tidelands and submerged lands along Pack Creek. Well-known location for watching brown bears. As many as 30 bears gather during July and August to feed on spawning salmon. Permit required. Access by floatplane or boat.

SUSITNA FLATS STATE GAME REFUGE – Anchorage – 300,800 acres – Page 82 C2 Expansive coastal lowlands bisected by Susitna River. Primary attraction spring and fall concentrations of migrating waterfowl and shorebirds. Popular for waterfowl hunting. Access by floatplane or boat.

TETLIN NATIONAL WILDLIFE REFUGE – Tok – 700,000 acres – Page 99 B6 Located in Upper Tanana River Valley encompassing thousands of lakes and ponds interspersed with rolling hills, forests and snowcapped mountains. One of highest densities of nesting waterfowl in Alaska. 143 nesting and 47 migrating bird species. Spectacular views of migrating sandhill cranes in spring and fall. Arctic and common loon, osprey, bald eagle and trumpeter swan. Hunting for moose and waterfowl. Fishing for northern pike, burbot and grayling. Two campgrounds and two cabins. Visitor center. Access along 70 miles of Alaska Highway.

TOGIAK NATIONAL WILDLIFE REFUGE – Dillingham – 4,105,000 acres – Page 56 D2 Mountain crags, fast-flowing rivers, deep lakes, estuaries, coastal lagoons, sea cliffs and sandy beaches. Resting and breeding area for migrating waterfowl and shorebirds. Spotted seals, walrus and seven whale species. 1,500 miles of streams and rivers for spawning salmon. River rafting. Excellent fishing for salmon and trout. Hunting for brown bear. Access by plane. Includes 2.3-million-acre Wilderness. *(See Unique Natural Features.)*

ALASKA MARITIME NATIONAL WILDLIFE REFUGE

With the most diverse wildlife species of all Alaska refuges, this 4.5-million-acre area encompasses more than 2,500 islands, islets, rocks and headlands. Divided into five units (listed below), the refuge extends from the Arctic Ocean to southeastern Alaska, including most lands in the Aleutian Islands and the Gulf of Alaska. 2.6 million acres are designated Wilderness.

In addition to thousands of sea mammals, including sea lions, seals, walruses and sea otters, 80 percent of the 50 million seabirds nesting in Alaska inhabit this area. Birds congregate in "bird cities" or colonies, each species having a specialized nesting site—rock ledge, crevice, boulder rubble, pinnacle or burrow—allowing them to use small areas of land. The 38 bird species using the refuge include puffins, murres, auklets, kittiwakes and storm-petrels.

For more information contact the refuge headquarters at 202 Pioneer Avenue, Homer, AK 99603, (907) 235-6546.

ALASKA PENINSULA UNIT – Sand Point – 139 B5 More than 700 islands, islets and rocks on south side of Alaska Peninsula. Many very small islands, including Semidi and Shumagin Islands and Sandman Reefs, support spectacular bird colonies.

ALEUTIAN ISLANDS UNIT–Amchitka Island – 140 D3 Volcanic, treeless island chain. Nesting area for tufted puffins, rare whiskered auklet and endangered Aleutian Canada goose. Asiatic species on central and western islands. WWII and Aleut historic sites.

BERING SEA UNIT – St. Matthew Island – 139 A4 Several islands and headlands on Norton Sound and extensive wilderness on St. Matthew Island. Well-known seabird cliffs and fur seal rookeries on Pribilof Islands and Hagemeister Island.

CHUKCHI SEA UNIT – Point Hope – 134 D1 Many barrier islands along Chukchi Sea, Capes Lisburne and Thompson and Chamisso Island in Kotzebue Sound. High escarpments on Lisburne Peninsula host largest seabird colonies along Alaska's northern coast.

GULF OF ALASKA UNIT – Port William – 53 A4 Includes islands surrounding Kodiak and Afognak Islands; Duck and Chisik Islands in Cook Inlet; Barren, Pye and Chiswell Islands off Kenai Peninsula; and Forrester, Hazy and St. Lazaria Islands of southeastern Alaska. Most accessible sea lion rookeries and seabird colonies in refuge. Charter boats, lodging and campgrounds available in Sitka, Seward and Homer.

TRADING BAY STATE GAME REFUGE – Shirleyville – 160,960 acres – Page 81 D4   Large, tidally influenced coastal marsh fed by six rivers. Used by thousands of waterfowl during spring and fall migration and for nesting during summer months. Fishing and waterfowl, moose and bear hunting. Access by small plane, boat or road from Tyonek.

TUGIDAK ISLAND STATE CRITICAL HABITAT AREA – Tugidak Island – 50,240 acres – Page 64 D1   Remote, uninhabited, treeless island with shallow lagoon and barrier spit at northern end. Renowned for one of largest harbor seal pupping and haulout areas in world. Also large concentrations of migrating and ground nesting birds. No public-use facilities. Access by floatplane from Kodiak Island.

WALRUS ISLANDS STATE GAME SANCTUARY – Walrus Islands – 9,728 acres – Page 47 B4   Group of seven craggy islands fronted by rocky beaches and steep sea cliffs. Best known, Round Island, only regularly used land-based walrus haulout on southern Bering Sea, where 8,000–12,000 male walruses return each spring. Also nesting ground for nearly 450,000 seabirds. Access by charter boat or floatplane, May–September. Permit required.

WILLOW MOUNTAIN STATE CRITICAL HABITAT AREA – Willow – 22,270 acres – Page 82 A3   In Talkeetna Mountains, established to protect high-quality moose habitat. As many as 1,000 moose seen along mid-level mountain slopes in summer, fall and early winter. Access on Peters–Purches Trail off Fishhook–Willow Road or Willow Mountain Trail off Willer–Kash Road.

YAKATAGA STATE GAME REFUGE – Cape Yakataga – 82,000 acres – Page 76 D2   Isolated, coastal lowlands surrounded by Chugach Mountains to north and glaciers, east and west. Critical mountain goat and moose winter habitat. Hundreds of wintering bald eagles. Rich salmon spawning and rearing habitat. Hunting for moose, black and brown bear, mountain goat and waterfowl. Fishing for coho salmon. Access by plane or boat.

YUKON DELTA NATIONAL WILDLIFE REFUGE – Bethel – 19,624,458 acres – Page 131 D4   Treeless, wetland plain dominated by Yukon and Kuskokwim Rivers. Noted for wildlife variety and abundance. Nesting and feeding habitat for more than 750,000 swans and geese, two million ducks and 100 million shorebirds and waterfowl.

Moose, caribou, black and grizzly bears and wolves. Herds of musk-ox and reindeer on 1.1-million-acre Nunivak Island. 42 Eskimo villages. Hunting, fishing, hiking and boating. Access by boat or plane. Includes 1.9-million-acre Wilderness.

YUKON FLATS NATIONAL WILDLIFE REFUGE – Fort Yukon – 8,630,000 acres – Page 137 D6   Most northerly point reached by Yukon River, where waters spread unconfined through vast floodplain. 40,000 lakes and ponds. One of highest waterfowl nesting densities in North America. Two million migrating ducks and geese. Longest salmon spawning run in US. Moose, caribou, wolves, black and grizzly bears. Canoe, kayak and rafting trips. Fishing for northern pike. Access by plane.

Alaska Marine Highway System

The Alaska Marine Highway System is a fleet of eight ferries, owned and operated by the state of Alaska. This fleet provides year-round service to southeast and southwest parts of the state, covering 3,500 miles. Most of the ferries carry vehicles as well as passengers, and offer food, observation lounges and staterooms. The vessels range in length from the 148-foot flagship M/V *Columbia* to the 193-foot M/V *Bartlett*. USDA Forest Service naturalists ride the larger ferries in summer, offering interpretive programs.

The ferries cover two separate routes which have been plotted in detail in this Atlas. The Southeast System offers trips from Bellingham, Washington, and Prince Rupert, British Columbia, to the northern tip of the Inside Passage. Stops at communities along the way include Ketchikan, Wrangell, Petersburg, Sitka and Juneau.

The Southwest System serves Prince William Sound, the Kenai Peninsula and Kodiak Island, including stops at Cordova, Valdez, Whittier, Seward, Seldovia, Homer, Kodiak and Port Lions. Service to remote ports of the Aleutian Chain is available May–September, including stops at Chignik, Sand Point, King Cove, Cold Bay and Dutch Harbor.

There are no connecting routes between the Southeast and Southwest Systems. Travelers can get from one system to the other overland via the road system; for example: Haines to Valdez, Haines to Fairbanks or Haines to Anchorage *(see Mileage Chart, page 5, for distances)*.

Routes, schedules and tariffs vary according to time of year. Reservations are required on all ferries for both passengers and vehicles. For more information contact the Alaska Marine Highway System at P.O. Box 25535, Juneau, AK 99802-5535, 1-800-642-0066; in Canada, (907) 465-3941.

A sampling of routes with approximate running times and traveling distances (measured in nautical miles) follows.

Bellingham, WA–Ketchikan	36 hours/619 miles
Prince Rupert, BC–Ketchikan	6 hours/92 miles
Ketchikan–Wrangell	5.7 hours/88 miles
Wrangell–Petersburg	3 hours/40 miles
Petersburg–Juneau/Auke Bay	7.75 hours/120 miles
Juneau/Auke Bay–Haines	4.5 hours/68 miles
Haines–Skagway	1 hour/14 miles
Juneau/Auke Bay–Sitka	8.7 hours/131 miles
Petersburg–Sitka	10 hours/156 miles
Homer–Kodiak	12 hours/155 miles
Homer–Dutch Harbor	72 hours/875 miles
Whittier–Valdez	7 hours/90 miles
Seward–Kodiak	12 hours/200 miles
Seward–Valdez	12 hours/200 miles

Scenic Drives

Alaska's highways provide access to adventure and endless scenic wonder—mountains, rivers, glaciers, parks, forests and wildlife. Many of the state's major roads have been included here. While most roads are well-maintained, road surfaces and conditions may vary, and some may require high-clearance vehicles. Be sure to check ahead for road and weather conditions before starting out. For more information contact one of the Public Lands Information Centers listed in Visitor Information Centers on page 6.

NAME	LENGTH	TRIP START	TRIP END	PAGE & GRID	COMMENTS
Alaska Highway	1422 miles	Delta Junction	Dawson Creek, BC	116 D3	Historic highway *(see Historic Sites/Museums)*. Open and maintained year-round. Only 302 miles actually within Alaska.
Denali Highway	133 miles	Paxson	Cantwell	106 D3	Original travel route to Denali National Park. Outstanding scenery. Gravel road most of length.
Elliott Highway	156 miles	Fox	Manley Hot Springs	115 A5	Well-maintained gravel road with steep hills and sharp turns. Parallels Trans-Alaska Pipeline for short distance.
George Parks Highway	324 miles	Matanuska	Fairbanks	83 B4	Heavily traveled, paved highway. Access to Denali National Park.
Glacier Highway	40 miles	Juneau	Echo Cove	33 C4	Follows Favorite Channel northward. Views of Chilkat Range. Gravel road last eight miles to Echo Cove.
Glenn Highway	124 miles	Anchorage	Tok	82 D3	Paved, heavily traveled road. Views of Talkeetna and Wrangell Ranges. Last 125 miles known as Tok Cut-off.
James Dalton Highway	416 miles	Livengood	Arctic Ocean	124 C3	Rough gravel road parallels Trans-Alaska Pipeline. Drive with headlights on at all times. Restricted use past Mile 211.
McCarthy Road	61 miles	Chitina Ranger Station	McCarthy	87 B4	Gravel road follows abandoned railroad bed. First 22 miles within Wrangell–St. Elias National Park.
Nabesna Road	46 miles	Slana Ranger Station	Nabesna	98 B1	Gravel road. Most of drive in Wrangell–St. Elias National Park. Last four miles to Nabesna not maintained (may be impassible).
Richardson Highway	368 miles	Valdez	Fairbanks	85 D5	Paved road leading through Alaska Range and Chugach Mountains. Passes spectacular glaciers.
Seward Highway	127 miles	Anchorage	Seward	82 D3	Passes through Kenai Mountains. Views of Chugach Mountains and Cook Inlet.
Steese Highway	162 miles	Fairbanks	Circle	115 A5	Used by gold rush prospectors to freight supplies by dog sled and wagon. Interior Alaska's oldest travel route.
Sterling Highway	137 miles	Junction with Seward Hwy	Homer	71 B3	Winds through Kenai Mountains in Kenai Peninsula. Excellent fishing opportunities along route.
Taylor Highway	160 miles	Tetlin Junction	Eagle	108 C3	Gravel road with steep hills and hairpin curves. Climbs three times to over 3,500 feet.

Hunting

Alaska is divided into 26 State Game Management Units within which various species can be hunted. For information on a specific unit call the closest regional office of the Alaska Department of Fish and Game, Division of Wildlife Conservation, as indicated below. Refer to the locater map below for approximate unit locations. Information provided here is subject to change. It is most important to be thoroughly familiar with all rules, regulations and restrictions before hunting in any area. For a copy of the current Alaska State Hunting Regulations booklet or more information contact any of the offices listed here.

GAME MANAGEMENT UNIT LOCATER MAP

ALASKA DEPARTMENT OF FISH AND GAME OFFICES

Headquarters
Capital Office Park, 1255 West 8th Street, P.O. Box 25526, Juneau, AK 99802-5526, (907) 465-4190 .... Page 33 C4

Regional Offices
Douglas Island Center Building, 802 3rd Street, P.O. Box 240020, Douglas, AK 99824, (907) 465-4265 ..... Page 33 C4
333 Raspberry Road, Anchorage, AK 99518, (907) 267-2180 .... Page 82 D3
1300 College Road, Fairbanks, AK 99701, (907) 456-5156 .... Page 115 A5

Continue on Page 18

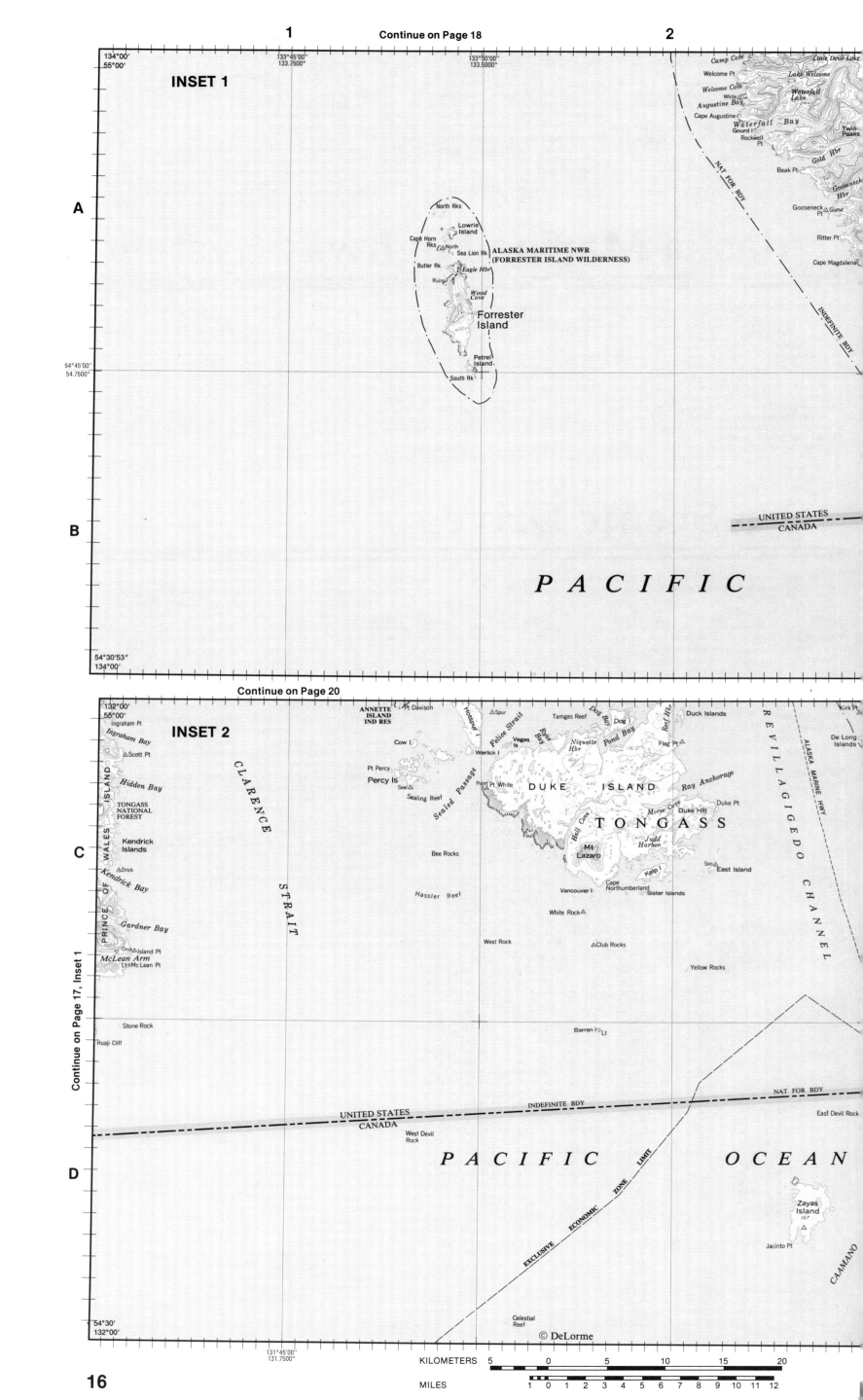

INSET 1

134°00'
55°00'

133°45'00"
133.7500°

133°00'00"
133.5000°

A

North Rks

Lowrie
Island

Cape Horn
Rks   North

Sea Lion Rk   ALASKA MARITIME NWR
(FORRESTER ISLAND WILDERNESS)

Butler Rk   Eagle Hbr

Ruin   Wood
Cove

Forrester
Island

Petrel
Island

54°45'00"
54.7500°

South Rk

B

UNITED STATES
CANADA

P A C I F I C

54°30'53"
134°00'

Camp Cove   Little Devil Lake
Welcome Pt   Lake Welcome

Welcome Cove   Waterfall
White   Lake
Augustine Bay
Cape Augustine   Waterfall Bay
Gourd I   Twin
Rockwell   Peaks
Pt

Beak Pt   Gold Hbr

Gooseneck
Hbr

Gooseneck   Goose
Pt

Ritter Pt

Cape Magdalena

NAT FOR BDY

INDEFINITE BDY

Continue on Page 20

132°00'
55°00'

INSET 2

Ingraham Pt   Pt Davison
Ingraham Bay   Spur   Tamgas Reef   Dog Bay Dog I   Duck Islands   Kirk Pt
                                  Felice Strait   Red Hbr
Scott Pt   Cow I   Vegas   Bold   Niquette   Flag Pt   R   De Long
Hidden Bay   Is   Bay   Hbr   Pond Bay   E   Islands
                                  Werlick I   V
TONGASS   Pt Percy   Point Pt White DUKE   ISLAND Ray Anchorage   I   ALASKA
NATIONAL   Percy Is   L   MARINE HWY
FOREST   Seal   Sealing Reef   Point Pt White   L
Kendrick   Morse Cove Duke Hill Duke Pt   A
Islands   CLARENCE   TONGASS   G
                                                  Hall Cove Duke Hbr   I
Drick   Bee Rocks   Foul   D   East Island
Kendrick Bay   Mt   Judd   E
                  STRAIT   Lazaro   Harbor   O   Son
                                                                                              East Island
Gardner Bay   Hassler Reef   Kelp I   C
                                                  Vancouver I Cape   Sister Islands   H
Orca Island Pt   Northumberland   A
McLean Arm   White Rock   N
Lt Mc Lean Pt   N
                                                                                          E
                                  West Rock   Club Rocks   L

Stone Rock   Barren I Lt   Yellow Rocks

Huaji Cliff

UNITED STATES   INDEFINITE BDY   NAT FOR BDY
CANADA
                  West Devil   East Devil Rock
                  Rock

P A C I F I C   EXCLUSIVE ECONOMIC ZONE LIMIT   *O C E A N*

Zayas
Island

Jacinto Pt   CAAMANO

Celestial
Reef   © DeLorme

54°30'
132°00'

131°45'00"
131.7500°

Continue on Page 17, Inset 1

KILOMETERS 5   0   5   10   15   20

MILES   1 0 1 2 3 4 5 6 7 8 9 10 11 12

16

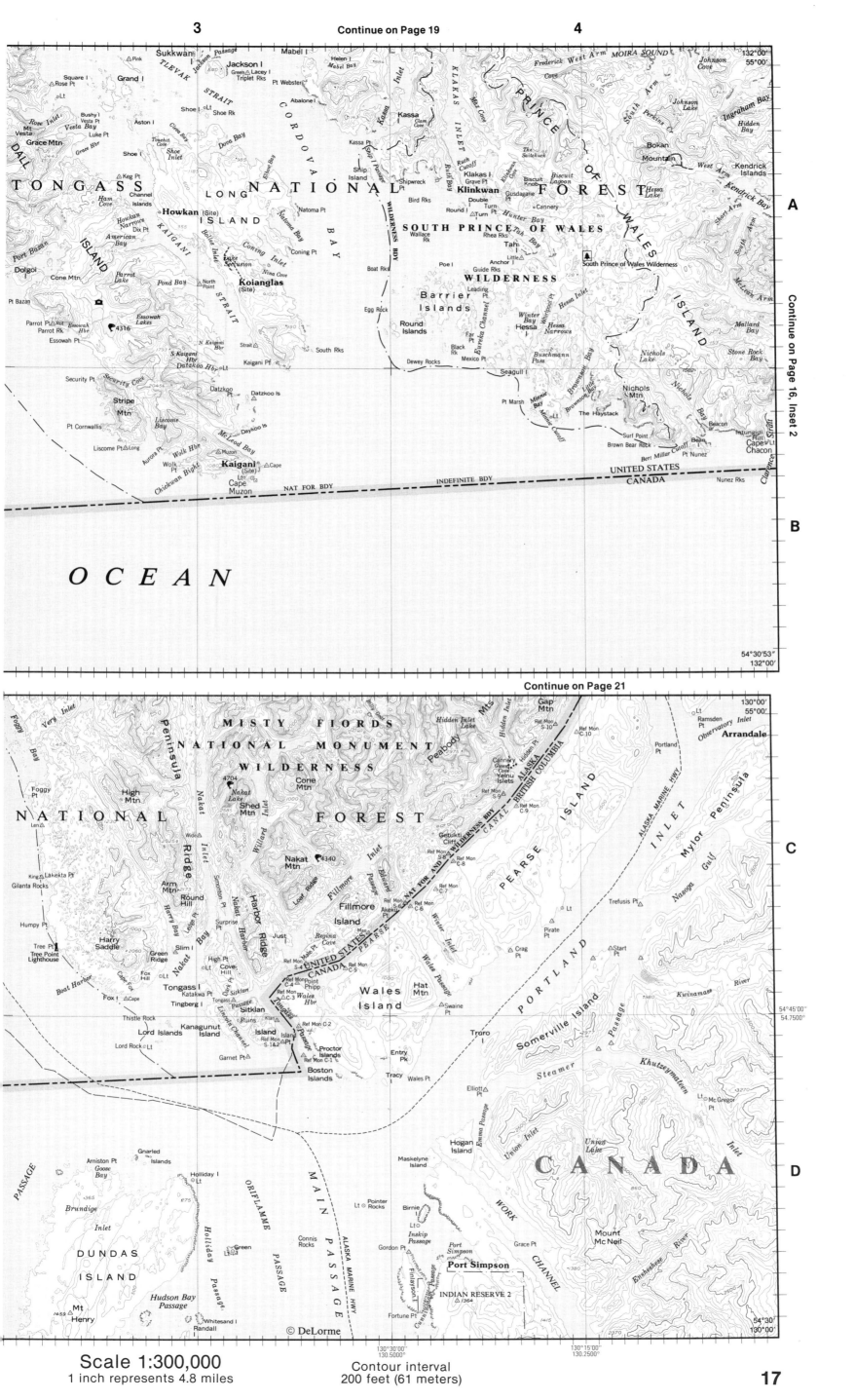

Continue on Page 16, Inset 2

Continue on Page 21

© DeLorme

Scale 1:300,000
1 inch represents 4.8 miles

Contour interval
200 feet (61 meters)

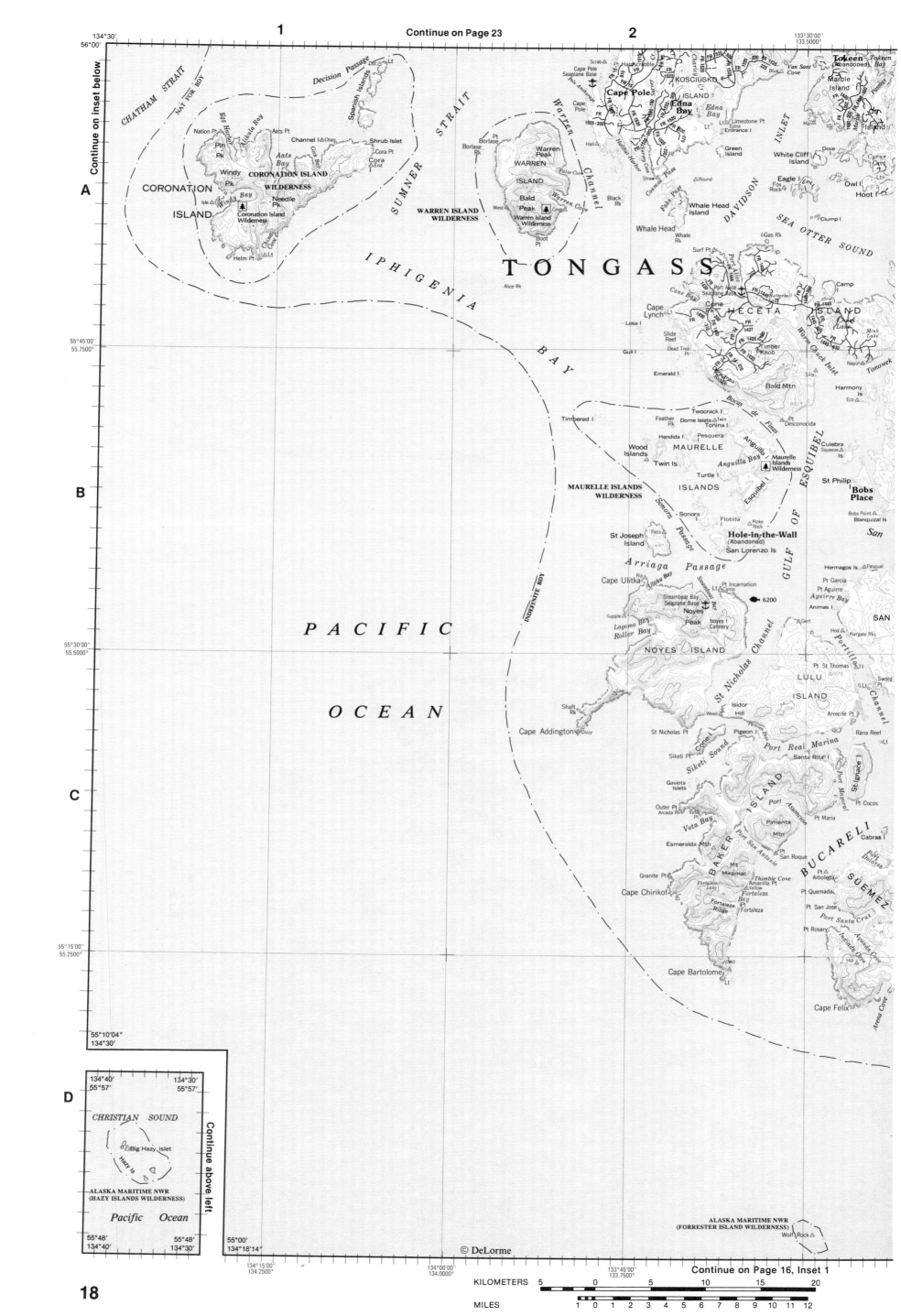

1 **2**

134°30'
56°00'

CHATHAM STRAIT

Continue on inset below

133°30'00''
133.5000°

Decision Passage   NAT FOR BDY   ·Lt

Spanish Islands

Tokeen   Tokeen
Bay
Marble
Island

Scrab Pt   Hardscrabble   FR 6
Cape Pole   Charlie   FR 1520   225
Seaplane Base   FR 15   1522   Blue

Van Sant
Cove

KOSCIUSKO

Egg Harbor   Alikula Bay   Aats Pt   Channel I △Chan   Shrub Islet
Nation Pt   Pin
Pk   Aata   Cora Pt   Cora
Bay   Gish Bay   △End

Pt Anchorage   Cape Pole   Cape Pole   ISLAND   Edna
Pt   Edna Bay   Bay

Limestone Pt
Edna
Entrance I

Marble
Island

Borlase   Warren   Charl   Island
Pt
Borlase   Halibut Harbor   Strawb   Green Island
Bay   Warren   Survey Point   Round   White Cliff
Peak   WARREN   False Cove   Island

SUMNER

Windy   CORONATION ISLAND   ISLAND   DAVIDSON   Dove
Pk   WILDERNESS   Warren Island   Cyrus
CORONATION   Needle   Wilderness   Eagle I   Owl I
Isle △   Windy   Pk   Fox   Fox   Hoot
Bay   2560   West   Bald   Warren Cove   Rock
ISLAND   China   Peak   △   Cove
Cove   Coronation Island   Warren Island   Whale Head   Clump I
Wilderness   Boot   Island
Helm Pt △Lt   Pt   Whale Head   Whale   Gas Rk

STRAIT

WARREN ISLAND
WILDERNESS

SEA OTTER SOUND

IPHIGENIA

T O N G A S S

Alice Rk

Surf Pt   Port   Camp
Cone Bay   Port Alice   FR   FR 1445
Cape   Port Alice   HECETA   ISLAND   Mink
Lynch △Lt   Cone   Seaplane Base   Butterball   Lake
FR   1427   Warm Chuck Inlet
Slide   FR 14   1425   Timber   Napu △
Reef   Dead Tree   Knob   Tonowek
Emerald I   Pt   Bald Mtn   Harmony
Is   Eco △

B A Y

Gull I

Twocrack I   Bocas de Finos   Desconocida
Timbered I   Feather   Dome Islets △Twin
Rk   Tonina I
Hendida I   Pesquera I   Anguilla   Culebra
Wood   MAURELLE   Maurelle   Squeeze △   Is
Islands   Islands   St Philip
Twin Is   Anguilla Bay   Wilderness   Bobs
Turtle I   ISLANDS   Esquibel I   Place
MAURELLE ISLANDS   Bobs Point △
WILDERNESS   Sonora   Blanquizal Is

GULF OF ESQUIBEL

Sonora   San
Pass △   Flotilla
St Joseph   497   Moke
Island   Hole-in-the-Wall   Rock
(Abandoned)   Hermagos Is △   Pasqual
San Lorenzo Is   Pt Garcia
Arriaga   Passage   Pt Aguirre △
Rio   Aguirre Bay
Cape Ulitka   Aluka Bay   Lt △ Pt Incarnation   Animas I △   SAN
Camp   Gert
Steamboat Bay   ● 6200   Hod △   Alargate Rks
Seaplane Base   Noyes   Portillo
Supple △   92106   Peak   Pt St Thomas
Lagoma Bay   Noyes I   1075
Roller Bay   Cannery   LULU   Sword
St Nicholas Channel   ISLAND   Lt   Channel
NOYES ISLAND   Pt St Thomas

P A C I F I C

O C E A N

Shaft
Rk   Arrecife Pt △
Cape Addington ·Dizzy   Isidor   Rana Reef
Weed   Hill   Pigeon I   Lt
St Nicholas Pt
Cone I   Port Real Marina
Siketi Pt   Santa Rita I   Port
Siketi Sound   Pt Cocos
Gaviota   Port   I Perez I △
Islets   Pt Mayoral
Outer Pt   Veta   Port   Pt
Arcada Rk   Asuncion   Pt Cocos
Veta Bay   Pimenta   BUCARELI
Pt Maria   Cabras I
Esmeralda Mtn   Mt   Pt △
Miramar   San Roque   Arboleda   Pt Dolores
Granite Pt   Thimble Cove   Pt Quemada
Amarilla   Yellow   SUEMEZ
Cape Chirikof   Fortaleza   Fortaleza   Pt San Jose
Lake   Bay   Port Santa Cruz
Fortaleza   Fortaleza
Ridge   Pt Rosary

55°45'00''
55.7500°

55°30'00''
55.5000°

55°15'00''
55.2500°

INDEFINITE BDY

55°10'04''
134°30'

Continue above left

134°40'   134°30'
55°57'   55°57'

CHRISTIAN SOUND

Big Hazy Islet
Hazy Is

ALASKA MARITIME NWR
(HAZY ISLANDS WILDERNESS)

Pacific   Ocean

Cape Bartolome

△Lt

Cape Felix

Arena Cove

55°48'   55°48'
134°40'   134°30'

55°00'
134°18'14''
134.2500°

134°00'00''
134.0000°

133°45'00''
133.7500°

ALASKA MARITIME NWR
(FORRESTER ISLAND WILDERNESS)
Wolf Rock △

© DeLorme

Continue on Page 16, Inset 1

18

KILOMETERS 5   0   5   10   15   20

MILES   1 0 1 2 3 4 5 6 7 8 9 10 11 12

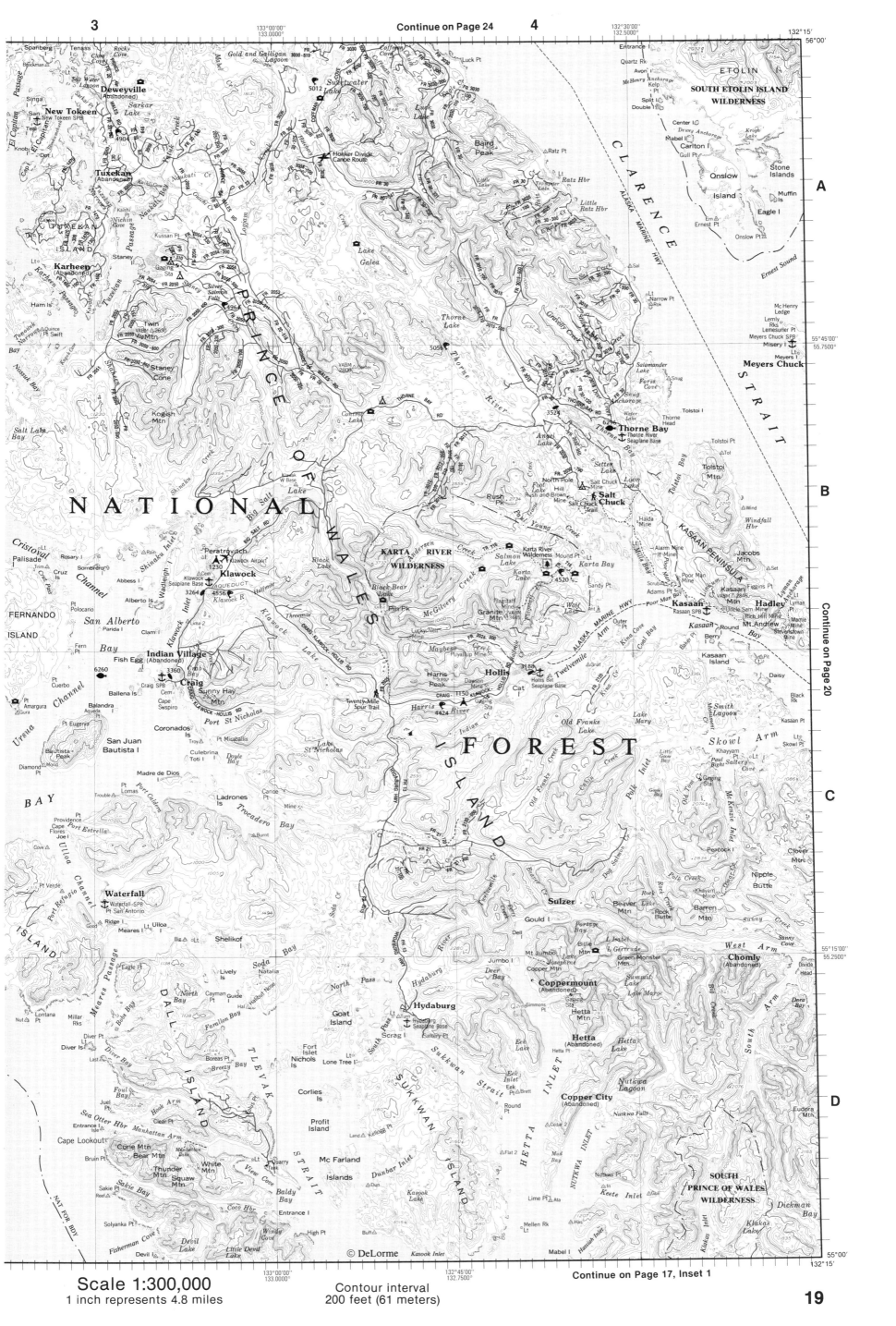

Continue on Page 20

Continue on Page 17, Inset 1

Scale 1:300,000
1 inch represents 4.8 miles

Contour interval
200 feet (61 meters)

© DeLorme

132°15'
132°00'00"
132.0000'
131°45'00"
131°45'0"
131°30'00"
131°30'00"
131°15'00"
131°15'00"

56°00'

A

B

Continue on Page 19

C

D

55°45'00"
55°45'0"

55°15'00"
55°25.0'

55°00'
132°15'

TONGASS

REVILLAGIGEDO ISLAND NATIONAL

Mt Shakes
TONGASS
NATIONAL
FOREST
Brownson
Pt
Brownson
Island
SOUTH ETOLIN ISLAND
WILDERNESS

Santa Anna
Bald Mtn
Twin Rift
4660
Bell Island
Hot Springs
Bell Island Hot Springs SPB
6004
6004

ERNEST SOUND
CLEVELAND PENINSULA

Yes Bay
Yes Bay Lodge
Seaplane Base

Spacious Bay
Square Island

Hassler
Island
WILDERNESS BDY

Mt
Burnett
Union
Bay
Cannery
Cannery

Vixen Pt
Sunshine
Vixen
Inlet

Neets
Bay
6196
4764
Orchard Lake
Cedar Lake
Bluff Lake
4436
Mt Reid

Helm
Bay
4840
Rainbow
Lake
Gold Mtn

Francis Cove
Escape Pt

4700
Orton Pt
Chamberlain
Lake
Emma
Lake
Jordan
Lake
4992
Swan Lake

Loring
Loring SPB
Orton
Ranch

Betton
Island
Betton
Head
Betton Pt
Tatoosh Pt
Tatoosh Islands

Grant
Island
Back I
Joe I
Hump

Leask
L
Salt
Lagoon
North Saddle Lake
Shelter
Cove

Settlers Cove
State Recreation Site

Clover
Pup Island
6048 Clover
1050
Survey Pt
Pt Higgins

4420
Harriet Hunt
Lake
Whitey River

6024

Painted
Peak

Guard Islands
Lighthouse
Guard Islands

Whipple
Totem Bight SHP
Perseverance
Lake Trail

5160
Thornton
Mtn
Talbet Lake
Coon I

Big Lake

Vallenar Rk
6316
Rock I Lt

4208
Connell Lake
Brown Mtn
Diana Mtn
John Mtn

Mud
Bay
Ward Cove
Refuge Cove
Danger I
Murphys SPB
Heliport
Signal Mtn

4152
4780
Upper Mahoney Lake
Mahoney Mtn

KETCHIKAN
4557
Tongass Historical Museum
Twin
Peaks
4536

S Vallenar Pt
Lewis Pt
High Mtn
Ketchikan
International Airport

Deer Mtn
Totem Heritage Center

6120

Gem Cove

6300

Grant Cove
Tongass
GRAVINA
NATIONAL
ISLAND
FOREST

House Mtn
Curve Mtn
Nipple
Mtn
Plain
Mtn
Smooth
Mtn

Pennock Island

Saxman
Dairy
6028
Mountain
Point
China
Town
6192
Red Mtn

Black Mtn
Notch
Mtn

PRINCE OF WALES ISLAND
TONGASS
NATIONAL
FOREST

Clover
Lake
Monte
Lake
Doctor I
Anderson Lt
Clover Bay
Skin I

Chasina
Chasina Pt

Spot Mtn
Flat Mtn
Bostwick Inlet

Mound
Hill
Cone I
Cone Pt

CHOLMONDELEY
Divide
Head
Dora Bay
Hump

Punch
Hill
Nelson Cove

Bingo
Mtn
Bush
Mtn

Round
Mtn
Chenango
Mtn

Lewis
Island
Hassler
Lake
Lucky Cove
Luck Pt
6216

D
Dolomi
(Abandoned)
FOREST

Adams I
Nest

Dall Bay
State Marine Park
Dall Bay
Dall Head

Hemlock
Pt

ANNETTE
ISLAND
Narrows
Mtn
Tired
Mtn
Brant
Mtn
Dubuque
Mtn

Twin Islands
South Twin

MARY
ISLAND
Mary I
Lighthouse

Niblack
(Abandoned)
4536
Kegan
Lake

Whiterock I
Menefee Anchorage
Rip Pt
Chichagof Bay

3376
Metlakatla
Metlakatla SPB

Yellow Hill
Purple
Mtn
Purple
Lake
Bell Is
Ridge

Trout
Hill

Davison Mtn

Cat Island

MOIRA SOUND
Polk Island
Bronaugh Is
Pt McCartey

Tamgas Harbor
Seaplane Base
Tamgas L

TONGASS
NATIONAL
FOREST

© DeLorme

132°00'00"
132.0000'
131°45'00"
131°45'00"
131°30'00"
131°30'00"

KILOMETERS   5   0   5   10   15   20

MILES   1 0   1   2   3   4   5   6   7   8   9 10 11 12

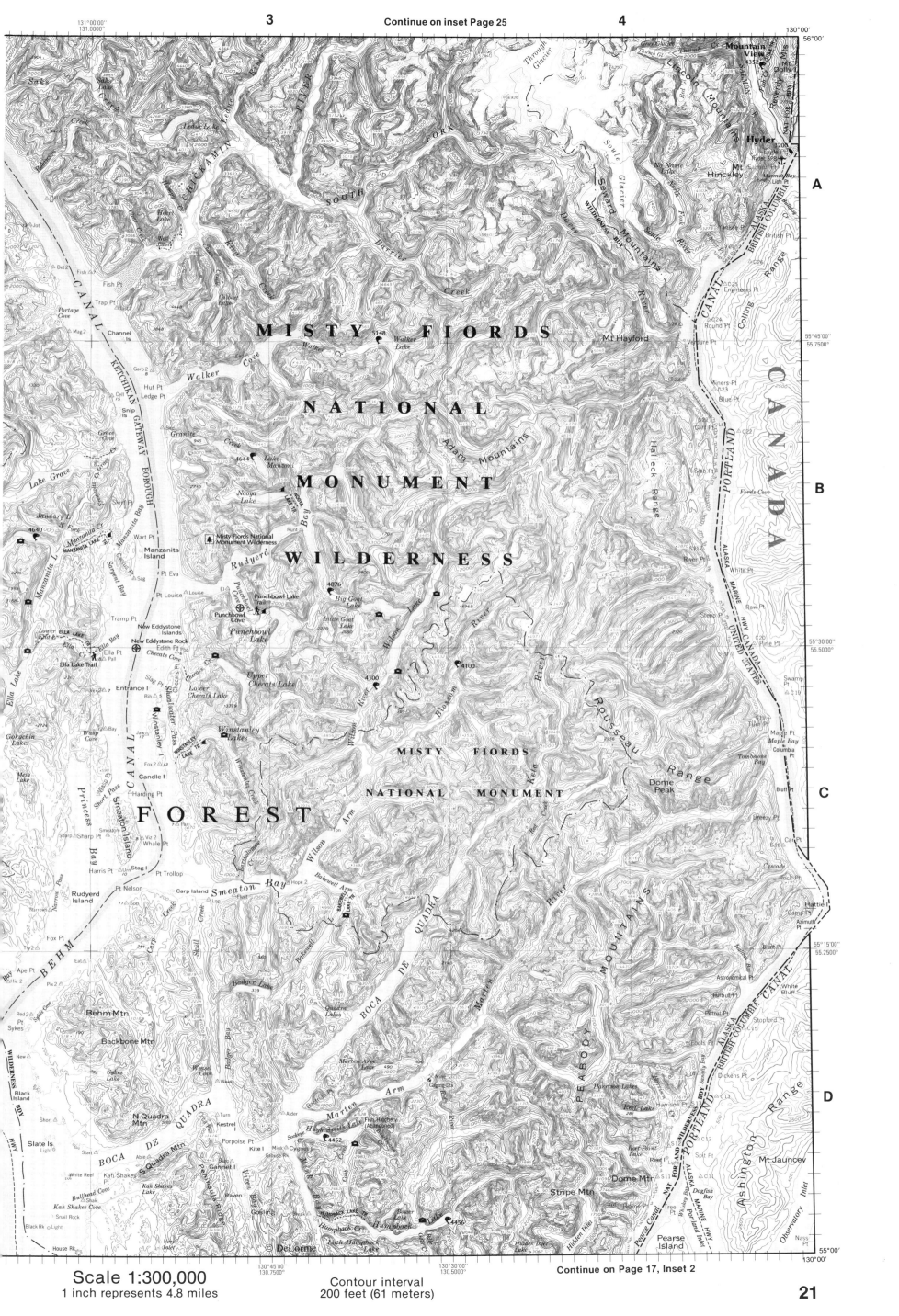

Continue on Page 17, Inset 2

Scale 1:300,000
1 inch represents 4.8 miles

Contour interval
200 feet (61 meters)

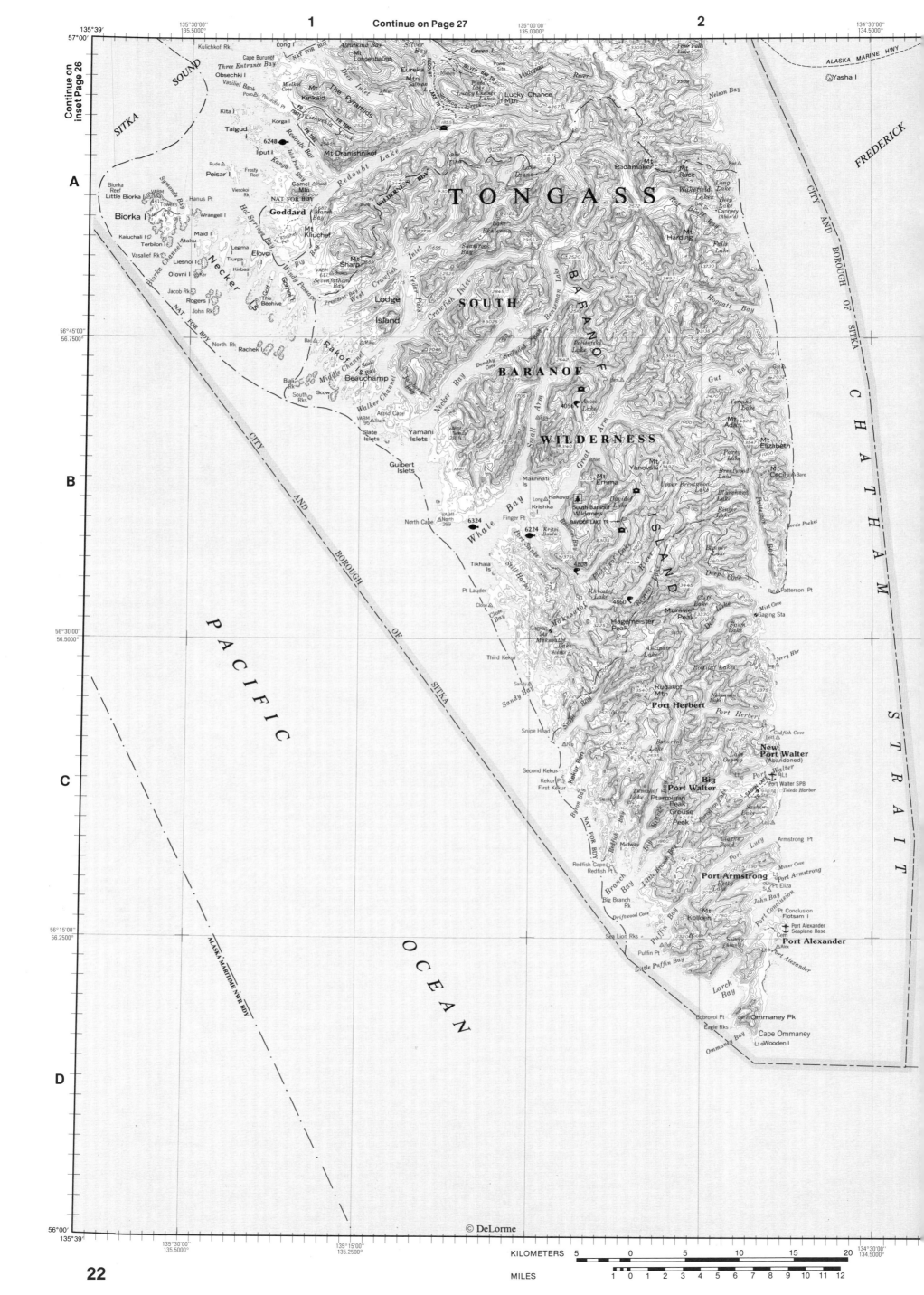

Continue on inset Page 26

135°39'

135°30'00''
135.5000°

135°00'00''
135.0000°

134°30'00''
134.5000°

57°00'

SITKA SOUND

FREDERICK

ALASKA MARINE HWY

Yasha I

A

T O N G A S S

S O U T H   B A R A N O F

B A R A N O F

WILDERNESS

I S L A N D

C H A T H A M

B

56°45'00''
56.7500°

South Baranof Wilderness

Whale Bay

P A C I F I C

O C E A N

56°30'00''
56.5000°

C

Port Herbert

New Port Walter (Abandoned)

Big Port Walter

Port Armstrong

56°15'00''
56.2500°

Port Alexander

S T R A I T

Cape Ommaney

D

56°00'

© DeLorme

135°39'

135°30'00''
135.5000°

135°15'00''
135.2500°

134°30'00''
134.5000°

KILOMETERS 5   0   5   10   15   20

MILES 1 0 1 2 3 4 5 6 7 8 9 10 11 12

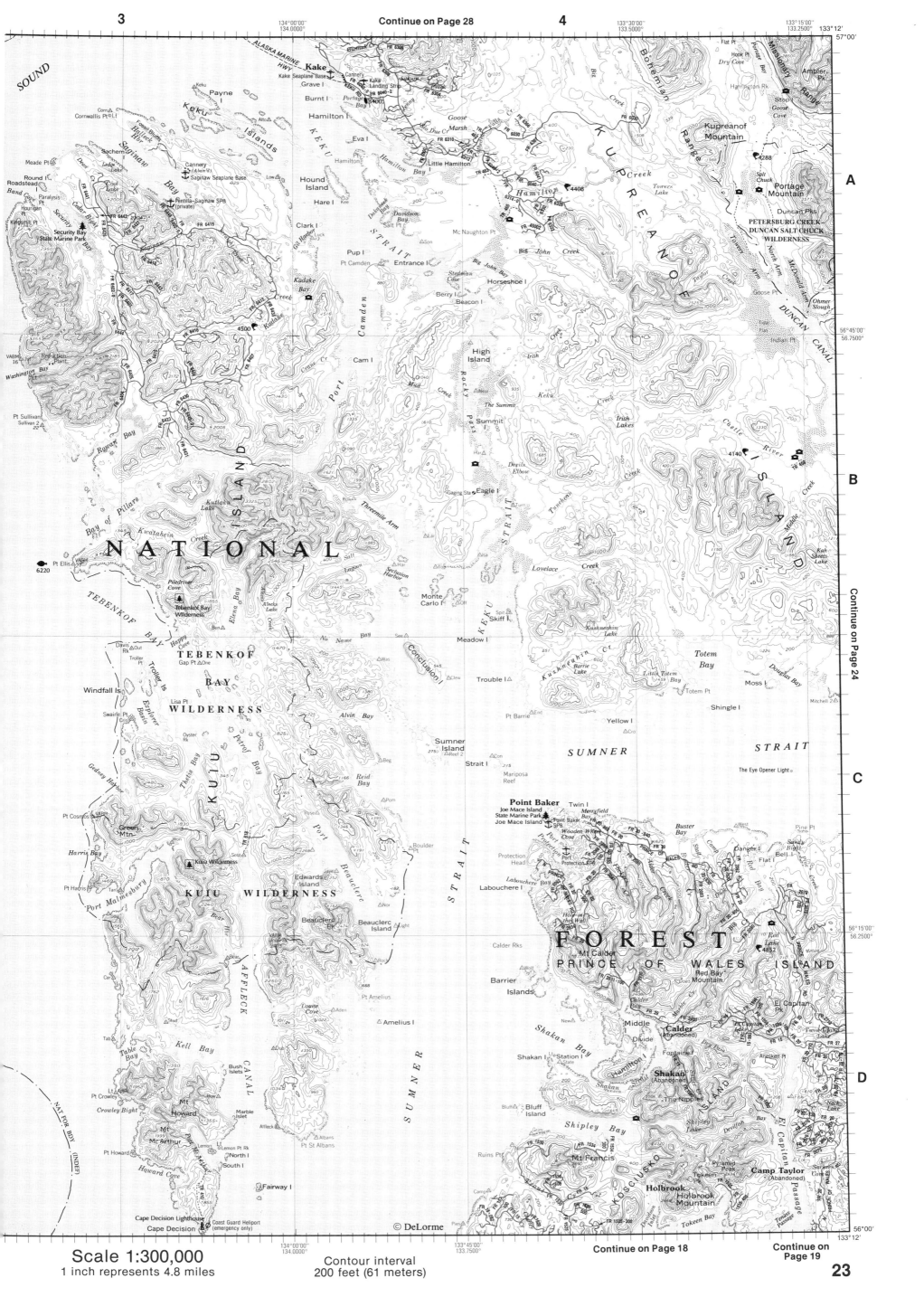

Continue on Page 24

Continue on Page 18　　Continue on Page 19

Scale 1:300,000
1 inch represents 4.8 miles

Contour interval
200 feet (61 meters)

© DeLorme

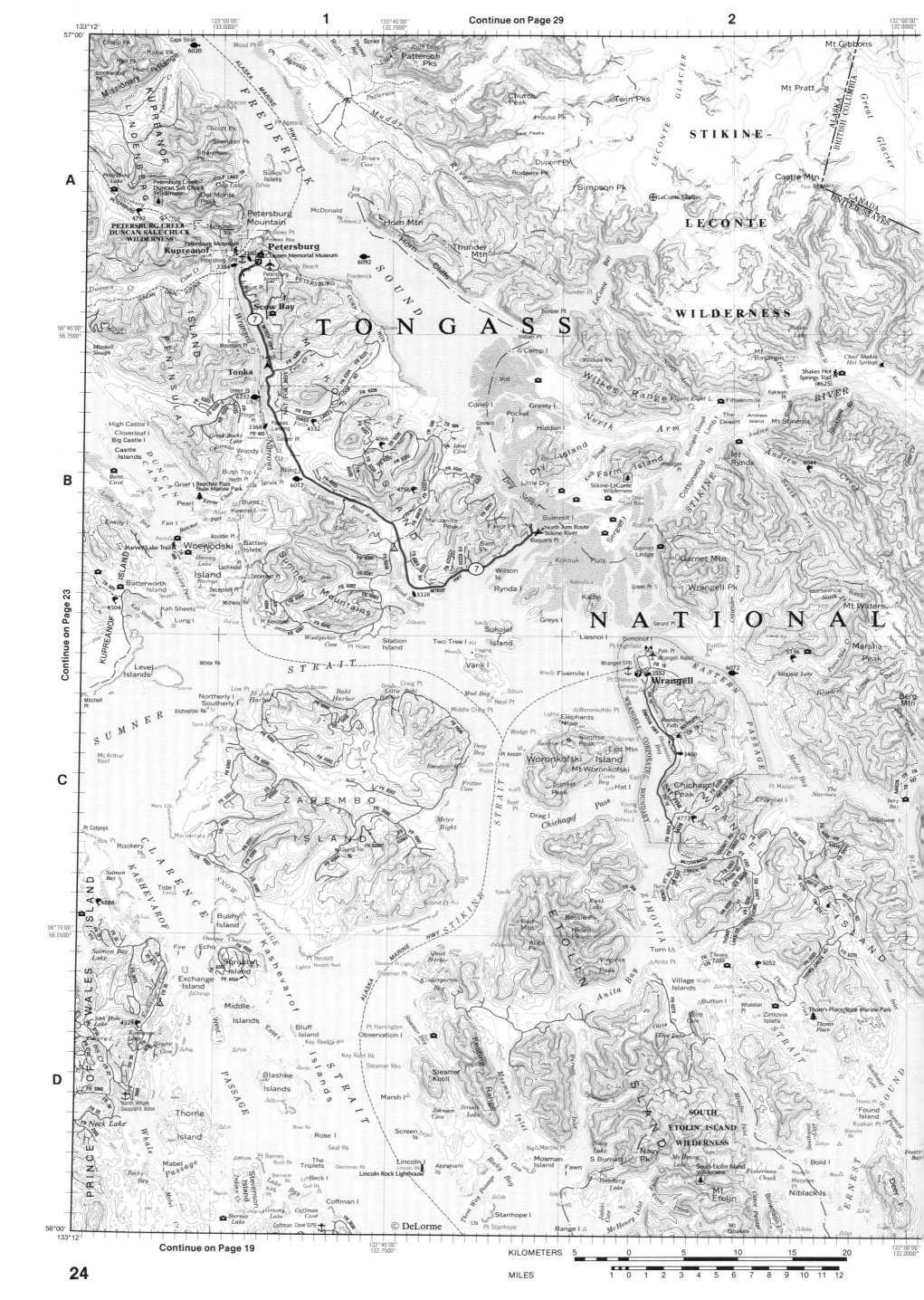

Continue on Page 23

© DeLorme

KILOMETERS 5   0   5   10   15   20

MILES   1 0 1 2 3 4 5 6 7 8 9 10 11 12

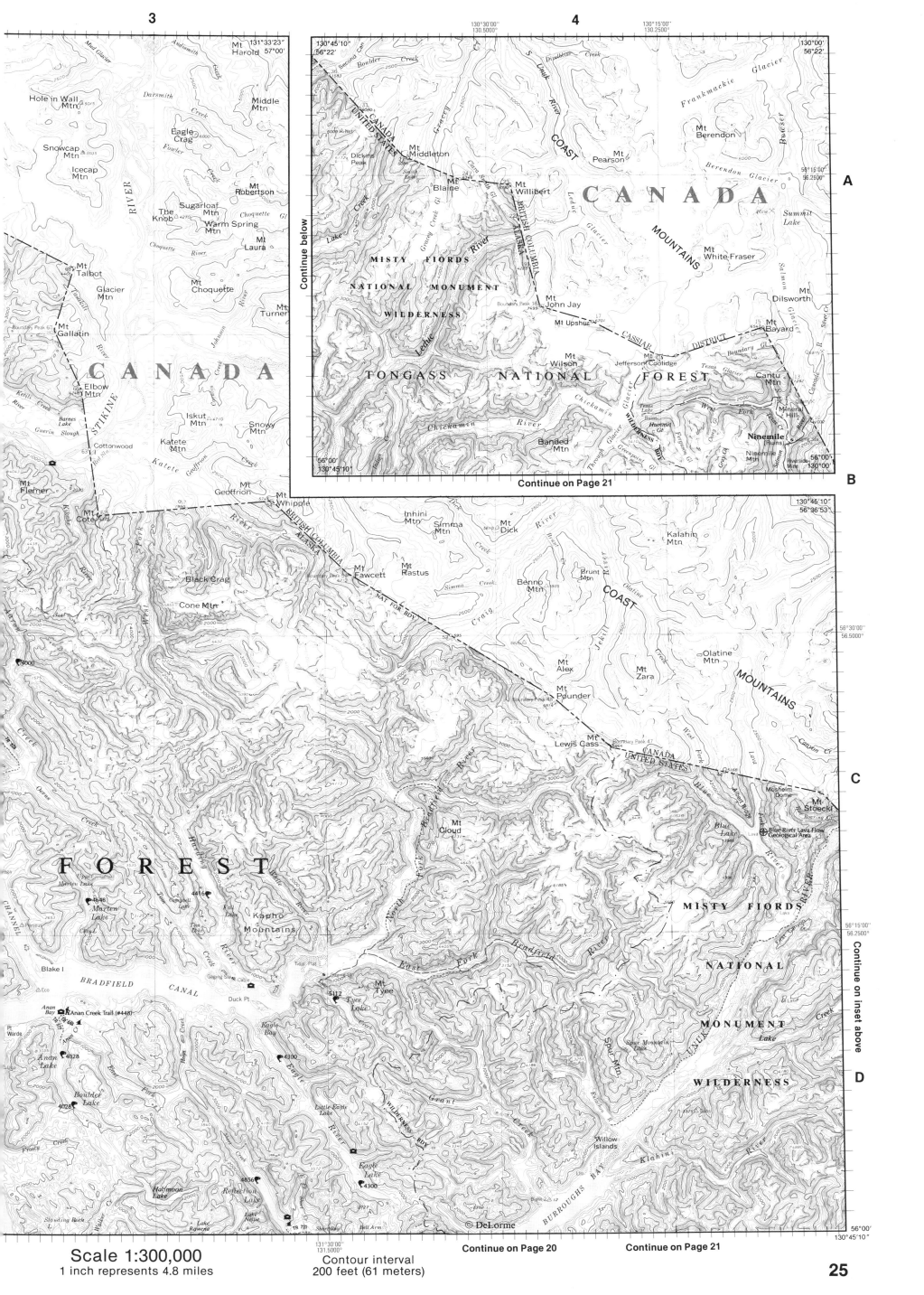

Scale 1:300,000
1 inch represents 4.8 miles

Contour interval
200 feet (61 meters)

Continue on Page 21

Continue on Page 20

Continue on Page 21

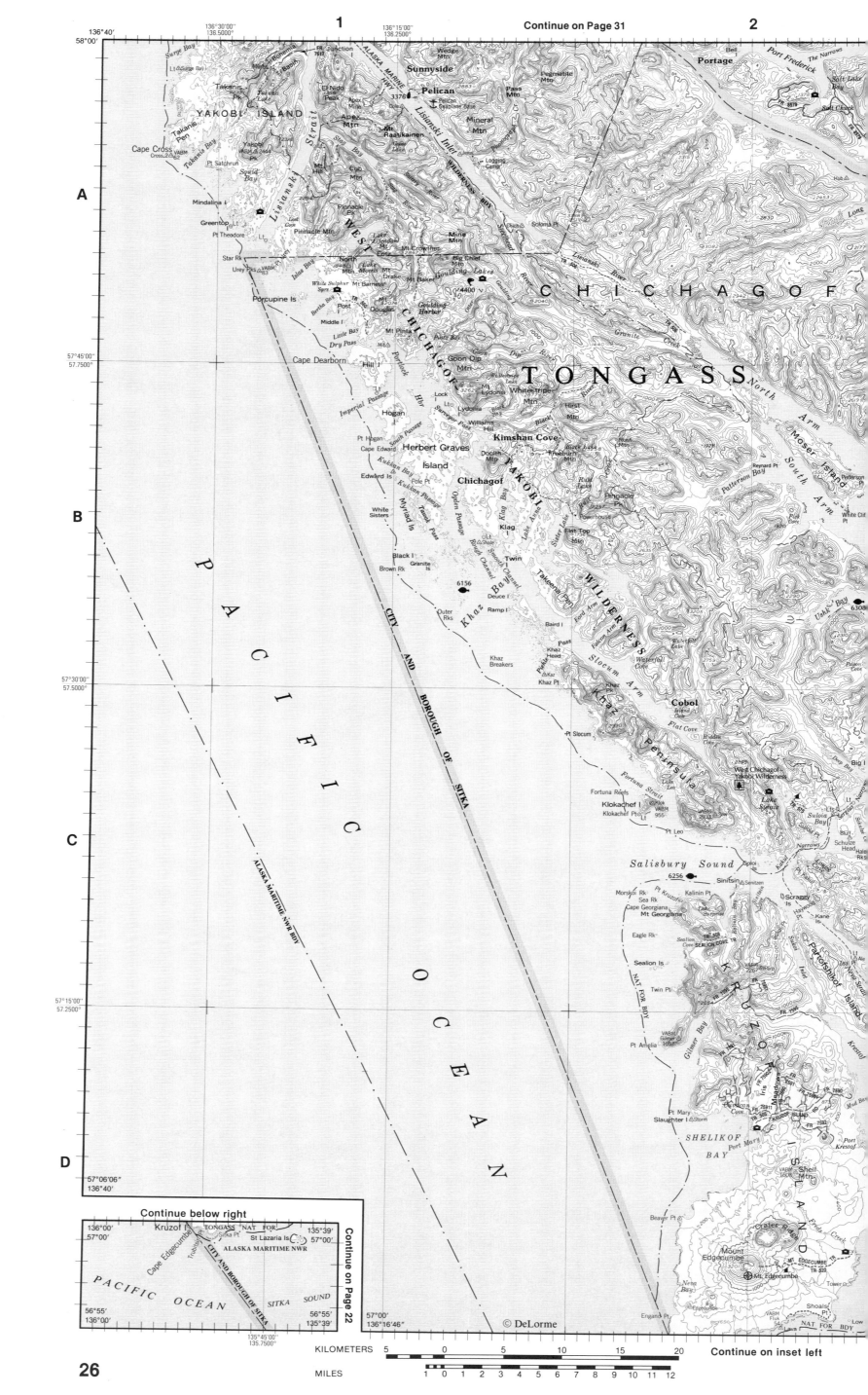

Continue below right

Continue on Page 22

© DeLorme

KILOMETERS   5   0   5   10   15   20

MILES   1 0 1 2 3 4 5 6 7 8 9 10 11 12

Continue on inset left

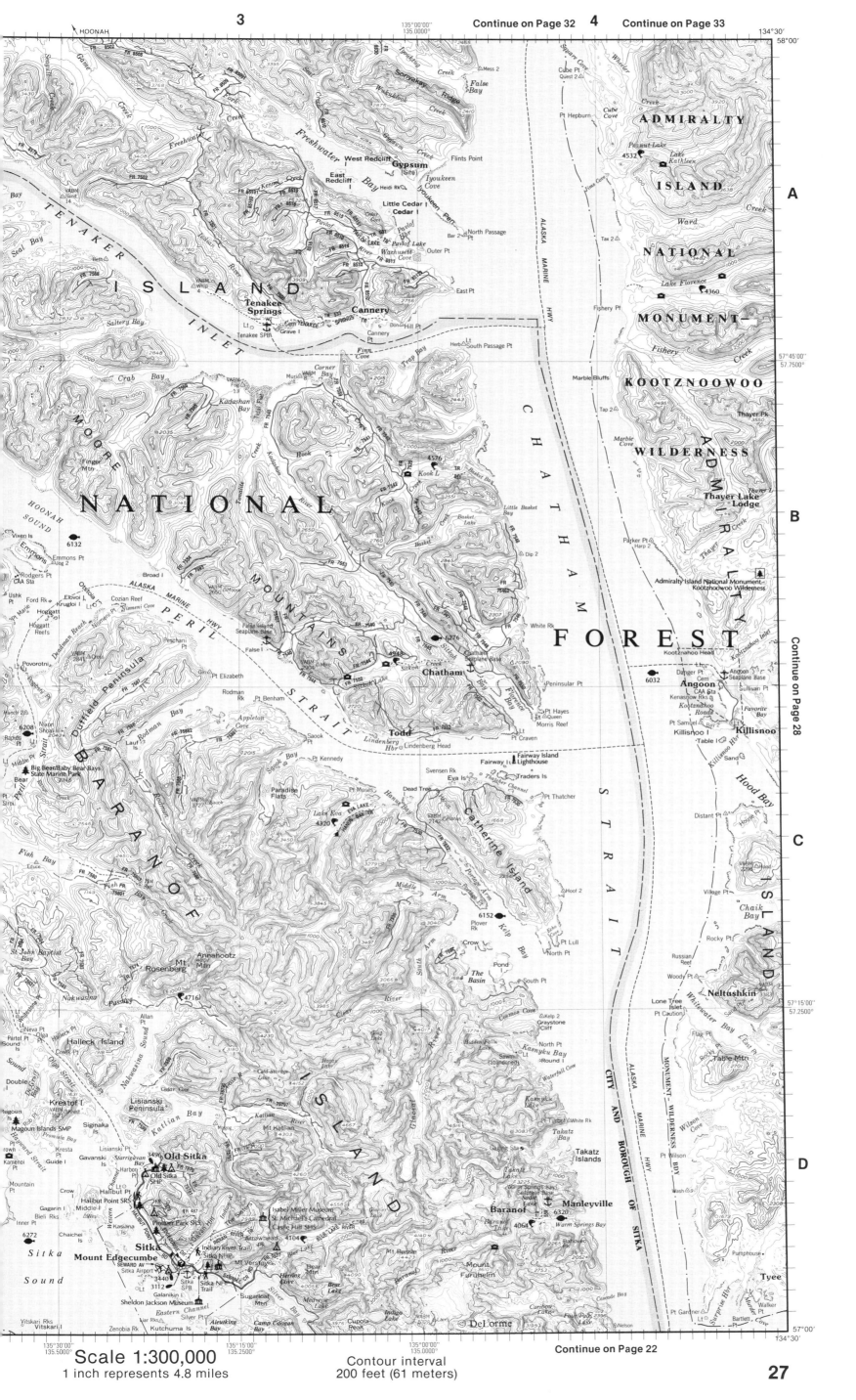

Continue on Page 28

Scale 1:300,000
1 inch represents 4.8 miles

Contour interval
200 feet (61 meters)

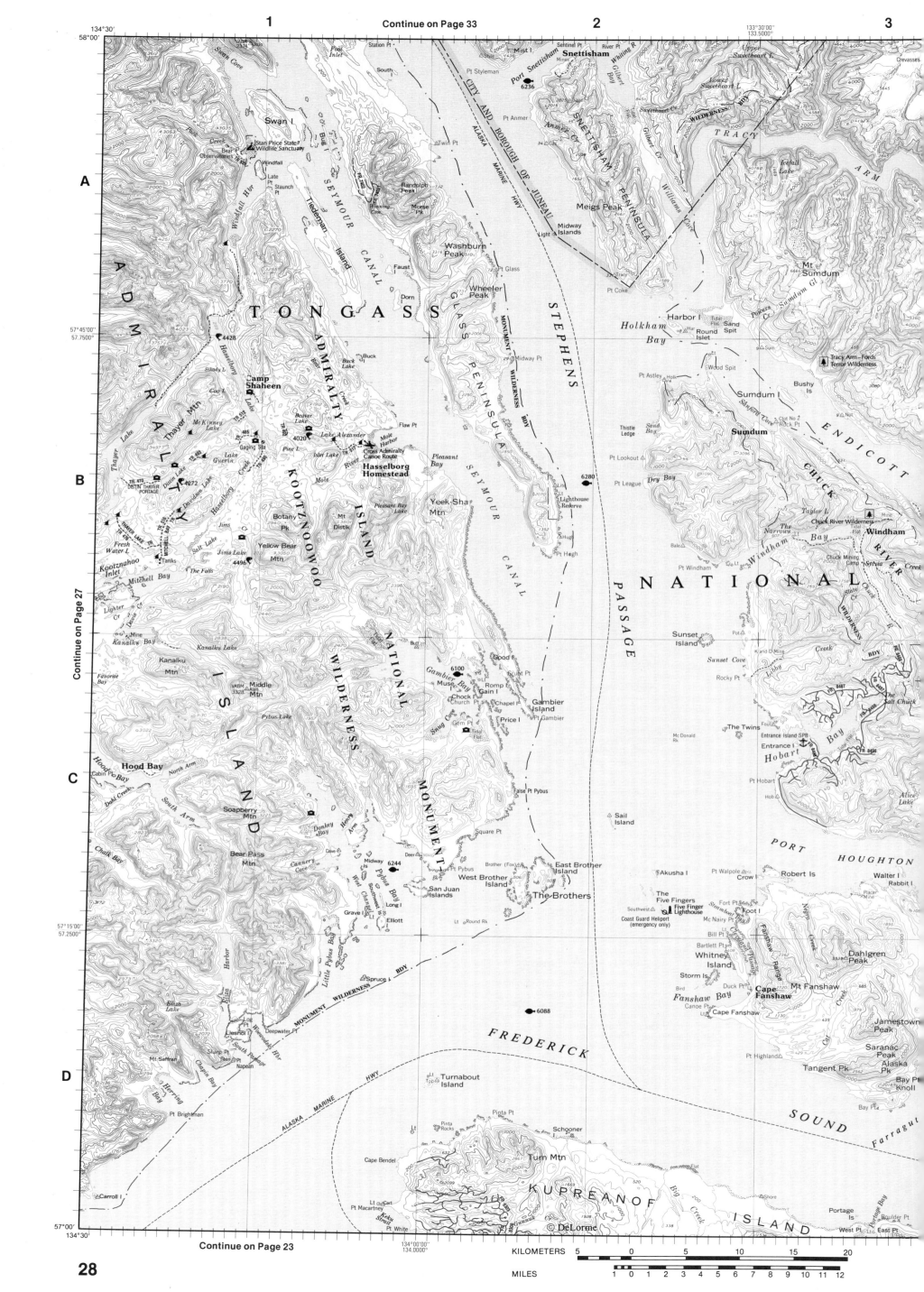

Continue on Page 33

Continue on Page 27

Continue on Page 23

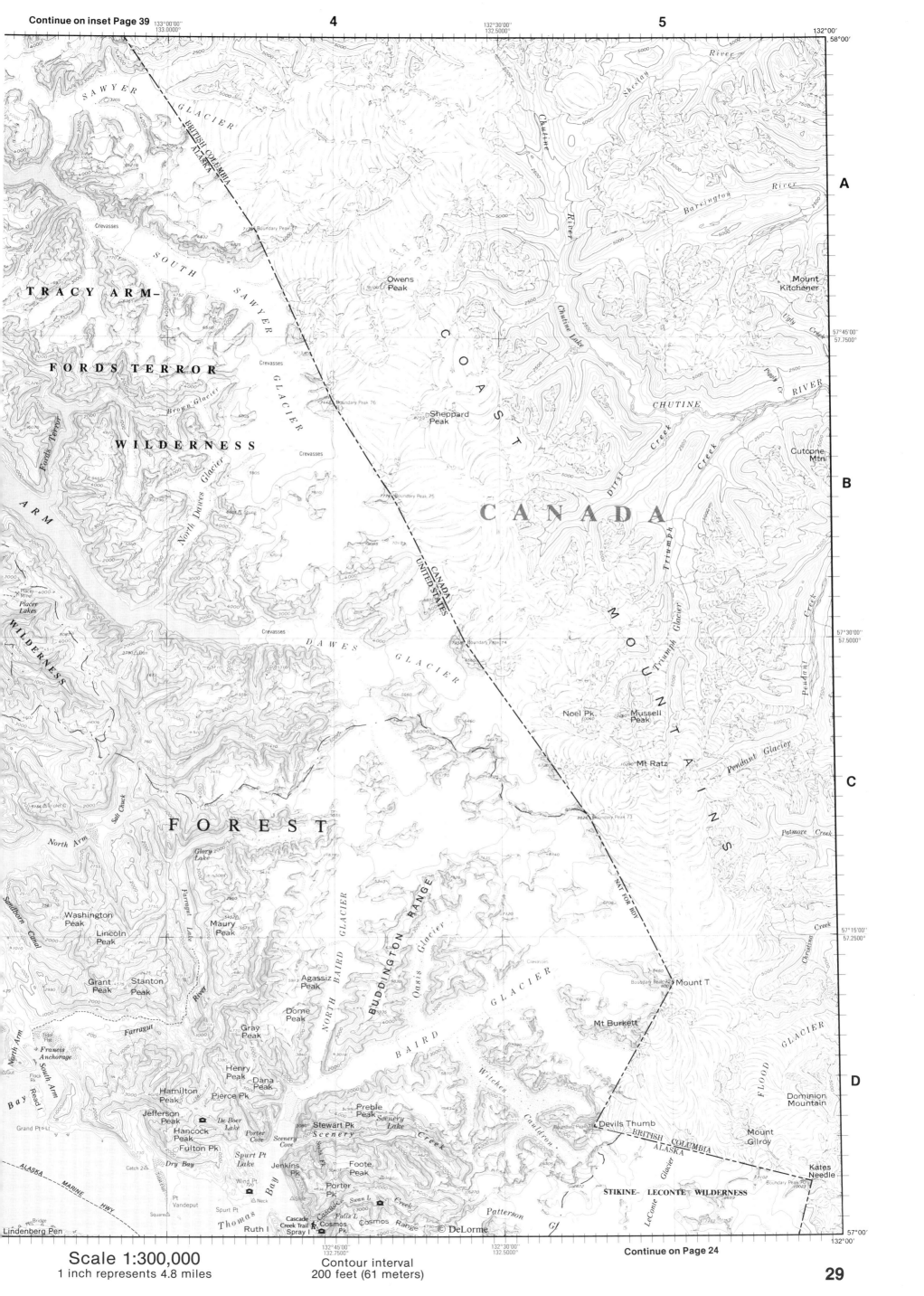

133°00'00"
133.0000°

4

132°30'00"
132.5000°

5

132°00'
58°00'

SAWYER

GLACIER

BRITISH COLUMBIA
ALASKA

Crevasses

SOUTH

TRACY ARM-

SAWYER

FORDS TERROR

GLACIER

Brown Glacier

WILDERNESS

Fords Terror

North Dawes Glacier

ARM

WILDERNESS

Placer Mine
Placer Lakes

Boundary Peak 77

Crevasses

Boundary Peak 76

Crevasses

Boundary Peak 75

Crevasses

CANADA
UNITED STATES

DAWES

GLACIER

Boundary Peak 74

Owens
Peak

Sheppard
Peak

C

O

A

S

T

Shestay River

River

Barrington
River

CANADA

Chutine

River

Chutine Lake

CHUTINE

Dirst

Creek

Creek

Triumph

Glacier

Triumph

Mount
Kitchener

Ugly

Creek

Pugsly Cr.

RIVER

Cutcone
Mtn

A

57°45'00"
57.7500°

B

FOREST

Glory
Lake

Washington
Peak

Lincoln
Peak

North Arm

Sandborn Canal

Grant
Peak

Stanton
Peak

Triplet C

Sell Chuck

Farragut

River

Maury
Peak

Agassiz
Peak

Dome
Peak

Gray
Peak

NORTH BAIRD GLACIER

BUDDINGTON RANGE

Oasis Glacier

Glacier

Noel Pk.

Mussell
Peak

Mt Ratz

Boundary Peak 73

M

O

U

N

T

A

I

N

S

Pendant Glacier

Pendant

Creek

Patmore Creek

Christina Creek

57°30'00"
57.5000°

57°15'00"
57.2500°

C

Farragut
Lake

Francis
Anchorage

South Arm

Bay

Grand Pt Lt

Henry
Peak

Hamilton
Peak

Jefferson
Peak

Hancock
Peak

Fulton Pk

Dry Bay

Catch 2

Dana
Peak

Pierce Pk

De Boer
Lake

Porter
Cove

Spurt Pt
Lake

BAIRD

GLACIER

Preble
Peak

Scenery
Lake

Stewart Pk

Scenery

Scenery
Cove

Creek

Wiches

Cauldron

Glacier

Boundary Peak

Boundary Peak 72

Mount T

Mt Burkett

Devils Thumb

BRITISH COLUMBIA
ALASKA

GLACIER

FLOOD

Dominion
Mountain

Mount
Gilroy

Kates
Needle

NAT FOR BDY

D

57°00'

North Arm

Tidal
Flat

Gut

Flock Rk

ALASKA

MARINE

HWY

Lindenberg Pen

Bridge

Jenkins
Pk

Porter
Pk

Pt
Vandeput

Square

Spurt Pt

Thomas

Bay

Ruth I

Foote
Peak

Cascade Creek Trail
Spray I

Cosmos
Pk

Falls L

Swan L

Cosmos

Range

Neck

Wind Pt

Patterson

© DeLorme

STIKINE- LECONTE WILDERNESS

LeConte Glacier

Gl

132°45'00"
132.7500°

132°30'00"
132.5000°

132°00'

Scale 1:300,000
1 inch represents 4.8 miles

Contour interval
200 feet (61 meters)

Continue on Page 24

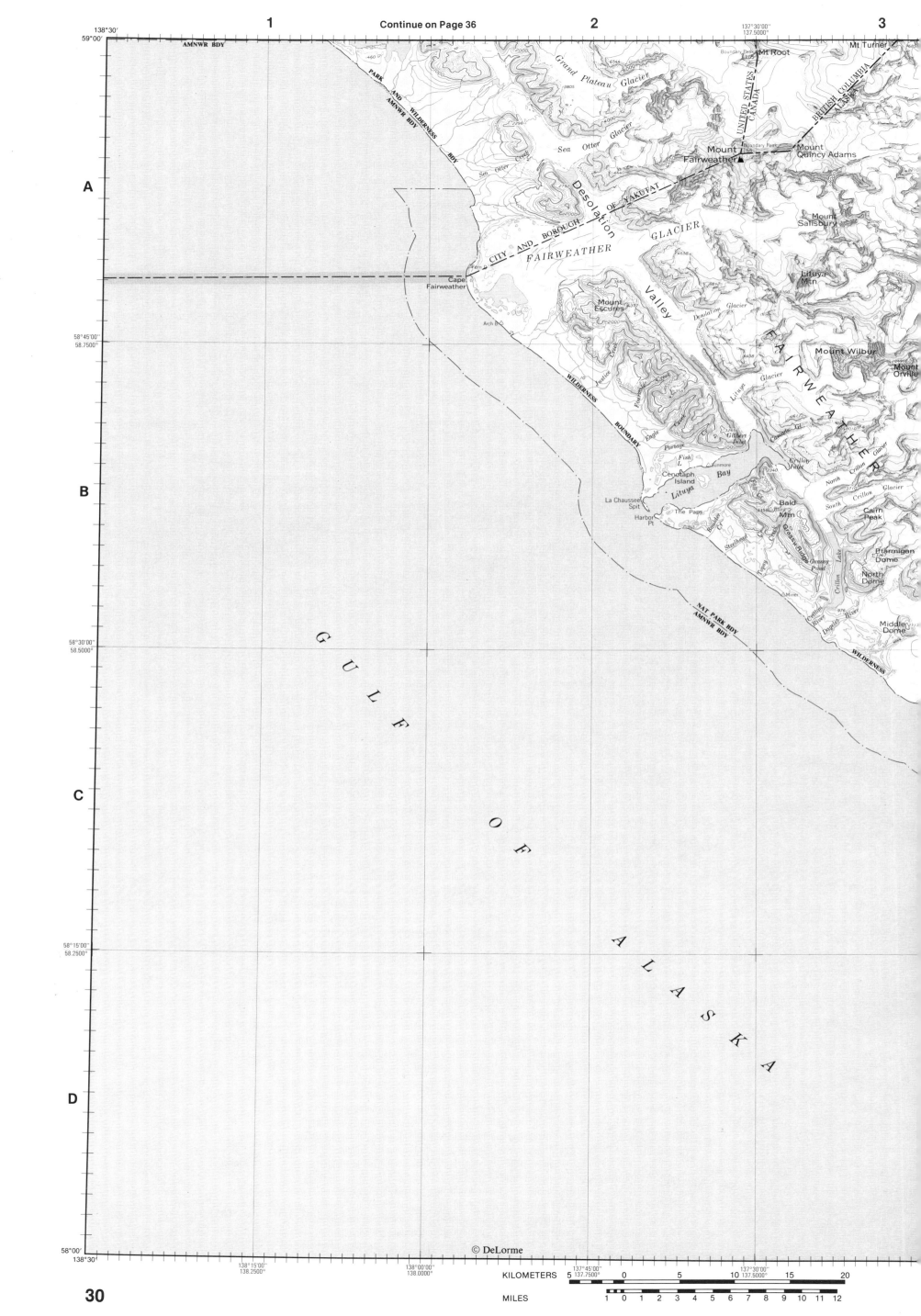

1

2

3

138°30'
59°00'

AMNWR BDY

PARK AND WILDERNESS BDY

AMNWR BDY

Grand Plateau Glacier

Boundary Peak

Mt Root

Mt Turner

UNITED STATES
CANADA

BRITISH COLUMBIA
ALASKA

Sea Otter Glacier

Sea Otter Creek

Mount
Fairweather ▲

Boundary Peak

Mount
Quincy Adams

A

Desolation

CITY AND BOROUGH OF YAKUTAT

FAIRWEATHER

GLACIER

Mount
Salisbury

Cape
Fairweather

Mount
Escures

Desolation Glacier

Lituya
Mtn

Arch Pt

Valley

58°45'00''
58.7500°

WILDERNESS

Flannigan Creek

Justice Creek

Lituya Glacier

Mount Wilbur

Mount
Orville

FAIRWEATHER

BOUNDARY

Eagle Creek

Portage

Fish
L

Gilbert
Inlet

Cascade Gl.

Crillon Inlet

North Crillon Glacier

B

La Chaussee
Spit

Cenotaph
Island

Dunmore

Lituya
Bay

Bald
Mtn

South Crillon
Glacier

Cairn
Peak

Harbor
Pt

The Paps

Boulder

Ptarmigan
Dome

Steelhead

Grassy
Ridge

Tongue

Grassy Point

Crillon River

North
Dome

Desolation River

Middle
Dome

NAT PARK BDY
AMNWR BDY

58°30'00''
58.5000°

G U L F

WILDERNESS

C

O F

58°15'00''
58.2500°

A L A S K A

D

58°00'
138°30'

138°15'00''
138.2500°

138°00'00''
138.0000°

137°45'00''
137.7500°

137°30'00''
137.5000°

© DeLorme

KILOMETERS 5   0   5   10   15   20

MILES   1 0 1 2 3 4 5 6 7 8 9 10 11 12

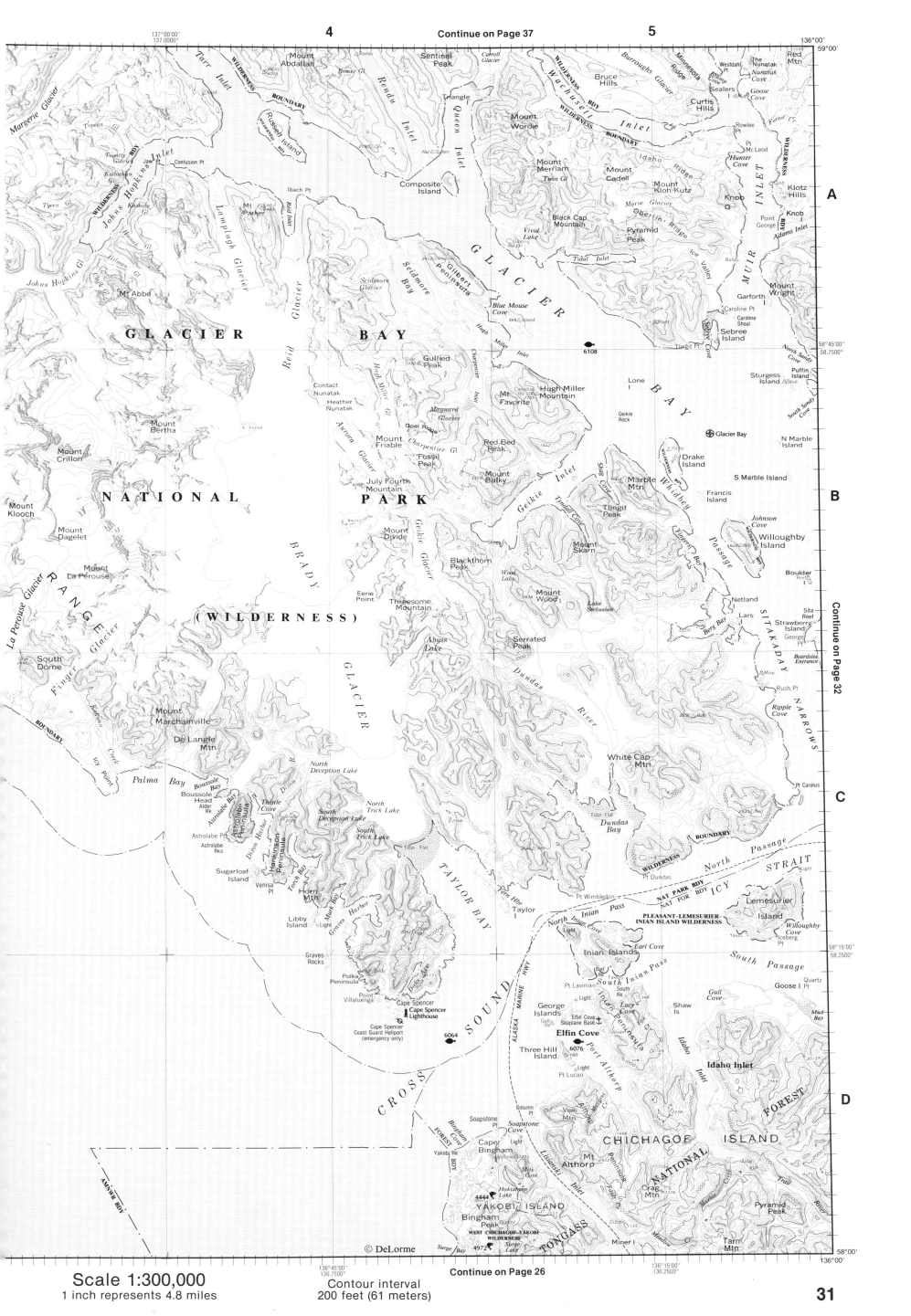

137°00'00"
137.0000°

136°00'

59°00'

A

58°45'00"
58.7500°

B

Continue on Page 32

C

D

GLACIER BAY

NATIONAL

PARK

(WILDERNESS)

GLACIER BAY

MUIR INLET

SITAKADAY NARROWS

ICY STRAIT

CROSS SOUND

CHICHAGOF ISLAND

NATIONAL FOREST

YAKOBI ISLAND

TONGASS

ALASKA MARINE HWY

PLEASANT-LEMESURIER INIAN ISLAND WILDERNESS

WEST CHICHAGOF-YAKOBI WILDERNESS

© DeLorme

58°15'00"
58.2500°

58°00'
136°00'

Scale 1:300,000
1 inch represents 4.8 miles

Contour interval
200 feet (61 meters)

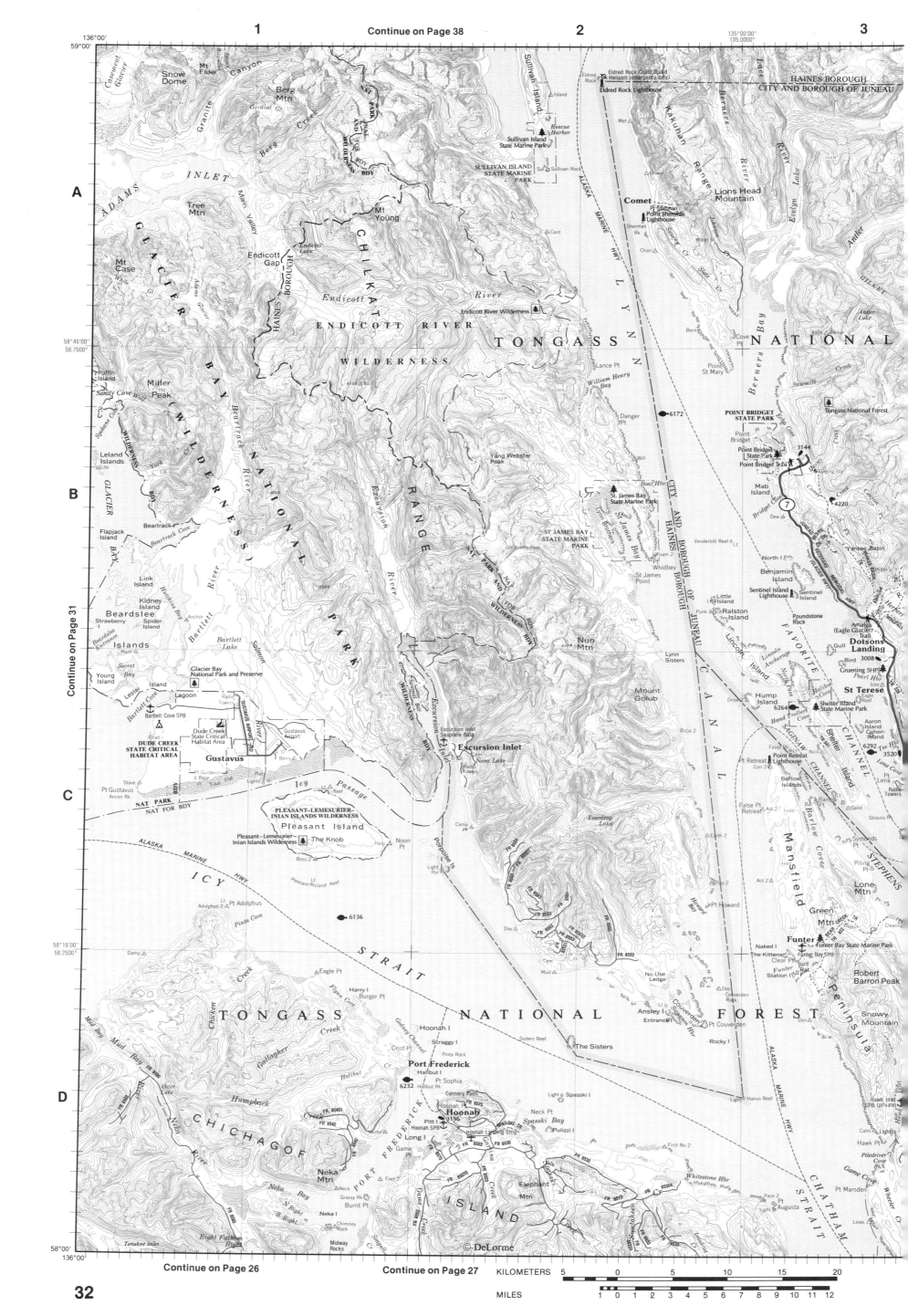

1 2 3

136°00'
59°00'

A

58°45'00"
58.7500°

B

Continue on Page 31

C

58°15'00"
58.2500°

D

58°00'
136°00'

135°00'00"
135.0000°

HAINES BOROUGH
CITY AND BOROUGH OF JUNEAU

KILOMETERS 5   0   5   10   15   20

MILES   1 0 1 2 3 4 5 6 7 8 9 10 11 12

32

©DeLorme

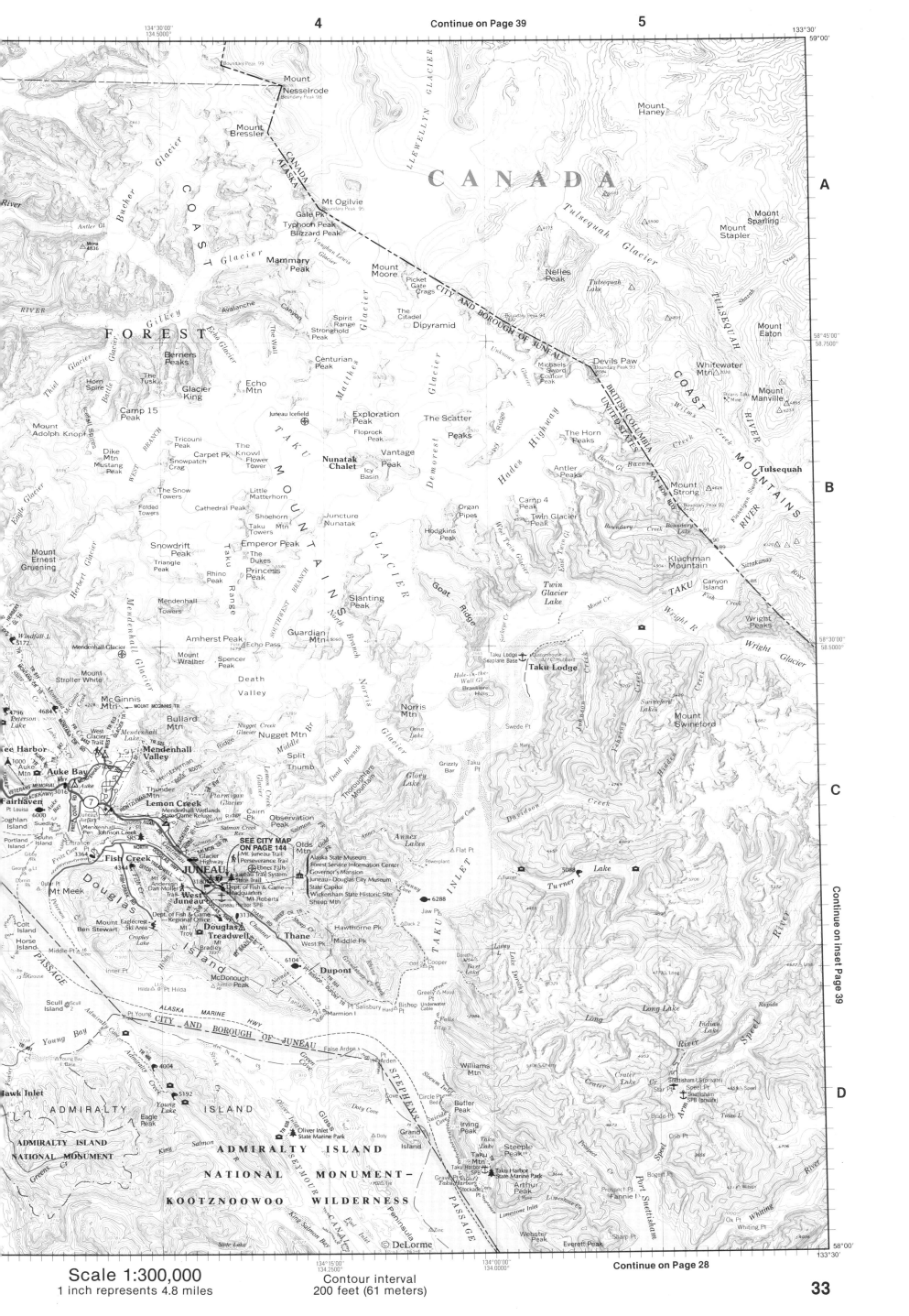

Continue on inset Page 39

Continue on Page 28

Scale 1:300,000
1 inch represents 4.8 miles

Contour interval
200 feet (61 meters)

© DeLorme

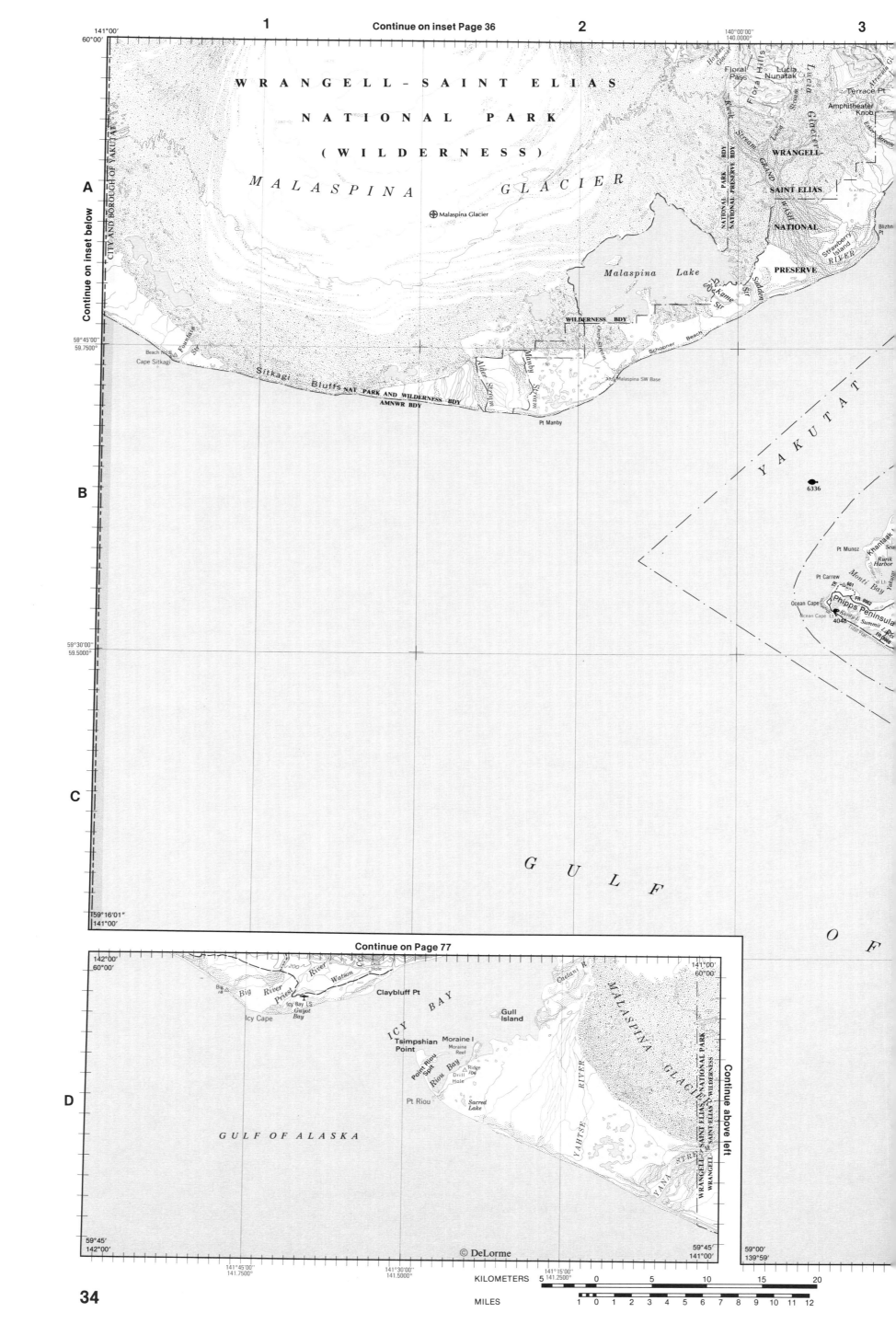

141°00'
60°00'

W R A N G E L L - S A I N T   E L I A S

N A T I O N A L   P A R K

(W I L D E R N E S S)

M A L A S P I N A   G L A C I E R

Malaspina Glacier
1200

Floral Hills
Floral Pass
Lucia Nunatak
Lucia Glacier
Terrace Pt
Amphitheater Knob
Hayden Glacier
Kulik Stream
Grand Stream
WRANGELL-
SAINT ELIAS
NATIONAL
PRESERVE
Strawberry Island
Blizhn
Malaspina Lake
Schooner Beach
Kame Str
Osar Stream
Sudden Str
Manby Stream
Alder Stream
WILDERNESS   BDY
Malaspina SW Base

A

Beach No 8
Cape Sitkagi
Fountain Str
59°45'00"
59.7500°
Sitkagi   Bluffs   NAT   PARK AND WILDERNESS   BDY
AMNWR BDY
Pt Manby

CITY AND BOROUGH OF YAKUTAT

Continue on inset below

B

Y A K U T A T

6336

Pt Munoz
Khantaak I
Rurik Harbor
Pt Carrew
Monti Bay
Ocean Cape
Phipps Peninsula
Ocean Cape L
4046

59°30'00"
59.5000°

C

G   U   L   F

O

F

59°16'01"
141°00'

Continue on Page 77

142°00'
60°00'

200
Big River
Priest River
Watson River
Hole
Claybluff Pt
Chetani R
141°00'
60°00'

Blu
18
Icy Bay LS
Gaijot Bay
Icy Cape
I C Y   B A Y
Gull Island
MALASPINA

Tsimpshian Point
Moraine I
Moraine Reef
Point Riou Spit
Riou Bay
Ridge Hole
Drill Hole
Pt Riou
Sacred Lake

RIVER

YAHTSE

GLACIER

WRANGELL-SAINT ELIAS NATIONAL PARK
WRANGELL-SAINT ELIAS NATIONAL PARK-WILDERNESS

D

G U L F   O F   A L A S K A

YANA STREAM

Continue above left

59°45'
142°00'

© DeLorme

141°45'00"
141.7500°
141°30'00"
141.5000°
141°15'00"
141.2500°

59°45'
141°00'
59°00'
139°59'

KILOMETERS   5   5   0   5   10   15   20

MILES   1   0   1   2   3   4   5   6   7   8   9   10   11   12

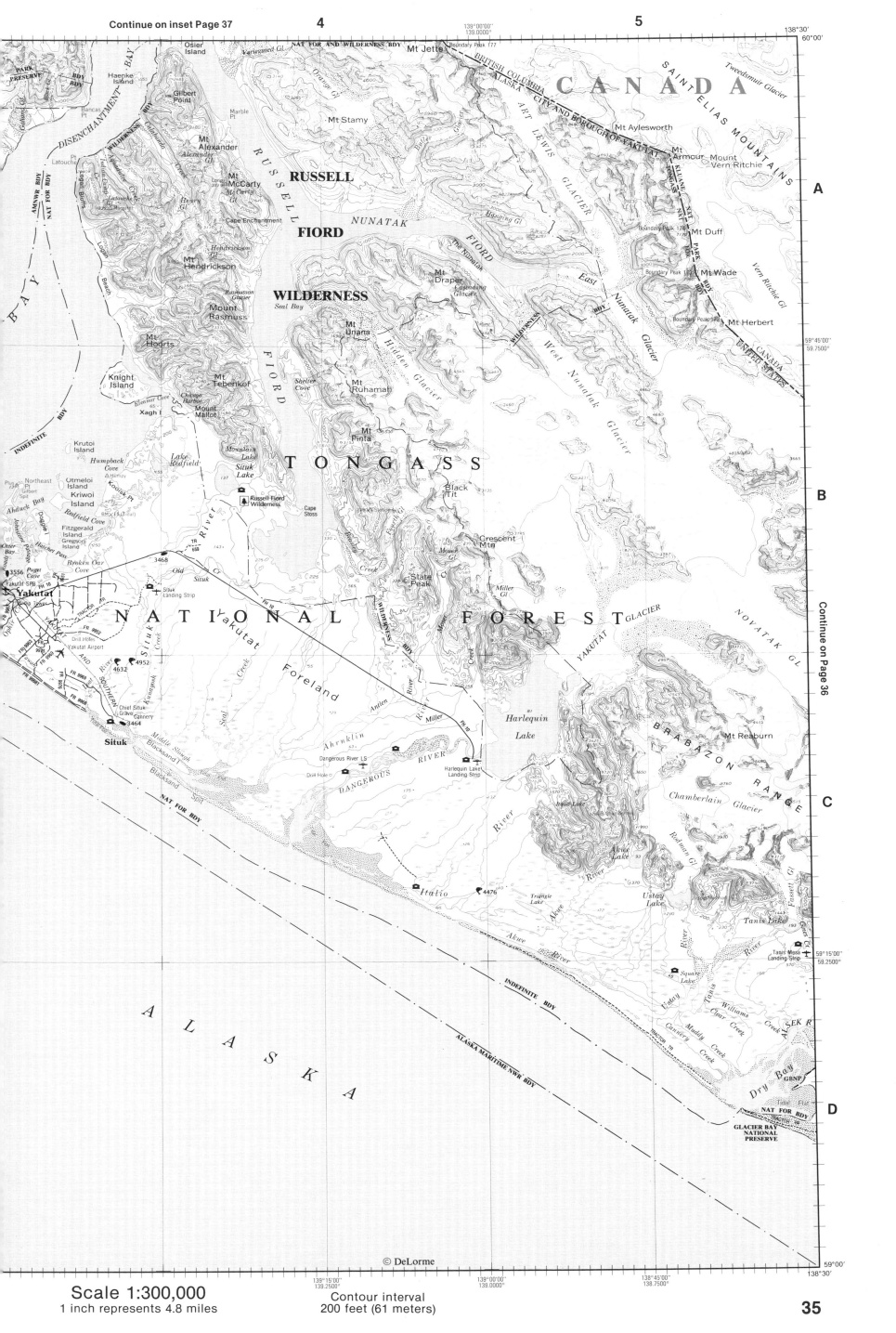

CANADA

BRITISH COLUMBIA
ALASKA

SAINT ELIAS MOUNTAINS

Tweedsmuir Glacier

60°00'

Mt Jette
Boundary Peak 177

Osier Island

Variegated Gl

NAT FOR AND WILDERNESS BDY

Haenke Island

Gilbert Point

Mt Stamy

Orange Gl

Mt Aylesworth

Mt Armour Mount Vern Ritchie

A

PARK PRESERVE

BDY BDY

Marble Pt

Boundary Peak 174

Mt Duff

Vern Ritchie Gl

Bancas

Mt Alexander
Alexander Gl

RUSSELL

Haning Gl

Boundary Peak 173

Mt Wade

DISENCHANTMENT BAY

Mt McCarty
McCarty Gl

NUNATAK

Boundary Peak 172

Mt Herbert

RUSSELL

FIORD

The Nunatak

59°45'
59.7500°

UNITED STATES

Latouche

Mt Hendrickson
Hendrickson Gl

Cape Enchantment

FIORD

Mt Draper
Cascading Glacier

East Nunatak Glacier

CANADA

AMNWR BDY
NAT FOR BDY

Mount Rasmuss

Rasmusson Glacier

WILDERNESS

Seal Bay

Mt Unana

West Nunatak Glacier

Mt Hoorts

Knight Island

Mt Tebenkof

Shelter Cove

Mt Ruhamah

B

INDEFINITE

BDY

Elenor Cove

Mount Mallot

Xagh I

Chicago Harbor

Mt Pinta

T O N G A S S

Black Tit

59°45'
59.7500°

Krutoi Island

Lake Redfield

Monotana Lake

Situk Lake

Russell Fiord Wilderness

Cape Stoss

Crescent Mtn

NOVATAK GL

Humpback Cove

Kodiak Pt

State Peak

Miller Gl

Otmeloi Island

Kriwoi Island

Redfield Cove

TR 659

GLACIER

Fitzgerald Island
Gregson Island

Old Situk

Situk Landing Strip

WILDERNESS BDY

YAKUTAT

Broken Oar Cove

3468

Mt Reaburn

Yakutat

N A T I O N A L

F O R E S T

BRABAZON RANGE

C

Puget Cove

Drill Holes

4632 4952

Harlequin Lake

Chamberlain Glacier

Yakutat Airport

Chief Situk Grave

Situk

Cannery

3464

Italio Lake

Akwe Lake

Ahrnklin

Dangerous River LS

Ustay Lake

Tanis Lake

Drill Hole

Harlequin Lake Landing Strip

Blacksand T

DANGEROUS RIVER

59°15'
59.2500°

Blacksand Spit

Akwe

Triangle Lake

Tanis Mesa Landing Strip

NAT FOR BDY

Italio

4476

Square Lake

A L A S K A

INDEFINITE BDY

ALASKA MARITIME NWR BDY

Williams Clear Creek

Cannery Creek

Muddy Creek

Dry Bay

GBNP

NAT FOR BDY

D

GLACIER BAY NATIONAL PRESERVE

59°00'

© DeLorme

Continue on Page 36

138°30'

139°00'00''
139.0000°

138°30'

139°15'00''
139.2500°

139°00'00''
139.0000°

138°45'00''
138.7500°

138°30'

Scale 1:300,000
1 inch represents 4.8 miles

Contour interval
200 feet (61 meters)

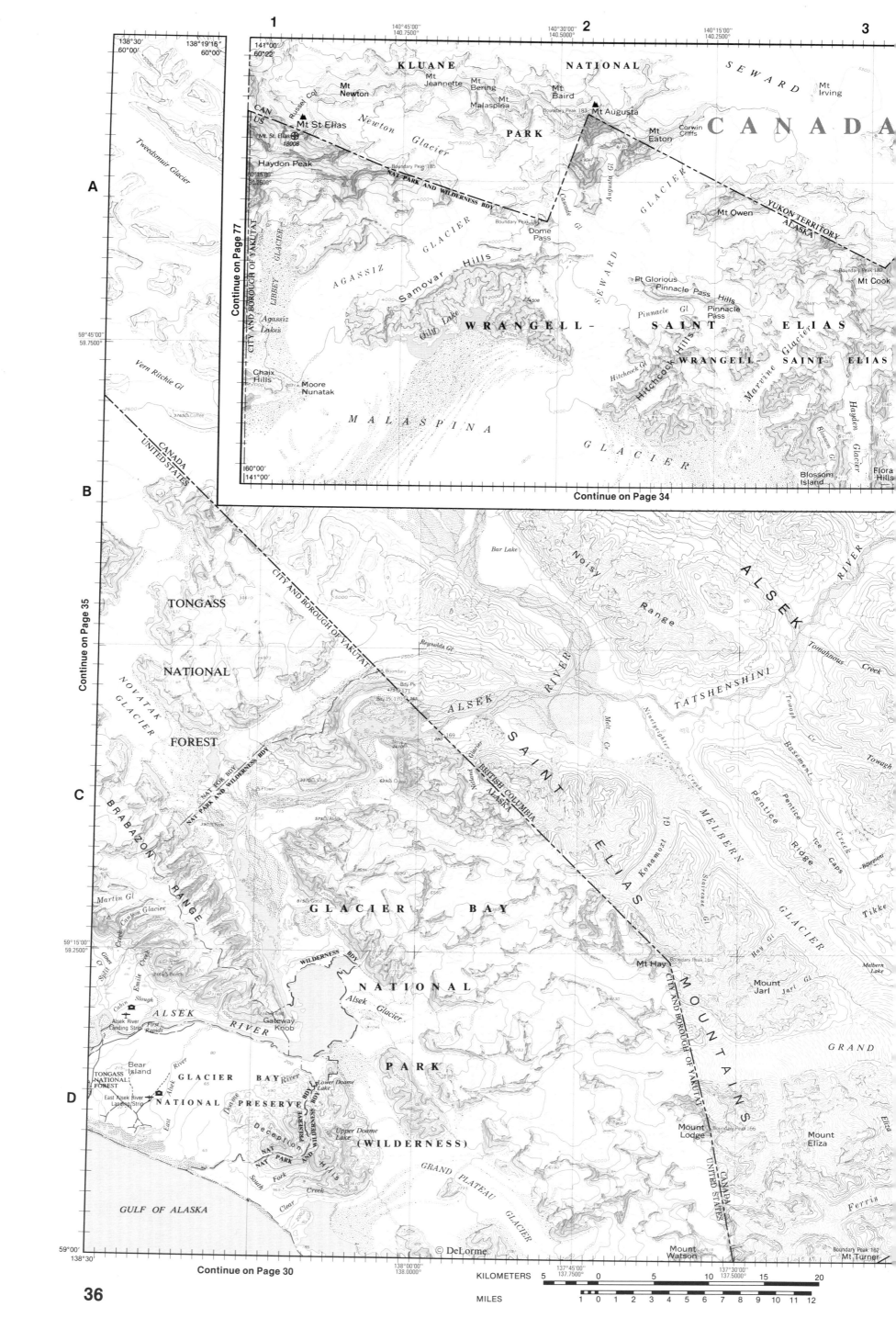

Continue on Page 77

Continue on Page 34

Continue on Page 35

Continue on Page 30

1 140°45'00" 140.7500°   **2** 140°30'00" 140.5000°   140°15'00" 140.2500°   **3**

138°30' 138°19'16"
60°00' 60°00'

141°00' 60°22'

KLUANE   NATIONAL

SEWARD

Mt
Newton
Mt
Jeannette
Mt
Bering
Malaspina
Mt
Baird
Mt Augusta
Mt
Irving

Mt St Elias

PARK

Mt
Eaton

CANADA

CAN
TUS

Mt. St. Elias
18008

Haydon Peak

Boundary Peak 185

Newton
Glacier

Mt Owen

YUKON TERRITORY
ALASKA

Boundary Peak 183

60°15'00"
60.2500°

NAT PARK AND WILDERNESS BDY

Boundary Peak 184

Dome
Pass

Cascade
Gl

Augusta Gl

Corwin
Cliffs

Boundary Peak 182

Mt Cook

AGASSIZ

Samovar Hills

Pt Glorious
Pinnacle Pass

Pinnacle Gl
Pinnacle
Pass

WRANGELL-   SAINT   ELIAS

Gilli Lake

GLACIER

Agassiz
Lakes

Hills

SEWARD

Hitchcock
Hills

WRANGELL- SAINT ELIAS

Hitchcock Gl

Marvine Glacier

Chaix
Hills

Hayden
Gl

Moore
Nunatak

MALASPINA

Blossom
Gl

Flora
Hills

160°00'
141°00'

GLACIER

Blossom
Island

59°45'00"
59.7500°

Tweedsmuir Glacier

Vern Ritchie Gl

3765 Coffee

CANADA
UNITED STATES

CITY AND BOROUGH OF YAKUTAT

LIBBEY GLACIER

A

Bar Lake

Noisy

ALSEK

RIVER

Range

TONGASS

Tomahnous
Creek

NATIONAL

TATSHENSHINI

Reynolds Gl

ALSEK

SAINT

Mel Cr

Tougali
Cr

NOVATAK GLACIER

FOREST

Boundary
Bdy Pk
170

RIVER

Nineteighteen Creek

Basement
Cr

Pentice
Ridge

Towagh
Cr

Ice Caps

Basement

C

BRABAZON RANGE

NAT PARK AND WILDERNESS BDY

ELIAS

Nelson
Glacier

Kanamuxt
Gl

MELBERN

Slatirease Gl

Tikke

Martin Gl

BRITISH COLUMBIA
ALASKA

Canyon Glacier

GLACIER   BAY

GLACIER

59°15'00"
59.2500°

Gina
Cr

Emile
Creek

WILDERNESS   BDY

NATIONAL

Mt Hay
Boundary Peak 162

Hay Gl

Melbern
Lake

Cabin
Slough

ALSEK

RIVER

Alsek Glacier

Mount
Jarl

Jarl Gl

MOUNTAINS

CITY AND BOROUGH OF YAKUTAT

Alsek River
Landing Strip

First
Rapids

Gateway
Knob

PARK

Bear
Island

TONGASS
NATIONAL
FOREST

East Alsek River
Landing Strip

GLACIER   BAY

River

Doame

Lower Doame

GRAND

Mount
Lodge

Boundary Peak 166

Mount
Eliza

D

NATIONAL   PRESERVE

East

South
Fork

Deception

Hills

Upper Doame
Lake

(WILDERNESS)

GRAND PLATEAU GLACIER

CANADA
UNITED STATES

Clear

Creek

© DeLorme

Mount
Watson

Boundary Peak 162
Mt Turner

59°00'
138°30'

138°00'00"
138.0000°

137°45'00"
137.7500°

137°30'00"
137.5000°

Ferris

KILOMETERS 5   0   5   10   15   20

MILES   1 0 1 2 3 4 5 6 7 8 9 10 11 12

36

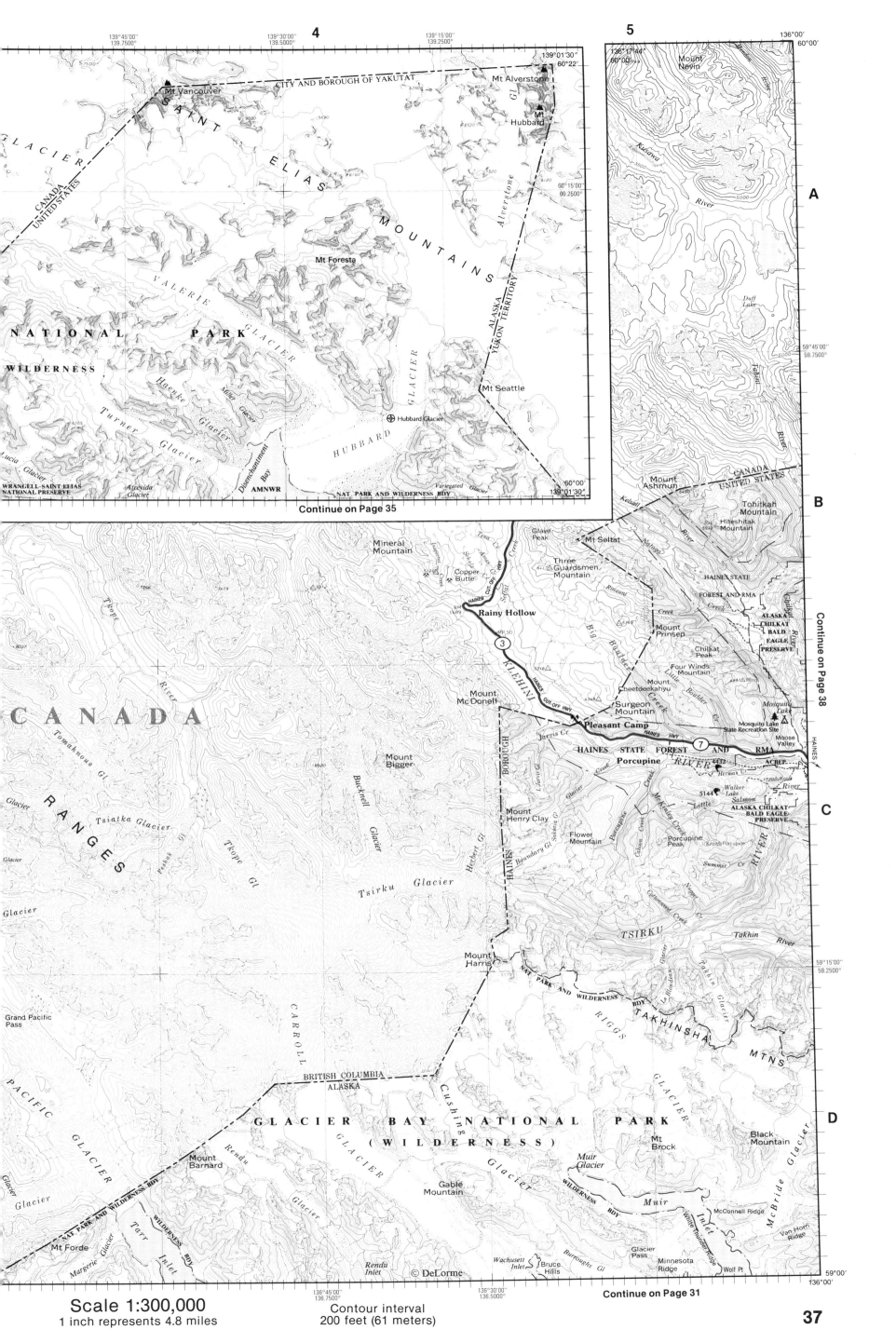

Continue on Page 35

Continue on Page 38

Continue on Page 31

Scale 1:300,000
1 inch represents 4.8 miles

Contour interval
200 feet (61 meters)

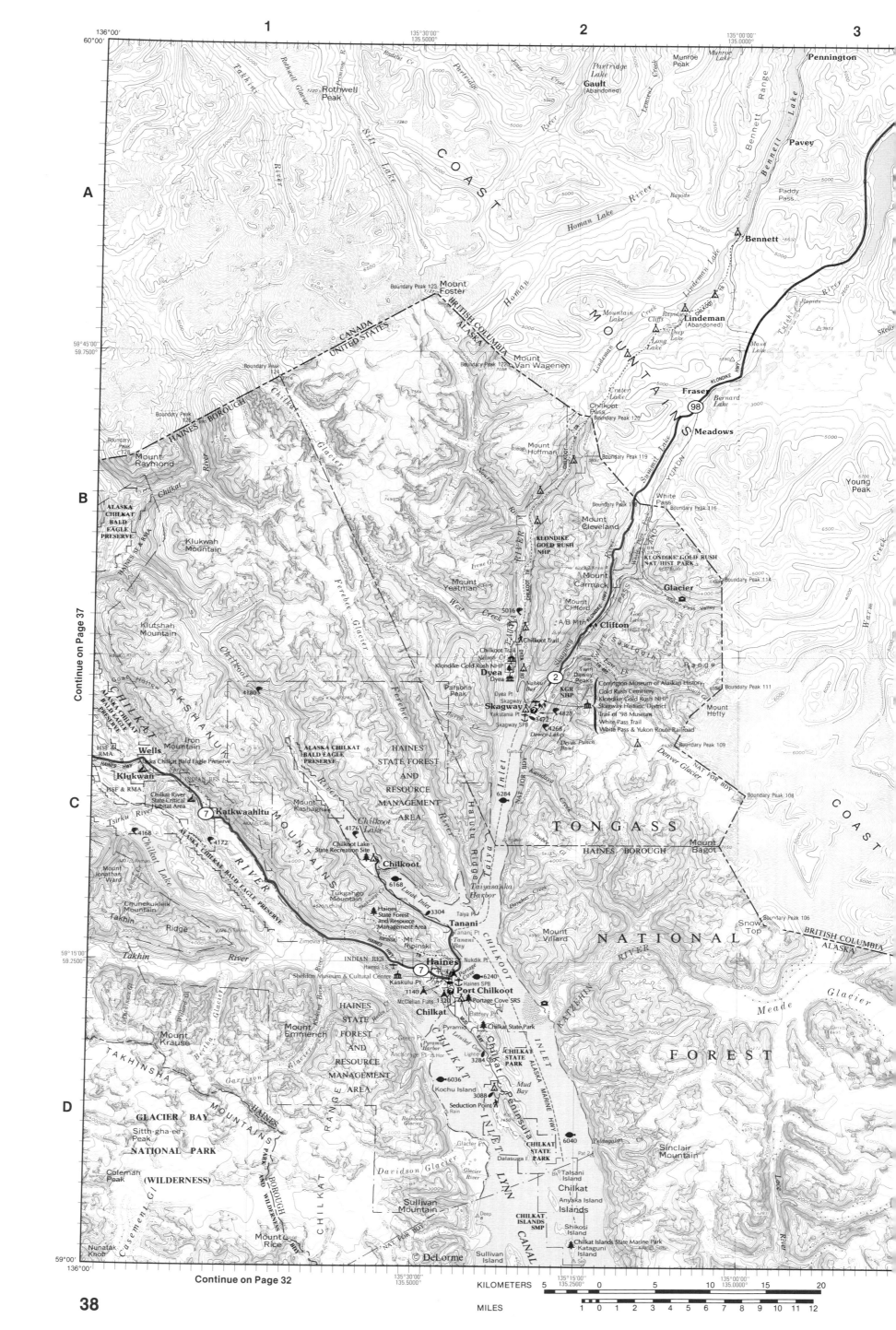

136°00'
60°00'

A

135°30'00"
135.5000'

135°00'00"
135.0000'

Munroe
Peak

Munroe
Lake

Pennington

*Partridge
Lake*

Gault
(Abandoned)

Bennett Range

Pavey

Paddy
Pass

Bennett

Rothwell
Peak

COAST

Mount
Foster
Boundary Peak 123

BRITISH COLUMBIA
ALASKA

Lindeman
(Abandoned)

59°45'00"
59.7500'

CANADA
UNITED STATES

Boundary Peak 124

Mount
Van Wagenen

Mount
Hoffman

Chilkoot
Pass
Boundary Peak 120

Fraser
(98)

Meadows

White
Pass

**Young
Peak**

HAINES BOROUGH

Boundary Peak
126

Boundary
Peak
128

Mount
Raymond

Boundary Peak 119

Boundary Peak 116

B

ALASKA
CHILKAT
BALD
EAGLE
PRESERVE

Klukwah
Mountain

KLONDIKE
GOLD RUSH
NHP

Mount
Cleveland

KLONDIKE GOLD RUSH
NAT HIST PARK

Boundary Peak 11A

Mount
Yeatman

Mount
Carmack

Glacier

Ferebee Glacier

Mount
Clifford

A/B Mtn

Clifton

Klutshah
Mountain

5016

Chilkoot Trail

Chilkoot Trail
Klondike Gold Rush NHP

4180

Dyea
Dyea

Corrington Museum of Alaskan History
Gold Rush Cemetery
Klondike Gold Rush NHP
Skagway Historic District
Trail of '98 Museum
White Pass Trail
White Pass & Yukon Route Railroad

Boundary Peak 111

Continue on Page 37

Parsons
Peak

Dyea Pt
Skagway

(2)
KGR
NHP

Skagway
Yakutania Pt
Skagway SPB

4472

4828

Mount
Hofty

CHILKAT
RIVER

TAKSHANUK

Wells

Iron
Mountain

HAINES
STATE FOREST
AND
RESOURCE
MANAGEMENT
AREA

6284

Twin
Dewey
Peaks

4268

Devils Punch
Bowl

Denver Glacier

NAT FOR BDY

Boundary Peak 109

C

HSF &
RMA

Klukwan

ALASKA CHILKAT
BALD EAGLE
PRESERVE

Chilkat River
State Critical
Habitat Area

HSF & RMA

(7) **Katkwaahltu**

4168

4172

Mount
Kashagnak

4176

Chilkoot
Lake

Chilkoot Lake
State Recreation Site

Chilkoot

Dewey Lake

Garbage

TONGASS

HAINES BOROUGH

Mount
Bagot

Boundary Peak 108

Mount Jonathan
Ward

Chunekukleik
Mountain

Takhin
Ridge

6168

3304

Lutak Inlet

Tukgahgo
Mountain

Haines
State Forest
and Resource
Management Area

Taiya

Tanani
Tanani Pt

Tanani
Bay

Taiyasanka
Harbor

Mount
Villard

NATIONAL

Snow
Top

Boundary Peak 106

**BRITISH COLUMBIA
ALASKA**

59°15'00"
59.2500'

Tsirku River

Zimovia

Mt
Ripinski

INDIAN RES
Haines LS

Sheldon Museum & Cultural Center

(7) **Haines**

Nukdik Pt

Portage
Cove

6240

Haines SPB

Port Chilkoot

Portage Cove SRS

KATAHIN RIVER

Glacier

Meade

Takhin

River

Kaskulu Pt

1140

McClellan Flats 1320

Chilkat

Battery Pt

HAINES
STATE
FOREST
AND
RESOURCE
MANAGEMENT
AREA

Mount
Emmerich

Green Pt

Chilkat State Park

Chilkat State Park

FOREST

Mount
Krause

Pyramid
Harbor

Pyramid
Island

Anchorage Pt

Lighter

3284

Letnikof Cove

CHILKAT
STATE
PARK

TAKHINSHA

Garrison

6036

Kochu Island

3088

Seduction Point

6040

Feldspage

Sinclair
Mountain

D

GLACIER BAY

Sitth-gha-ee
Peak

NATIONAL PARK

Rainbow
Glacier

Rain

Mud
Bay

Pat Pt

Dalasuga I

Talsani
Island

CHILKAT
STATE
PARK

LYNN

Chilkat

Anyaka Island
Islands

Coleman
Peak

(WILDERNESS)

Davidson Glacier

Glacier
River

Glacier Pt

Deep

Shikosi
Island

CHILKAT
ISLANDS
SMP

Chilkat Islands State Marine Park
Kataguni
Island

Nunatak
Knob

Mount
Rice

NAT FOR BDY

Sullivan
Mountain

Sullivan
Island

CANAL

© DeLorme

59°00'
136°00'

Continue on Page 32

135°30'00"
135.5000'

KILOMETERS   5   0   5   10   15   20

135°00'00"
135.0000'

MILES   1 0 1 2 3 4 5 6 7 8 9 10 11 12

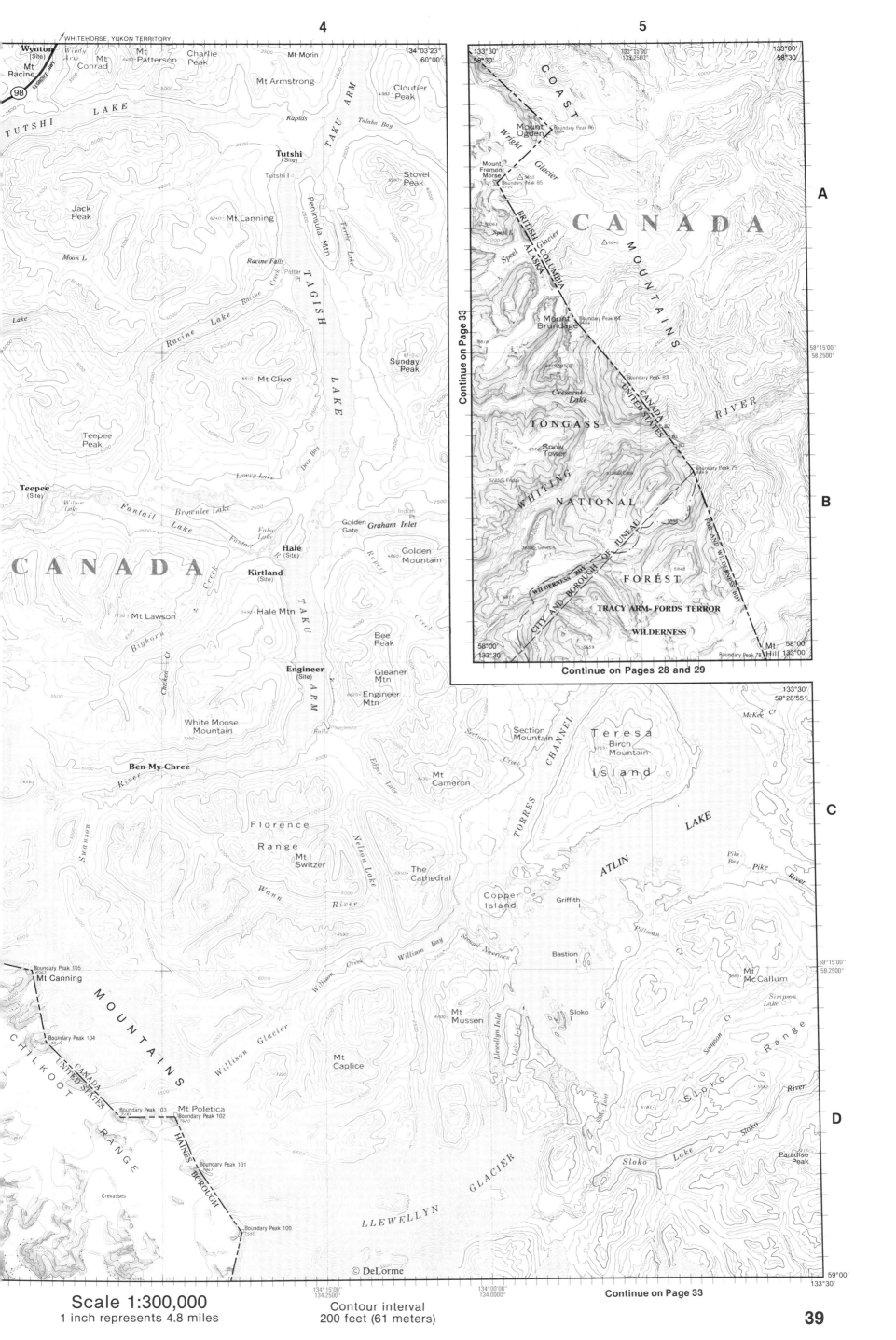

WHITEHORSE, YUKON TERRITORY

Wynton
(Site)

Mt
Racine

98

Windy
Arm

Mt
Conrad

Mt
Patterson

Charlie
Peak

Mt Morin

Mt Armstrong

Cloutier
Peak

TUTSHI LAKE

Rapids

Talahn Bay

Tutshi
(Site)

Tutshi I

Stovel
Peak

Jack
Peak

Mt Lanning

Peninsula Mtn

Moon L

Racine Falls

Potter
Pt

TAGISH   LAKE

TAKU   ARM

Racine Lake

Racine Creek

Lake

Sunday
Peak

Mt Chve

Teepee
Peak

Lowery Lake

Deep Bay

Teepee
(Site)

Willow
Lks

Fantail Lake

Brownlee Lake

False
Lake

Golden
Gate

Graham Inlet

CANADA

Hale
R (Site)

Golden
Mountain

Chicken Cr

Kirtland
(Site)

Bighorn

Mt Lawson

Hale Mtn

Bee
Peak

Engineer
(Site)

Gleaner
Mtn

Engineer
Mtn

White Moose
Mountain

TAKU   ARM

Ben-My-Chree

River

Swanson

Florence

Range

Mt
Switzer

Nelson Lake

The
Cathedral

Wann

River

Willison Creek

Willison Bay

Stroud Narrows

Edgar Inlet

Boundary Peak 105
Mt Canning

MOUNTAINS

Willison Glacier

Mt
Mussen

Mt
Caplice

Boundary Peak 104

CANADA
UNITED STATES

CHILKOOT

RANGE

Boundary Peak 103
Mt Poletica
Boundary Peak 102

HAINES BOROUGH

Boundary Peak 101

Crevasses

Boundary Peak 100

LLEWELLYN

© DeLorme

COAST

Mount
Ogden

Boundary Peak 86

Glacier

Wright

Mount
Fremont
Morse

Boundary Peak 85

Speel

BRITISH COLUMBIA
ALASKA

Glacier

Speel L.

CANADA

MOUNTAINS

Mount
Brundage

Boundary Peak 84

CANADA
UNITED STATES

Boundary Peak 83

RIVER

Crescent
Lake

TONGASS

Snow
Tower

WHITING

NATIONAL

FORFST   AND   WILDERNESS   BDY

FOREST

Boundary Peak 79

WILDERNESS   BDY   AND   CITY   AND   BOROUGH   OF   JUNEAU

TRACY ARM- FORDS TERROR

WILDERNESS

Mt
Hill

Boundary Peak 78

Continue on Page 33

Continue on Pages 28 and 29

Section
Mountain

Section Creek

TORRES   CHANNEL

Teresa

Birch
Mountain

Island

McKee Cr

Mt
Cameron

ATLIN

LAKE

Copper
Island

Griffith

Pike
Bay

Pike

River

Pillman Cr

Bastion

Mt
McCallum

Simpson
Lake

Llewellyn Inlet

Sloko

Simpson Cr

Sloko   Range

Lake Inlet

Sloko   Lake

River

GLACIER

Sloko River

Paradise
Peak

Continue on Page 33

Scale 1:300,000
1 inch represents 4.8 miles

Contour interval
200 feet (61 meters)

A

B

C

D

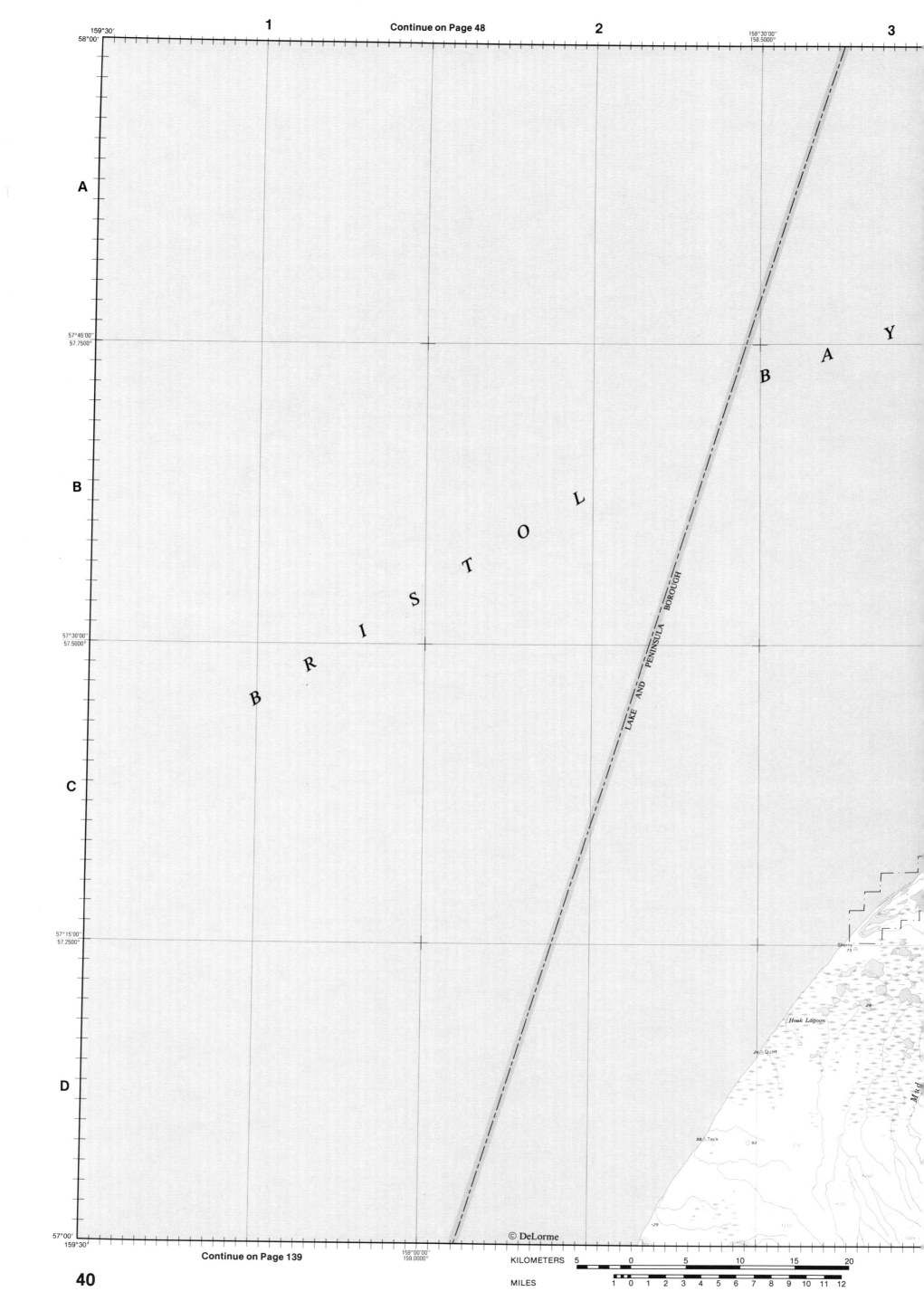

Continue on Page 48

159°30'
58°00'

159°30'00"
158.5000°
158°30'00"

1

2

3

A

B

Y

B

A

B

R

I

S

T

O

L

LAKE AND PENINSULA BOROUGH

57°45'00"
57.7500°

B

57°30'00"
57.5000°

C

Sherry
75

Hook Lagoon

Quirt

Mud

57°15'00"
57.2500°

D

Teck

93

© DeLorme

57°00'
159°30'

159°00'00"
159.0000°

Continue on Page 139

40

KILOMETERS 5 0 5 10 15 20

MILES 1 0 1 2 3 4 5 6 7 8 9 10 11 12

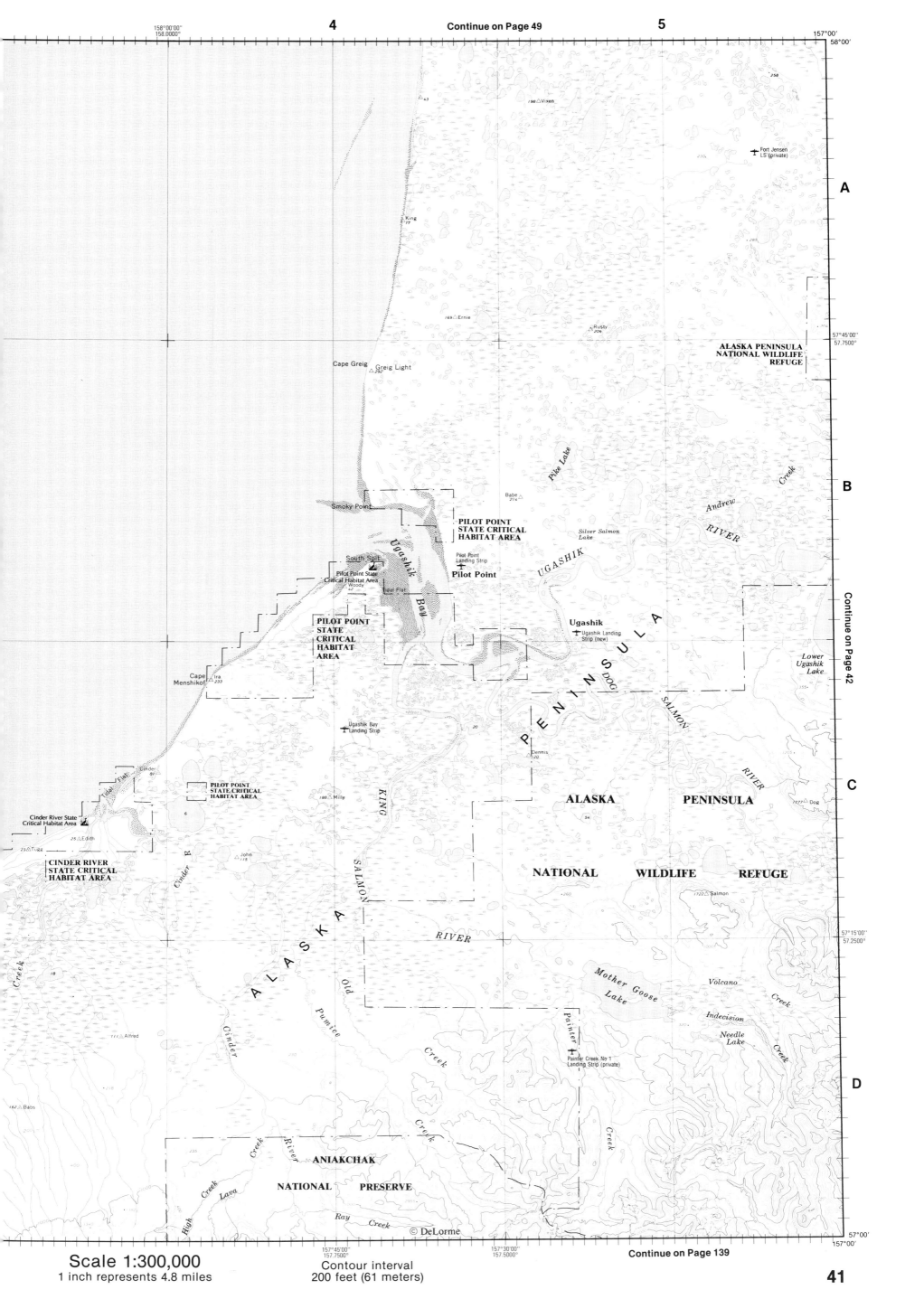

158°00'00"
158.0000°
157°00'
58°00'

258

198 △Vixen

✈ Fort Jensen
LS (private)

43

A

*King
17*

169 △Ernie

*Rusty
204*

Continue on Page 42

57°45'00"
57.7500°

**ALASKA PENINSULA
NATIONAL WILDLIFE
REFUGE**

Cape Greig Greig Light
△292

Pike Lake

Andrew

*Babe △
214*

B

Smoky Point

**PILOT POINT
STATE CRITICAL
HABITAT AREA**

*Silver Salmon
Lake*

Creek

RIVER

South Spit
Pilot Point State
Critical Habitat Area
Woody

*Ugashik
Bay*

Pilot Point
Landing Strip

Pilot Point

UGASHIK

Tidal Flat

**PILOT POINT
STATE
CRITICAL
HABITAT
AREA**

Ugashik
✈ Ugashik Landing
Strip (new)

*Lower
Ugashik
Lake*

155

Cape
Menshikof △Ira
233

PENINSULA

DOG

SALMON

RIVER

C

Ugashik Bay
✈ Landing Strip

20

*Dennis
720*

ALASKA   PENINSULA

1277 △ Dog

188 △ Milly

KING

54

Cinder River State
Critical Habitat Area

**PILOT POINT
STATE CRITICAL
HABITAT AREA**

Tidal Flat Cinder
81 △

6

Cinder R.

SALMON

NATIONAL   WILDLIFE   REFUGE

1729 △ Salmon

233 △Tuzz *25 △Edith*

**CINDER RIVER
STATE CRITICAL
HABITAT AREA**

ALASKA

*△John
115*

260

57°15'00"
57.2500°

Creek

18

RIVER

*Mother Goose
Lake*

Volcano

Creek

Indecision

Old

Pumice

*Needle
Lake*

711 △ Alfred

Cinder

Creek

Painter

D

762 △ Babs

Creek

River

Lava

235

Creek

✈ Painter Creek No 1
Landing Strip (private)

ANIAKCHAK

NATIONAL   PRESERVE

High

Ray   Creek

© DeLorme

57°00'

157°45'00"
157.7500°

157°30'00"
157.5000°

Continue on Page 139

Scale 1:300,000
1 inch represents 4.8 miles

Contour interval
200 feet (61 meters)

157°00'
58°00'
156°00'00"
156.0000'

BECHAROF   **NATIONAL**   **WILDLIFE**

BECHAROF

A

LAKE

KEJULIK

The Gas Rocks

Ukinrek
Maars

Severson Peninsula

BECHAROF

57°45'00"
57.7500'

Featherly Creek

LAVA

Mount Peulik

Camp Cr

Seal Point
Bellim Bay

Cleo

Blue Mountain

Featherly
Pass

Simeon
Creek

Mount
Simeon

Burls
Pass

Mount
Burls

Burls

WILDERNESS BDY

Sulphur Cr

B

ALASKA   Upper   **PENINSULA**

Mount
Demian

Mount
Lee

South Fork

Otter Salmon

Oil Well

Dry Bay

Mount
Ugashik

APPROXIMATE BDY

Ruth
Lake

Kanatak
Pass

Summit
Lake

5124

Crooked

Moore Creek

Deer Creek

Kanatak

Kanatak
Lake

Kelp
Point

1804

Lower

NATIONAL

Mount
Becharof

Kanatak
Lagoon

Jute
Bay

Ugashik   Lake

Becharof

Jute
Is
Bay

Cape Kanatak

Portage Bay

WILDLIFE

Black Creek

631 Ridge

Coal Point

Cape
Igvak

REFUGE

Deer
Mountain

Mount
Shannon
Pass

Lee
Cabin

East Channel I

Lenora Lake

Elizabeth
Lake

Sids
Pass

Short Creek

Creek

Channel Rock

West Channel I

Terrace I

C

**ALASKA MARITIME
NATIONAL WILDLIFE
REFUGE**

Hartman I

Figure Eight

Alai Cr

Spit

Wide Bay

Titcliff I

Dog Salmon River

Goblet Creek

Creek

Mount
Alai

Tidal Flat

Lone
Hill

Creek

Icy
Peak

Wide
2198

Cape Kayakliut

Gob
3393

57°15'00"
57.2500'

Kialagvik Creek

AMNWR

Imuya Bay

Wandering Creek

Mount
Kialagvik

Kiukak Creek

Cape Kilokak
Kilokak Rocks

PACIFIC

Imuya

Gunter Creek

KODIAK ISLAND BOROUGH
LAKE AND PENINSULA BOROUGH

D

Mount
Chiginagak

AMNWR

Agripina Bay

Agripina River

Lagoon

Ashiiak I

Lone Rock

AMNWR
*Chiginagak
Bay*

Tidal Flat

Port Wrangell

Flat I
AMNWR

David I

Poltava I

© DeLorme

57°00'
157°00'

Continue on Page 41

Continue on Page 139

156°30'00"
156.5000'

KILOMETERS   5   0   5   10   15   20

MILES   1 0 1 2 3 4 5 6 7 8 9 10 11 12

155°30'00''
155.5000°

154°30'

58°00'

KATMAI NATIONAL PARK

(WILDERNESS)

Katmai Bay

Atmo Mtn

Kashvik Bay

REFUGE

Cape Kubugakli

R E F U G E

A

PENINSULA AND BOROUGH

East Fork

Albert Cr

PARK REFUGE AND WILDERNESS

PENINSULA

Mt Kubugakli

BDY BDY

RIVER

Margaret Creek

KATMNE ISLAND

AMNWR

Big Alinchak Cr

Beah Bay

WILDERNESS AND

LAKE KODIAK

Portage Creek

Helen Creek

Moose Creek

Big Alinchak Bay

Alinchak Cr

Alinchak Bay

P U A L E   B A Y

57°45'00''
57.7500°

Cape Kekurnoi

VABM 96

Cape Aklek

S
T
R
A
I
T

B

Dry 39

Cape Karluk

Cape Unalishagvak

Continue on Page 44

Sturgeon Head

VABM 1323

S
H
E
L
I
K
O
F

Grant Lagoon

ISLAND

Cape Grant

VABM Grant 1236

1520

1602

1520

Halibut Bay

KODIAK

C

Middle Cape

VABM 118

Tombstone Rks

Cannery

KODIAK

1275

VABM 150A Dales

Ayakulik

NATIONAL

Mushroom Reef

762

1120

Outer Seal Rk

Gurney Bay

WILDLIFE REFUGE

1020

VABM 100

Inner Seal Rk

Cape Ikolik

Bumble Bay

Anvil Mtn

1530

Red River

Little Bear Rk

1057

1225

57°15'00''
57.2500°

1335

Ayakulik I Yak 2

Oval Mtn

Ayakulik

Cem

O C E A N

REFUGE BDY

Mud

D

© DeLorme

155°15'00''
155.2500°

155°00'00''
155.0000°

Continue on Page 64, Inset 1

57°00'
154°30'

Bluff

Scale 1:300,000
1 inch represents 4.8 miles

Contour interval
200 feet (61 meters)

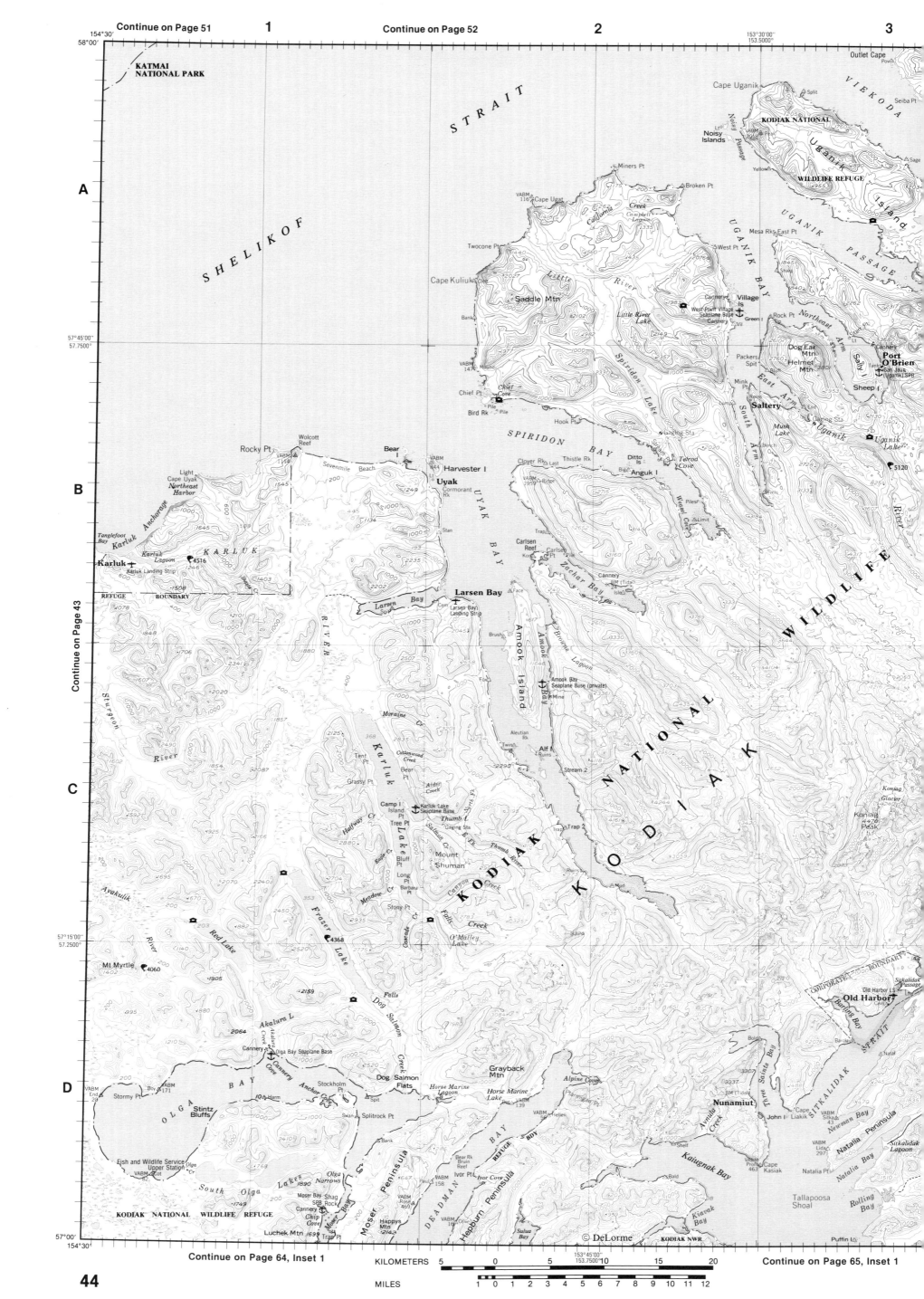

Continue on Page 43

KILOMETERS   5   0   5   10   15   20

MILES   1   0   1   2   3   4   5   6   7   8   9   10   11   12

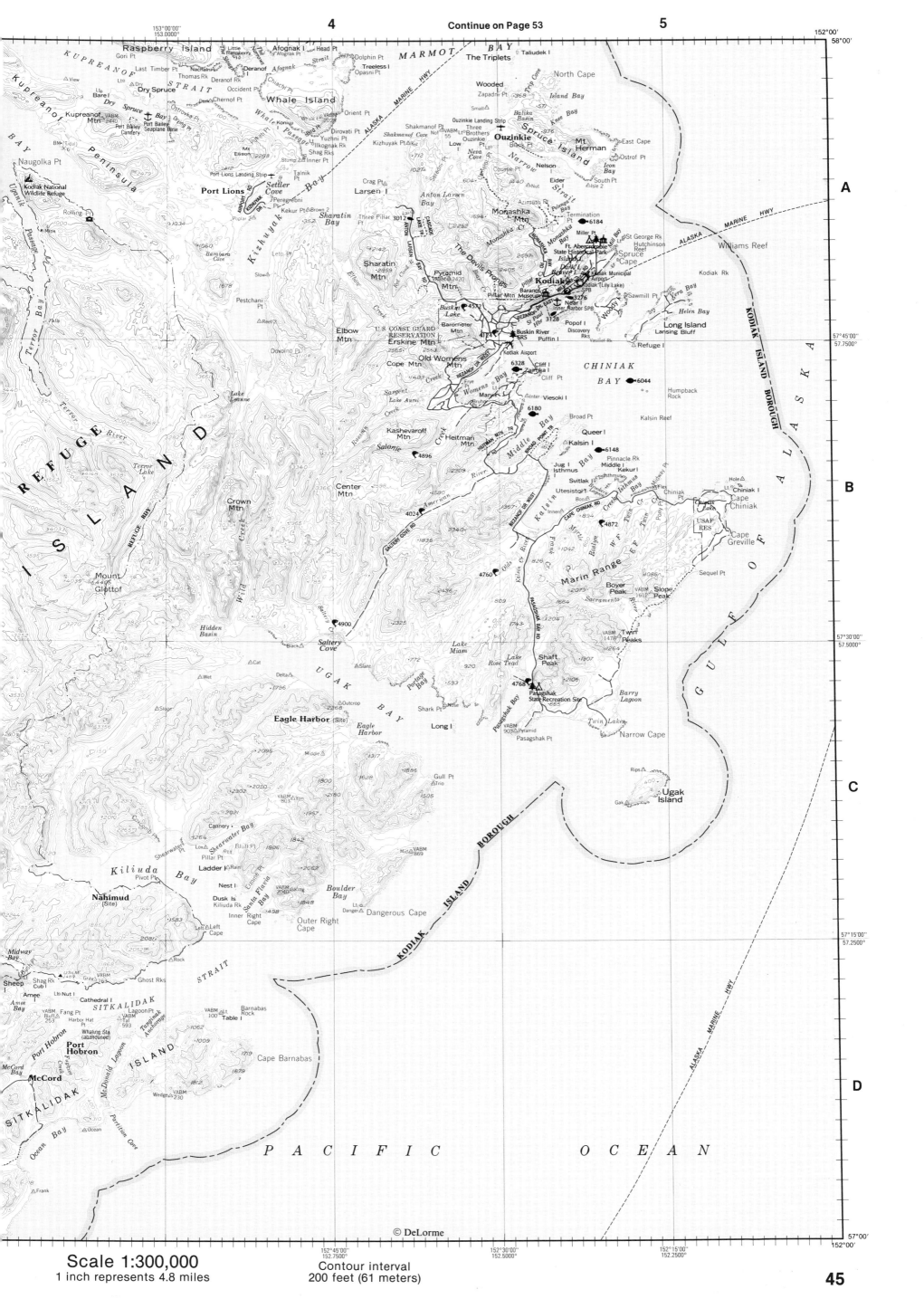

Scale 1:300,000
1 inch represents 4.8 miles

Contour interval
200 feet (61 meters)

© DeLorme

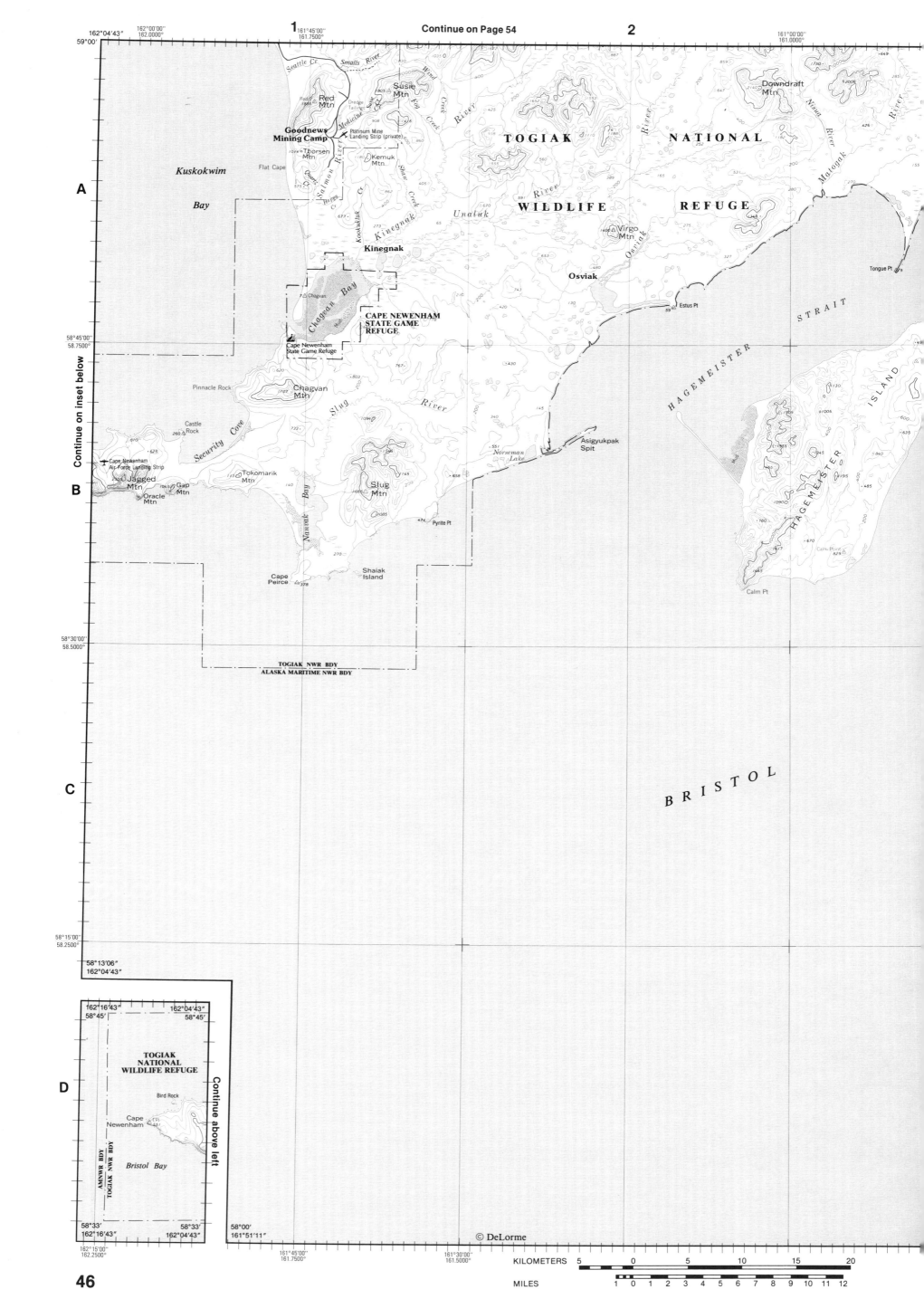

162°04'43"
162°00'00"
162.0000°

1
161°45'00"
161.7500°

2

161°00'00"
161.0000°

59°00'

Seattle Cr
Smalls River
Wind
Creek
Susie Mtn
Fog Creek
River
Downdraft Mtn
Red Mtn
Goodnews Mining Camp
Platinum Mine Landing Strip (private)
Dredge Tailings
Medicine
Kemuk Mtn
Thorsen Mtn
Flat Cape
Salmon River
Shan Creek

TOGIAK   NATIONAL

Kuskokwim

A

Bay

Kookukluk
Kinegnak
River
Unaluk
River

WILDLIFE   REFUGE

Virgo Mtn
Osviak
River
Matogak River
Nisua River

Tongue Pt

Kinegnak

Chagvan
Chagvan Bay
CAPE NEWENHAM STATE GAME REFUGE
Cape Newenham State Game Refuge

Osviak

Estus Pt

H A G E M E I S T E R   S T R A I T

58°45'00"
58.7500°

Pinnacle Rock
Castle Rock
Security Cove
Chagvan Mtn
Slug
River
Norseman Lake
Asigyukpak Spit

B

Cape Newenham Air Force Landing Strip
Jagged Mtn
Oracle Mtn
Gap Mtn
Tokomarik Mtn
Nanvak Bay
Slug Mtn
Pyrite Pt

H A G E M E I S T E R   I S L A N D

Calm Point

Cape Peirce
Shaiak Island
Calm Pt

58°30'00"
58.5000°

TOGIAK NWR BDY
ALASKA MARITIME NWR BDY

C

B R I S T O L

58°15'00"
58.2500°

58°13'06"
162°04'43"

162°16'43"
58°45'
162°04'43"
58°45'

TOGIAK NATIONAL WILDLIFE REFUGE

D

Bird Rock

Cape Newenham

AMNWR BDY
TOGIAK NWR BDY

Bristol Bay

58°33'
162°16'43"
162.2500°

58°33'
162°04'43"

58°00'
161°51'11"

161°45'00"
161.7500°

161°30'00"
161.5000°

© DeLorme

KILOMETERS   5   0   5   10   15   20

MILES   1 0 1 2 3 4 5 6 7 8 9 10 11 12

160°30'00"
160.5000°

159°30'
59°00'

Quigling River

Aeolus
Mtn

T O G I A K   B A Y

Anchor Pt

Owen

Negukthlik River

Ungalikthluk R.

Ungalikthluk

TOGIAK   NATIONAL

WILDLIFE   REFUGE

Kulukak

Kulukak River

Konik River

VABM
Ualik
370

Rocky Pt

Nunavachak Lake

VABM
Amyko
1092

Kulukak Bay

VABM
Kulukak
956

A

Summit
Island

Kulukak
Pt

Fyativak Bay

Rocky Pt   Strait
38

INDEFINITE   BDY

58°45'00"
58.7500°

W a l r u s   I s l a n d s

Melotak
Bay

VABM
245   Right Hand Pt

High
Island

128 Black Rock

Crooked
Island

WALRUS ISLANDS
STATE GAME SANCTUARY

404

Crooked
Az Mark
236

B

VABM
1410   Round I

Walrus Islands
State Game Sanctuary

436
The Twins

Continue on Page 48

B A Y

C

58°15'00"
58.2500°

B E R I N G   S E A

D

58°00'
159°30'

© DeLorme

160°45'00"
160.7500°

160°15'00"
160.2500°

160°00'00"
160.0000°

159°45'00"
159.7500°

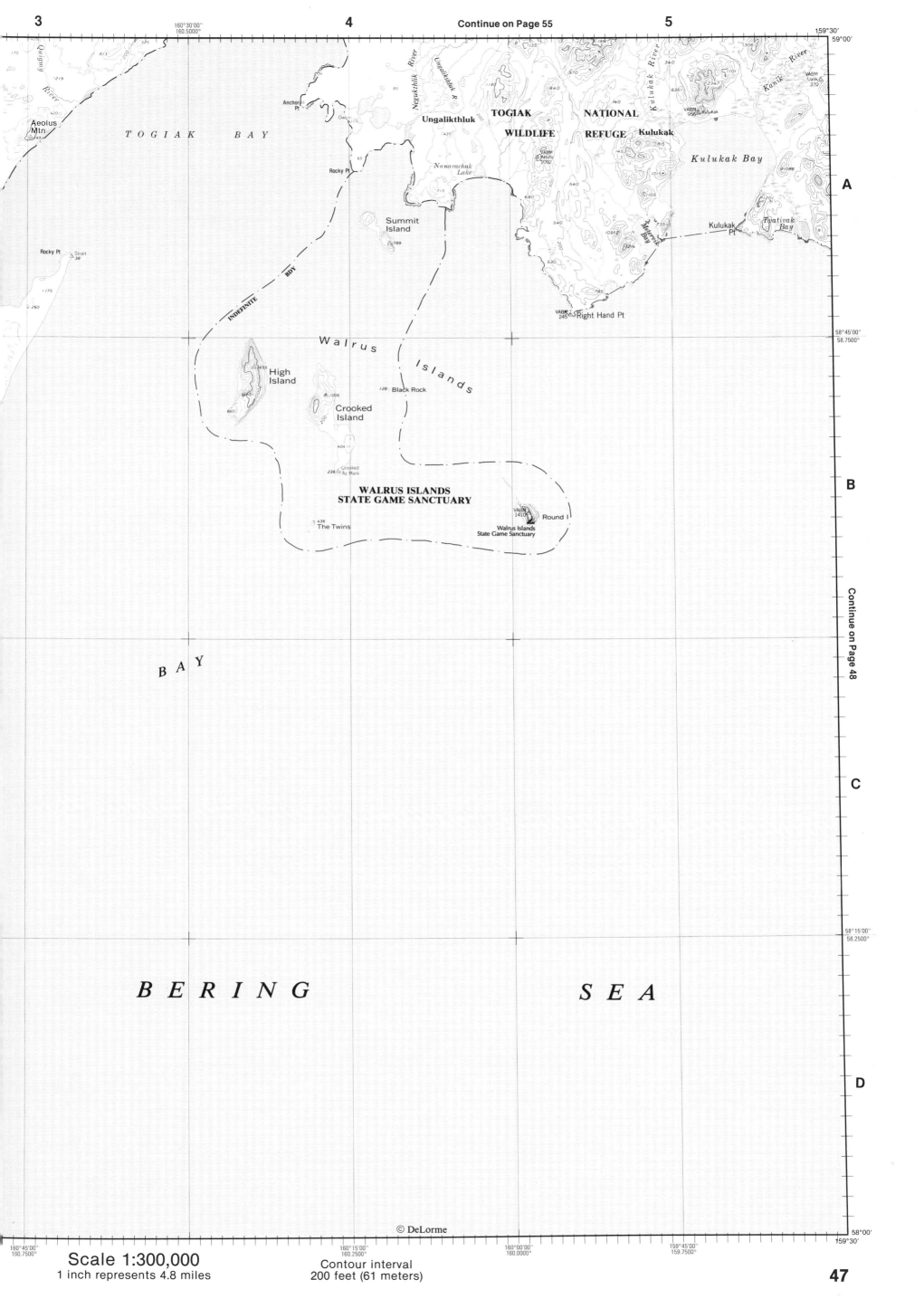

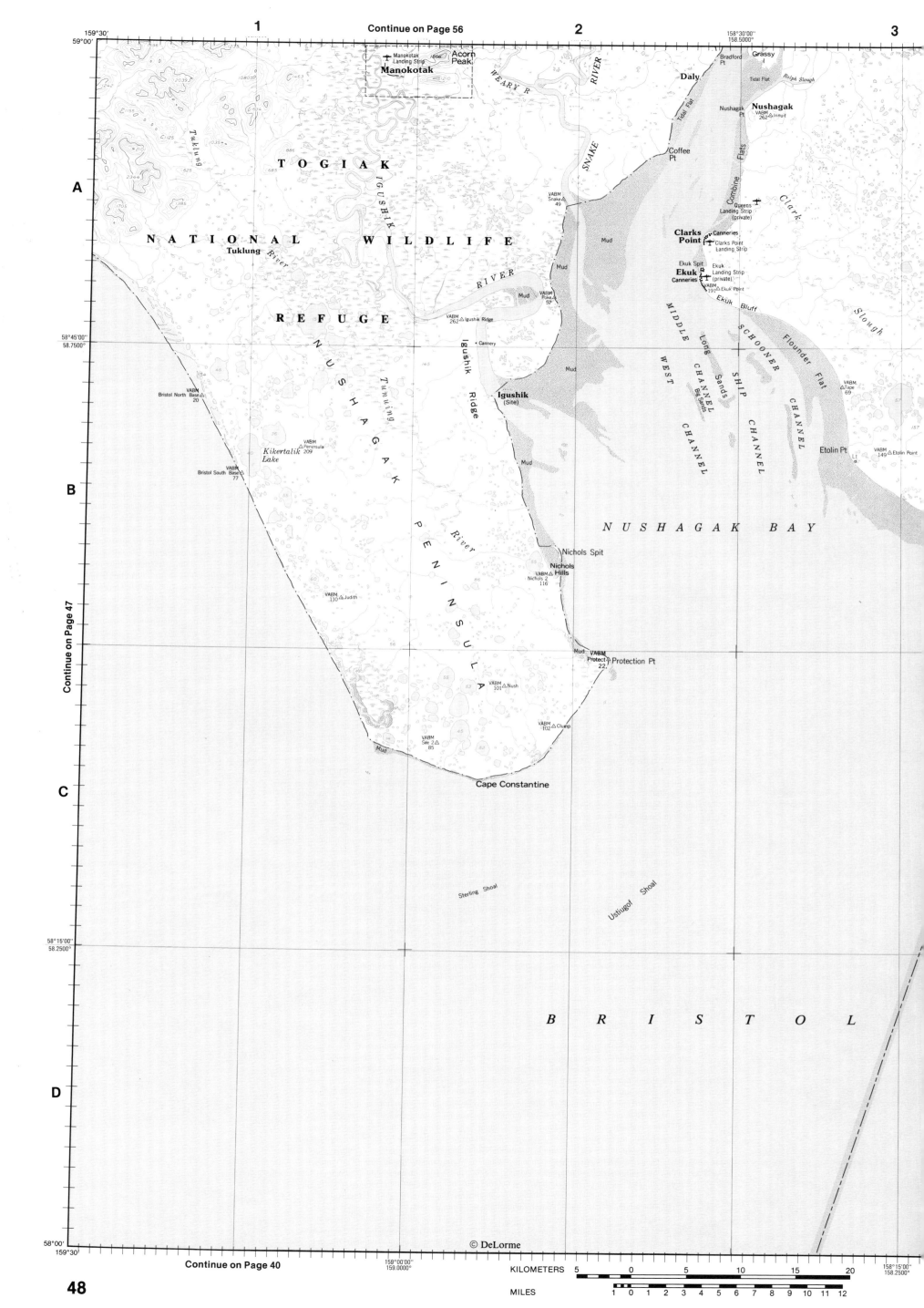

159°30'
59°30'
59°00'

158°30'00"
158.5000°

Bradford
Pt

Grassy

Daly

Tidal Flat

Ralph Slough

Nushagak
Pt

Nushagak
VABM
262 △ Innuit

Manokotak
Landing Strip

Acorn
Peak

Manokotak

WEARY R

SNAKE

RIVER

Coffee
Pt

Tidal Flat

Combine

Queens
Landing Strip
(private)

Clark

T O G I A K

VABM
Snake △
49

Igushik

Mud

A

Mud

**Clarks
Point**

Canneries

Clarks Point
Landing Strip

Combine

Flats

N A T I O N A L   **W I L D L I F E**

Tuklung

River

RIVER

Mud

Ekuk Spit

Ekuk
Landing Strip
(private)

Ekuk
Canneries

VABM
191 △ Ekuk Point

R E F U G E

VABM
262 △ Igushik Ridge

VABM
Poke △
59

Mud

Ekuk Bluff

M I D D L E

Slough

Igushik

• Cannery

58°45'00"
58.7500°

N U S H A G A K

Tuning

Ridge

Igushik
Ridge

Igushik
(Site)

Mud

L O N G

C H A N N E L

Big Sands

Sands

W E S T

S H I P *C H A N N E L*

S C H O O N E R

F l o u n d e r   F l a t

C H A N N E L

VABM
△ Tape
69

VABM
△ Peninsula
209

*Kikertalik
Lake*

VABM
Bristol North Base △
20

River

C H A N N E L

VABM
△ Etolin Point
149

Etolin Pt
Lt

B

VABM
Bristol South Base △
77

P E N I N S U L A

VABM
110 △ Judith

Nichols Spit

**Nichols
Hills**

VABM
Nichols 2 △
116

N U S H A G A K   *B A Y*

Mud

VABM
Protect △
22

Protection Pt

VABM
101 △ Nush

VABM
102 △ Clump

C

VABM
Sale 2 △
85

Mud

Cape Constantine

Sterling Shoal

Ustiugof Shoal

58°15'00"
58.2500°

B   R   I   S   T   O   L

D

159°00'00"
159.0000°

58°00'
159°30'

© DeLorme

158°15'00"
158.2500°

Continue on Page 47

KILOMETERS 5   0   5   10   15   20

MILES 1 0 1 2 3 4 5 6 7 8 9 10 11 12

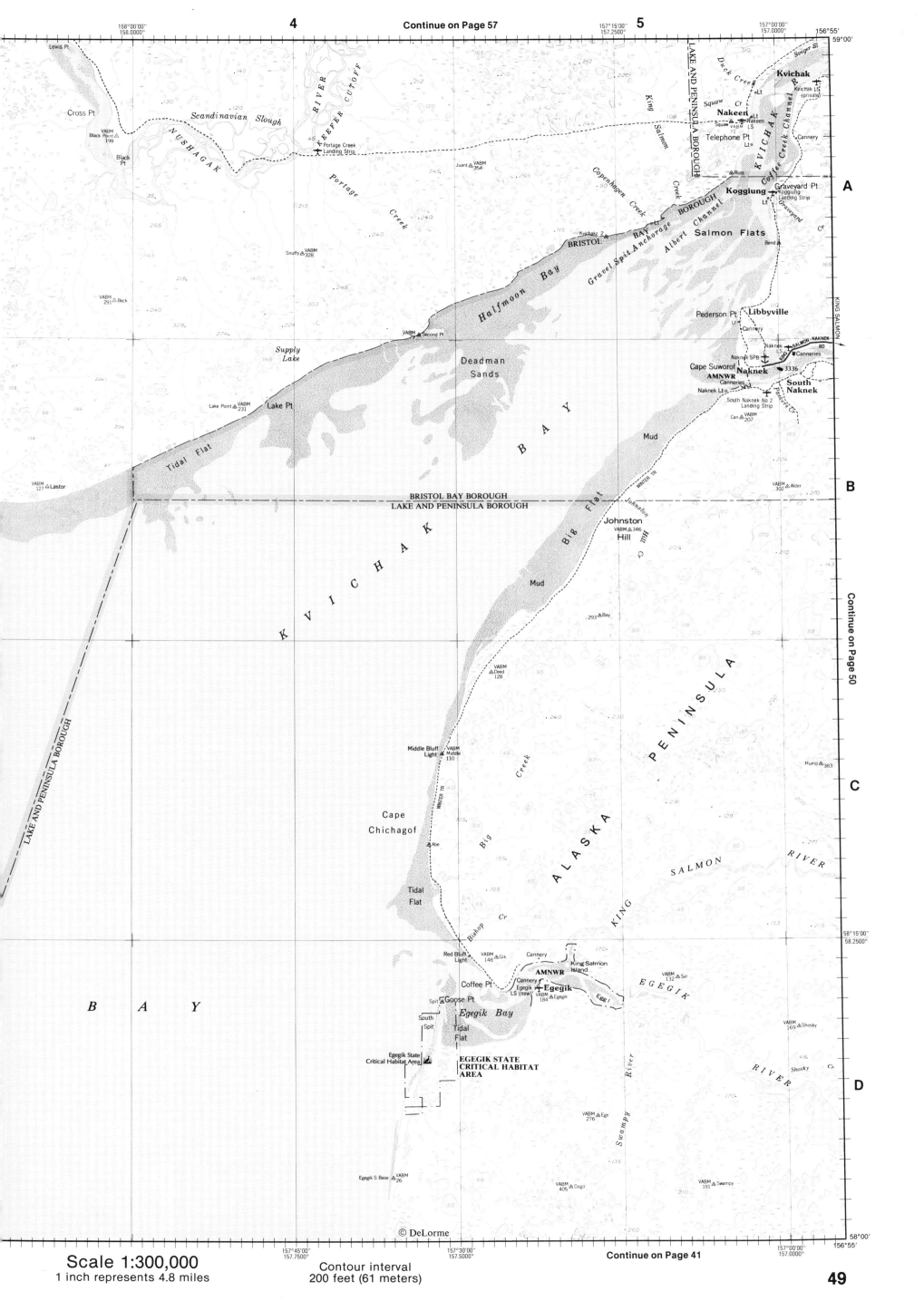

Continue on Page 50

Continue on Page 41

© DeLorme

Scale 1:300,000
1 inch represents 4.8 miles

Contour interval
200 feet (61 meters)

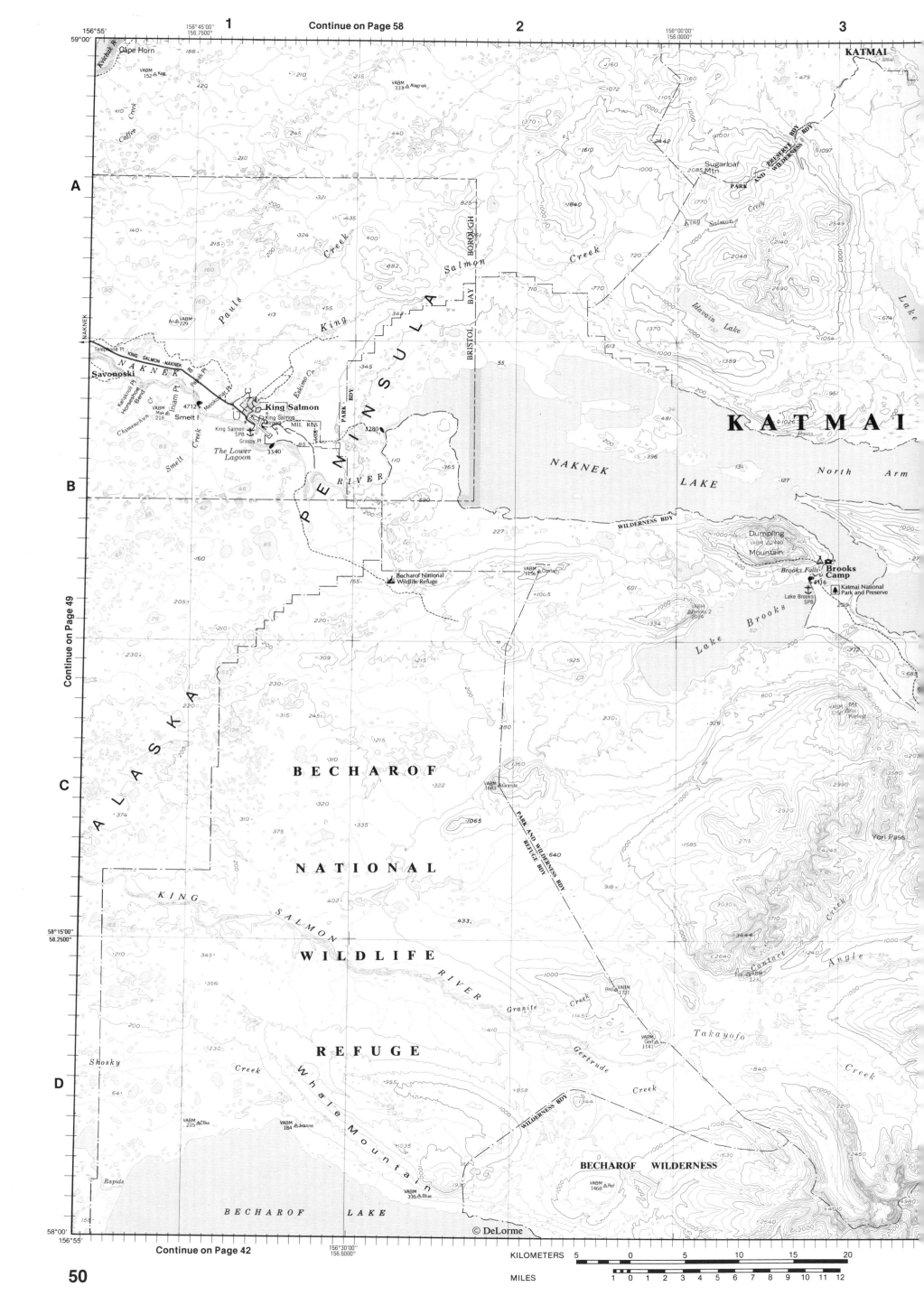

156°55'
59°00'
156°45'00"
156.7500°
156°00'00"
156.0000°

KATMAI

Cape Horn

A

NAKNEK   **PENINSULA**

Savonoski

King Salmon
MIL. RES.

Sugarloaf Mtn

Idavain Lake

K A T M A I

B

NAKNEK   LAKE

North Arm

Continue on Page 49

Dumpling Mountain

Brooks Falls
Brooks Camp
Lake Brooks SPB
Katmai National Park and Preserve

Becharof National Wildlife Refuge

WILDERNESS BDY

Lake   Brooks

A L A S K A

C

B E C H A R O F

PARK AND WILDERNESS BDY
REFUGE BDY

Yori Pass

N A T I O N A L

58°15'00"
58.2500°

W I L D L I F E

KING   SALMON   RIVER

Granite   Creek

Takayofo

R E F U G E

Shosky   Creek

Gertrude   Creek

D

Whale Mountain

BECHAROF   WILDERNESS

WILDERNESS BDY

Rapids

B E C H A R O F   L A K E

© DeLorme

58°00'
156°55'

Continue on Page 42

156°30'00"
156.5000°

KILOMETERS   5   0   5   10   15   20

MILES   1 0 1 2 3 4 5 6 7 8 9 10 11 12

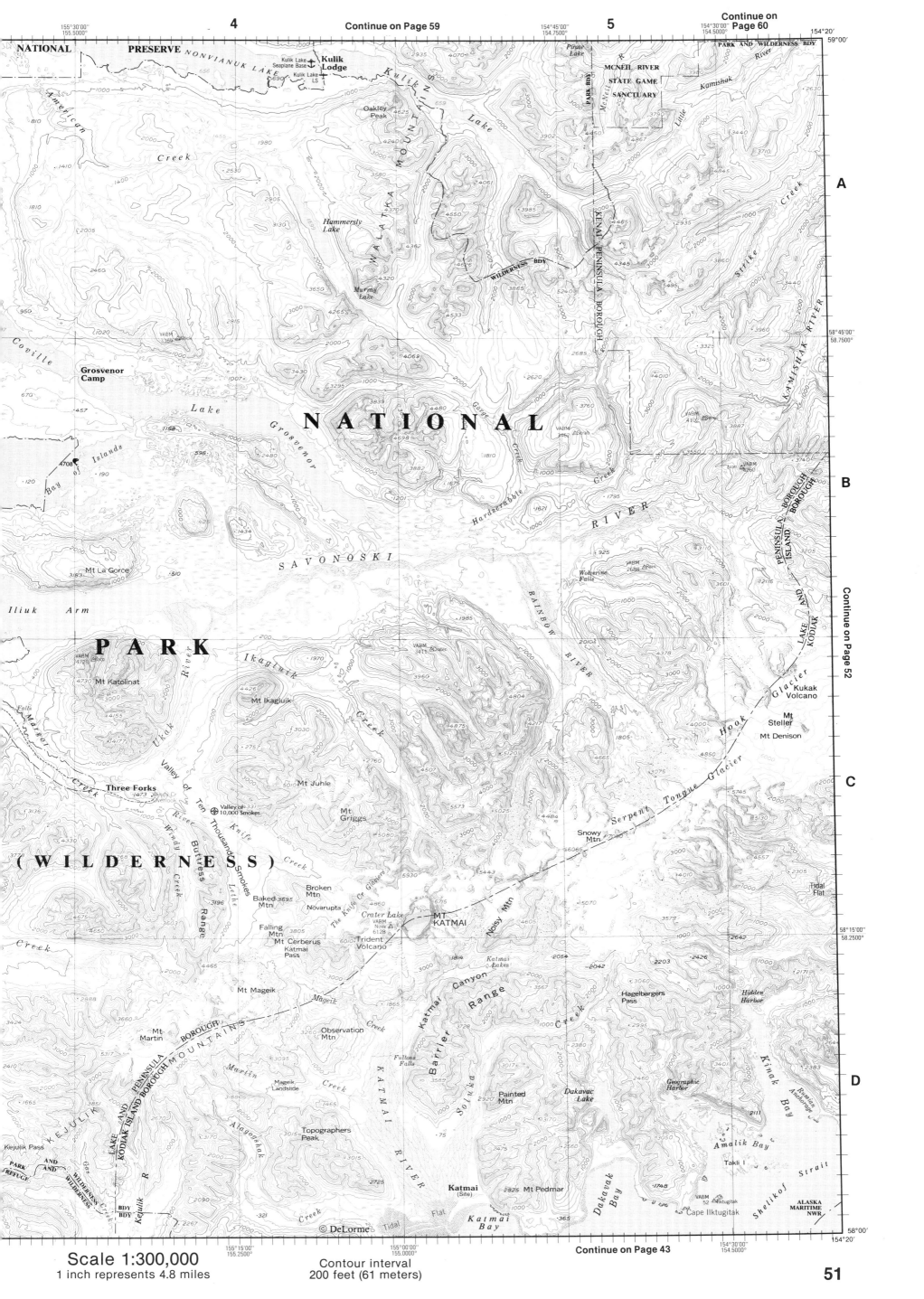

Continue on Page 52

Scale 1:300,000
1 inch represents 4.8 miles

Contour interval
200 feet (61 meters)

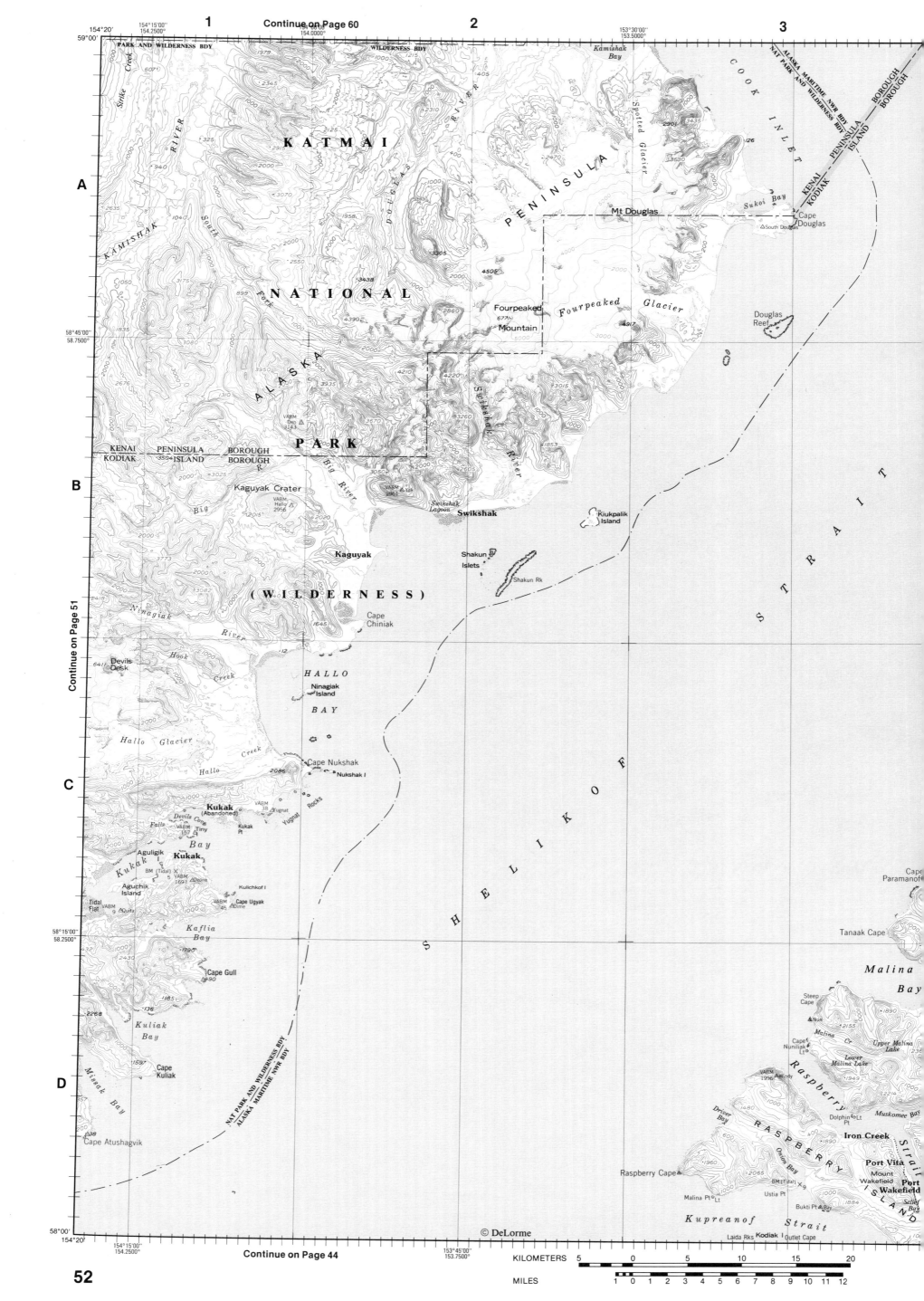

154°20'
154°15'00"
154.2500°
154°00'00"
154.0000°
153°30'00"
153.5000°
59°00'

PARK AND WILDERNESS BDY
WILDERNESS BDY

A

K A T M A I

DOUGLAS RIVER

PENINSULA

Kamishak Bay

Spotted Glacier

COOK INLET

ALASKA MARITIME NWR NAT PARK AND WILDERNESS BDY

KENAI PENINSULA BOROUGH BOROUGH
KODIAK ISLAND

Mt Douglas

Sukoi Bay

△South Douglas

Cape Douglas

N A T I O N A L

Fourpeaked Mountain

Fourpeaked Glacier

Douglas Reef

58°45'00"
58.7500°

A L A S K A

KENAI PENINSULA BOROUGH BOROUGH
KODIAK ISLAND

P A R K

Big River

Suklekshak River

B

Kaguyak Crater

VABM Hallo 2956

Swikshak Lagoon

Swikshak

Kiukpalik Island

S T R A I T

Kaguyak

Shakun Islets

Shakun Rk

(W I L D E R N E S S)

Ninagiak River

Cape Chiniak

Devils Desk

Hook Creek

H A L L O

Ninagiak Island

B A Y

S H E L I K O F

Continue on Page 51

Hallo Glacier

Hallo Creek

Cape Nukshak

Nukshak I

Rocks

C

Kukak (Abandoned)

Devils Cove

Kukak Pt

Yugnat

Kukak Bay

Tiny

Aguligik

Kukak

BM (Tidal)

Aguchik Island

Kulichkof I

Tidal Flat

Cape Ugyak

Kaflia Bay

S

Cape Paramanof

58°15'00"
58.2500°

Tanaak Cape

Cape Gull

Malina Bay

Steep Cape

Kuliak Bay

Malina Cr

Cape Nuniliak Lt

Upper Malina Lake

Lower Malina Lake

D

Missak Bay

Cape Kuliak

NAT PARK AND WILDERNESS BDY
ALASKA MARITIME NWR BDY

R A S P B E R R Y

Driver Bay

Dolphin Pt

Muskomee Bay

Iron Creek

Cape Atushagvik

Port Vita

Raspberry Cape

Onion Bay

Mount Wakefield

Port Wakefield

Malina Pt Lt

Ustia Pt

Bukti Pt & Bay

Kupreanof

Strait

58°00'
154°20'

Laida Rks
Kodiak

Outlet Cape

© DeLorme

154°15'00"
154.2500°
153°45'00"
153.7500°

KILOMETERS 5   0   5   10   15   20

MILES   1 0 1 2 3 4 5 6 7 8 9 10 11 12

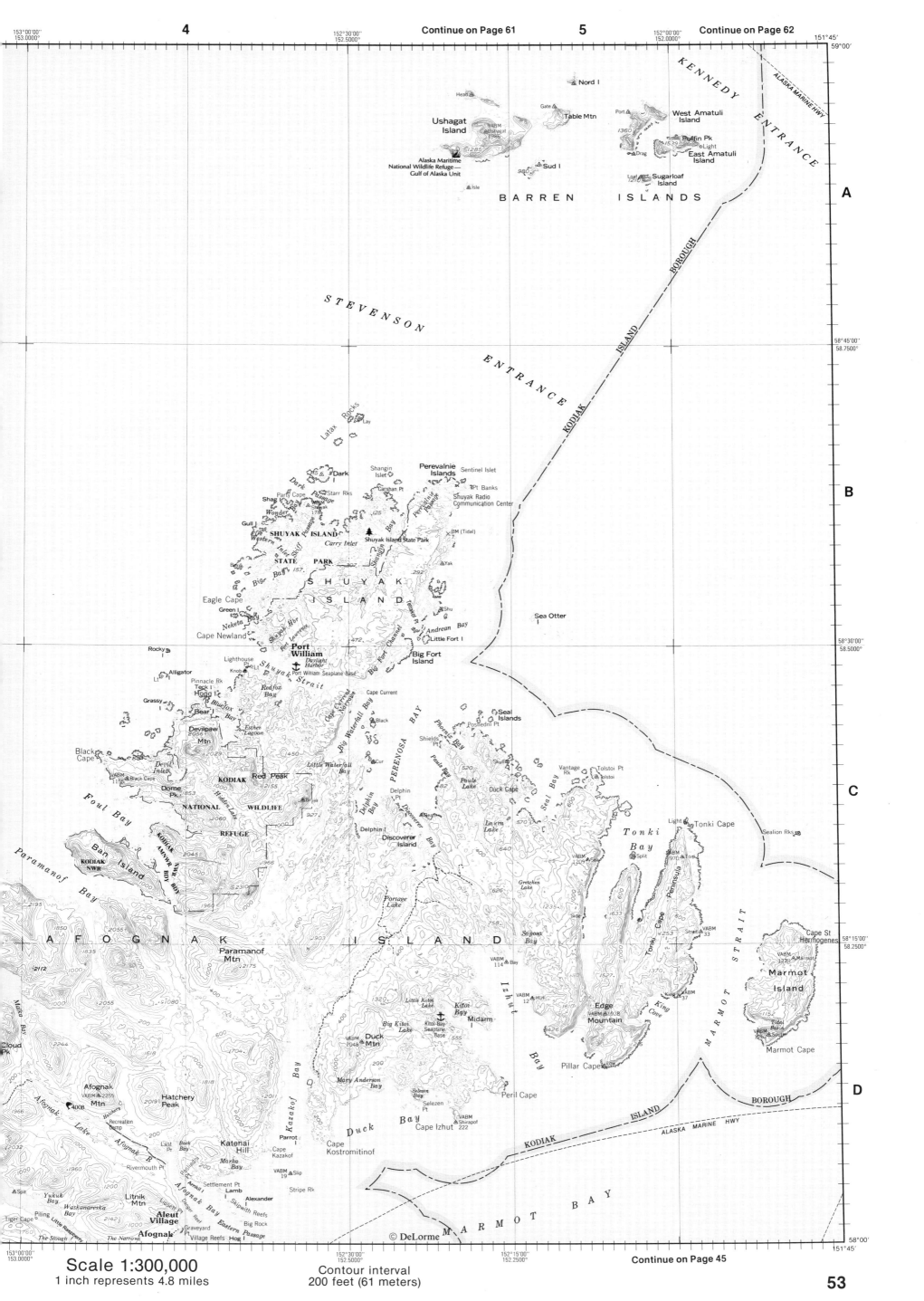

Continue on Page 45

Scale 1:300,000
1 inch represents 4.8 miles

Contour interval
200 feet (61 meters)

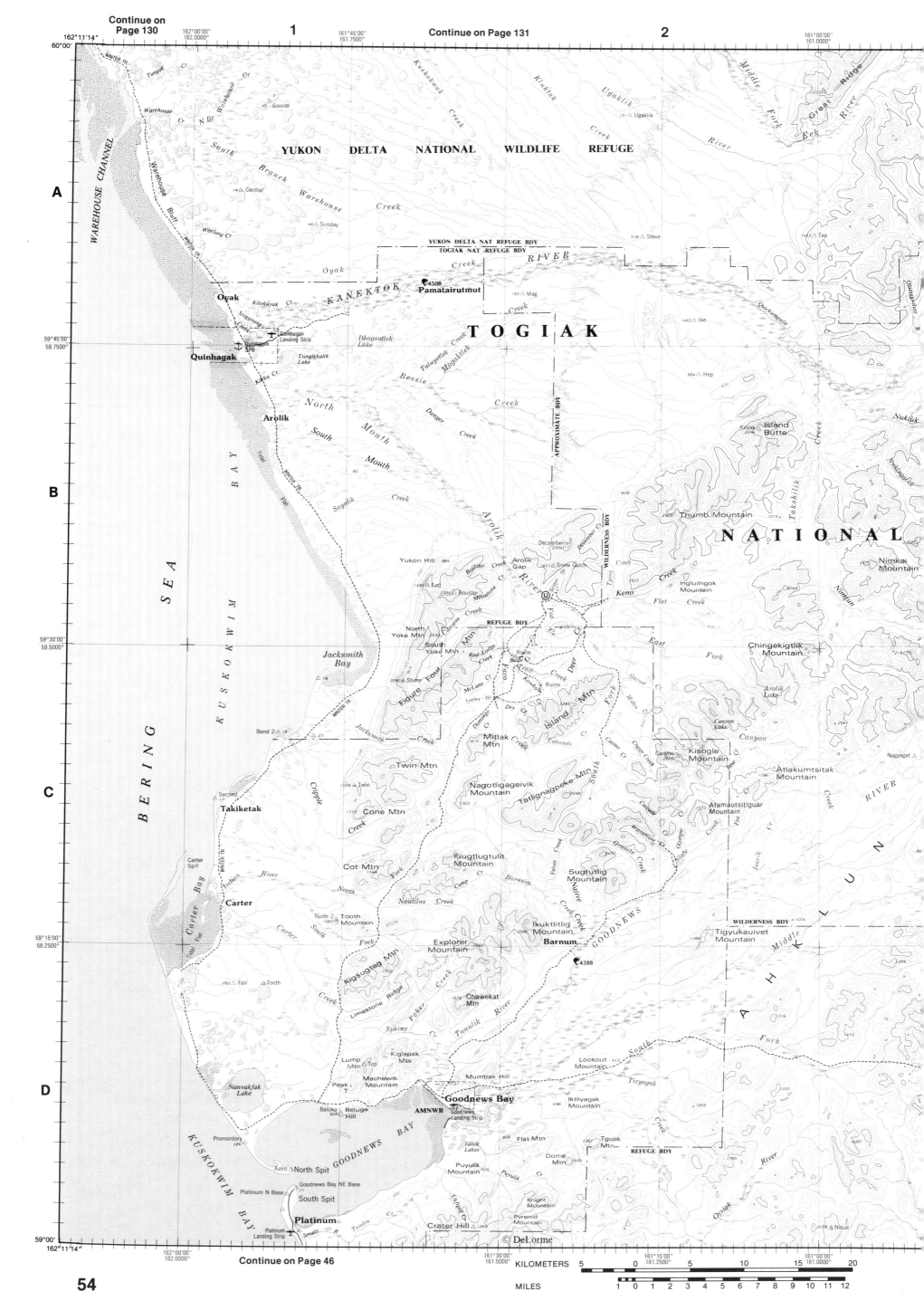

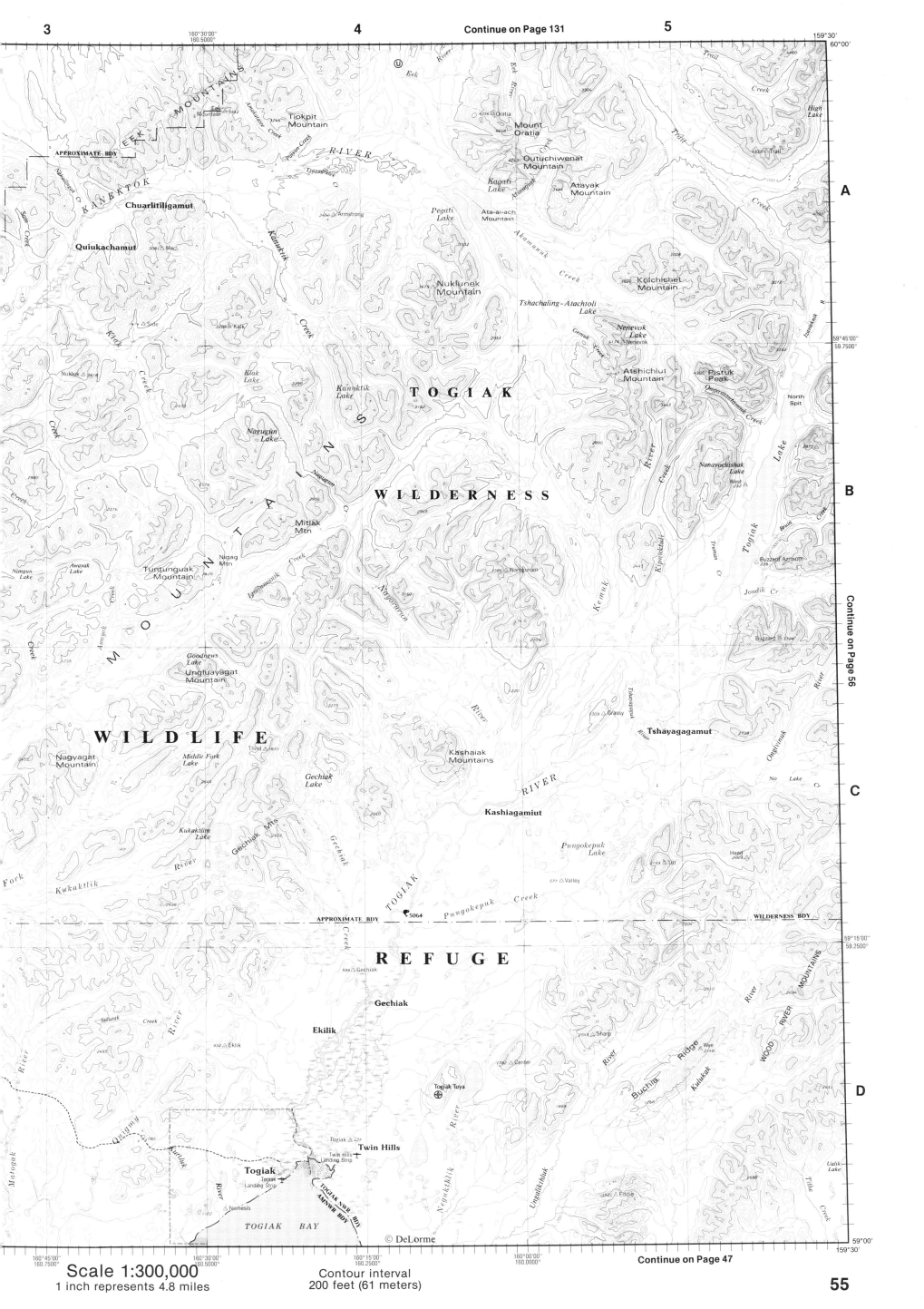

160°30'00"
160.5000°

159°30'
60°00'

EEK MOUNTAINS

Eek Mountain △ 3542

Tiokpit Mountain

Amasukause Creek

RIVER

Kanuktik Creek

Panyan Creek

Tsayyarlak Cr

KAAEKTOK

Nadlingat Creek

Chuarlitiligamut

Quiukachamut

3067 △ Mac

Sam Creek

New Armstrong

Pegati Lake

Ata-ai-ach Mountain

Eek River

(U)

Eek

Eek River

3356 Oratia

Mount Oratia
4668

Outuchiwenat Mountain

Kagati Lake

Abumjuk

3644

Atayak Mountain

Trail

Creek

High Lake

4360

4350 Trail

Creek

Akamanuk Creek

3008

Kolchichet Mountain
3625

3075

Izavieknik R

A

59°45'00"
59.7500°

Klink Creek

Nukluk 2914

Side

3296 Kalik

2478

Blak Lake
3294

Kanuktik Lake

3162

3679 Nuklunek Mountain

2953

Tshachaling–Atachtoli Lake

Nenevok Lake
5174 Nenevok

3443

Gemuk Creek

Atshichlut Mountain

Ougunmuttamuk Creek

Pistuk Peak

North Spit

3975

TOGIAK

Creek

Nagugun Lake

2576

2955

Naugun Cr

2162

WILDERNESS

2645

2690

Nanavochishak Lake

West 232

Togiak Lake

Bruin

Buzzard Azimuth 236

B

59°45'00"
59.7500°

2980

2376

Mitlak Mtn

Nigag Mtn

Nimgun Lake

Awayak Lake

Tuntunguak Mountain

2325

Aiwnyk Creek

2275

2576

Igmimnuuk Creek

Nagomrun

Nagomrun River

3586 Nargkurun

3160

Kemuk Cr

2463

Kipnatnut

2604

Truman Cr

Jondik Cr

Buzzard 3 2304

River

Continue on Page 56

Goodnews Lake

Ungluayagat Mountain

2275

River

220

309 Grassy

Tsharugagamut River

Tshayagagamut 2730

Onguivinuk River

WILDLIFE

Nagyagat Mountain
2652

Middle Fork Lake

Third △ 2830

Gechiak Lake

Kukaktlim Lake

Gechiak Mts
2652

2656

2663

2438

Gechiak River

Kashaiak Mountains

Kashiagamiut

RIVER

Pungokepuk Lake

2759 Tift

No Lake Cr

Head 2669

C

Fork

Kukaktlik

2498

Gechiak River

TOGIAK

APPROXIMATE BDY △ 5064

Pungokepuk Creek

577 △ Valley

2304

WILDERNESS BDY

59°15'00"
59.2500°

REFUGE

599 △ Gechiak

Gechiak

Ekilik

932 △ Eklik

2510

2549 △ Sharp

River

Buchia Ridge

Kulukak River

WOOD RIVER MOUNTAINS

2404

2445

D

Suturak Creek

River

2495

Quigmy River

Kurluk River

2085

Togiak △ 477

Twin Hills Landing Strip

Twin Hills

Togiak

Togiak Landing Strip

1742 △ Center

1869

Togiak Tuya

Neguklthik River

Ungalikthluk

2561 △ Eddie

Wye

Ualik Lake

2586

Tilik Creek

Matogak River

Nemesis

TOGIAK NWR BDY

TOGIAK BAY

© DeLorme

Continue on Page 47

160°45'00"
160.7500°

160°30'00"
160.5000°

160°15'00"
160.2500°

160°00'00"
160.0000°

159°30'
59°00'

Scale 1:300,000
1 inch represents 4.8 miles

Contour interval
200 feet (61 meters)

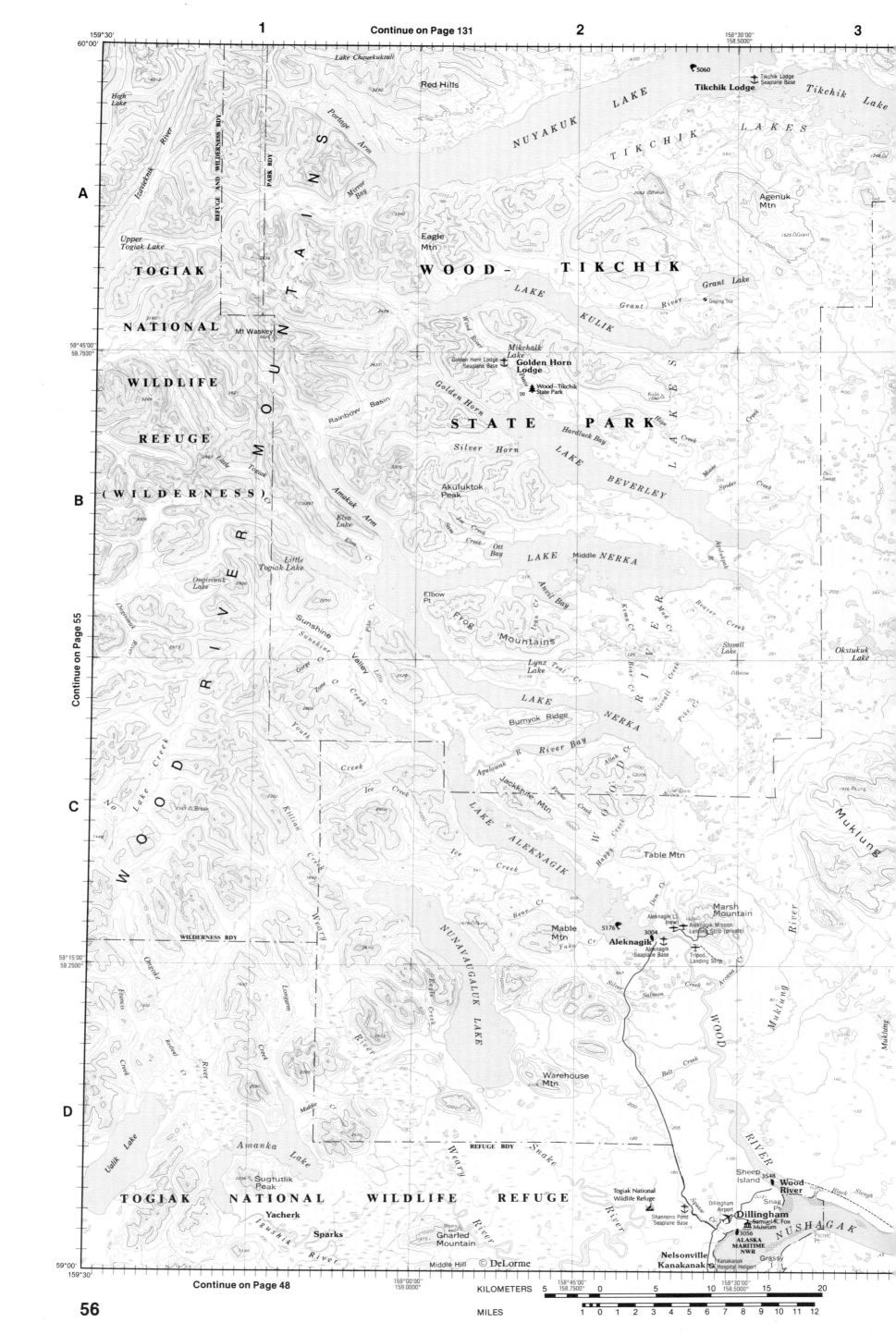

159°30'
60°00'
159°30'

A

B

Continue on Page 55

C

D

TOGIAK

NATIONAL

WILDLIFE

REFUGE

(WILDERNESS)

High
Lake

Upper
Togiak Lake

Igugigiamik

Portage
Arm

Lake Chauekuktuli

Red Hills

Mirror
Bay

Eagle
Mtn

Mt Waskey

REFUGE AND WILDERNESS BDY

PARK BDY

Rainbow Basin

Little Togiak

Amakuk Arm

Elva
Lake

Elva Cr

Little
Togiak Lake

Ongivinuk
Lake

Sunshine

Sunshine

Gorge Cr

Zone Cr

Youth Creek

Valley Little

Pike Cr

WOOD RIVER MOUNTAINS

No Lake Creek

Ice Creek

Break

Killian

Creek

Weary

WILDERNESS BDY

Ongoke

Francis

Redleaf Cr

River

Longarm

Creek

River

Middle Cr

Uqlik Lake

Amanka Lake

Sugtutlik
Peak

Yacherk

Sparks

Igushik River

Gnarled
Mountain

Middle Hill

© DeLorme

TOGIAK NATIONAL WILDLIFE REFUGE

WOOD – TIKCHIK

STATE PARK

NUYAKUK LAKE

TIKCHIK LAKES

Tikchik Lake

🐾 5060

Tikchik Lodge

Tikchik Lodge
Seaplane Base

Agenuk
Mtn

Yakuk

Grant

Grant Lake

Gaging Sta

Grant River

KULIK

Mikchalk
Lake

Golden Horn Lodge
Seaplane Base

Golden Horn
Lodge

Wood–Tikchik
State Park

Kulik

Golden Horn

Silver Horn

Akuluktok
Peak

Hardluck Bay

LAKE BEVERLEY

LAKES

Hope Creek

Moose
Creek

Spider Creek

Sweat

Joe Creek

Sam Creek

Ott
Bay

LAKE Middle NERKA

Elbow
Pt

Frog
Mountains

Anvil Bay

Lynx Trail
Lake

Kema Cr

Bear Cr

WOOD RIVER

Mud Cr

Beaver
Creek

Stovall
Lake

Below

Okstukuk
Lake

LAKE NERKA

Bumyok Ridge

River Bay

Aguliowak

Pike Cr

Stovall

Jackknife Mtn

Perito

Allah Cr

Low Gone

W Creek

LAKE ALEKNAGIK

Ice
Creek

Happy Cr

Table Mtn

Muklung
River

Dam Cr

Marsh
Mountain

Bear Cr

Aleknagik LS
(new)

Aleknagik Mission
Landing Strip (private)

Mable
Mtn

5176

3004

Aleknagik

Aleknagik
Seaplane Base

Tripod
Landing Strip

Yako

NUNAVAUGALUK LAKE

Bear Cr

Silver

Salmon Creek

Arcana Cr

WOOD

Muklung

RIVER

Eagle Creek

Warehouse
Mtn

Belt Creek

REFUGE BDY

Weary

Snake

River

Sheep
Island

3548

Wood
River

RIVER

Snag
Pt

Togiak National
Wildlife Refuge

Shannons Pond
Seaplane Base

Dillingham
Airport

Dillingham

Samuel K. Fox
Museum

3056

ALASKA
MARITIME
NWR

Kanakanak
Hospital Heliport

Nelsonville
Kanakanak

NUSHAGAK

Black Slough

Grassy

Picnic

59°45'00"
59.7500°

59°15'00"
59.2500°

59°00'
159°30'

158°30'00"
158.5000°

Continue on Page 48

159°00'00"
159.0000°

KILOMETERS   5   0   5   10   15   20

158°45'00"
158.7500°

158°30'00"
158.5000°

MILES   1 0 1 2 3 4 5 6 7 8 9 10 11 12

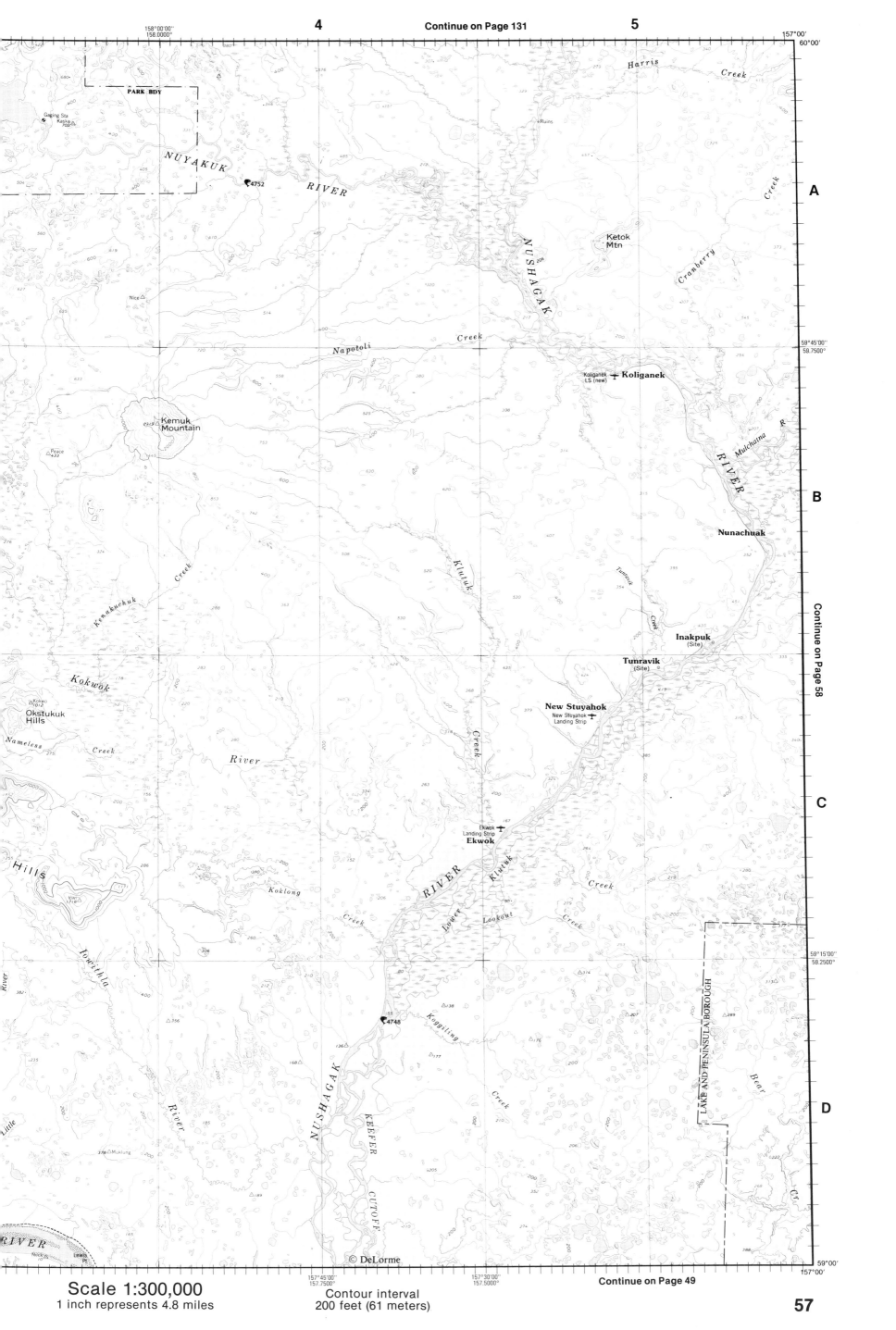

Continue on Page 58

Scale 1:300,000
1 inch represents 4.8 miles

Contour interval
200 feet (61 meters)

© DeLorme

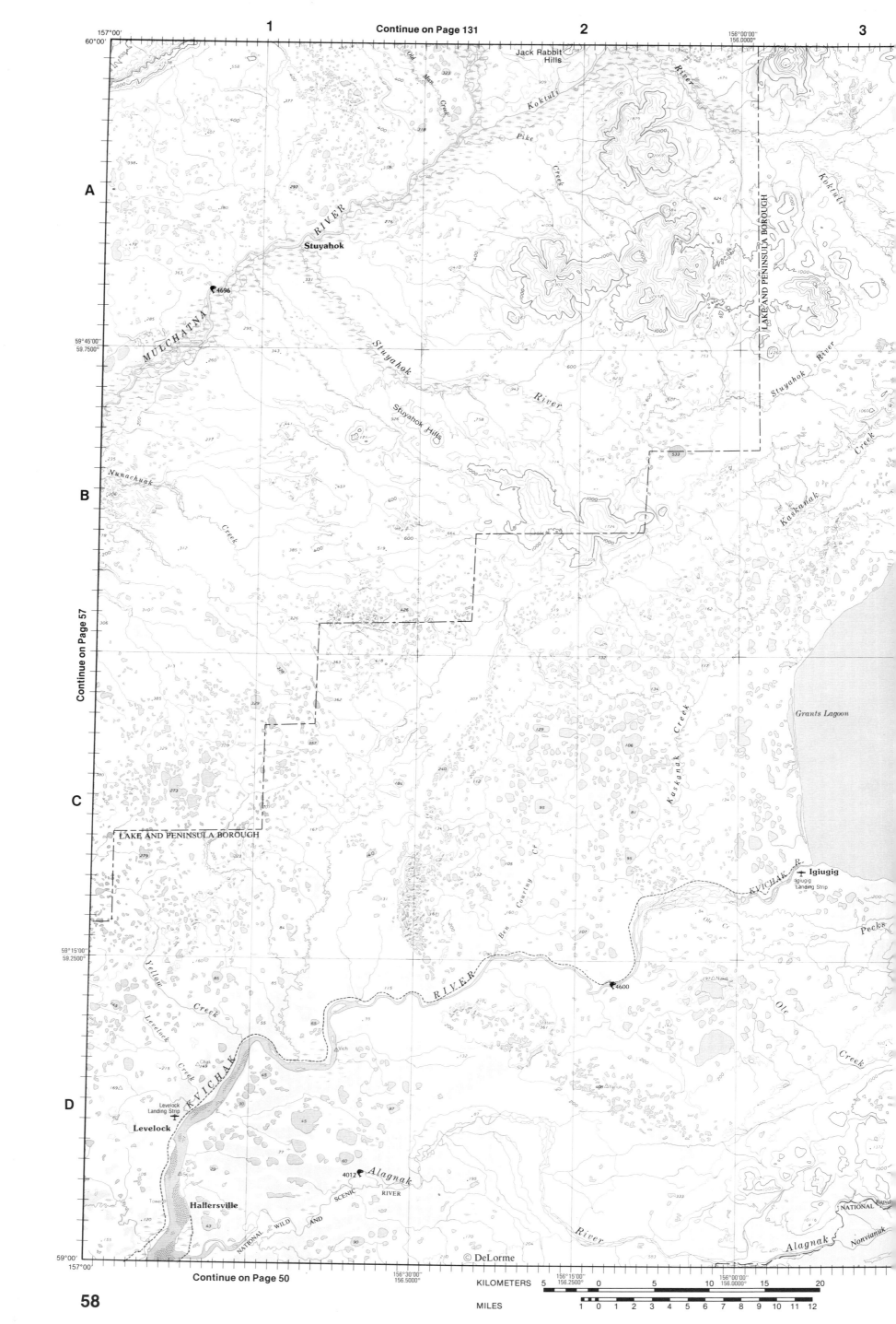

A

Jack Rabbit
Hills

Kokuli

Pike

Creek

River

Kokuli

LAKE AND PENINSULA BOROUGH

Stuyahok

*4696

MULCHATNA

RIVER

Stuyahok

River

Stuyahok River

Kaskanak Creek

59°45'00''
59.7500°

Stuyahok Hills

B

Nunachuak

Creek

Continue on Page 57

Grants Lagoon

Kaskanak Creek

C

Igiugig

KVICHAK R.
Igiugig
Landing Strip

LAKE AND PENINSULA BOROUGH

KVICHAK

Ben Courtny Cr

Ole Cr

Pecks

59°15'00''
59.2500°

*4600

Yellow

Creek

Ole

RIVER

Creek

Levelock

Creek

KVICHAK

*Vich

Statem

D

Levelock
Landing Strip

Levelock

4012 *

Alagnak

RIVER

SCENIC

NATIONAL

Hallersville

NATIONAL WILD AND

River

Alagnak

Nonvianuk

59°00'
157°00'

© DeLorme

Continue on Page 50

156°30'00''
156.5000°

KILOMETERS
156°15'00''
156.2500°
5   0   5   10   15   20

MILES
1 0 1 2 3 4 5 6 7 8 9 10 11 12

156°00'00''
156.0000°

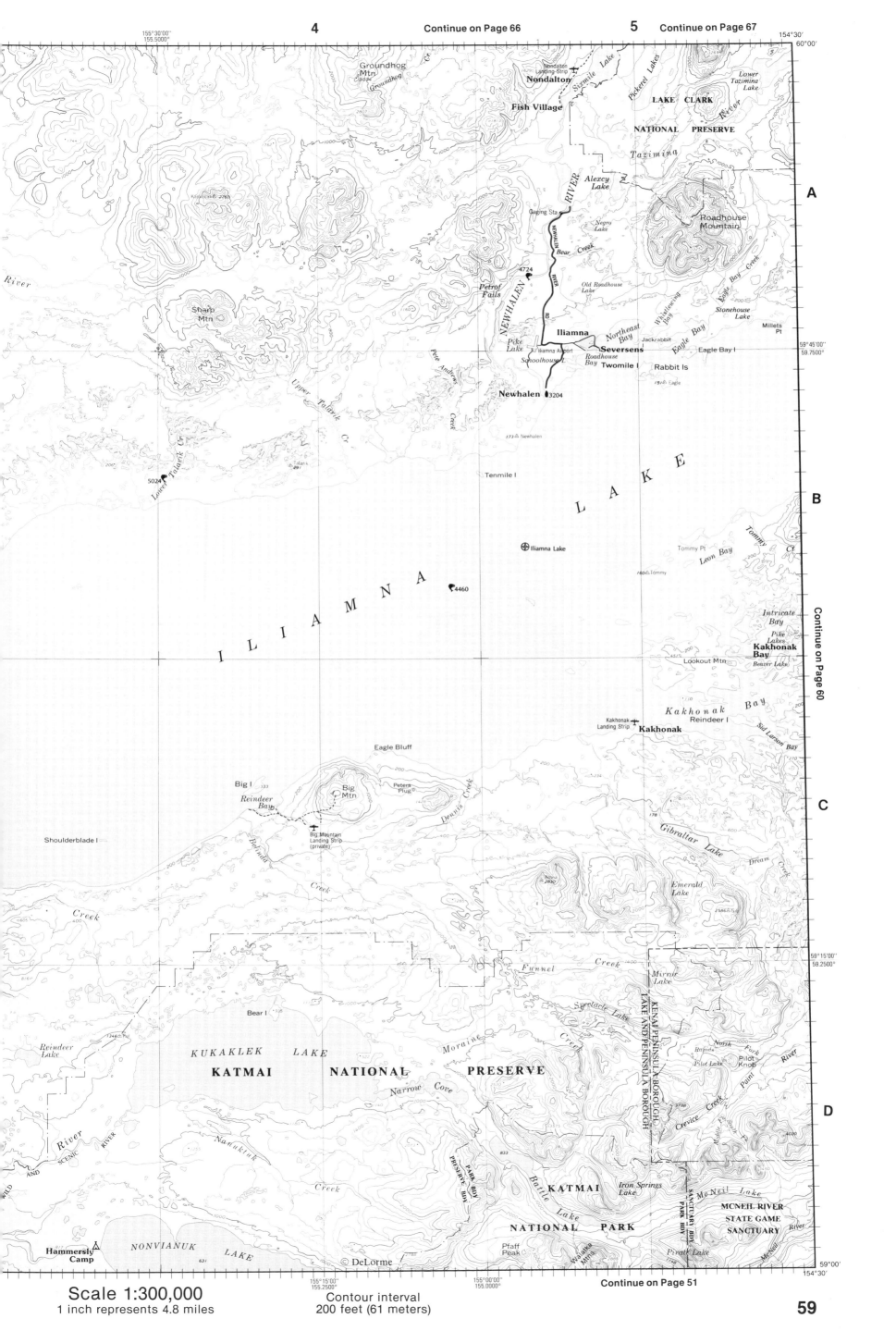

155°30'00"
155.5000°

154°30'
60°00'

Groundhog Mtn
Groundhog Cr

Nondalton Landing Strip
Nondalton
Sixmile Lake
Pickerel Lakes
LAKE CLARK
Lower Tazimina Lake

Fish Village

NATIONAL PRESERVE

Tazimina River

RIVER

Alexcy Lake

Tazimina

A

Gaging Sta
Negro Lake
Roadhouse Mountain

NEWHALEN

Bear Creek

River

4724
Petrof Falls
Old Roadhouse Lake
Whitewing Bay
Eagle Bay Creek
Stonehouse Lake

Sharp Mtn

NEWHALEN RIVER

RD

Pike Lake
Iliamna
Iliamna Airport
Seversens
Northeast Bay
Jackrabbit
Eagle Bay
Millets Pt

59°45'00"
59.7500°

Schoolhouse L
Roadhouse Bay
Twomile I
Eagle Bay I
Rabbit Is

Pete Andrews

Upper Talarik Cr

Newhalen 3204
151& Eagle

173 & Newhalen

Lower Talarik Cr

5024

Talarik
Talarik Cr 291

Tenmile I

I L I A M N A   L A K E

B

Iliamna Lake

Tommy Pt
Leon Bay
Tommy Cr

4460

160& Tommy

Intricate Bay
Pike Lakes
Kakhonak Bay
Beaver Lake

451/5 200
Lookout Mtn

Kakhonak Bay

710

Kakhonak Landing Strip
Kakhonak
Reindeer I
Sid Larson Bay

Eagle Bluff

Big I
133
Reindeer Bay
Big Mtn
Peters Plug
180
Dennis Creek
234

Gibraltar Lake

C

600

Shoulderblade I
Big Mountain Landing Strip (private)
Belinda
Creek

Dream Cr

Nikoli 2830

Emerald Lake
2586&S.5

200

59°15'00"
59.2500°

Funnel Creek
Mirror Lake

Creek

Bear I
138
Moraine Creek
Spectacle Lake

KENAI PENINSULA BOROUGH

LAKE AND PENINSULA BOROUGH

Reindeer Lake
1346 Pal

KUKAKLEK LAKE

North Fork
Pilot Knob
Pilot Lake
Funk River

KATMAI NATIONAL PRESERVE

Narrow Cove

3700
Crevice Creek

D

River
SCENIC RIVER

Nanuktuk

WILD AND

Creek

PARK BDY
PRESERVE BDY

833

KATMAI
Iron Springs Lake
McNeil Lake

MCNEIL RIVER

SANCTUARY BDY
PARK BDY

Hammersly Camp
NONVIANUK LAKE
631

© DeLorme

NATIONAL PARK
Pfaff Peak
Battle Lake
Walatka Mtns
Pirate Lake
Pfaff Peak

STATE GAME SANCTUARY
McNeil River

155°15'00"
155.2500°
155°00'00"
155.0000°

Continue on Page 51

154°30'
59°00'

Continue on Page 60

Scale 1:300,000
1 inch represents 4.8 miles

Contour interval
200 feet (61 meters)

154°30'
60°00'

A

B

Continue on Page 59

C

59°15'00''
59.2500°

D

59°00'
154°30'

LAKE   **CLARK**   **NATIONAL**   **PRESERVE**

Lower
Tazimina
Lake

Chekok
Lake

Three Sisters Mountain

LAKE   **CLARK**

PRESERVE BDY
NAT PARK AND WILDERNESS BDY

KENAI PENINSULA BOROUGH
LAKE AND PENINSULA BOROUGH

Chekok
Creek

Creek

Knutson
Creek

Pile Creek

Iliamna River

Holland Creek

Right Creek

Creek

Knutson
Mtn

Knutson
Valley

Long
Lake

Pile
Bay

Clearwater
Creek

Creek

Hedlunds
(Site)

Knutson   Bay

Pedro Bay
Landing Strip

Pedro
Mtn

**Pedro
Bay**

Dumbbell
Lake

+

Lonesome
Pt

**Pile Bay
Village**

Sugarloaf
Mtn

Mt
Eleanor

Roscoe
Peak

Rosewood
Gl

Roscoe Creek

Portage
Pass

Antlimonuk
Creek

Chekok
Pt

Fox Bay

Hat
I

Pedro   Bay

Big Chutes

Lonesome Bay

Old Iliamna
(Site)

Slippery
Creek

Range
Peak

ILIAMNA

Flat I

Porcupine I

PILE   BAY

Summit
Lakes

Chinkelyes Creek

Williams Creek

Back Range

Iliamna Bay

Bower Creek

Seal Is

FRI Camp

Durants
Cove

Williamsport

Mid

Cy
Peak

Pavloff
Creek

LAKE

Triangle I

Squirrel
Point

Creek

NATIVE TR

Ptarmigan
Cr

Dutton

Cottonwood
Bay

Mud

AC Pund

Knoll
Head

Mushroom
Islets

Scott

Mt
Pomeroy

Well Cr

Oil
Bay

Oil Islets

Meadow Lake

Moose Lake

Lto White Gull I

Inlet Rk
Inlet Shoal

Vert I

Inlet I

Pomeroy I

Oil Reef

Big Rock

Tommy   Creek

Upper
Copper Lake

Lower
Copper Lake

Boot
Lake

**North
Head**

South Head

Turtle
Reef

Tidal
Flat

Copper   River

Kakhonak

Fog Lake

Lake

The Cone

Brown
Peak

Ursus
Head

Ursus   Cove

Kakhonak   R

Kakhonak

1060 g

Stadau
Creek

Rocky Cove

Burr Pt

Burr
52

Seven
Sisters

Big Hill

Kirschner
Lake

Step
Mtn

Tignagvik Pt

Augustine   Island

Augustine
Volcano

Mound
268

LAKE AND PENINSULA BOROUGH
KENAI PENINSULA BOROUGH

Venturi
Lake

Fortification Bluff

South Augustine 52

A   L   E   U   T   I   A   N

Amakdedori
Creek

Bruin   Bay

Contact Point

Amakdedori
(Site)

Dwandedak

Chenik
Mtn

K   A   M   I   S   H   A   K

Chenik

Chenik
Lake

Chenik Head

Amakdedulia Cove

Nordyke I

B   A   Y

Lake Fork
Paint

Creek

River

Akjemguiga
Cove

Mc Neil
Cove

AMWR BDY
NAT PARK BDY

Kenty
Creek

Middle
Mtn

Shakpak Cr

Kamishak
(Site)

Mc Neil Islet

Tidal Flat

Maple Cr

McNeil
Head

McNeil River
State Game Sanctuary

Horseshoe Cove

Akumwarvik   Bay

Tidal Flat

WILDERNESS BDY

KATMAI

MCNEIL RIVER
STATE GAME SANCTUARY

McNeil

Little   Kamishak

River

Pintuhia Cove

Sitka Cr

Ashivak
(Site)

Tidal
Flat

Douglas   River

NATIONAL   *PARK*

© DeLorme

Shaw I

KATMAI WILDERNESS

153°30'00''
153.5000°

153°30'00''
153.5000°

59°45'00''
59.7500°

59°15'00''
59.2500°

154°15'00''
154.2500°

153°45'00''
153.7500°

153°30'00''
153.5000°

KILOMETERS   5   0   5   10   15   20

MILES   1 0 1 2 3 4 5 6 7 8 9 10 11 12

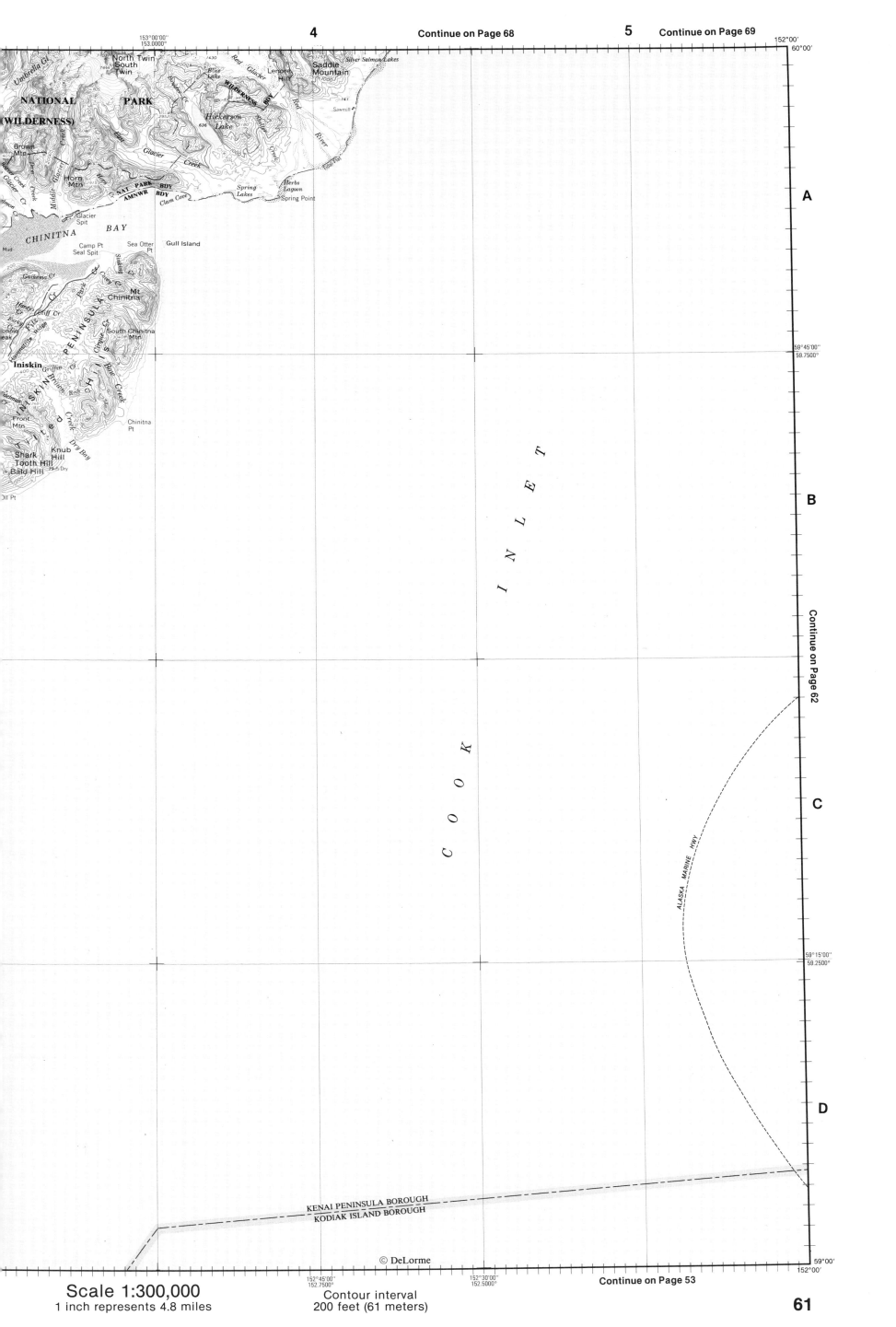

153°00'00''
153.0000°

152°00'
60°00'

North Twin
South
Twin

1430

Red
Glacier

Lenore
Hill

Saddle
Mountain

Silver Salmon Lakes

Umbrella Gl.

Blue
Lake

NATIONAL   PARK

WILDERNESS

Red

River

(WILDERNESS)

Hickerson
Lake

636

952

Sawmill

747

Brown
Mtn

Glacier   Creek

Creek

Red

Horn
Mtn

Glacier
Cr

NAT PARK BDY

Spring
Lakes

Herbs
Lagoon

AMNWR   BDY

Spring Point

A

Glacier
Spit

Clam Cove

CHINITNA   BAY

Camp Pt

Sea Otter
Pt

Gull Island

Mud

Seal Spit

Gakeena Cr

PENINSULA

Mt
Chinitna

Hardy
Cr

Cliff Cr

Fitz
Cr

South Chinitna
Mtn

59°45'00''
59.7500°

Iniskin

Griffin
Cr

Sophie
Peak

Rich   Creek

INISKIN

Brown   Creek

Chinitna
Pt

Front
Mtn

Dry Bay

B

Shark
Tooth Hill

Knub
Hill

Dry

Bald Hill

Oil Pt

I
N
L
E
T

Continue on Page 62

C

O
O
K

ALASKA MARINE HWY

C

59°15'00''
59.2500°

D

KENAI PENINSULA BOROUGH

KODIAK ISLAND BOROUGH

© DeLorme

59°00'
152°00'

152°45'00''
152.7500°   152°30'00''
152.5000°   Continue on Page 53

Scale 1:300,000
1 inch represents 4.8 miles

Contour interval
200 feet (61 meters)

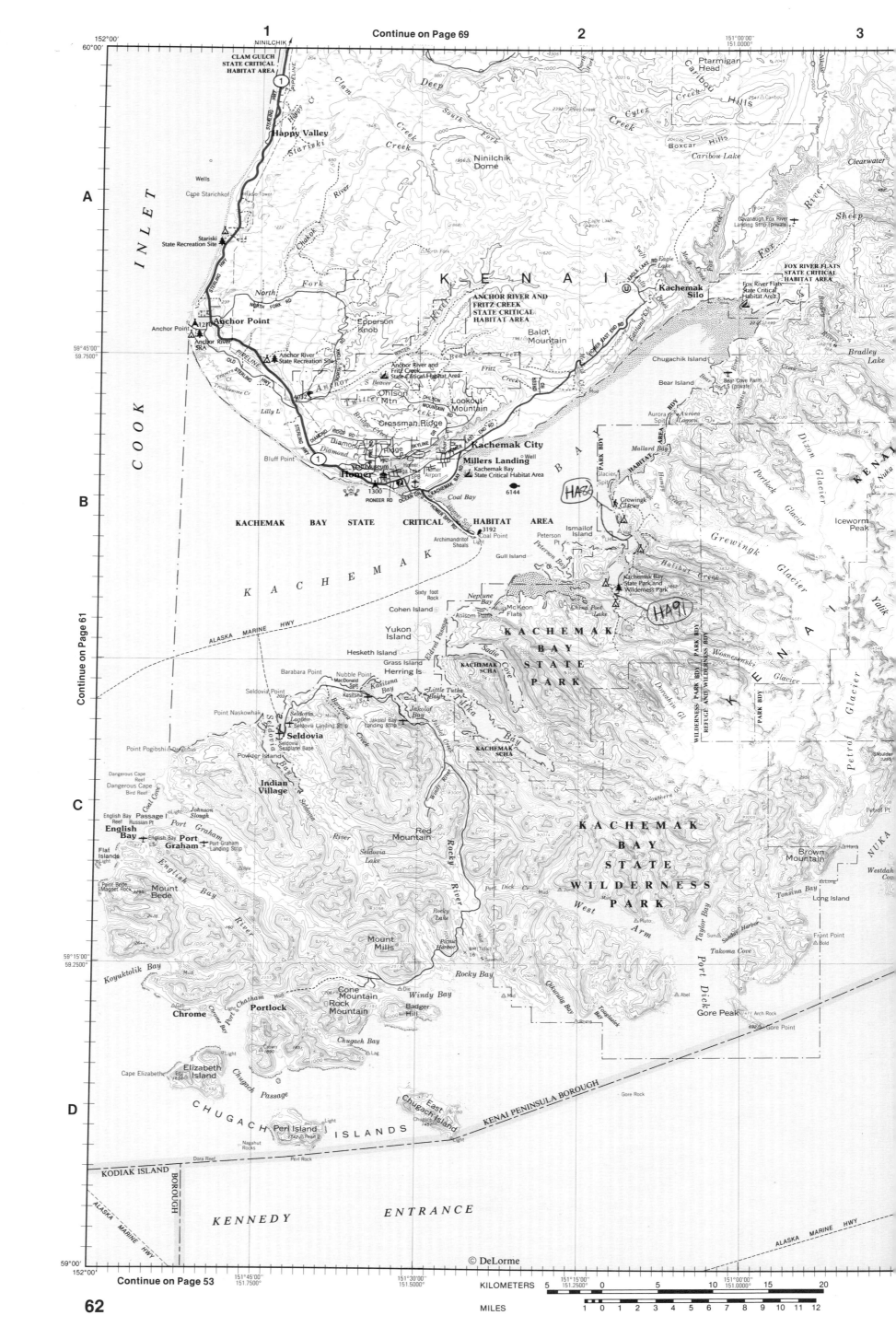

Continue on Page 61

Continue on Page 53

© DeLorme

KILOMETERS 5   0   5   10   15   20

MILES   1 0 1 2 3 4 5 6 7 8 9 10 11 12

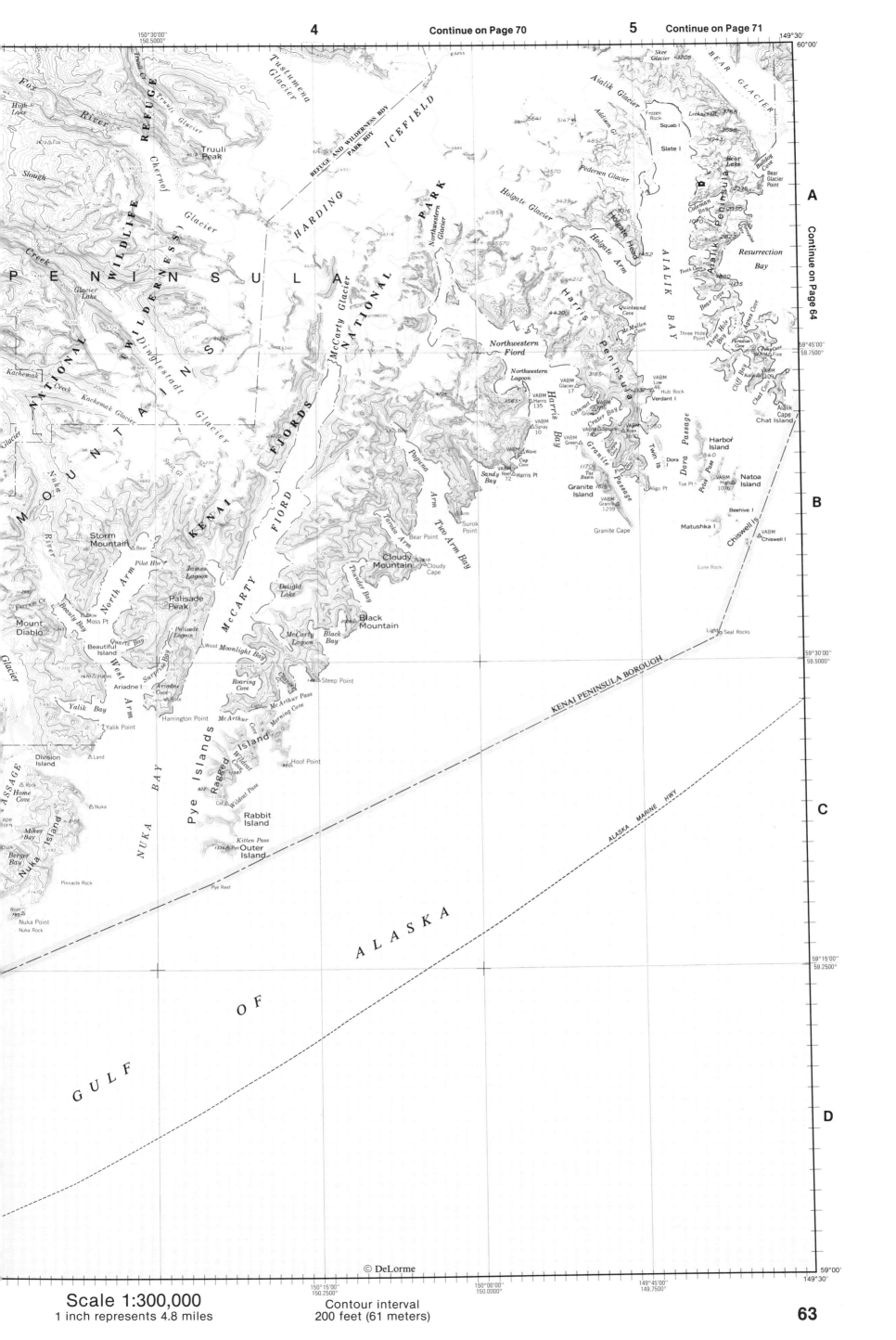

Continue on Page 64

Scale 1:300,000
1 inch represents 4.8 miles

Contour interval
200 feet (61 meters)

© DeLorme

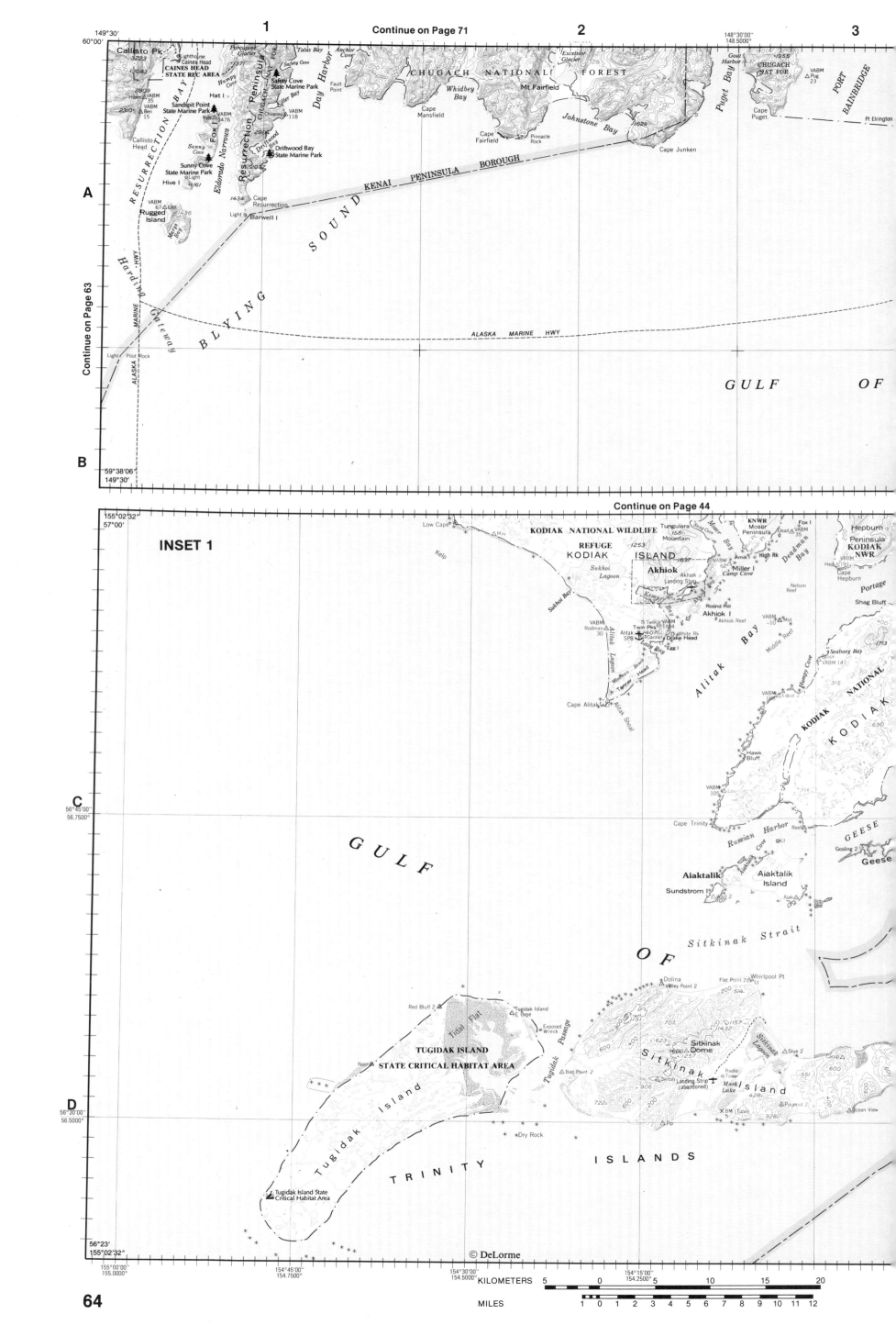

Continue on Page 63

Continue on Page 44

INSET 1

© DeLorme

KILOMETERS   5   0   5   10   15   20

MILES   1 0 1 2 3 4 5 6 7 8 9 10 11 12

148°00'00"
148.0000°
147°00'

MONTAGUE STRAIT

Squirrel Bay
Evans I
Lonetree Pt
Lt
VABM 62
CHUGACH
LIGHTHOUSE RESERVE
Elrington Passage
Elrington I
N Twin Bay
S Twin Bay
LIGHTHOUSE RESERVE
Latouche Passage
NAT FOR
Latouche I
1649
Latouche Peak
VABM Farnen 1926

Danger I

NAT FOR BDY (INDEF)
ALASKA MARITIME NWR BDY

Pt Bazil
Hanning Bay
2037
2986
Box Pt
Box I

Fault Cove
CHUGACH ISLAND
Patton River
Patton Bay
6206

Pt Woodcock
1685
2673
Martin River
Nettie
Pointed Rock

MacLeod Harbor
Pilings
Jeanie
2049
1690
Wooded Is
Fish I
Tanker I

Pt Bryant
Jeanie Pk 772
1850
NATIONAL FOREST
Slide
Tortuous Cr
Slide Creek

VABM 1732
Stair Mtn
Deception Cr
Strike Cr
Jeanie Cove
Jeanie Pt

San Juan Bay
1975
Neck Pt

Cape Cleare

A L A S K A

ALASKA MARINE HWY

59°45'00"
59.7500°

A

B
59°38'06"
147°00'

KNWR
Suby Bay
Dog
1057
400
Bert Pt
Peep
Cape Kiavak
Ship Rock
Black Pt
Sitkalidak I

PENINSULA
1895
BM (Tidal) 8'
Shu

ALIULIK
1782
1945
Knoll Bay
Japanese Bay
1743
1898
Knoll Pt
Sitkalidak Strait

1718
1955
WILDLIFE
1888
1586
Yak

ISLAND
VABM 1390
Tok
1837
Twoheaded Island

Kaguyak Bay
Cape Kaguyak
Kagu

Kaguyak
3215 P

CHANNEL
Old Kaguyak Bay
Boot Pt
East
Flat Island

BOROUGH

KODIAK ISLAND

slands

A L A S K A

Cape Sitkinak

ALASKA MARINE HWY

© DeLorme

56°23'
153°13'05"

153°30'00"
153.5000°

153°15'00"
153.2500°

Continue on Page 75

144°40'
60°00'
144°10'
60°00'

INSET 2

Wingham I
Kayak Entrance
Kayak Island State Marine Park

Pyramid Peak

Kayak
CHUGACH NATIONAL ISLAND FOREST

Sea Ranger Reef

NAT FOR BDY (INDEF)
ALASKA MARITIME NWR BDY

GULF OF ALASKA

Cape St. Elias Lighthouse
Cape St Elias
Pinnacle Rock 490

P A C I F I C

Southeast Rk

O C E A N

C
59°45'00"
59.7500°

59°39'11"
144°40'

144°30'00"
144.5000°

59°39'11"
144°10'

See back cover map for inset location

146°30'
59°30'
146°00'
59°30'

INSET 3

Radio Tower
Lt
Middleton Island Landing Strip
Middleton
Middleton Island

GULF OF ALASKA

P A C I F I C

O C E A N

D

59°15'
146°30'

146°15'00"
146.2500°

59°15'
146°00'

Scale 1:300,000
1 inch represents 4.8 miles

Contour interval
200 feet (61 meters)

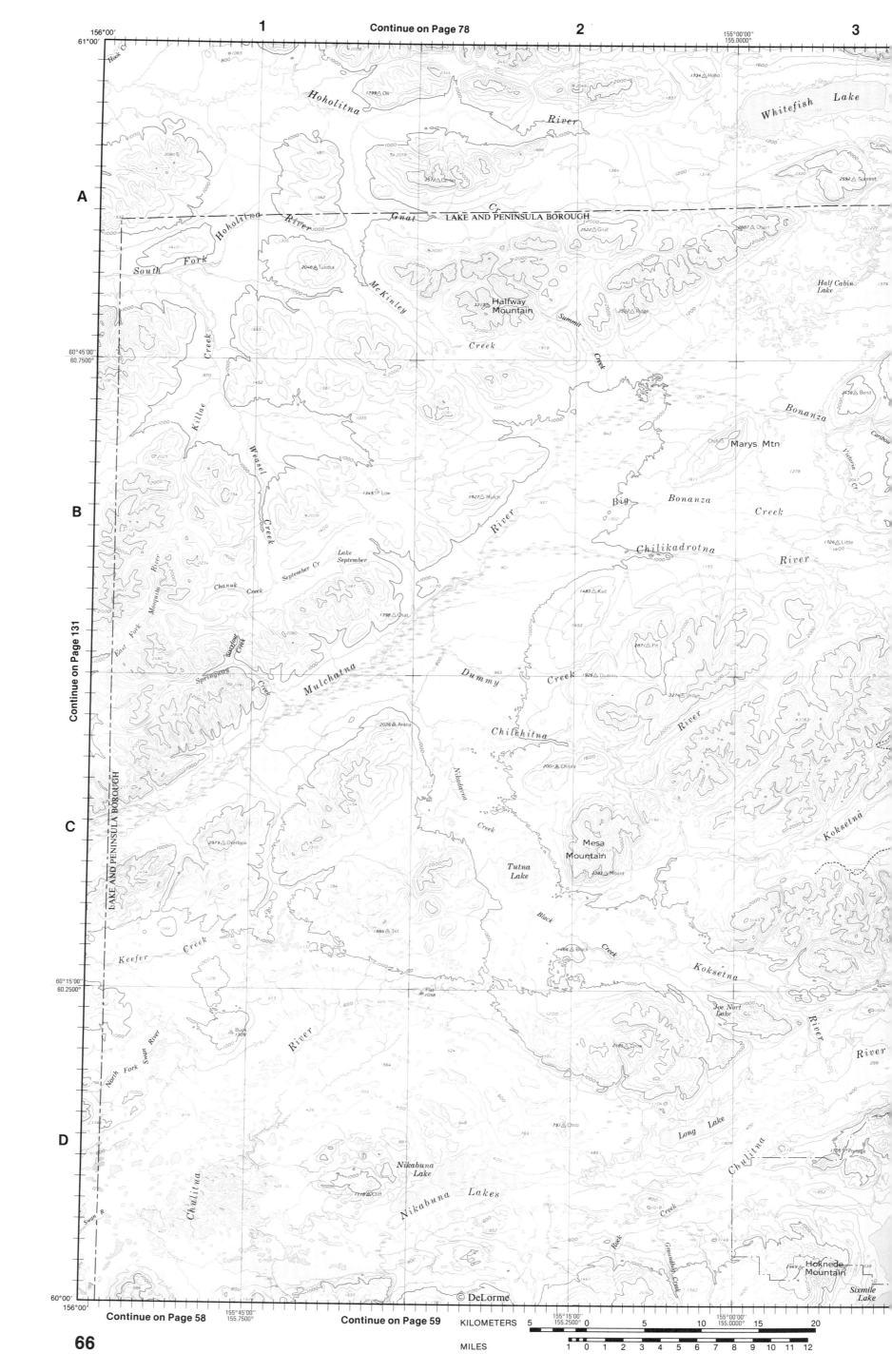

156°00'
61°00'

A

60°45'00"
60.7500°

B

Continue on Page 131

C

60°15'00"
60.2500°

D

60°00'
156°00'

LAKE AND PENINSULA BOROUGH

Hoholitna

River

Whitefish Lake

Half Cabin Lake

Bonanza

Marys Mtn

Big Bonanza Creek

Chilikadrotna River

Mulchatna

Dummy Creek

Chilchitna

Mesa Mountain

Tutna Lake

Black Creek

Koksetna

Koksetna River

Joe Nort Lake

Long Lake

Chulitna

Nikabuna Lake

Nikabuna Lakes

Hoknede Mountain

Sixmile Lake

Halfway Mountain

Summit Creek

McKinley Creek

Killue Creek

Weasel Creek

September Cr

Lake September

Chanuk Creek

Keefer Creek

North Fork Swan River

Chulitna River

© DeLorme

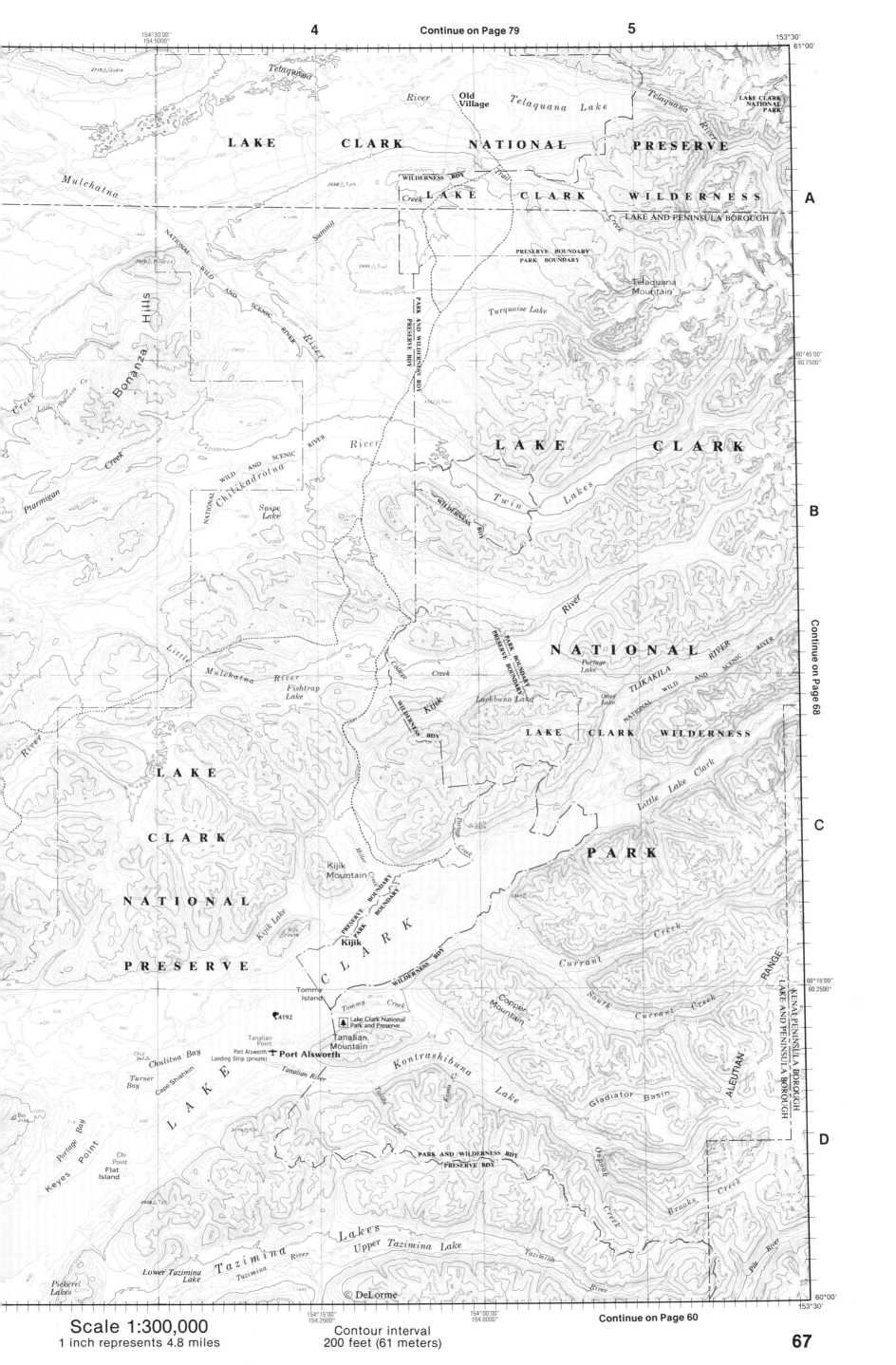

154°30'00''
154.5000°

153°30'
61°00'

A

B

Continue on Page 68

C

60°45'00''
60.7500°

60°15'00''
60.2500°

D

60°00'
153°30'

LAKE CLARK NATIONAL PRESERVE

LAKE CLARK WILDERNESS

LAKE AND PENINSULA BOROUGH

LAKE CLARK NATIONAL PARK

LAKE CLARK NATIONAL PRESERVE

Port Alsworth

Kijik

KENAI PENINSULA BOROUGH
LAKE AND PENINSULA BOROUGH

ALEUTIAN RANGE

Continue on Page 60

Scale 1:300,000
1 inch represents 4.8 miles

Contour interval
200 feet (61 meters)

© DeLorme

67

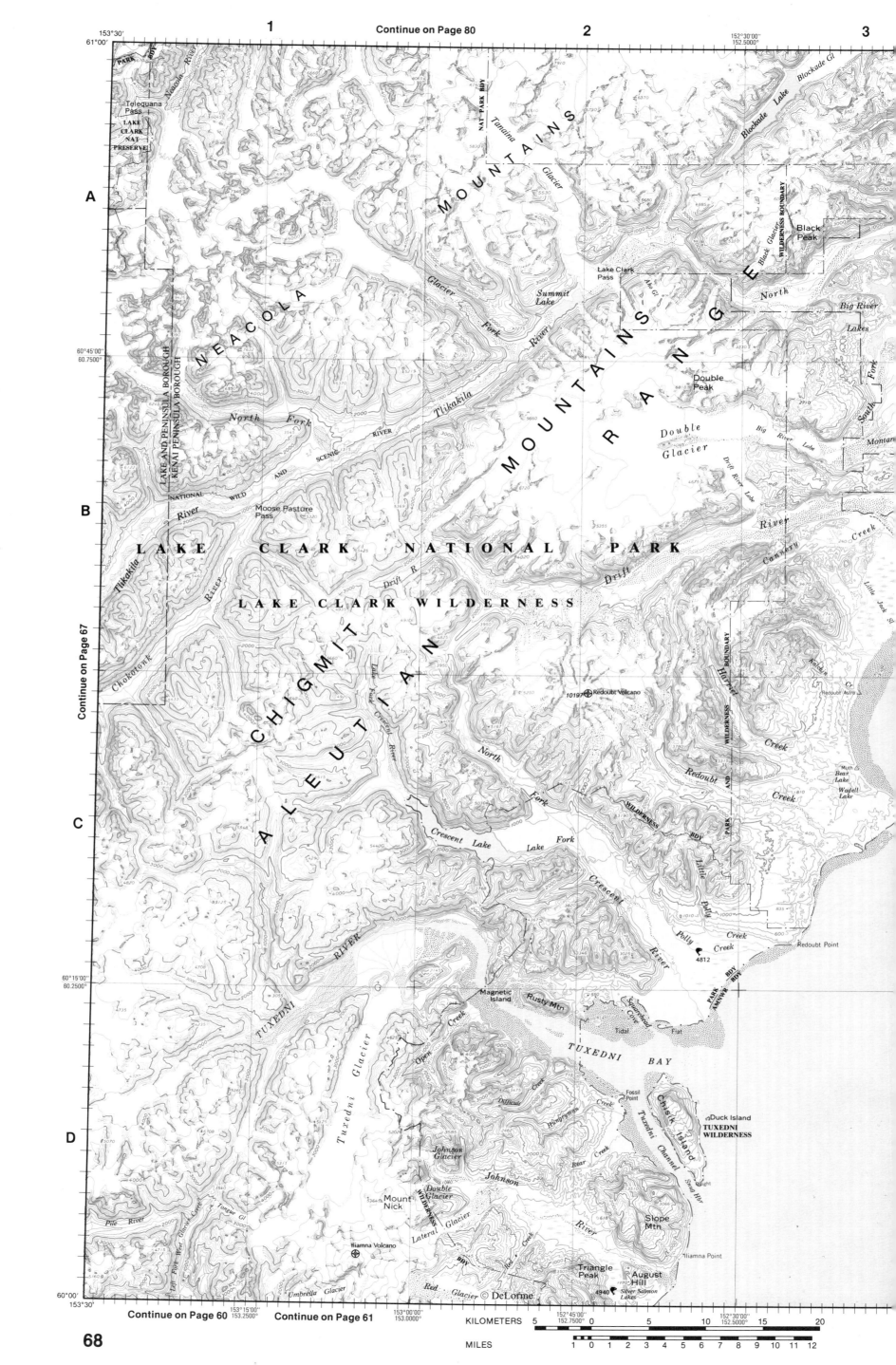

153°30'
61°00'

152°30'00"
152.5000°

PARK BDY

Naudlia River

Telequana
Pass

LAKE
CLARK
NAT
PRESERVE

A

NEACOLA

LAKE AND PENINSULA BOROUGH
KENAI PENINSULA BOROUGH

NAT PARK BDY

Tanaina

Glacier

MOUNTAINS

Blockade Lake

Blockade Gl

Black Glacier

Black
Peak

WILDERNESS BOUNDARY

Lake Clark
Pass

Summit
Lake

Glacier

Fork

River

Tlikakila

Aka Gl

North

RANGE

Big River
Lakes

South

Fork

Montan

60°45'00"
60.7500°

North

Fork

Moose Pasture
Pass

NATIONAL

River

AND

WILD

SCENIC

RIVER

Double
Peak

MOUNTAINS

Double
Glacier

Big River Lobe

Drift River Lobe

River

B

Tlikakila

River

Chokotonk

LAKE   CLARK   NATIONAL   PARK

LAKE CLARK WILDERNESS

CHIGMIT

Drift R

Drift

Cannery

Creek

Little Jack Sl

Continue on Page 67

Redoubt Volcano
10197

PARK AND WILDERNESS BDY

ALEUTIAN

North

Fork

Crescent

River

Redoubt

Creek

Redoubt Astro

Muth
Bear
Lake

Wadell
Lake

C

Crescent Lake

Lake

Fork

WILDERNESS
BDY

Little

Polly

Crescent

River

Polly

Creek

4812

Creek

Redoubt Point

60°15'00"
60.2500°

RIVER

TUXEDNI

Magnetic
Island

Rusty Mtn

Squarehead
Cove

PARK AND WIL BDY

PARK BDY

Turedni Glacier

Open

Creek

TUXEDNI

BAY

Tidal

Flat

Fossil
Point

Chisik Island

Duck Island
TUXEDNI
WILDERNESS

Tuxedni Channel

Snug Hbr

D

Johnson
Glacier

Mount
Nick

Double
Glacier

Lateral Glacier

WILDERNESS

Difficult

Creek

Johnson

Bear

Creek

Hungryman

Creek

River

Slope
Mtn

Iliamna Point

Pile

River

Tongue Gl

Drift

West Glacier Creek

Iliamna Volcano

BDY

Red

Creek

Triangle
Peak

4940

August
Hill

Silver Salmon
Lakes

60°00'
153°30'

Umbrella Glacier

Red

Glacier

© DeLorme

153°15'00"
153.2500°

153°00'00"
153.0000°

152°45'00"
152.7500°

152°30'00"
152.5000°

KILOMETERS 5   0   5   10   15   20

MILES   1 0 1 2 3 4 5 6 7 8 9 10 11 12

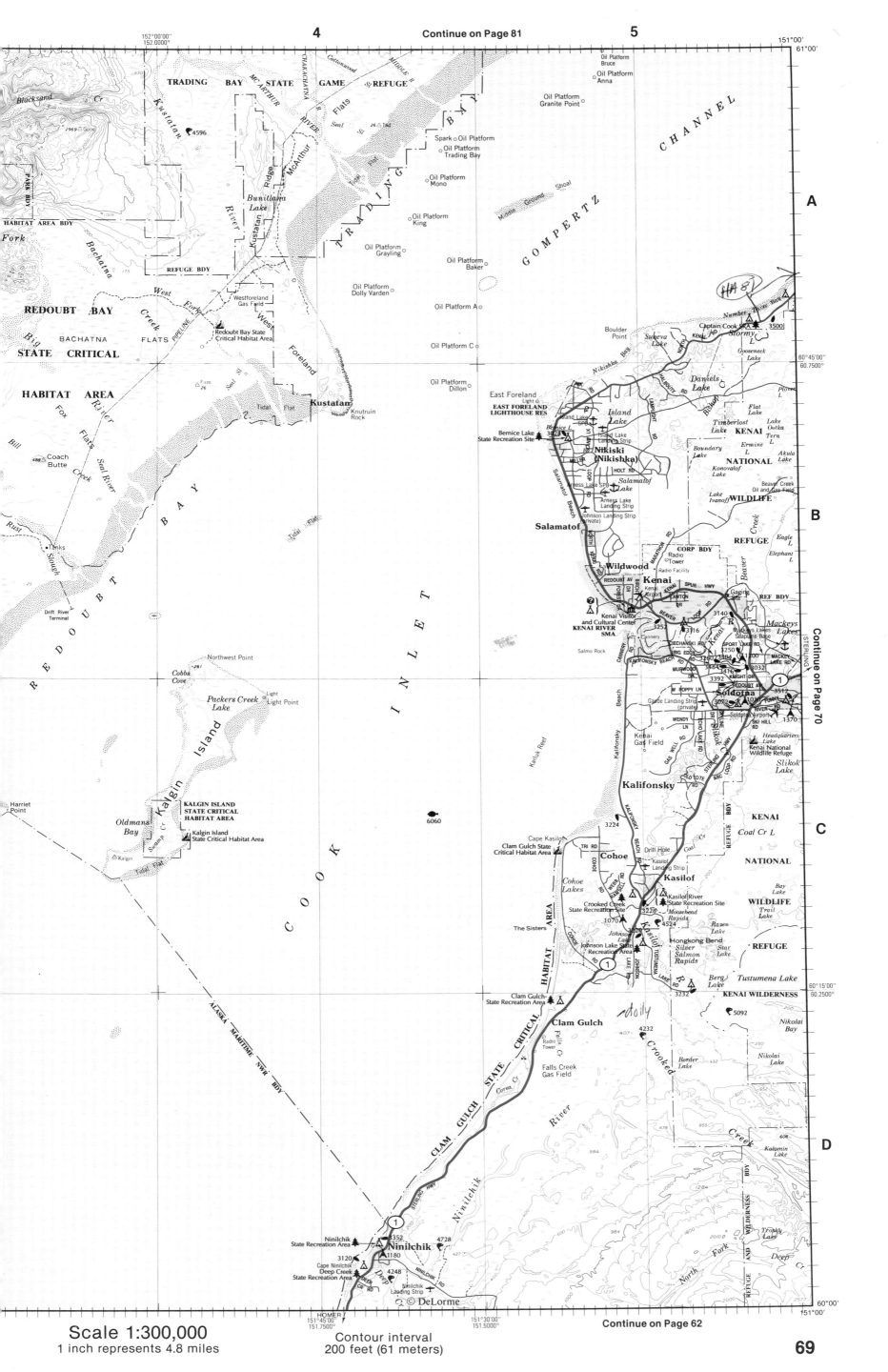

Continue on Page 70

Continue on Page 62

Scale 1:300,000
1 inch represents 4.8 miles

Contour interval
200 feet (61 meters)

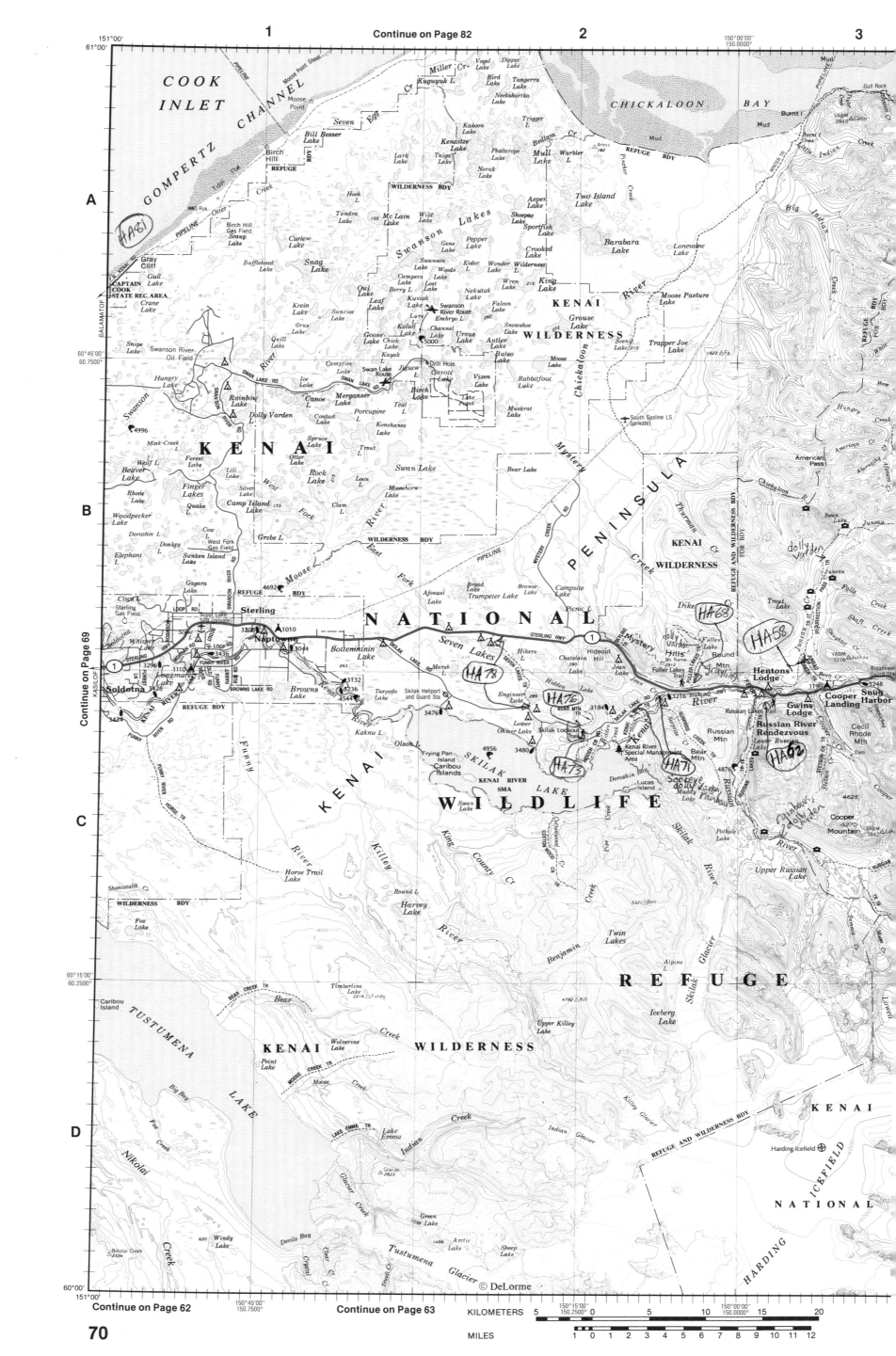

COOK
INLET

CHICKALOON BAY

COOK INLET

GOMPERTZ CHANNEL

KENAI

WILDERNESS

Swanson Lakes

KENAI

PENINSULA

KENAI

WILDERNESS

Continue on Page 69

Sterling

Naptowne

Soldotna

N A T I O N A L

Sterling Hwy

Seven Lakes

Hentons
Lodge

Gwins
Lodge

Cooper
Landing

Snug
Harbor

Russian River
Rendezvous

K E N A I

W I L D L I F E

Kenai River
Special Management
Area

R E F U G E

TUSTUMENA

LAKE

KENAI   WILDERNESS

Skilak

Lake

KENAI
RIVER
SMA

HARDING

ICEFIELD

KENAI

NATIONAL

Harding Icefield

© DeLorme

Continue on Page 63

KILOMETERS 5   0   5   10   15   20

MILES   1 0 1 2 3 4 5 6 7 8 9 10 11 12

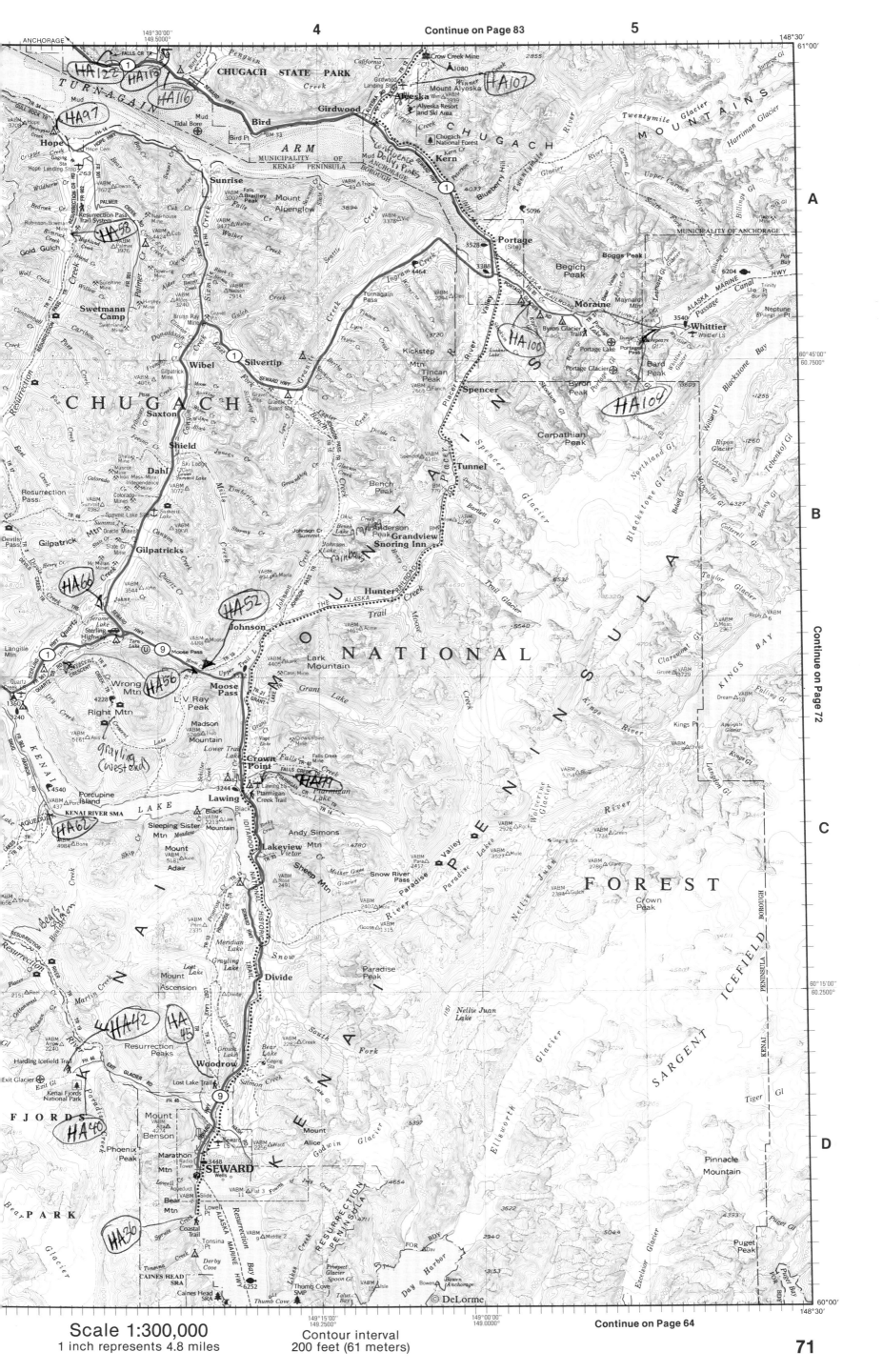

ANCHORAGE

149°30'00''
149.5000°

148°30'
61°00'

HA122 HA119
HA116

TURNAGAIN

HA97

Hope

CHUGACH STATE PARK

Girdwood

Bird

Alyeska Resort and Ski Area

Mount Alyeska

HA107

ARM
MUNICIPALITY OF KENAI PENINSULA BOROUGH

Kern

Sunrise

Mount Alpenglow

Portage (Site)

MUNICIPALITY OF ANCHORAGE

HA58

CHUGACH MOUNTAINS

Twentymile Glacier
Harriman Glacier

ALASKA MARINE

A

Begich Peak

Boggs Peak

6204

Moraine

Whittier

HA100

Swetmann Camp

Wibel Silvertip

Saxton

C H U G A C H

Shield

Dahl

Gilpatrick

Gilpatricks

Portage Lake
Portage Glacier

Spencer

HA109

Carpathian Peak

B

Tunnel

Bench Peak

Snoring Inn
Grandview

Anderson Peak

KINGS BAY

HA66

HA52

Johnson

Hunter

N A T I O N A L

P E N I N S U L A

Langille Mtn

Moose Pass

Sterling Highway

HA56

Wrong Mtn

Right Mtn

Moose Pass

Lark Mountain

grayling (west end)

L.V. Ray Peak

Madson Mountain

Crown Point

HA44

Lawing

HA62

KENAI RIVER SMA

Sleeping Sister Mtn

Porcupine Island

Andy Simons Mtn

F O R E S T

Crown Peak

C

Lakeview

Mount Adair

Sheep Mtn

Snow River Pass

Paradise

K E N A I

Mount Ascension

Lost Lake

Grayling Lake

Divide

Snow

Paradise Peak

Nellie Juan Lake

SARGENT ICEFIELD

60°15'00''
60.2500°

HA42

HA45

Resurrection Peaks

Bear Lake

Woodrow

Lost Lake Trail

Harding Icefield Trail

Exit Glacier
Kenai Fjords National Park

FJORDS

HA40

Phoenix Peak

Mount Benson

Marathon Mtn

SEWARD

Mount Alice

Pinnacle Mountain

D

Bear Mtn

PARK

HA30

CAINES HEAD SRA

Puget Peak

© DeLorme

60°00'
148°30'

Scale 1:300,000
1 inch represents 4.8 miles

Contour interval
200 feet (61 meters)

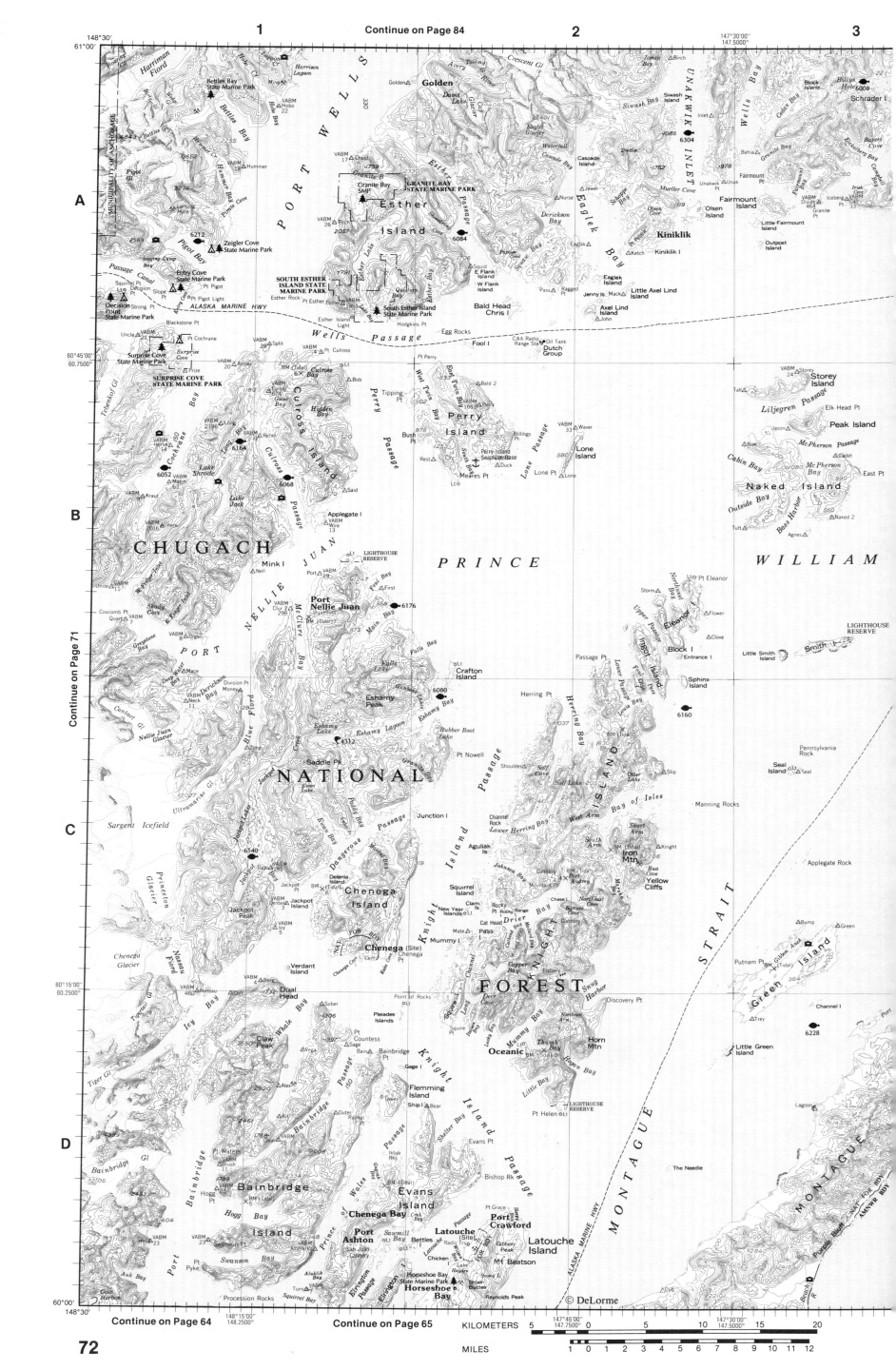

Continue on Page 71
Continue on Page 64
Continue on Page 65

© DeLorme

KILOMETERS

MILES

Continue on Page 74

Scale 1:300,000
1 inch represents 4.8 miles

Contour interval
200 feet (61 meters)

© DeLorme

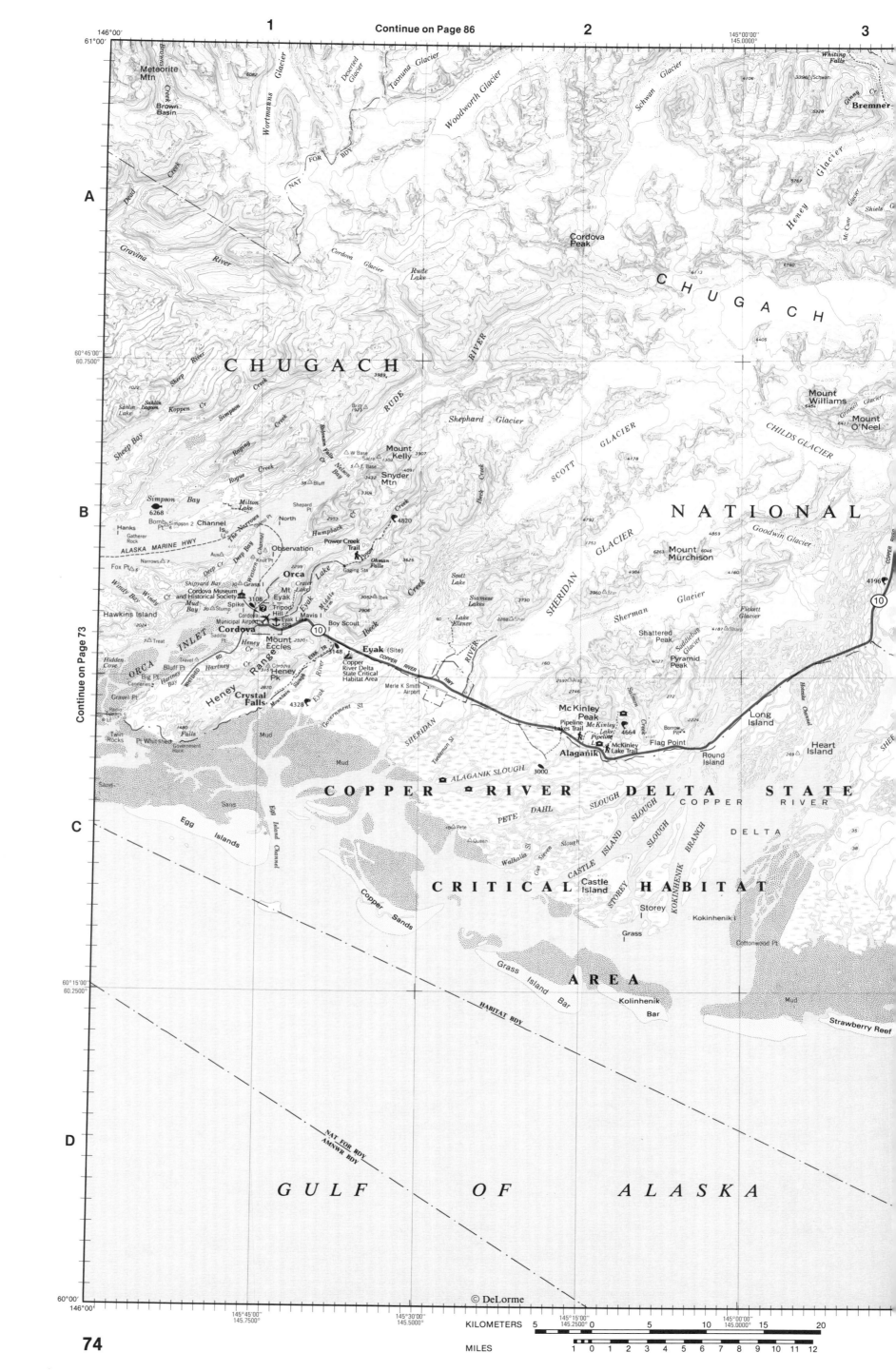

1

2

3

146°00'
61°00'
145°00'00''
145.0000°
60°45'00''
60.7500°
60°15'00''
60.2500°
60°00'00''
146°00'
145°45'00''
145.7500°
145°30'00''
145.5000°
145°15'00''
145.2500°
145°00'00''
145.0000°

A

B

C

D

Continue on Page 73

Meteorite
Mtn
Brown
Basin
Dead Creek
Gravina River
Wortmanns Glacier
Deserted Glacier
Tasnuna Glacier
Woodworth Glacier
Schwan Glacier
Whiting Falls
Bremner
Heney Glacier
Mt Cune
Shiels Glacier

Cordova
Peak

C H U G A C H

C H U G A C H

RUDE RIVER

Rude
Lake

Mount
Williams
Mount
O'Neel
Grinnell Glacier
CHILDS GLACIER

Sheep Bay
Sahlin
Lake
Sahlin
Lagoon
Koppen Cr
Simpson Creek
Rogue Creek
Shepard Glacier
Mount
Kelly
Snyder
Mtn
Scott Creek
Ibeck Creek
SCOTT GLACIER
N A T I O N A L

Simpson Bay
Hanks
Gatherer
Rock
Fox Pt
Milton
Lake
Channel Is
The Narrows
Deep Bay
Western Channel
Observation
North
Humpback
Shepard
Power Creek
Trail
Ohman
Falls
4820
Goodwin Glacier
Mount
Murchison
SHERIDAN GLACIER
Sherman Glacier
Pickett Glacier

Windy Bay
Windy Cr
Mud Bay
Hawkins Island
Shipyard Bay
Cordova Museum
and Historical Society
Spike
Orca
Mt
Eyak
Craig
Lake
Eyak Lake
Mavis I
Middle Creek
Ibeck
Scott
Lake
Siamese
Lakes
Lake
Elaner
Shattered
Peak
Saddlebag
Glacier
Sharp
4196
10

Cordova
Municipal Airport
Tripod
Hill
Cordova
Boy Scout
COPPER

Pyramid
Peak

Hidden
Cove
Big Pt
Bluff Pt
Hartney Bay
Saddle Pt
Mount
Eccles
Heney
Pk
Eyak River
Eyak
Eyak (Site)
Copper
River Delta
State Critical
Habitat Area
Merle K Smith
Airport
COPPER RIVER HWY
McKinley
Peak
4664
McKinley
Lake
Pipeline Lakes Trail
McKinley
Lake Trail
Flag Point
Long
Island
Heart
Island

ORCA INLET
Twin
Rocks
Pt Whitshed
Government
Rock
Crystal
Falls
4328
Mud
Mud
SHERIDAN
Alaganik
Round
Island
COPPER RIVER

Gravel Pt
Radio
Towers
Egg Island Channel
Sand
Egg
Islands
Sand
Mud
Sand
C O P P E R   R I V E R   D E L T A   S T A T E
PETE DAHL SLOUGH
ALAGANIK SLOUGH
Pete
Queen
Walhalla
STOREY SLOUGH
CASTLE ISLAND
Castle
Island
Storey
KOKINHENIK SLOUGH
KOKINHENIK BRANCH
Grass
Kokinhenik I
Cottonwood Pt
COPPER RIVER
D E L T A

Copper
Sands

C R I T I C A L   H A B I T A T

Grass Island Bar
A R E A
Kolinhenik
Bar
Kolinhenik
Bar
Mud
Strawberry Reef

HABITAT BDY

NAT FOR BDY
AMNWR BDY

G U L F   O F   A L A S K A

© DeLorme

KILOMETERS   5   0   5   10   15   20

MILES   1 0   1   2   3   4   5   6   7   8   9 10 11 12

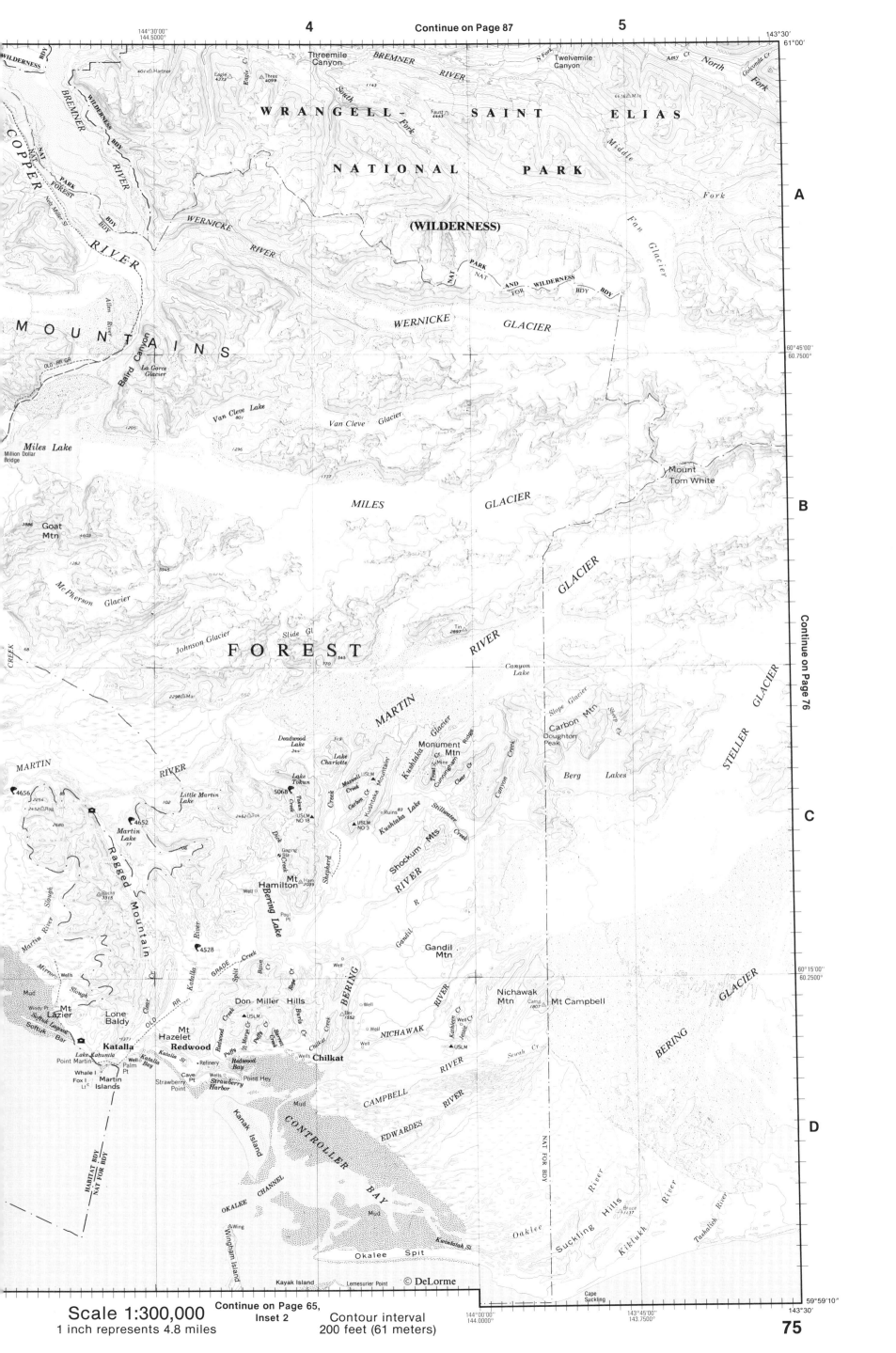

Continue on Page 76

Scale 1:300,000
1 inch represents 4.8 miles

Continue on Page 65,
Inset 2

Contour interval
200 feet (61 meters)

© DeLorme

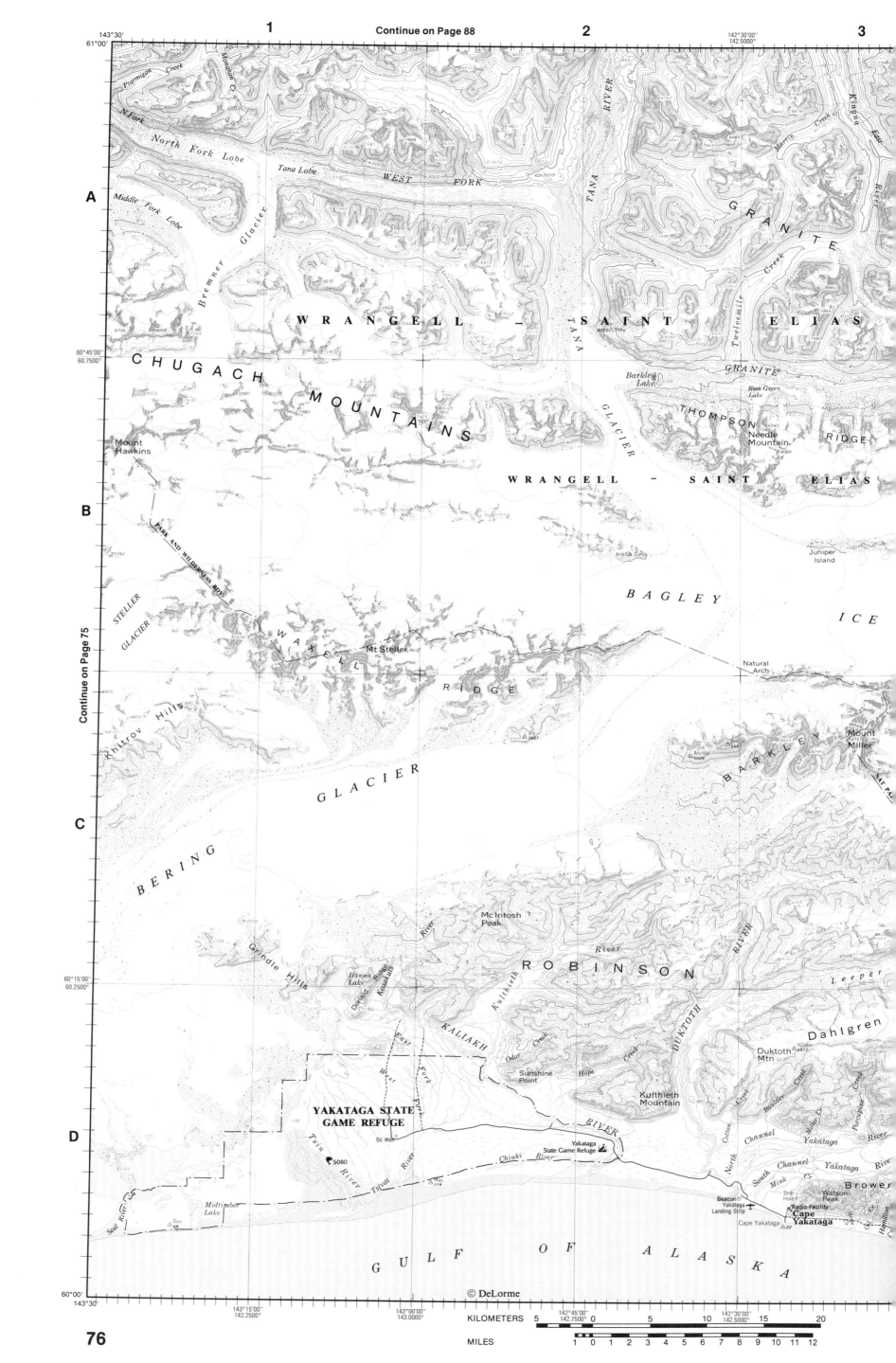

Continue on Page 88

Continue on Page 75

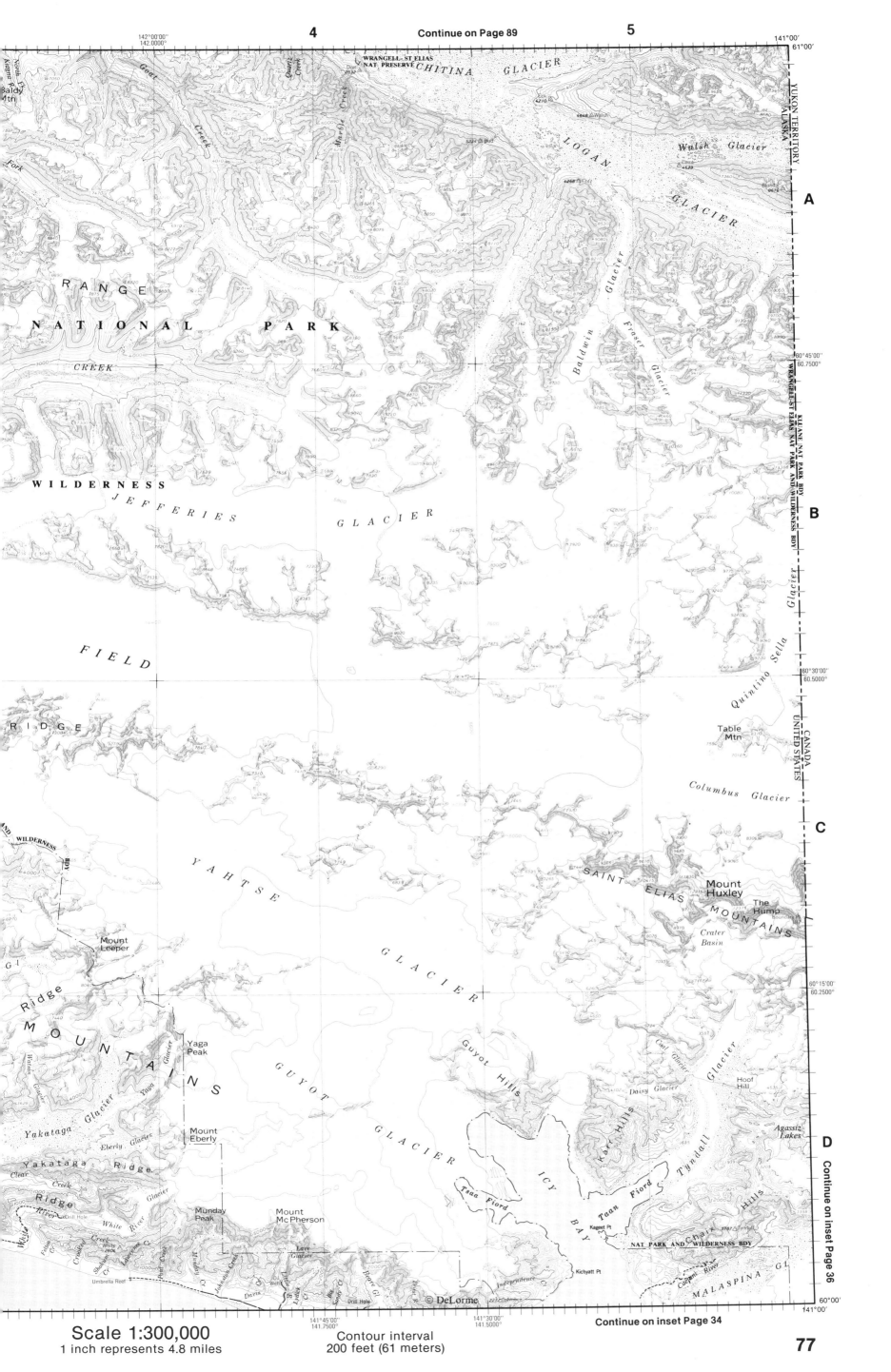

Scale 1:300,000
1 inch represents 4.8 miles

Contour interval
200 feet (61 meters)

Continue on inset Page 36

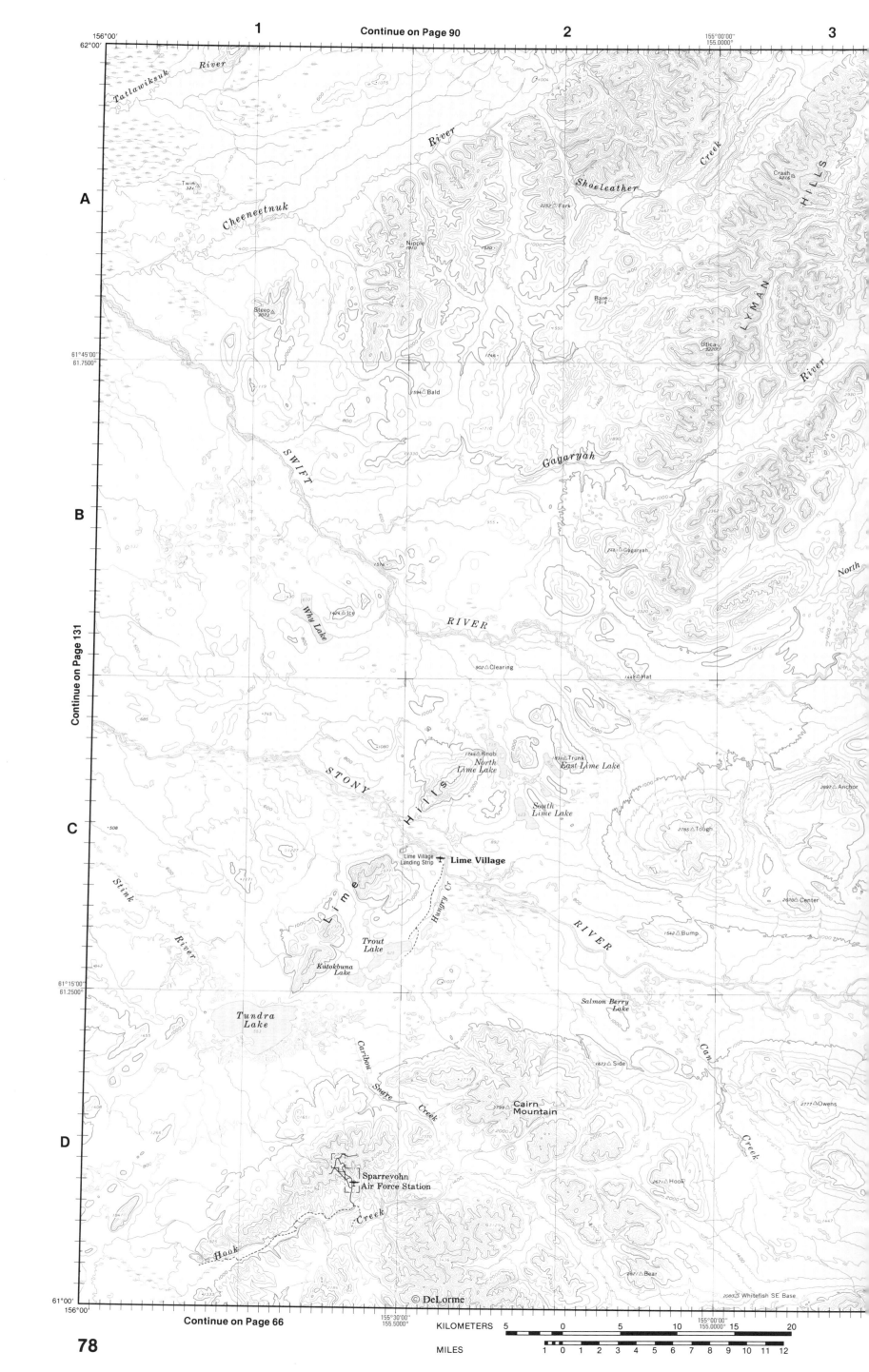

156°00'
62°00'

155°00'00"
155.0000'

A

61°45'00"
61.7500°

B

Continue on Page 131

C

61°15'00"
61.2500°

D

61°00'
156°00'

155°30'00"
155.5000°

155°00'00"
155.0000°

Lime Village

Tattawiksuk River

Cheeneetnuk

River

Shoeleather

Twin
321

Fork
2252

Nipple
1910

Crash
4216

LYMAN

HILLS

Steep
3072

Bare
1919

River

Utica
3220

1594 Bald

SWIFT

Gogaryah

1746

1710

1890

Gogaryah
1521

Why Lake

1624 Ice

RIVER

955

North

902 Clearing

1446 Hat

STONY

Knob *1744*

1832 Trunk
East Lime Lake

2897 Anchor

1080

North Lime Lake

508

Hills

South Lime Lake

2785 Tough

Lime Village Landing Strip

Lime Village

2470 Center

Stink

Lime

Hungry Cr

RIVER

1542 Bump

River

Trout Lake

Kutokbuna Lake

1037

Salmon Berry Lake

Can

Tundra Lake

1673 Side

Caribou

Snare

Creek

2759 Cairn Mountain

2771 Owens

Creek

1761 Hook

D

Sparrevohn Air Force Station

Creek

Hook

787 Bear

2080 Whitefish SE Base

© DeLorme

KILOMETERS 5   0   5   10   15   20

MILES 1 0 1 2 3 4 5 6 7 8 9 10 11 12

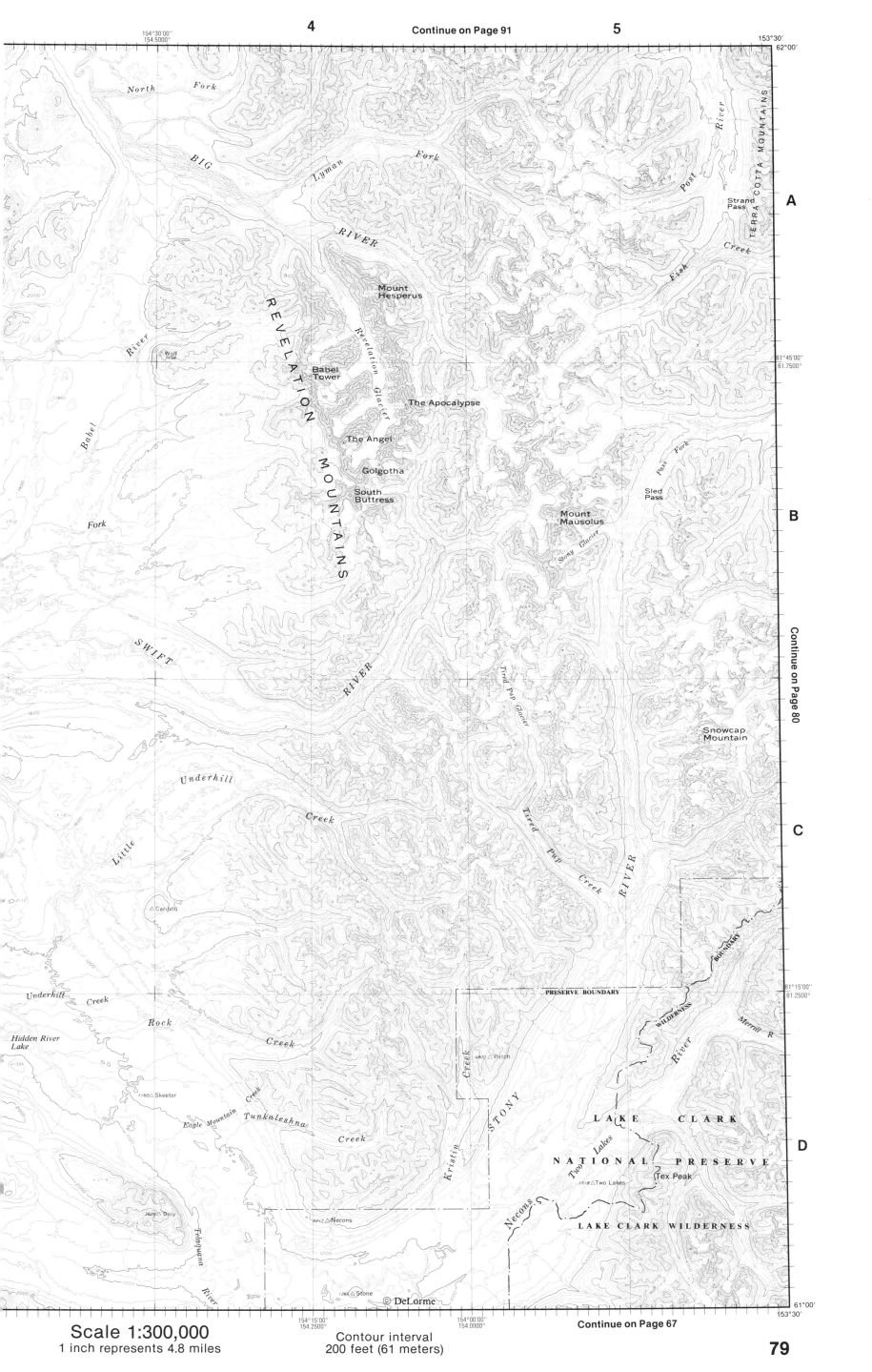

154°30'00''
154.5000°

153°30'
62°00'

North   Fork

B I G

Lyman   Fork

R I V E R

River

Mount
Hesperus

A

61°45'00''
61.7500°

Babel
Tower

The Apocalypse

R E V E L A T I O N

Revelation   Glacier

The Angel

Golgotha

South
Buttress

Mount
Mausolus

Stony   Glacier

Strand
Pass

Creek

Fish

Post

River

TERRA   COTTA   MOUNTAINS

Pass   Fork

Sled
Pass

B

M O U N T A I N S

Babel

Fork

Wolf

SWIFT

RIVER

Tired   Pup   Glacier

Snowcap
Mountain

Continue on Page 80

C

Underhill

Creek

Little

Caribou

Tired

Pup

Creek

RIVER

BOUNDARY

WILDERNESS

61°15'00''
61.2500°

Underhill   Creek

Rock

Creek

Hidden River
Lake

Skeeter

Eagle Mountain

Tunkaleshna

Creek

Creek

Creek

PRESERVE BOUNDARY

Patch

River

Merrill R

D

STONY

Kristin

Necons

L A K E   C L A R K

Two   Lakes

Two Lakes

Tex Peak

N A T I O N A L   P R E S E R V E

Telaquana

River

Only

Necons

Stone

© DeLorme

L A K E   C L A R K   W I L D E R N E S S

61°00'
153°30'

154°15'00''
154.2500°

154°00'00''
154.0000°

Continue on Page 67

Scale 1:300,000
1 inch represents 4.8 miles

Contour interval
200 feet (61 meters)

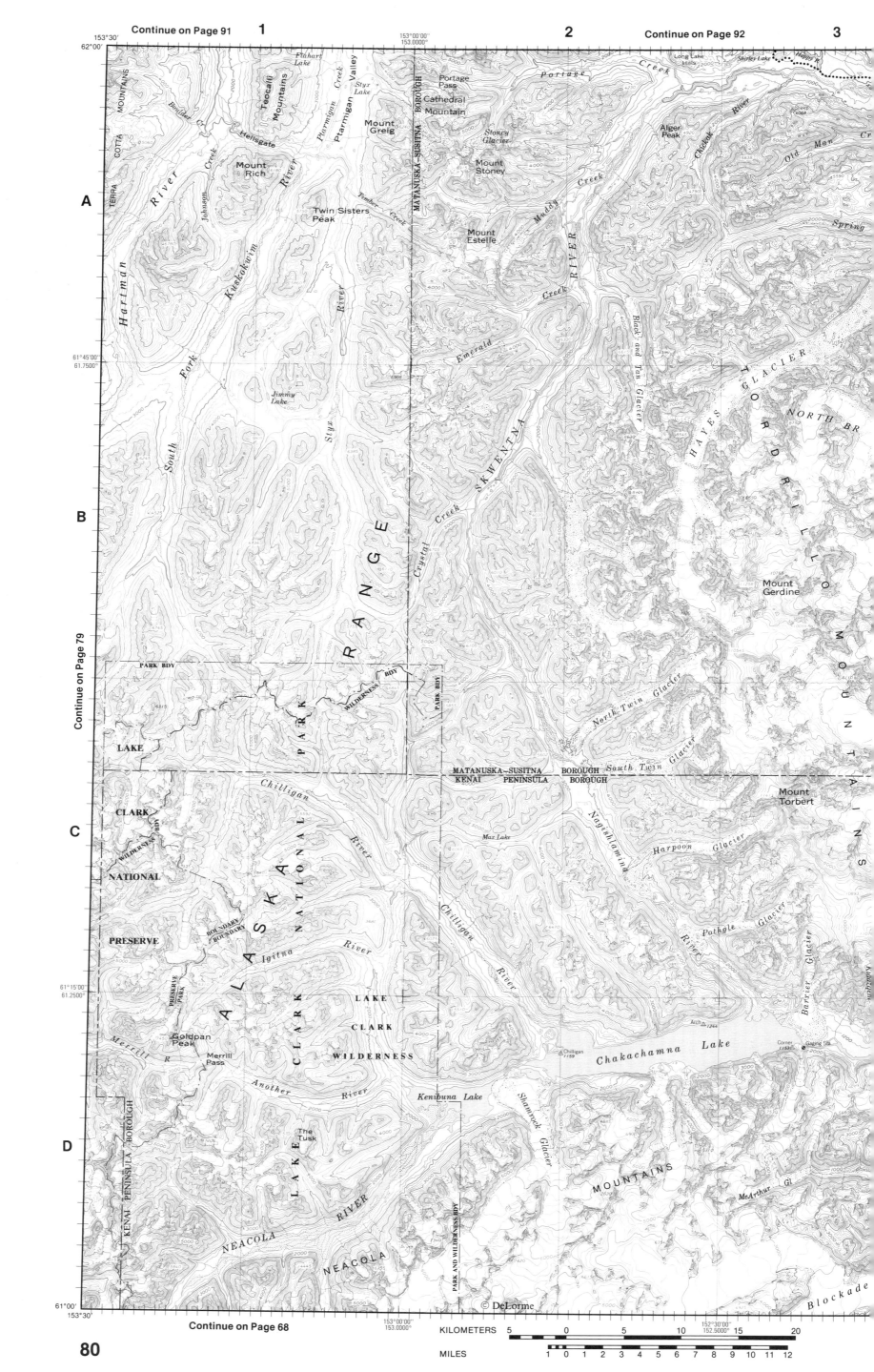

153°30'
62°00'

Flahart
Lake

Teocalli
Mountains

Hellsgate

Mount
Rich

Mount
Greig

Twin Sisters
Peak

Ptarmigan Creek

Ptarmigan
Valley

Styx
Lake

TERRA COTTA MOUNTAINS

Bonihid Cr.

Hartman

Kuskokwim

River

Johnson Creek

River

Tember Creek

Portage Pass

Cathedral
Mountain

Stoney
Glacier

Mount
Stoney

Mount
Estelle

MATANUSKA–SUSITNA BOROUGH

Portage

Creek

Long Lake
Hills

Shirley Lake

Happy R.

Alger
Peak

Chichuk

River

Muddy

Creek

Emerald

Creek

SKWENTNA

RIVER

Black and Tan Glacier

Old Man

Cr

Spring

A

61°45'00'
61.7500°

Jimmy
Lake

South Fork

Styx

Crystal Creek

HAYES

GLACIER

NORTH BR

T O R D R I L L O

NORTH

B

Continue on Page 79

PARK BDY

WILDERNESS BDY

PARK BDY

LAKE

PARK RANGE

North Twin Glacier

Mount
Gerdine

M O U N

C

CLARK

WILDERNESS BDY

NATIONAL

PRESERVE

BOUNDARY
BOUNDARY

PRESERVE
PARK

Chilligan

Igitna

River

River

MATANUSKA–SUSITNA BOROUGH
KENAI PENINSULA BOROUGH

South Twin Glacier

Max Lake

Nagishlamina

Harpoon Glacier

Mount
Torbert

Glacier

C

61°15'00'
61.2500°

Goldpan
Peak

Merrill R.

Merrill
Pass

Another

River

A L A S K A   N A T I O N A L

LAKE

CLARK

WILDERNESS

Chilligan

River

Pothole Glacier

River

△ Chilligan
1159

Arch △ 1244

Chakachamna

Lake

Barrier Glacier

Corner
1534

Gaging Sta.

Glacier

T A I N S

D

Kenibuna Lake

The Tusk

NEACOLA

RIVER

NEACOLA

PARK AND WILDERNESS BDY

Shamrock Glacier

M O U N T A I N S

McArthur Gl

Blockade

KENAI PENINSULA BOROUGH

© DeLorme

61°00'
153°30'

Continue on Page 68

153°00'00"
153.0000°

152°30'00"
152.5000°

KILOMETERS   5   0   5   10   15   20

MILES   1 0 1 2 3 4 5 6 7 8 9 10 11 12

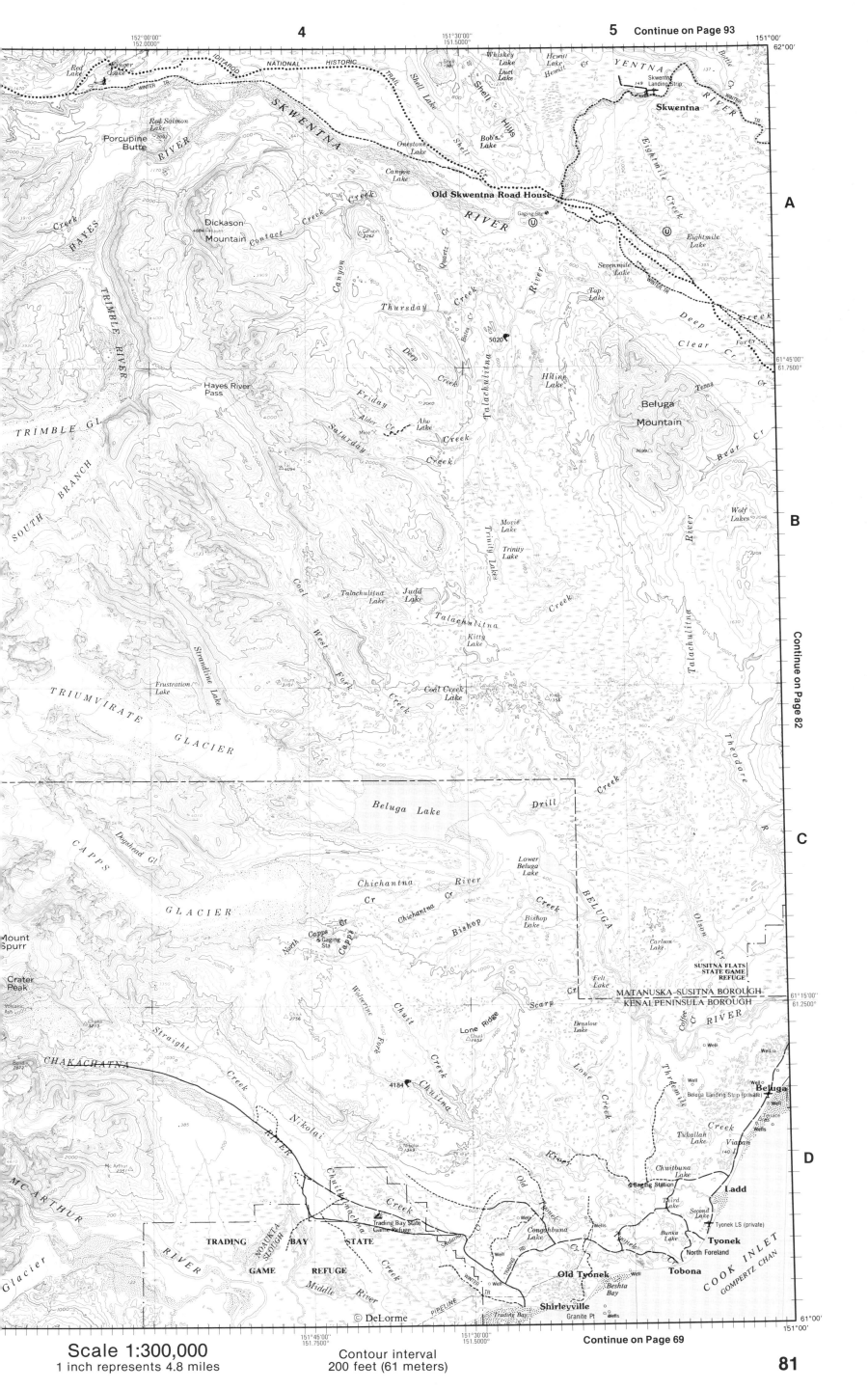

152°00'00"
152.0000'
151°30'00"
151.5000'
151°00'
62°00'

A

61°45'00"
61.7500'

B

Continue on Page 82

C

61°15'00"
61.2500'

D

61°00'
151°00'

Skwentna

Old Skwentna Road House

Red Lake
Yenger Lake
Porcupine Butte
Red Salmon Lake
Dickason Mountain
Hayes River Pass

TRIMBLE RIVER
HAYES RIVER
SKWENTNA RIVER

SOUTH BRANCH
TRIMBLE GL.

TRIUMVIRATE GLACIER

Strandline Lake
Frustration Lake

Talachulitna Lake
Judd Lake
Kitty Lake
Coal Creek Lake

Whiskey Lake
Luci Lake
Shell Lake
Bob's Lake
Onestone Lake
Canyon Lake

Hewitt Lake
Hewitt Cr.
YENTNA RIVER
Skwentna Landing Strip

Shell Hills
Shell Cr.

Thursday Creek
Deep Creek
Friday Creek
Saturday Creek
Alder Cr.
Ahn Lake

Talachulitna River
Trinity Lakes
Movie Lake
Trinity Lake

Talachulitna

Eightmile Creek
Sevenmile Lake
Top Lake
Eightmile Lake

Deep Creek
Clear Cr.
Fox Cr.

Beluga Mountain
Texas Cr.
Bear Cr.

Wolf Lakes

Theodore River

CAPPS GLACIER
Dogshead Gl.
Capps Gaging Sta.
North Capps Cr.
Capps Creek

Beluga Lake
Drill Creek

Chichantna River
Chichantna Cr.
Bishop Cr.
Bishop Lake

Lower Beluga Lake

BELUGA

Olson Cr.

Carlson Lake

SUSITNA FLATS
STATE GAME
REFUGE

Felt Lake

MATANUSKA-SUSITNA BOROUGH
KENAI PENINSULA BOROUGH

Mount Spurr
Crater Peak

Straight Creek

Nikolai River

Wolverine Fork
Chuit Creek
Lone Ridge
Chuitna

Scarp

Benslow Lake

Lone Creek

Coffee Cr.
RIVER

Well
Well

Threemile Cr.
Beluga Landing Strip (private)
Beluga
Well
Wells

CHAKACHATNA

MCARTHUR
McArthur
Glacier

Nikolai River
Nolurta Slough
Chakachatna Creek
Middle River

TRADING BAY STATE
GAME REFUGE

Trading Bay State
Game Refuge

Congahbuna Lake
Old Nikolai RD.
TRADING RD.

Wells
Well
Well

PIPELINE
WINTER TR.
Trading Bay
Granite Pt.

Old Tyonek
Shirleyville

Beshta Bay

Tukallah Lake
Viapan Lake
Chuitbuna Lake
Gaging Station
Ladd
Third Lake
Second Lake
Tyonek LS (private)
Bunk Lake
Tyonek
North Foreland
Tobona

COOK INLET
GOMPERTZ CHAN.

© DeLorme

Continue on Page 69

Scale 1:300,000
1 inch represents 4.8 miles

Contour interval
200 feet (61 meters)

81

151°45'00"
151.7500'
151°30'00"
151.5000'

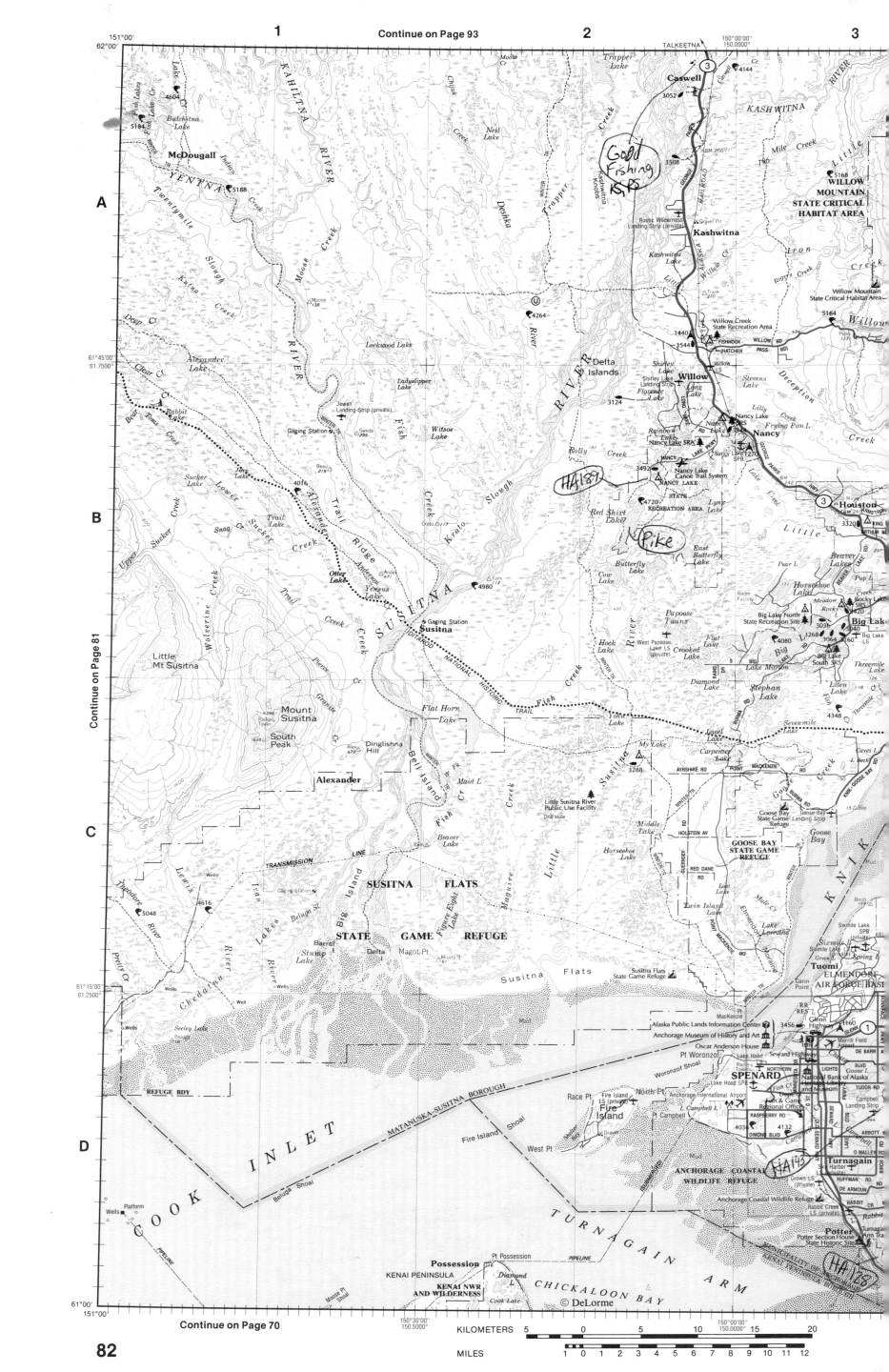

151°00'
62°00'

A

B

Continue on Page 81

C

D

61°45'00'
61.7500°

61°15'00'
61.2500°

61°00'
151°00'

KAHILTNA RIVER

YENTNA

RIVER

SUSITNA

Talkeetna

Caswell

KASHWITNA

Kashwitna

WILLOW MOUNTAIN STATE CRITICAL HABITAT AREA

Willow Mountain State Critical Habitat Area

Willow Creek State Recreation Area

Willow

Nancy Lake SRS

Nancy

Nancy Lake Canoe Trail System

NANCY LAKE STATE RECREATION AREA

Houston

Big Lake

Big Lake North State Recreation Site

Big Lake South SRS

Susitna

Alexander

Mount Susitna

South Peak

Little Mt Susitna

SUSITNA   FLATS

STATE   GAME   REFUGE

Susitna Flats State Game Refuge

GOOSE BAY STATE GAME REFUGE

Goose Bay State Game Refuge

Goose Bay

Tuomi

ELMENDORF AIR FORCE BASE

Alaska Public Lands Information Center
Anchorage Museum of History and Art
Oscar Anderson House

SPENARD

Anchorage International Airport

National Bank of Alaska

Fish & Game Regional Office

Fire Island

Turnagain

ANCHORAGE COASTAL WILDLIFE REFUGE

Anchorage Coastal Wildlife Refuge

Potter
Potter Section House State Historic Site

COOK   INLET

TURNAGAIN   ARM

Possession

KENAI PENINSULA
KENAI NWR AND WILDERNESS

CHICKALOON BAY

© DeLorme

MATANUSKA-SUSITNA BOROUGH

REFUGE BDY

150°30'00''
150.5000°

150°00'00''
150.0000°

KILOMETERS   5   0   5   10   15   20

MILES   1   0   1   2   3   4   5   6   7   8   9   10   11   12

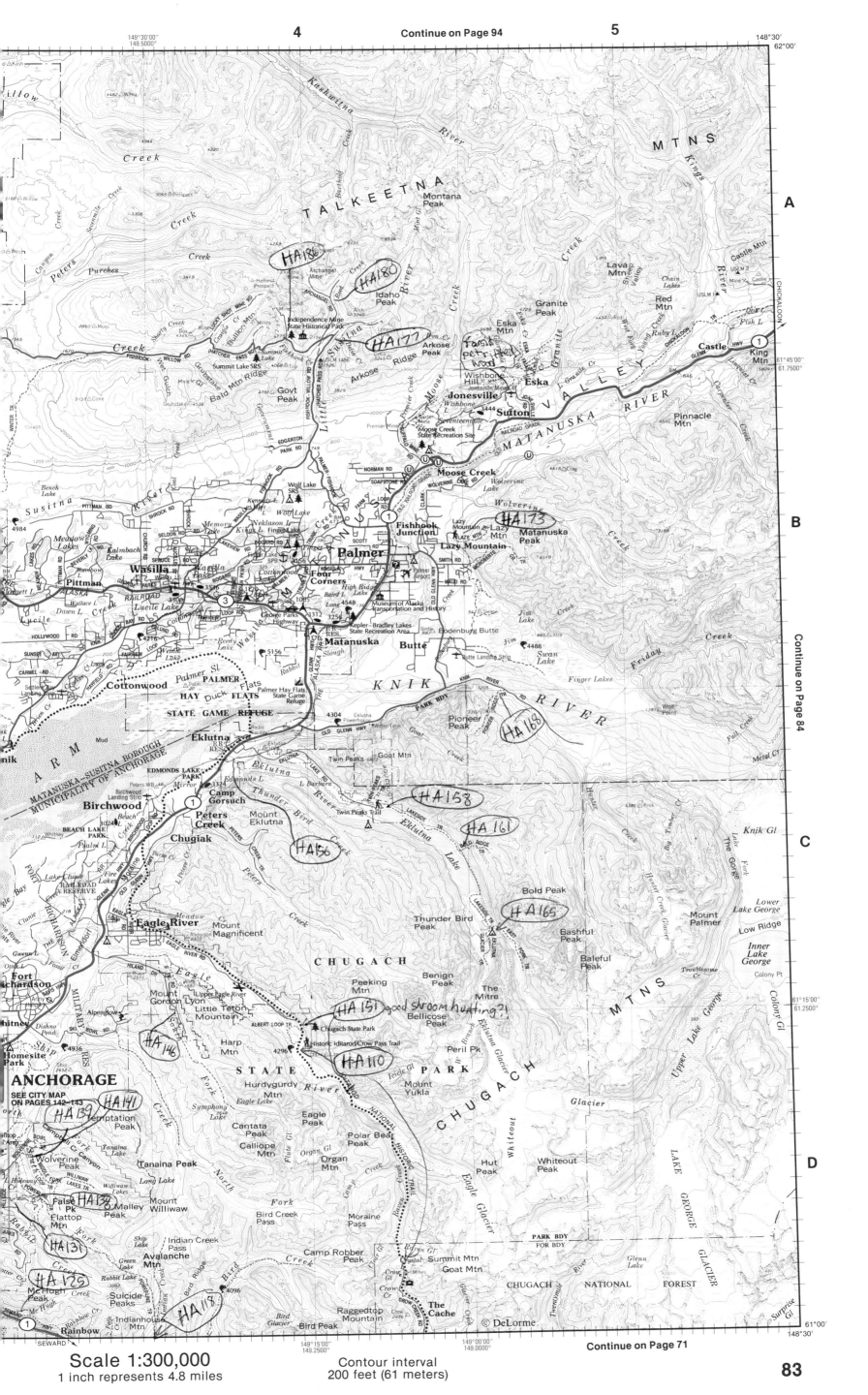

62°00'
149°30'00"
149.5000°
148°30'
A

T A L K E E T N A M T N S

Kings River

Montana Peak

Castle Mtn

Lava Mtns

Granite Peak

Red Mtn

Eska Mtn

HA180

HA185

Idaho Peak

Independence Mine State Historical Park

HA177

Arkose Peak

Chickaloon

Castle

King Mtn

1

61°45'00"
61.7500°

Jonesville

Eska

Sutton

Pinnacle Mtn

Govt Peak

Bald Mtn Ridge

M A T A N U S K A V A L L E Y R I V E R

Moose Creek State Recreation Site

Wishbone Hill

Moose Creek

HA173

Lazy Mountain

Matanuska Peak

B

Wolf Lake SRS

Fishhook Junction

1

Palmer

Lazy Mtn

Wasilla

Four Corners

Palmer Airport

Museum of Alaska Transportation and History

Jim Lake

Pittman

3

George Parks Highway

Kepler-Bradley Lakes State Recreation Area

Bodenburg Butte

Jim Creek

Friday Creek

Finger Lakes

Swan Lake

Matanuska

Butte

Cottonwood

PALMER
HAY FLATS

Palmer Sl

Duck FLATS

K N I K

R I V E R

Wolf Point

C

STATE GAME REFUGE

Palmer Hay Flats State Game Refuge

PARK BDY

Eklutna

HA168

Pioneer Peak

Eklutna

Matanuska-Susitna Borough
Municipality of Anchorage

A R M

Mud

Edmonds Lake Park

Camp Gorsuch

Thunder Bird River

HA158

Twin Peaks Trail

Goat Mtn

Knik Gl

Birchwood

1

Peters Creek

Mount Eklutna

HA161

Lower Lake George

Chugiak

HA156

Bold Peak

HA165

Mount Palmer

Low Ridge

C

Eagle River

Mount Magnificent

Thunder Bird Peak

Bashful Peak

Inner Lake George

Fort Richardson

C H U G A C H

Benign Peak

Baleful Peak

Troublesome Cr

Colony Pt

61°15'00"
61.2500°

Peeking Mtn

The Mitre

M T N S

Peril Pk

Colony Gl

Mount Gordon Lyon

Little Teton Mountain

HA151 good shroom hunting?!

Bellicose Peak

HA146

Albert Loop Tr

Chugach State Park

Historic Iditarod/Crow Pass Trail

HA110

Harp Mtn

Mount Yukla

Eklutna Glacier

C H U G A C H

Glacier

Whiteout Peak

ANCHORAGE
SEE CITY MAP
ON PAGES 142-143

S T A T E

Hurdygurdy Mtn

Eagle River

P A R K

HA141

HA139

Temptation Peak

Cantata Peak

Symphony Lake

Eagle Lake

Eagle Peak

Polar Bear Peak

Organ Gl

Hut Peak

Whiteout Peak

LAKE

D

Wolverine Peak

Tanaina Peak

Calliope Mtn

Organ Mtn

Homesite Park

North Fork

Long Lake

Mount Williwaw

Bird Creek Pass

Moraine Pass

GEORGE

HA135

O'Malley Peak

False Pk

Flattop Mtn

Ship Lake

Indian Creek Pass

Camp Robber Peak

Bird Ridge

Summit Mtn

Goat Mtn

Glenn Lake

HA131

Avalanche Mtn

Green Lake

Rabbit Lake

GLACIER

HA125

McHugh Peak

Suicide Peaks

HA118

Bird Peak

The Cache

CHUGACH NATIONAL FOREST

Rainbow

1

Indianhouse Mtn

Raggedtop Mountain

Bird Glacier

© DeLorme

PARK BDY
FOR BDY

61°00'

SEWARD

149°15'00"
149.2500°

149°00'00"
149.0000°

148°30'

Continue on Page 71

Scale 1:300,000
1 inch represents 4.8 miles

Contour interval
200 feet (61 meters)

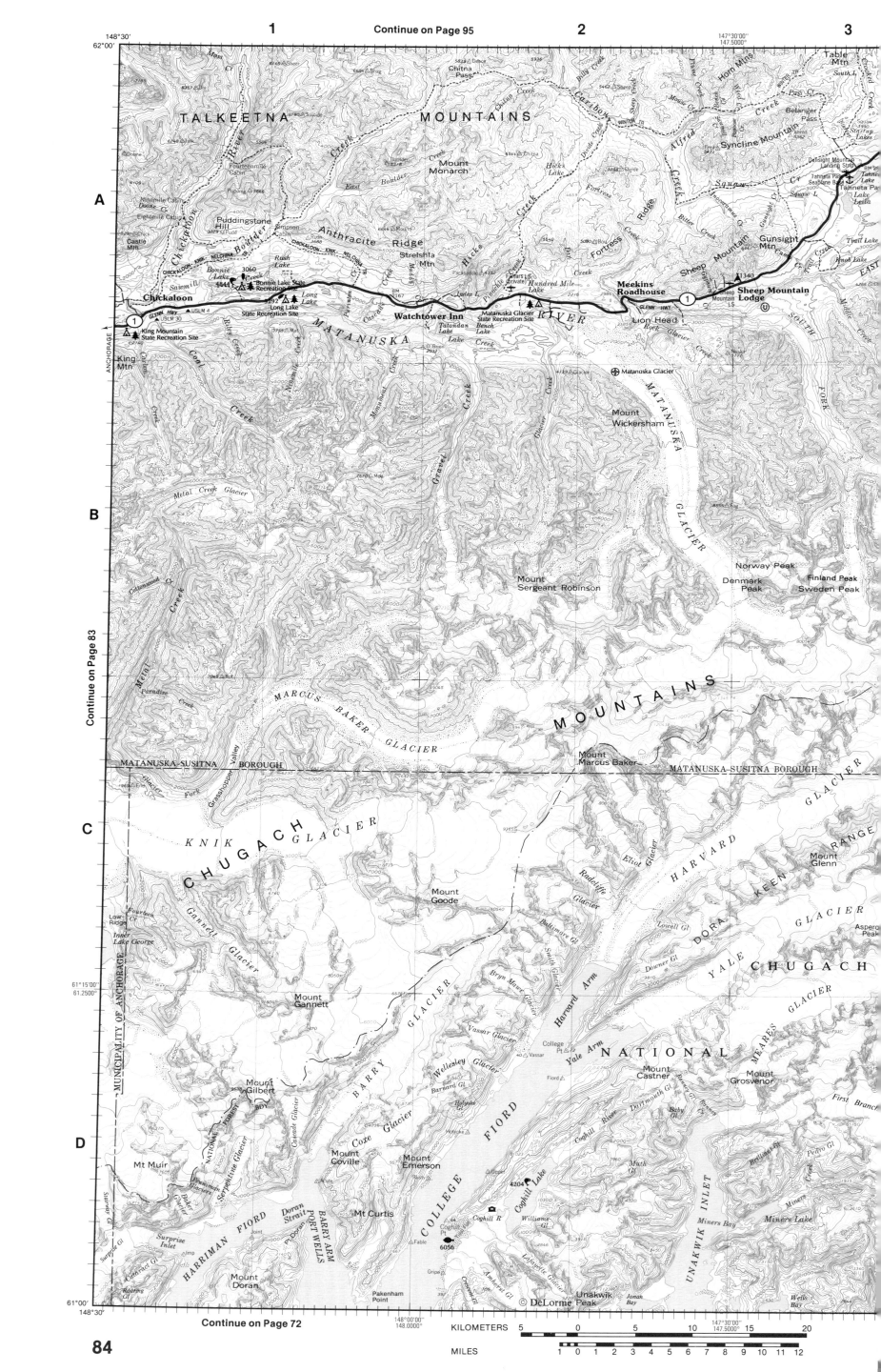

148°30'
62°00'

A

B

Continue on Page 83

C

61°15'00''
61.2500°

D

61°00'
148°30'

147°30'00''
147.5000°

TALKEETNA   MOUNTAINS

Mount Monarch

Syncline Mountain

Anthracite Ridge

Strelshla Mtn

Chickaloon

Bonnie Lake State Recreation Site

Long Lake State Recreation Site

King Mountain State Recreation Site

King Mtn

Watchtower Inn

Meekins Roadhouse

Sheep Mountain Lodge

Gunsight Mtn

Lion Head

Matanuska Glacier State Recreation Site

MATANUSKA

Mount Wickersham

MATANUSKA GLACIER

Metal Creek Glacier

Mount Sergeant Robinson

Norway Peak

Denmark Peak

Finland Peak
Sweden Peak

MARCUS BAKER GLACIER

MOUNTAINS

Mount Marcus Baker

MATANUSKA-SUSITNA BOROUGH

KNIK GLACIER

CHUGACH

Mount Goode

HARVARD GLACIER

Mount Glenn

DORA KEEN

RANGE

YALE GLACIER

CHUGACH

Gannett Glacier

Mount Gannett

Radcliffe Glacier

Barry Glacier

MUNICIPALITY OF ANCHORAGE

Harvard Arm

College Pt

Yale Arm

NATIONAL

Mount Castner

Mount Grosvenor

MEARES GLACIER

Mount Gilbert

Coxe Glacier

Cascade Glacier

Mount Coville

Mount Emerson

COLLEGE FIORD

Mt Muir

NATIONAL FOREST

Serpentine Glacier

Mt Curtis

Coghill Lake

Coghill R

UNAKWIK INLET

HARRIMAN FIORD

BARRY ARM PORT WELLS

Mount Doran

Doran Strait

Pakenham Point

DeLorme

Unakwik Peak

Miners Bay

Miners Lake

© DeLorme

Continue on Page 72

148°00'00''
148.0000°

147°30'00''
147.5000°

KILOMETERS   5   0   5   10   15   20

MILES   1   0   1   2   3   4   5   6   7   8   9   10   11   12

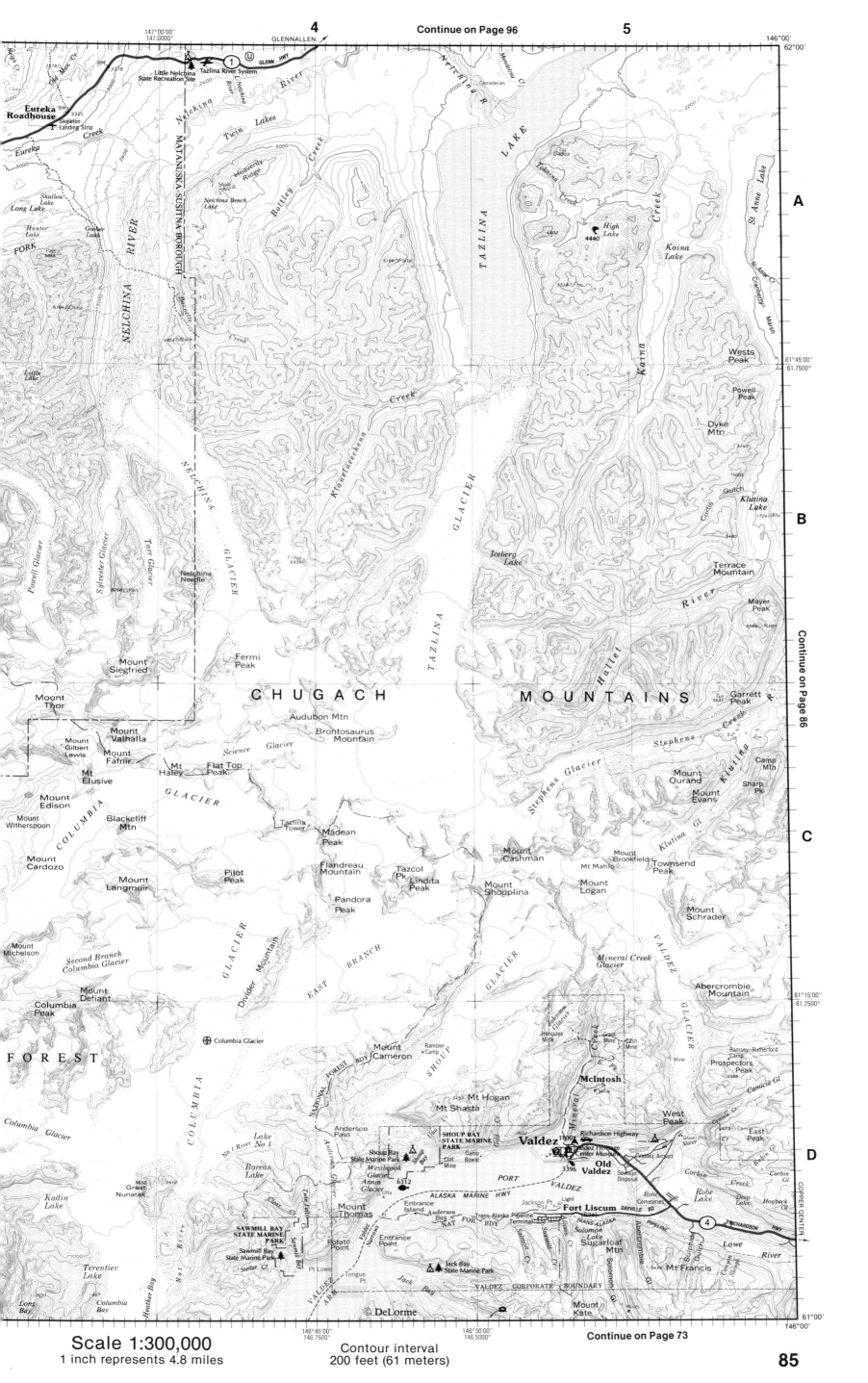

Continue on Page 86

Continue on Page 73

Scale 1:300,000
1 inch represents 4.8 miles

Contour interval
200 feet (61 meters)

© DeLorme

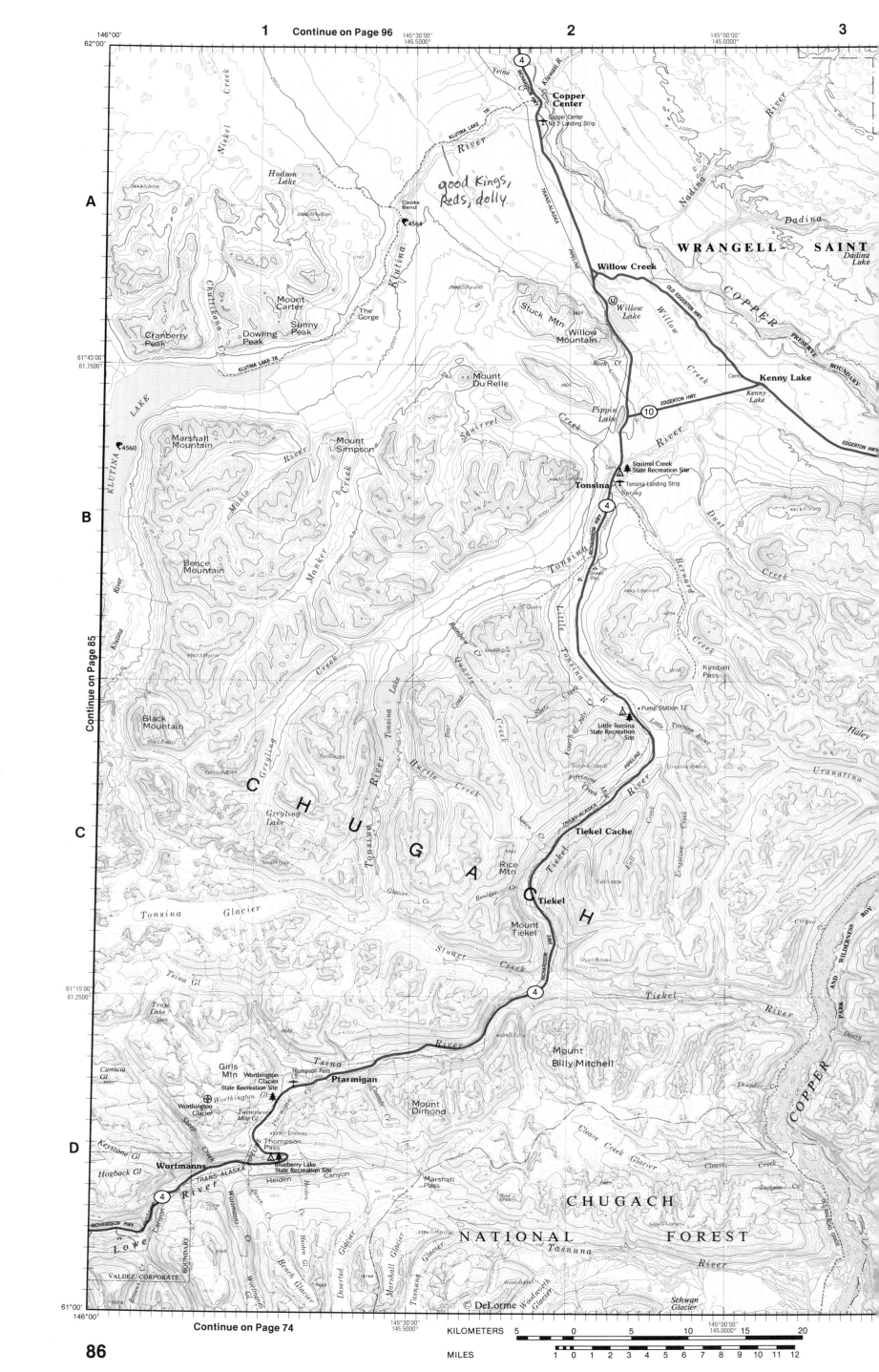

146°00'
145°30'00''
145.5000°

Continue on Page 85

good Kings,
Reds, dolly

WRANGELL — SAINT

Copper
Center

Willow Creek

Kenny Lake

Tonsina

Tiekel Cache

Tiekel

C H U G A C H

Ptarmigan

Wortmanns

CHUGACH

NATIONAL   FOREST

© DeLorme

145°00''
145.0000°

KILOMETERS 5   0   5   10   15   20

MILES   1 0 1 2 3 4 5 6 7 8 9 10 11 12

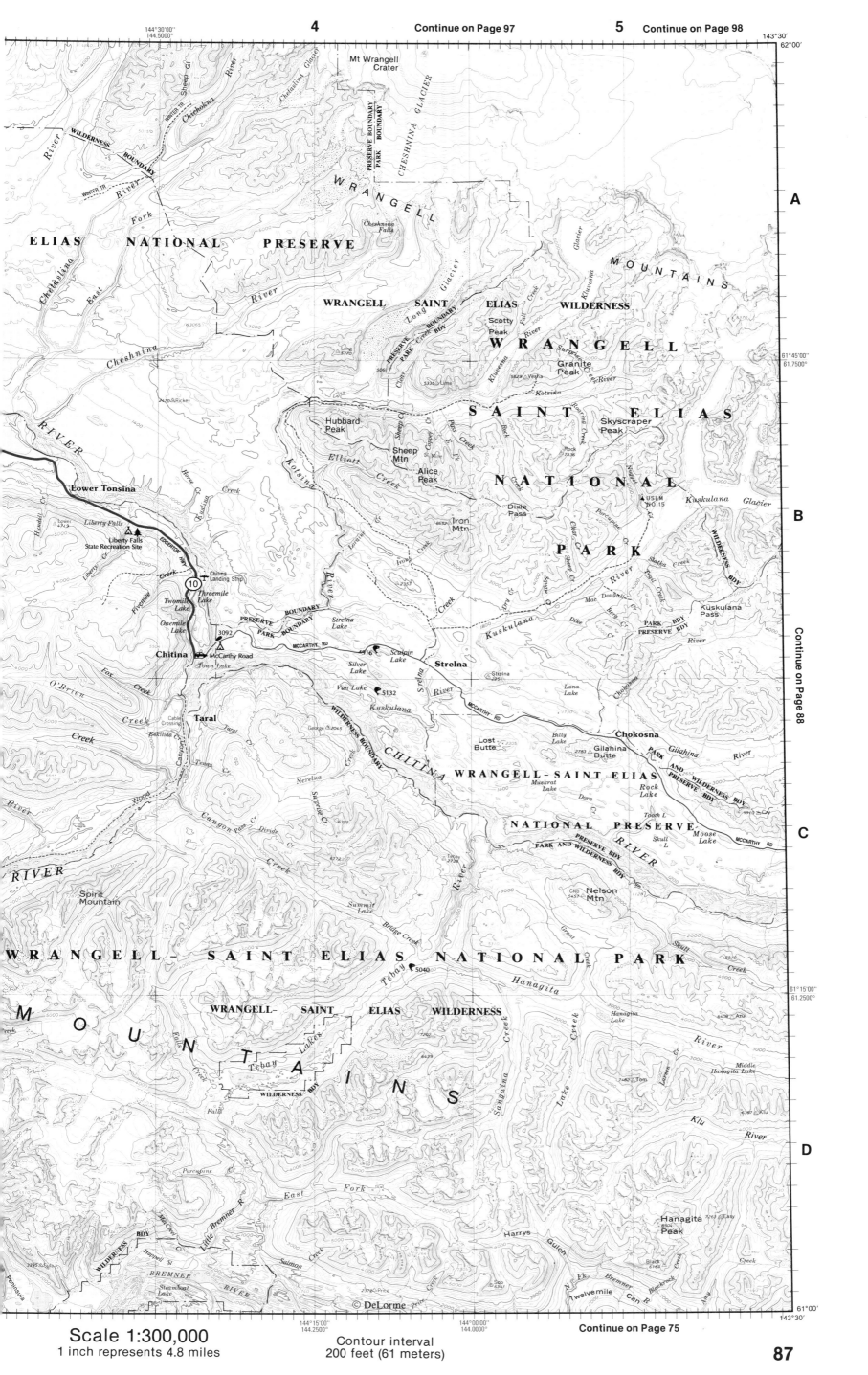

Mt Wrangell Crater

WRANGELL

CHESHNINA GLACIER

ELIAS NATIONAL PRESERVE

Cheshnina Falls

WRANGELL– SAINT ELIAS WILDERNESS

Scotty Peak

MOUNTAINS

Granite Peak

Skyscraper Peak

WRANGELL–

SAINT ELIAS

NATIONAL

PARK

Hubbard Peak

Sheep Mtn

Alice Peak

Iron Mtn

Dixie Pass

USLM NO 15

Kuskulana Glacier

WILDERNESS BDY

Kuskulana Pass

PARK BDY
PRESERVE BDY

Kuskulana River

Lower Tonsina

Liberty Falls

Liberty Falls State Recreation Site

Chitina Landing Strip

10

Twomile Lake
Threemile Lake

Onemile Lake

3092

Chitina
Town Lake

McCarthy Road

PRESERVE BOUNDARY
PARK BOUNDARY

Strelna Lake

MCCARTHY RD

Silver Lake
Scalpin Lake

Van Lake

Kuskulana

Strelna

Strelna River

MCCARTHY RD

Lana Lake

Taral

CHITINA

WILDERNESS BOUNDARY

Nerelna

Surprise Cr

Lost Butte

Billy Lake

WRANGELL–SAINT ELIAS

Gilahina Butte

Chokosna

PARK AND WILDERNESS BDY

Gilahina River

O'Brien Creek

Fox Creek

Eskilida Cr

Cabin Crossing

Canyon Cr

Tenas Cr

Wood Canyon

RIVER

Canyon Pass Cr

Divide Creek

NATIONAL PRESERVE RIVER

Muskrat Lake
Dora Cr
Rock Lake
Tooth L
Skull L
Moose Lake

MCCARTHY RD

PRESERVE BDY
PARK AND WILDERNESS BDY

Nelson Mtn

Spirit Mountain

Summit Lake

Bridge Creek

WRANGELL– SAINT ELIAS NATIONAL PARK

MOUNTAINS

WRANGELL– SAINT ELIAS WILDERNESS

Tebay Lakes

Tebay

WILDERNESS BDY

Hanagita

Sanjaina Creek

Lake Creek

Hanagita Lake

River

Middle Hanagita Lake

Falls Creek

MacColl Cr

Porcupine Cr

East Fork

Little Bremner R

BREMNER RIVER

Hanagita Peak

WILDERNESS BDY

Steamboat Lake

Harrys Gulch

Salmon Creek

Twelvemile Can R

Blackrock Creek

N Fk Bremner R

© DeLorme

Continue on Page 75

Continue on Page 88

Scale 1:300,000
1 inch represents 4.8 miles

Contour interval
200 feet (61 meters)

87

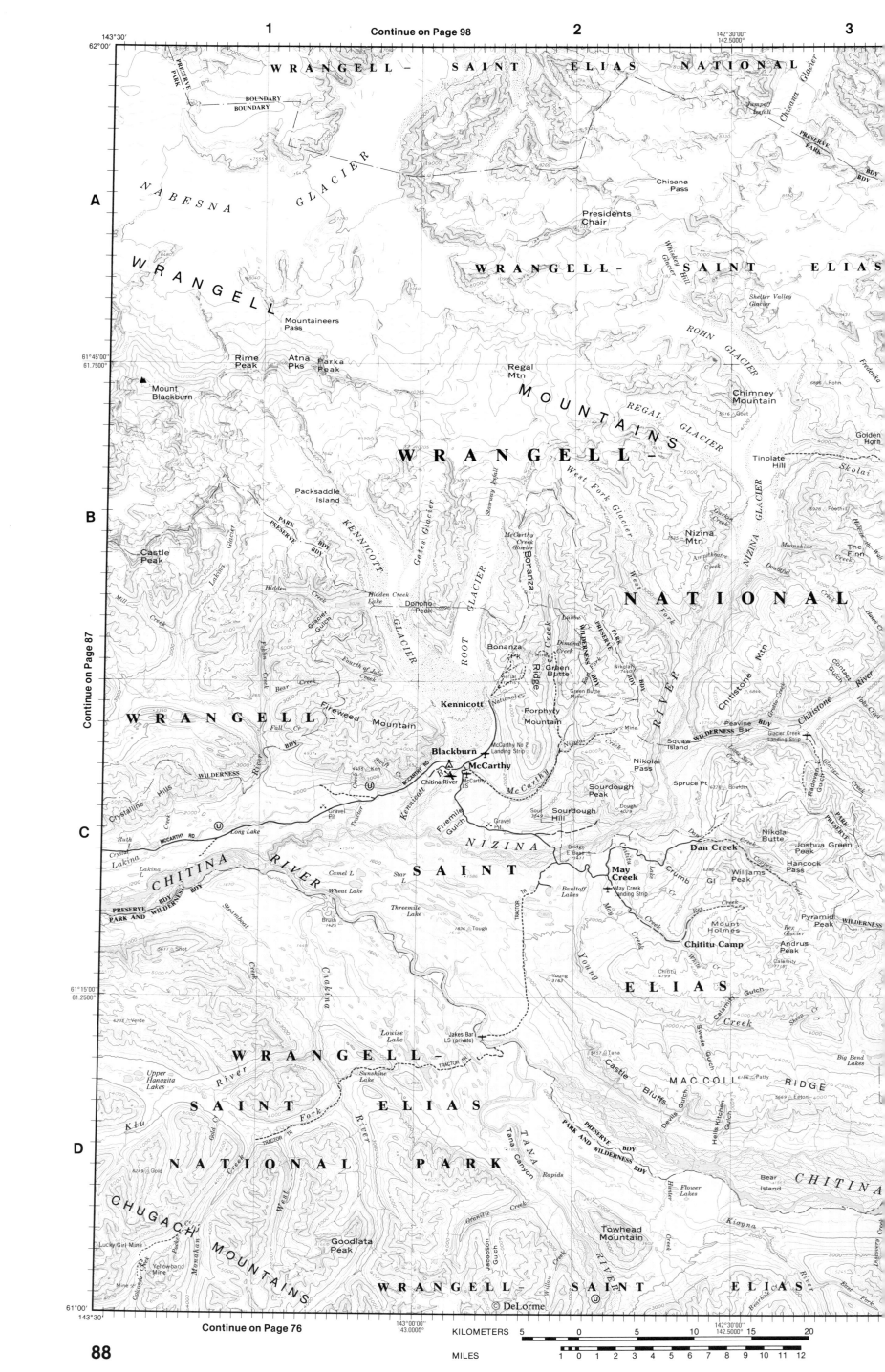

Continue on Page 87

© DeLorme

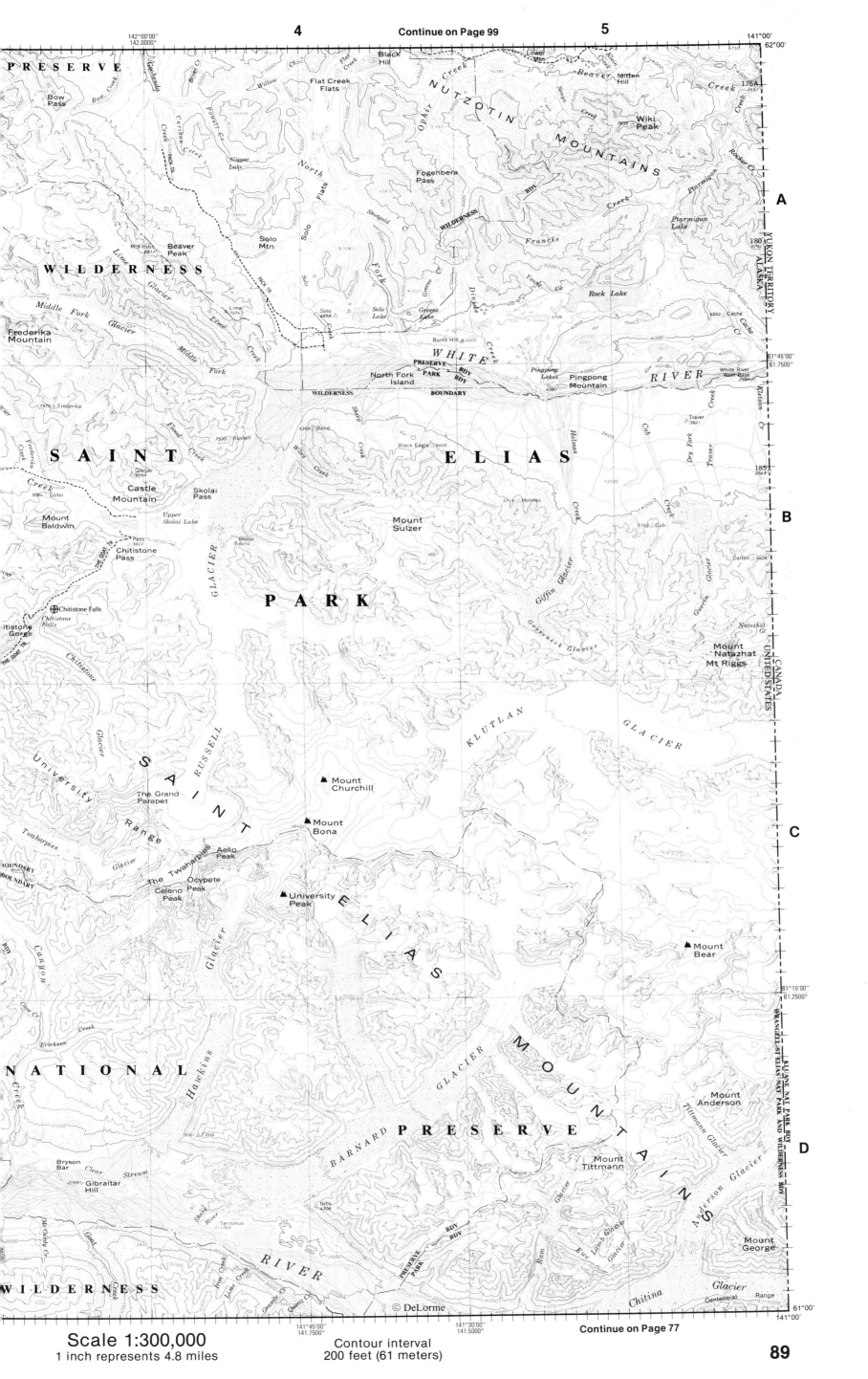

Scale 1:300,000
1 inch represents 4.8 miles

Contour interval
200 feet (61 meters)

Continue on Page 77

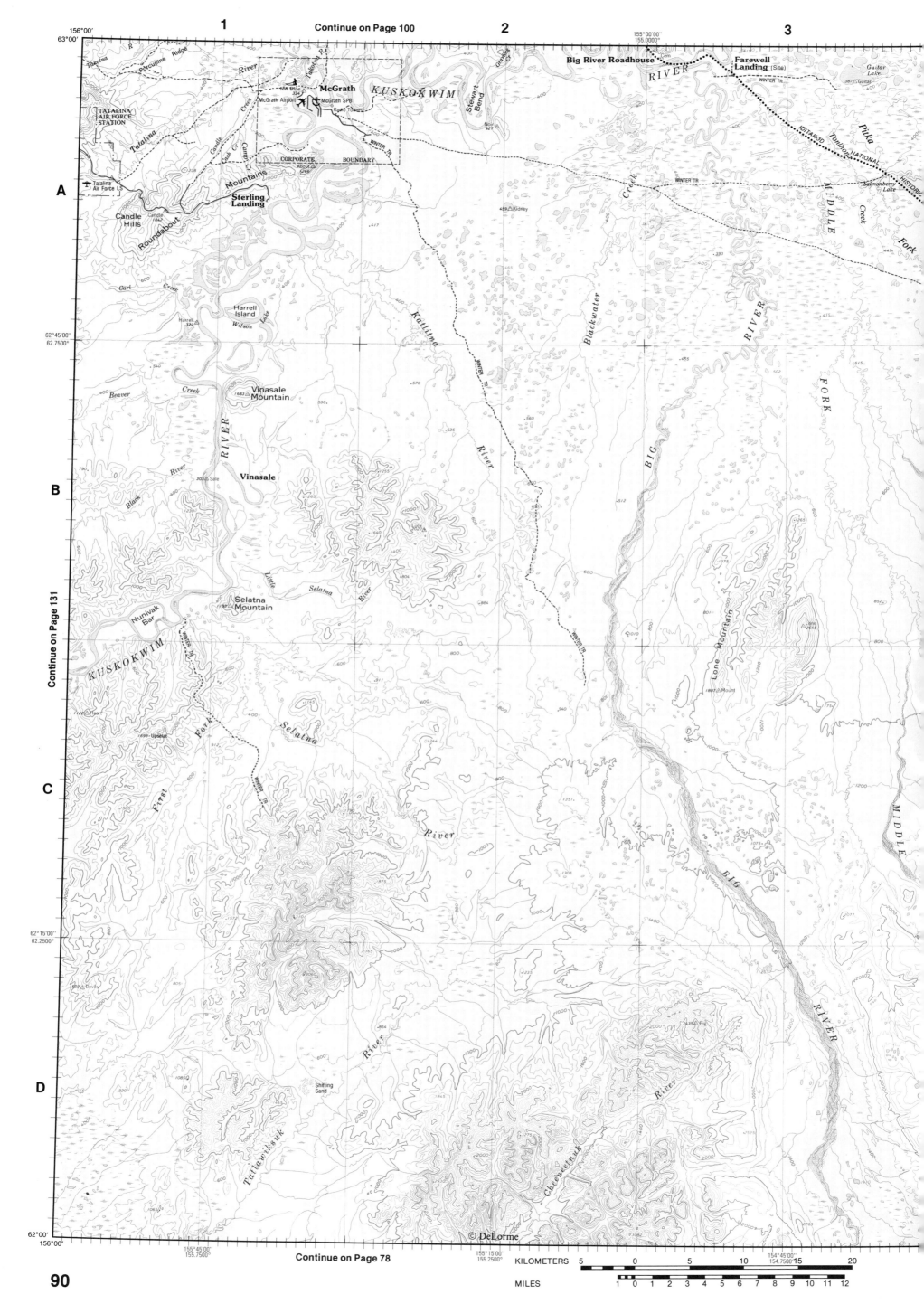

1 2 3

156°00'
63°00'

155°00'00"
155.0000°

A

B

Continue on Page 131

C

62°45'00"
62.7500°

62°15'00"
62.2500°

D

62°00'
156°00'

TATALINA
AIR FORCE
STATION

Tatalina
Air Force LS

Candle
Hills

Roundabout

Sterling
Landing

Takotna R.

Porcupine Ridge

River

Takotna R.

McGrath

McGrath Airport

McGrath SPB

KUSKOKWIM

Big River Roadhouse

Farewell
Landing (Site)

RIVER

Guitar
Lake

IDITAROD

Tonzona

NATIONAL

MIDDLE

HISTORIC

Pitka

Fork

Salmonberry
Lake

Stewart
Bend

Creek

CORPORATE

BOUNDARY

WINTER TR

Kidney

Candle

Camp Cr

Mountains

Carl

Creek

Harrell Island

Wilson

Inlet

Beaver

Creek

Vinasale
Mountain

RIVER

River

Black

Vinasale

Sale

Katlina

River

Blackwater

Creek

BIG

FORK

RIVER

Selatna

River

Little

Selatna

Mountain

Nunivak
Bar

KUSKOKWIM

First

Fork

Upshot

WINTER TR

WINTER TR

Selatna

River

Lone Mountain

Mount

Lone

BIG

RIVER

MIDDLE

Devil

Tatlawiksuk

River

Shifting
Sand

River

Cheeneetnuk

© DeLorme

155°45'00"
155.7500°

155°15'00"
155.2500°

154°45'00"
154.7500°

KILOMETERS 5 0 5 10 15 20

MILES 1 0 1 2 3 4 5 6 7 8 9 10 11 12

90

154°00'00''
154.0000''

153°00'

63°00'

NIKOLAI
CORP BDY

Lined Creek
Spruce

Little

South

Fork

Jones

Creek

Birch
Hills

Pingston

Birch Hills

Clear

Jones Creek

Fork

Salmon

River

A

SOUTH

FORK

Tonzona

No

River

Deepbank

Creek

WINTER TR

62°45'00''
62.7500''

Bear

Creek

KUSKOKWIM

RIVER

Big

Salmon

Fork

Creek

MATANUSKA-SUSITNA BOROUGH

B

Sullivan

WINTER TR

Sheep Creek

Creek

Dillinger

River

WINDY

Pitka

Creek

Submarine
Lake

Steele
Lake

Continue on Page 92

Khuchaynik

FORK

White

Mound

JEEP TR

JEEP TR

John R

Farewell
Lake

Farewell Lake
SPB

Farewell Lake Lodge

Tin Creek Landing Strip

Farewell
Mtn

Joken

River

TEOCALLI

C

Radio
Towers

Towers

Farewell Landing Strip

St Johns
Hill

High Lakes

Egypt
Mtn

Charlie
Lake

NATIONAL

HISTORIC

SOUTH

Tatina

River

Well

Veleska
Lake

Tin

Creek

Tuna
Mtn

River

Automatic

Creek

FORK

Iditarod

Trail

Tatina

Dalzell

62°15'00''
62.2500''

Smith
Lake

Rohn
Roadhouse

Tatina Landing Strip
(emergency only)

MOUNTAINS

KUSKOKWIM

Knox
Peak

Widgeon
Lake

Rainy
Pass

Rainy Pass
Lake

FORK

WINDY

Post

TERRA

COTTA

RIVER

Wolverine

Brush Cr

Pass

Fork

D

STRIMOKISH

FORK

Creek

Post
Lake

MOUNTAINS

Denny
Creek

ALASKA

Goodman
Pass

Happy

Hagen L

North Fork Big River

River

FORK

Ptarmigan Valley

Ptarmigan Creek

Houston
Pass

Marsh
L

Sheep
Lake

RANGE

Puntilla Cr

62°00'
153°00'

© DeLorme

154°00'00''
154.0000''

Scale 1:300,000
1 inch represents 4.8 miles

Contour interval
200 feet (61 meters)

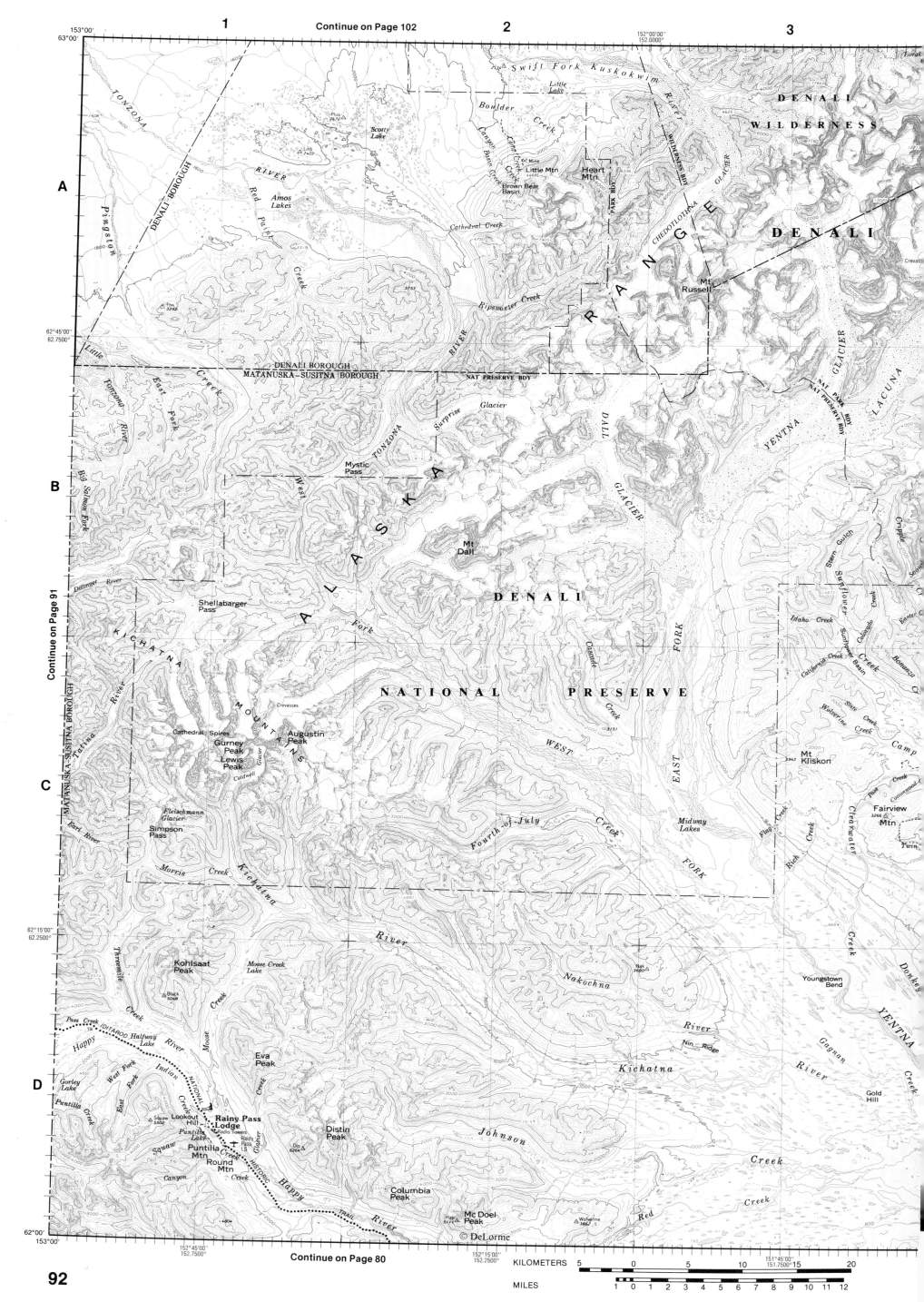

153°00'
63°00'

152°00'00"
152.0000"

A

TONZONA

Pingston

DENALI BOROUGH

RIVER

Red Paint

Amos Lakes

Creek

Scotty Lake

Log 2420

Plus 2470

Canyon

Gann Creek

Boulder

Creek

Little Lake

Swift Fork Kuskokwim

River

Little Mtn

Mine

Brown Bear Basin

Heart Mtn

Cathedral Creek

Ripsnorter Creek

River

CHEDOTLOTHNA

GLACIER

RANGE

Mt Russell

DENALI

WILDERNESS

DENALI

Crevass

62°45'00"
62.7500"

Little

Creek

DENALI BOROUGH
MATANUSKA-SUSITNA BOROUGH

TONZONA

East Fork

Tonzona River

River

NAT PRESERVE BDY

Surprise

Glacier

Mystic Pass

West

A L A S K A

DALL

GLACIER

Mt Dall

NAT PARK BDY
NAT PRESERVE BDY

YENTNA

GLACIER

LACUNA

B

Big Salmon Fork

Dillinger River

Shellabarger Pass

KICHATNA

Fork

Creek

D E N A L I

EAST

FORK

Stern Gulch

Cripple

Creek

Idaho Creek

Sunflower

Sunflower Basin

California Creek

Colorado

Eastern

Bonanza

Creek

C

Earl River

Tatina

River

A
L
A
S
K
A

M
O
U
N
T
A
I
N
S

Crevasses

Cathedral Spires

Gurney Peak

Lewis Peak

Augustin Peak

Caldwell Glacier

Fleischmann Glacier

Simpson Pass

Morris Creek

Kichatna

N A T I O N A L   P R E S E R V E

WEST

Creek

Fourth-of-July

Creek

EAST

FORK

Mt Kliskon

Midway Lakes

Share Creek

Wolverine Creek

Flag Creek

Rich Creek

Clearwater

Camp

Cottonwood

Creek

Fairview Mtn

Twin

62°15'00"
62.2500"

Threemile

Creek

Kohlsaat Peak

Black 5048

Moose Creek Lake

Creek

Moose

River

Nakochna

Nak

Youngstown Bend

River

YENTNA

Donkey

Creek

D

Gorley Lake

Puntilla Creek

West Fork

East Fork

Happy

Pass Creek

IDITAROD

Halfway Lake

Squaw 5502

Squaw Lake

Puntilla Mtn

Canyon

Lookout Hill

Rainy Pass Lodge

Round Mtn

Puntilla Creek

Rainy Pass LS

Indian

Creek

NATIONAL

Eva Peak

Distin Peak

Os 6264

Columbia Peak

Hap 5188

Mc Doel Peak

Johnson

HISTORIC

Happy

Creek

TRAIL

River

Wolverine 3061

Gagnan

River

Kichatna

Creek

Gold Hill

Red

Creek

© DeLorme

62°00'
153°00'

152°45'00"
152.7500"

152°15'00"
152.2500"

151°45'00"
151.7500"

KILOMETERS   5   0   5   10   15   20

MILES   1 0 1 2 3 4 5 6 7 8 9 10 11 12

Continue on Page 91

MATANUSKA-SUSITNA BOROUGH

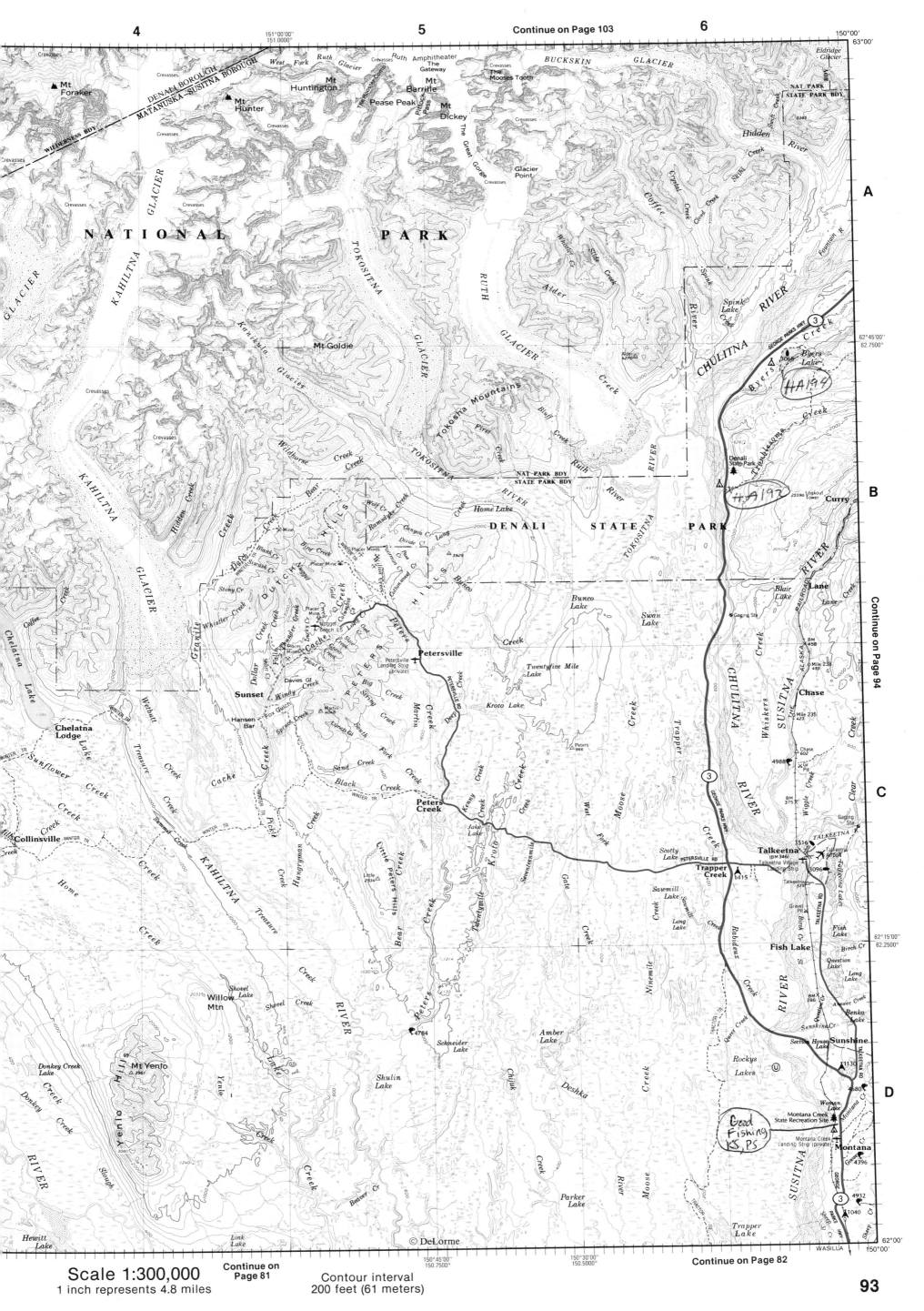

Continue on Page 103

Continue on Page 94

Continue on Page 81

Continue on Page 82

Scale 1:300,000
1 inch represents 4.8 miles

Contour interval
200 feet (61 meters)

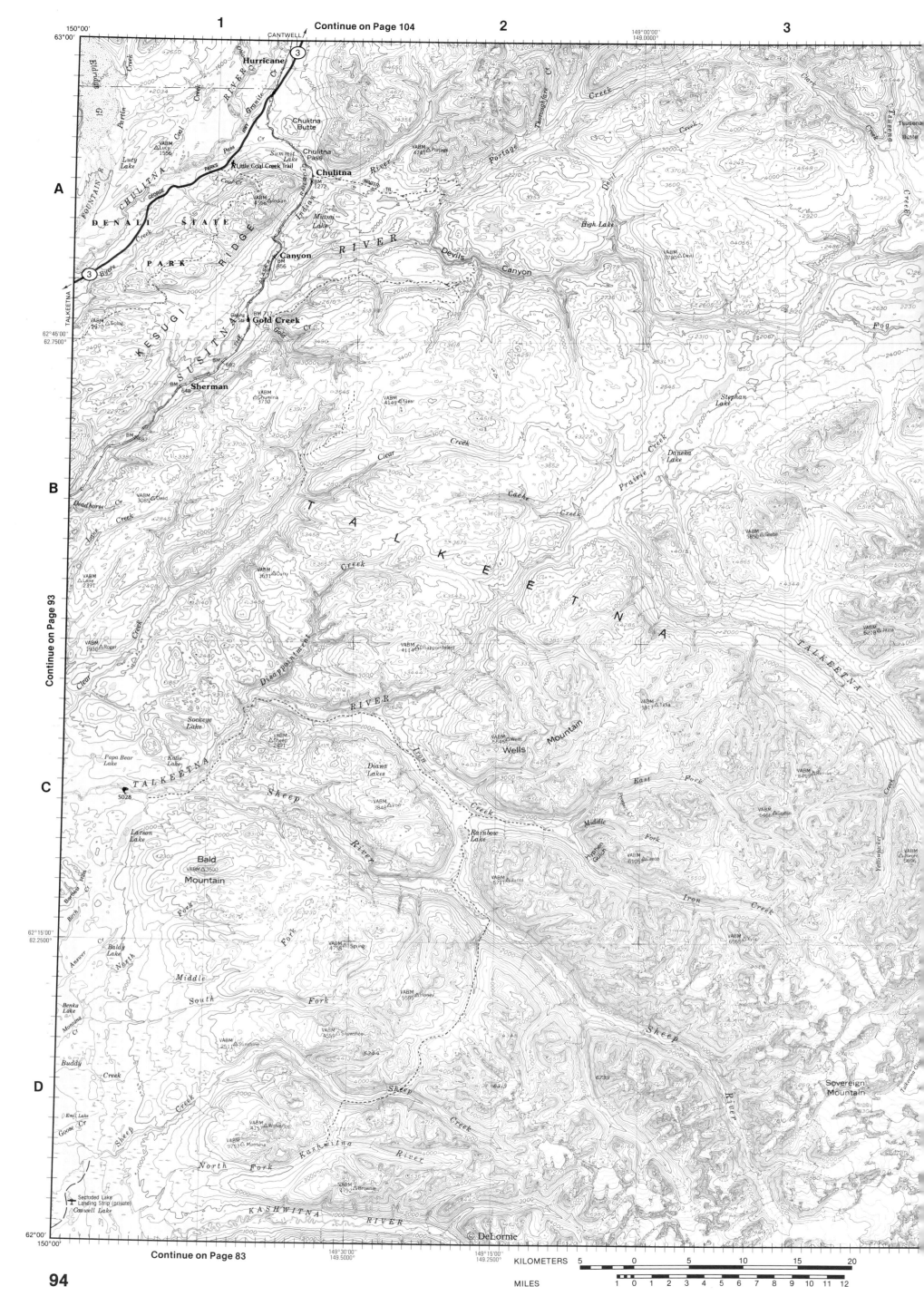

Continue on Page 93

Continue on Page 83

© DeLorme

KILOMETERS　5　0　5　10　15　20

MILES　1　0　1　2　3　4　5　6　7　8　9　10　11　12

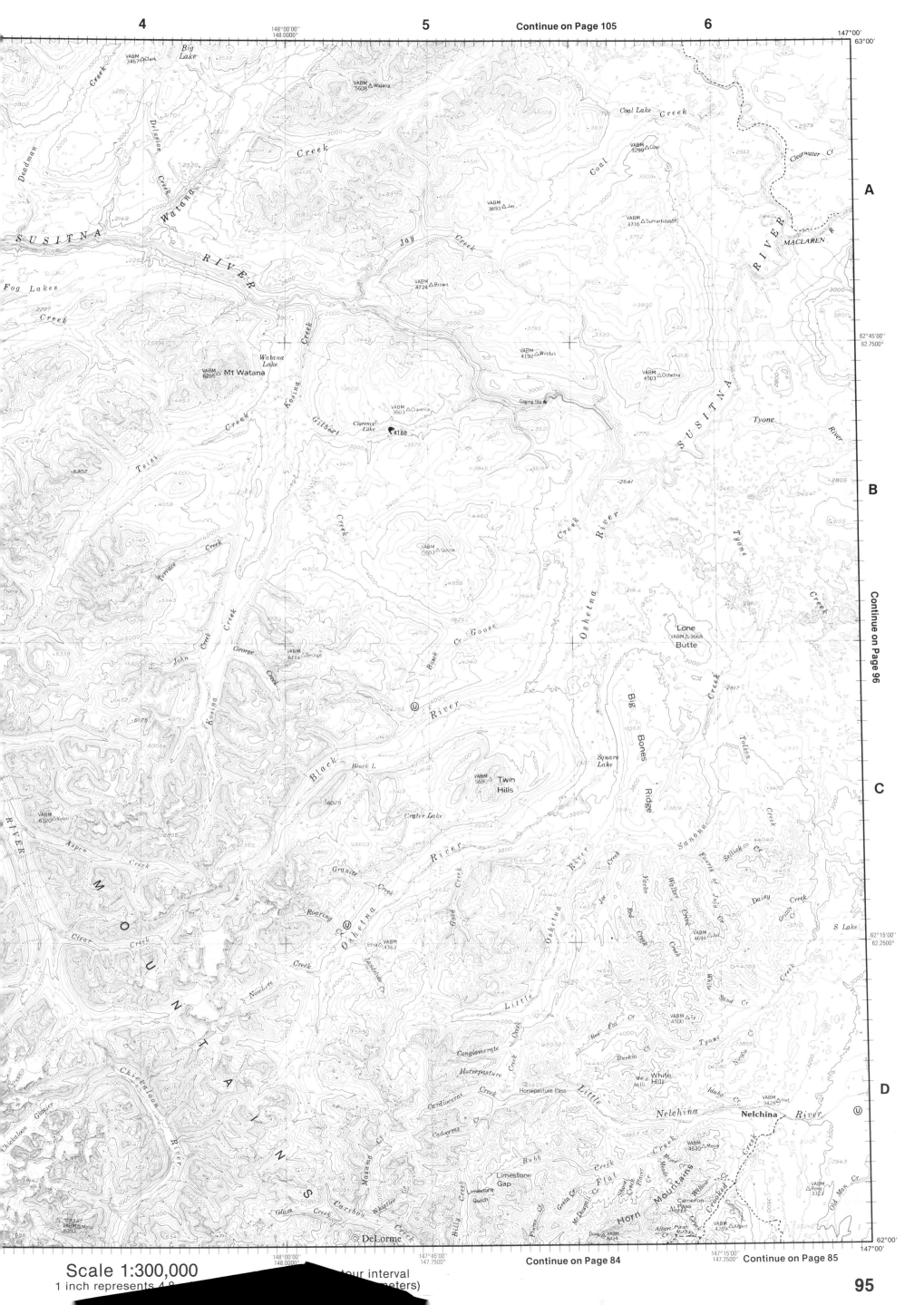

Continue on Page 96

Continue on Page 84   Continue on Page 85

Scale 1:300,000
1 inch represents 4.8

Contour interval

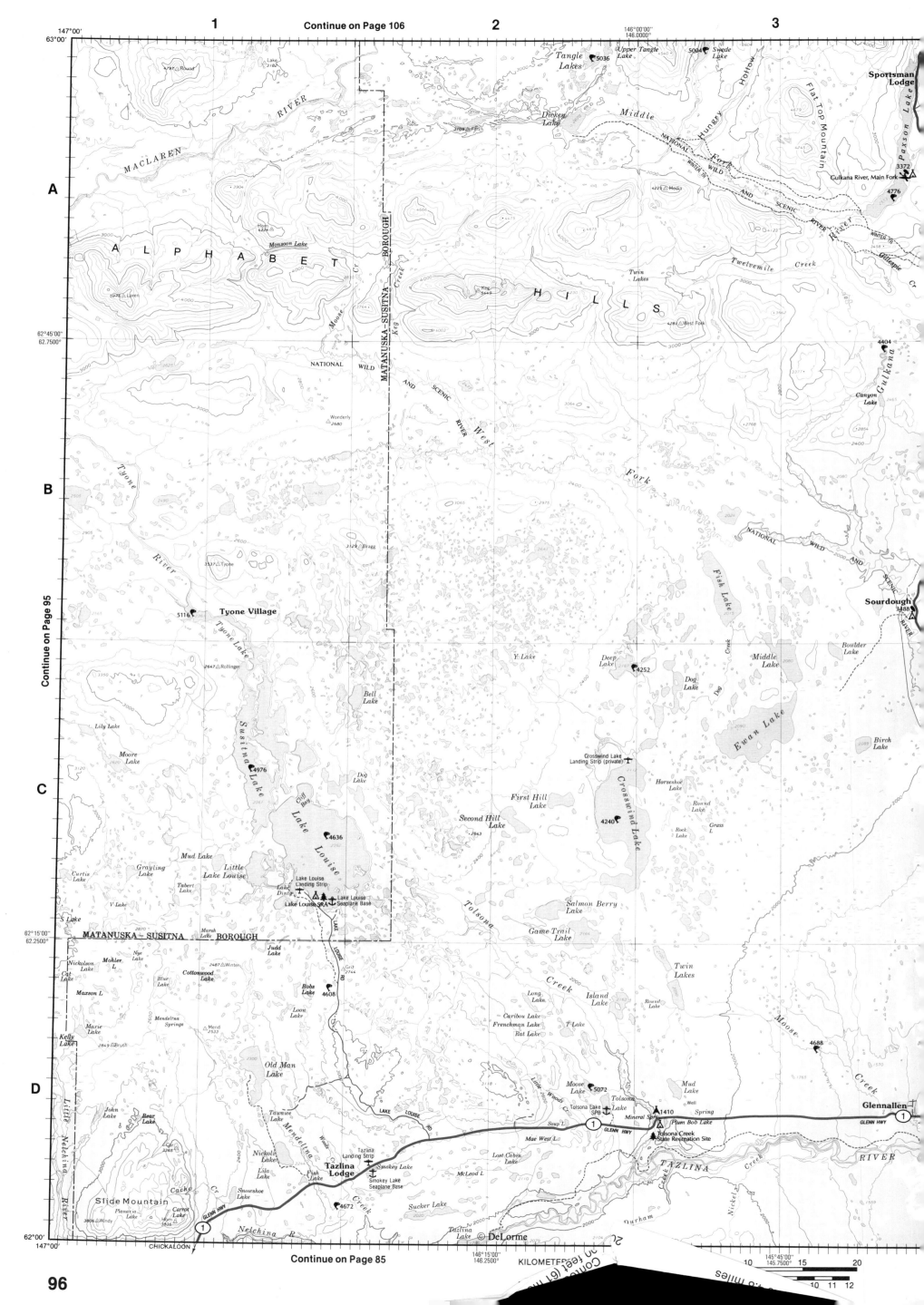

147°00'
63°00'

A

MACLAREN

ALPHABET

HILLS

Monsoon Lake

Keg Creek

NATIONAL WILD AND SCENIC RIVER

West Fork

Tangle Lakes

Upper Tangle Lake

Swede Lake

Sportsman Lodge

Gulkana River, Main Fork

Dickey Lake

Middle Fork

Hungry Hollow

Flat Top Mountain

Paxson Lake

Twelvemile Creek

Gillespie Cr

Twin Lakes

62°45'00"
62.7500°

4404

Gulkana River

Canyon Lake

B

Tyone River

Tyone Village

5116

Tyone Lake

Rollinger

Susitna Lake

NATIONAL WILD AND SCENIC RIVER

Fish Lake

Sourdough

3488

Boulder Lake

Middle Lake

Deep Lake

Dog Lake

Ewan Lake

Birch Lake

Continue on Page 95

Bell Lake

Y Lake

Lily Lake

Moore Lake

Dog Lake

Cliff Bay

Lake Louise

Crosswind Lake Landing Strip (private)

First Hill Lake

Second Hill Lake

Crosswind Lake

Horseshoe Lake

Round Lake

Grass L

Rock Lake

C

Curtis Lake

Grayling Lake

Mud Lake

Little Lake Louise

Tabert Lake

V Lake

Lake Dinty

Lake Louise Landing Strip

Lake Louise SRA

Lake Louise Seaplane Base

Tolsona

Salmon Berry Lake

Game Trail Lake

62°15'00"
62.2500°

MATANUSKA - SUSITNA BOROUGH

Marsh Lake

Judd Lake

S Lake

Nickolson Lake

Mohler L

Nye Lake

Blue Lake

Cottonwood Lake

Winter

Bob Lake

4608

Creek

Twin Lakes

Long Lake

Island Lake

Round Lake

Cat Lake

Maxson L

Loon Lake

Mendeltna Springs

Mend

Caribou Lake

Frenchman Lake

Rat Lake

T Lake

Moose Creek

Marie Lake

Brush

Kelly Lake

Old Man Lake

Little Woods

Moose Lake

5072

Mud Lake

Spring

4688

D

Little Nelchina River

John Lake

Bear Lake

Tavenire Lake

Mendeltna Creek

Nickoli Lake

Lila Lake

LAKE LOUISE RD

Tolsona Lake SPB

Tolsona Lake

1410

Well

Mineral Spring

Plum Bob Lake

Tolsona Creek State Recreation Site

Soup L

Mae West L

Lost Cabin Lake

GLENN HWY

Glennallen

GLENN HWY

1

TAZLINA

RIVER

Slide Mountain

Cache Cr

Carrot Lake

Planavin Lake

Windy

Tazlina Landing Strip

Fish Lake

Snowshoe Lake

Smokey Lake

Smokey Lake Seaplane Base

McLeod L

Sucker Lake

Nickel Creek

Durham Creek

Tazlina Lodge

62°00'
147°00'

CHICKALOON

Nelchina R.

4672

Tazlina Lake © DeLorme

146°15'00"
146.2500°

KILOMETERS

145°45'00"
145.7500°

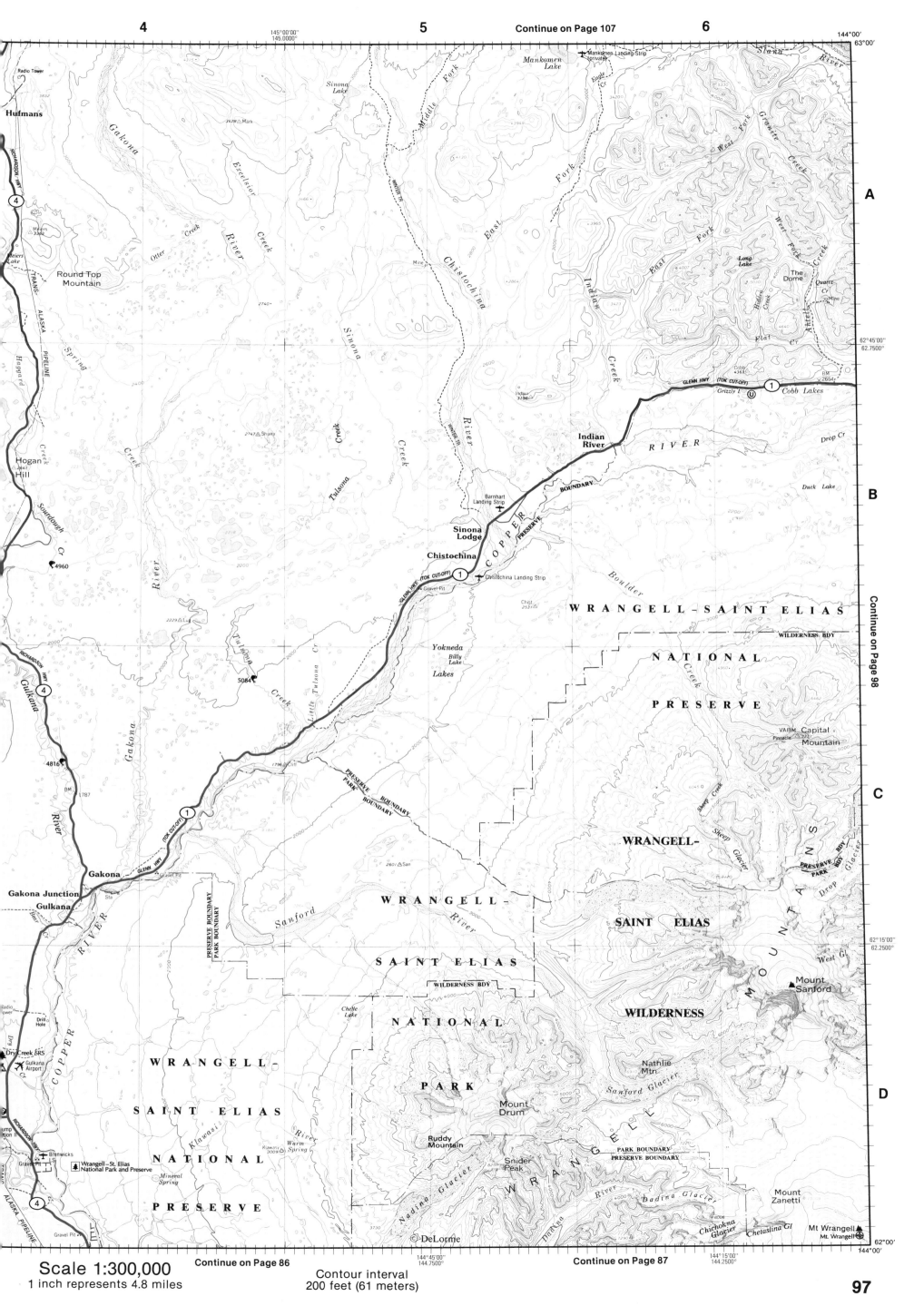

145°00'00''
145.0000°

144°00'
63°00'

A

62°45'00''
62.7500°

B

Hufmans

Radio Tower

Meiers
Lake
3832

Round Top
Mountain

Hogan
Hill
3647

4960

Gakona

Otter

Excelsior

Creek

River

Creek

River

Sourdough   Cr

TRANS-
ALASKA
PIPELINE

RICHARDSON HWY

4

Gakona

River

2229 Lua

5084

Tulsona

Creek

River

Spring

Creek

Creek

Creek

Tulsona

Sinona
Lake

2678 Mark

2740

2747 Shuna

Little Tulsona   Cr

Sinona

Creek

WHITE TR.

Chistochina

Middle

East

Fork

Fork

WINTER TR.

River

Barnhart
Landing Strip

Sinona
Lodge

Chistochina

GLENN HWY. (TOK CUT-OFF)

1

Gravel Pit

Chistochina Landing Strip

Indian
River

Indian
3298

2600

Indian

Mankomen
Lake

Mankomen Landing Strip
(private)

Eagle
Cr

Stann

River

Grizzly L

GLENN HWY. (TOK CUT-OFF)

1

Cobb Lakes
BM
2654

Cobb
4363

West Fork

Indian

Creek

RIVER

PRESERVE

BOUNDARY

COPPER

Boulder

Chet
2531

Long
Lake

The
Dome

Hidden Cr

Quartz
Cr
Mine

Ahtell

Creek

Drop Cr

Duck Lake

Flat   Cr

5332

West Fork

Granite   Creek

4256

WRANGELL-SAINT ELIAS

WILDERNESS BDY

NATIONAL

PRESERVE

VABM Capital
Pinnacle   Mountain

Sheep   Creek

Sheep
Glacier

PRESERVE PARK BDY

Drop   Glacier

62°15'00''
62.2500°

C

62°00'
144°00'

D

4

4

4816
BM
1787

Gulkana

River

RICHARDSON HWY

COPPER

RIVER

1

Gakona

Gakona Junction

Gulkana

Gravel Rd

GLENN HWY.

(TOK CUT-OFF)

Service
Sta.

PRESERVE BOUNDARY
PARK BOUNDARY

Yokneda
Billy
Lake
Lakes

2601 △San

PRESERVE   PARK
PARK   BOUNDARY
BOUNDARY

1796 △ Cliff

1

WRANGELL-

SAINT ELIAS

WILDERNESS BDY

Sanford

River

Chelle
Lake

NATIONAL

PARK

Mount
Drum

Ruddy
Mountain

Radio
Tower

Drill
Hole

Dry Creek SRS

Gulkana
Airport

Bear   Cr

Pump
Junction

RICHARDSON HWY

ALASKA
PIPELINE

Brenwicks
LS

Gravel Pit

4

Gravel Pit

Klawasi   River

Klawasi
3009

Warm
Spring

Klawasi

WRANGELL-

SAINT   ELIAS

NATIONAL

PRESERVE

Wrangell–St. Elias
National Park and Preserve

Mineral
Spring

Chitina

River

Nadina   Glacier

Snider
Peak

WRANGELL-

SAINT ELIAS

Nathlie
Mtn

Sanford   Glacier

WILDERNESS

Mount
Sanford

West Gl

MOUNTAINS

Sanford Glacier

PARK BOUNDARY
PRESERVE BOUNDARY

WRANGELL

Dadina   Glacier

River

Chichokna
Glacier

Chetaslina Gl

© DeLorme

Mount
Zanetti

Mt Wrangell ▲
Mt. Wrangell

3770

7790

Continue on Page 98

Continue on Page 86

Continue on Page 87

Scale 1:300,000
1 inch represents 4.8 miles

Contour interval
200 feet (61 meters)

144°45'00''
144.7500°

144°15'00''
144.2500°

1   2   3

144°00'   63°00'

TOK

143°00'00"
143.0000°

Meiklejohn
Pass

A

Mentasta
Lake

BM 2280

Mentasta Pass

GLENN HWY (TOK CUTOFF)

Forty
BM 2137

Mineral
Lake

M E N T A S T A

Indian
Pass

GLENN HWY (TOK CUTOFF)

Suslosina Creek

Suslota
Pass

Mineral Cairn

Tok River

Buck Creek

Tuck Creek

Moose Creek

Mice Creek

Bear Cr

River

62°45'00"
62.7500°

Porcupine Creek
State Recreation Site

**Duffys
Tavern**

Carlson
Lake

Suslota
Lake

Suslota

Susitna River

Bear
Lake

Bean
Lake

M O U N T A I N S

B

Slana
Copper River

Nabesna Road

Rufus Creek

Copper River

Batzulnetas

PRESERVE BDY
PARK BDY

Caribou Cr

NABESNA RD

Old Suslota (Site)

Suslota Creek

Noyes
Mountain

PRESERVE BDY

PRESERVE BDY

GLENNALLEN

Drop Creek

Tanada Creek

Gravel
Pit

Rock
Creek

Long Lake

Gravel
Pit

Little Jack Creek

Peggy
Lake

Lost Cr

Chulk Creek

Big
Grayling
Lake

Karen
Lake

Soda Cr Spr

Soda
Lake

Platinum

Totschunda Creek

W R A N G E L L -

SAINT ELIAS

NATIONAL

PRESERVE

WILDERNESS   BOUNDARY

Boomerang
Lake

Jack Lake

Sportsman's Paradise
Landing Strip
(private)

Boyden Creek

B o y d e n   H i l l s

Jack Creek

NABESNA RD

Gillam
Lake

Punk
Lake

Jimmy
Brown L

R I V E R

C

PRESERVE BOUNDARY
PARK BOUNDARY

Drop Glacier

West Glacier

Copper River

Copper Lake

N A T I O N A L   P A R K

4212

5032

Tanada
Lake

Bob
5679

Devils Mountain Lodge
Landing Strip (private)

Skookum Cr

WINTER

Cabin
Mine Cr

**Devils
Mountain**

**Devils
Mountain Lodge**

White
Mtd

Nabesna

Raven Hills

Windy
Lake

Virginia
Lake

Camp Creek

Copper Cr

Nimente

WRANGELL - SAINT ELIAS

Goat Creek

Whitham L

Gold
Hill

Keenan
Pk

Blue
Creek

62°15'00"
62.2500°

Tanada
Peak

PARK   BOUNDARY
PRESERVE   AND   WILDERNESS

PRESERVE BDY

Wait Creek

Caribou Creek

W R A N G E L L -

Sheep
Lake

Fish Creek

NABESNA

N A B E S N A

S A I N T   E L I A S

Whit L

Orange Hill
Landing Strip
(private)

Orange
Hill

East Fk

D

Copper Glacier

PRESERVE PARK BOUNDARY

Grizzly
Lake

Jacksina Creek

Jaeger Mesa

Monte Cristo Creek

Mt Gordon

Cone   Ridge

Mend Creek

GLACIER

Nikonda Glacier

Stone Creek

Middle Fk

Nikonda Creek

South Fk

WILDERNESS   BOUNDARY

W R A N G E L L -

Tumble Creek

Jacksina Glacier

Lakes Plateau

WILDERNESS

Ice Fields Plateau

Cross Creek

Cross Glacier

SAINT ELIAS

Mt Jarvis

W R A N G E L L

East
Crater

M O U N T A I N S

© DeLorme

144°00'   62°00'

143°30'00"
143.5000°

143°15'00"
143.2500°

KILOMETERS   5   0   5   10   15   20

MILES   1 0 1 2 3 4 5 6 7 8 9 10 11 12

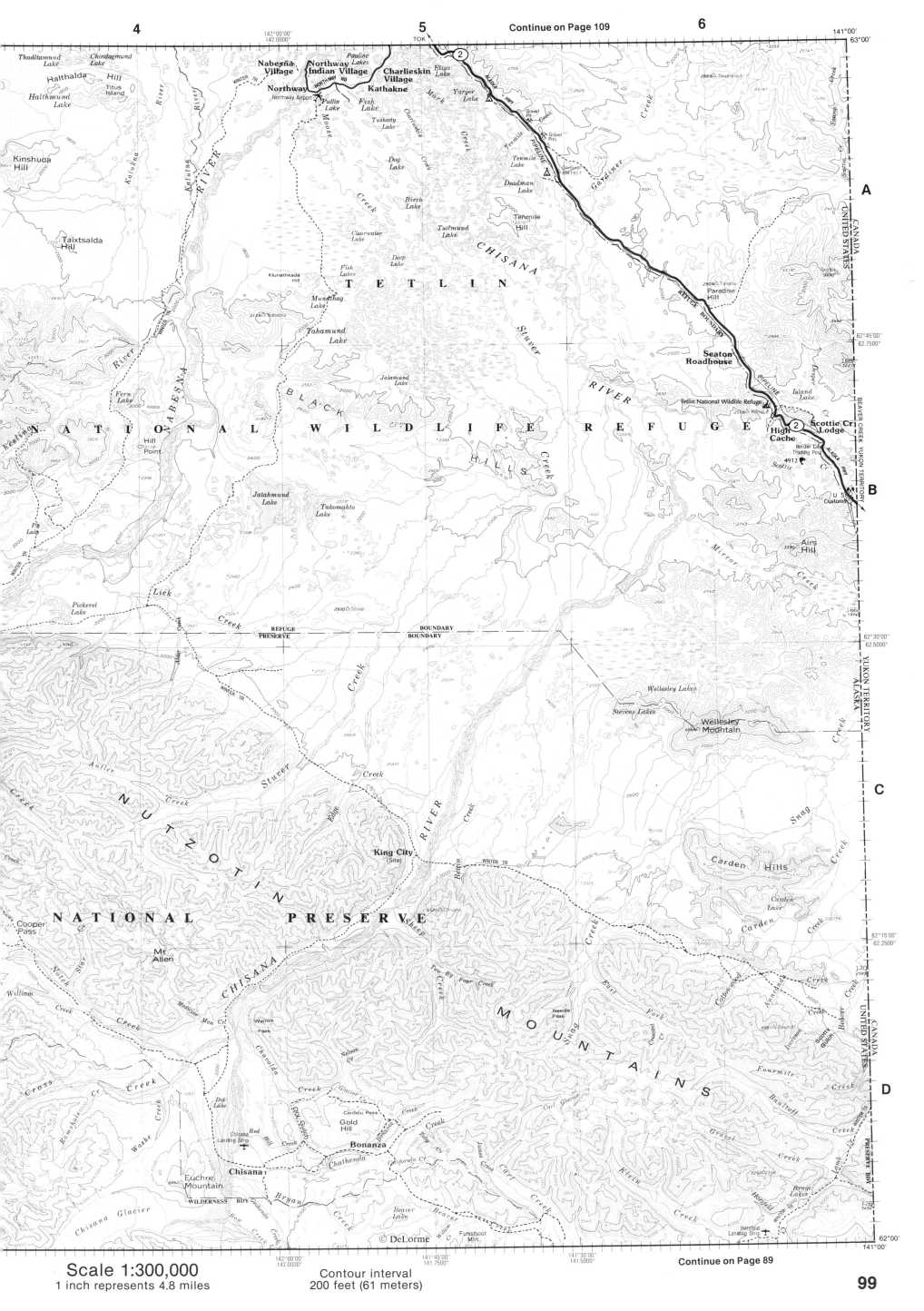

Continue on Page 89

Scale 1:300,000
1 inch represents 4.8 miles

Contour interval
200 feet (61 meters)

© DeLorme

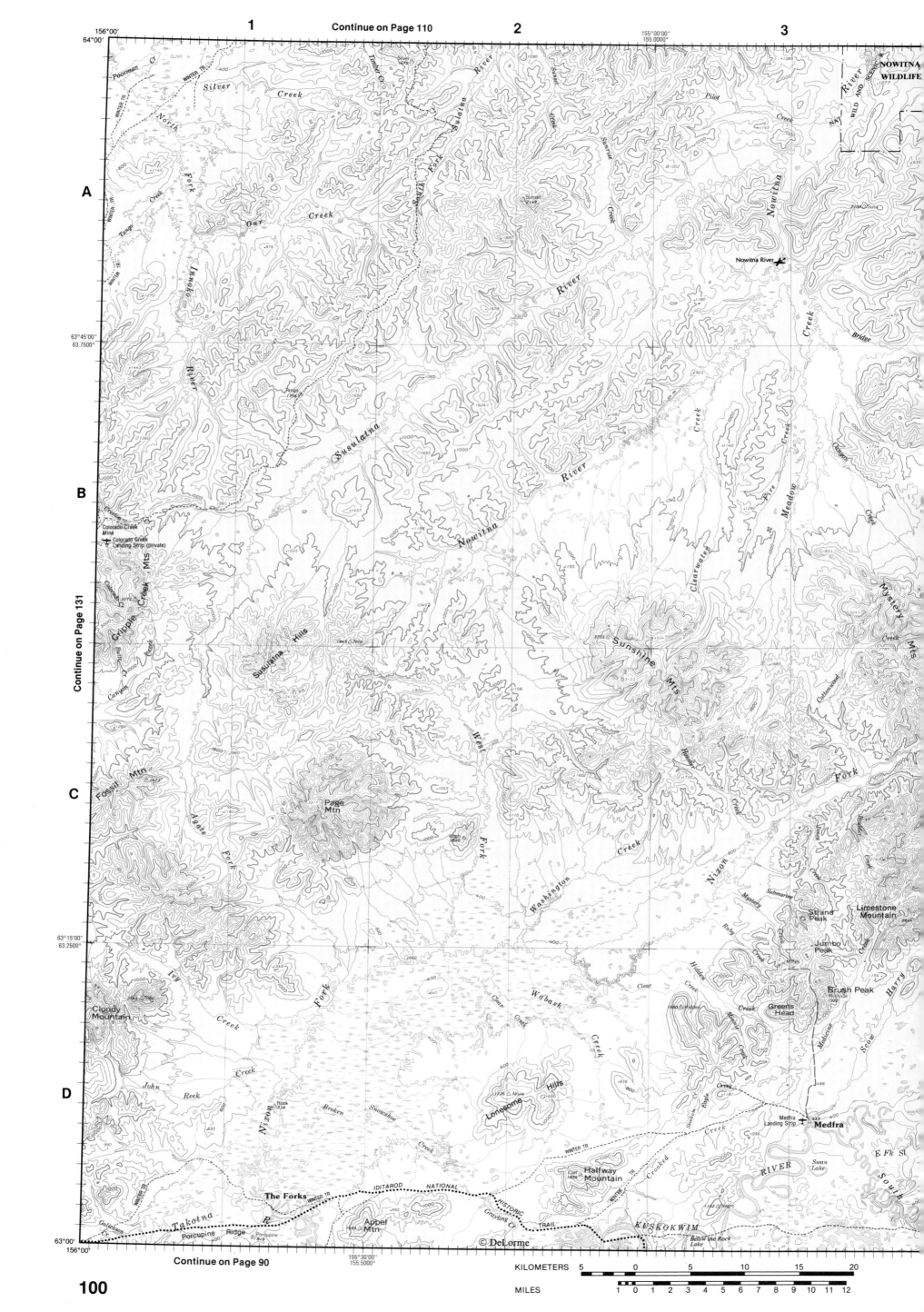

156°00'
64°00'

A

63°45'00''
63.7500°

B

Continue on Page 131

C

63°15'00''
63.2500°

D

63°00'
156°00'

155°30'00''
155.5000°

100

© DeLorme

155°00'00''
155.0000°

KILOMETERS   5   0   5   10   15   20

MILES   1 0 1 2 3 4 5 6 7 8 9 10 11 12

NOWITNA
WILDLIFE

Colorado Creek
Mine
Colorado Creek
Landing Strip (private)

Fossil Mtn

Susulatna Hills

Page Mtn

Sunshine Mts

Cloudy Mountain

Lonesome Hills

Halfway Mountain

The Forks

Appel Mtn

Medfra Landing Strip   Medfra

Greens Head

Brush Peak

Jumbo Peak

Limestone Mountain

Strand Peak

IDITAROD NATIONAL HISTORIC TRAIL

KUSKOKWIM

RIVER

Swan Lake

Below the Rock Lake

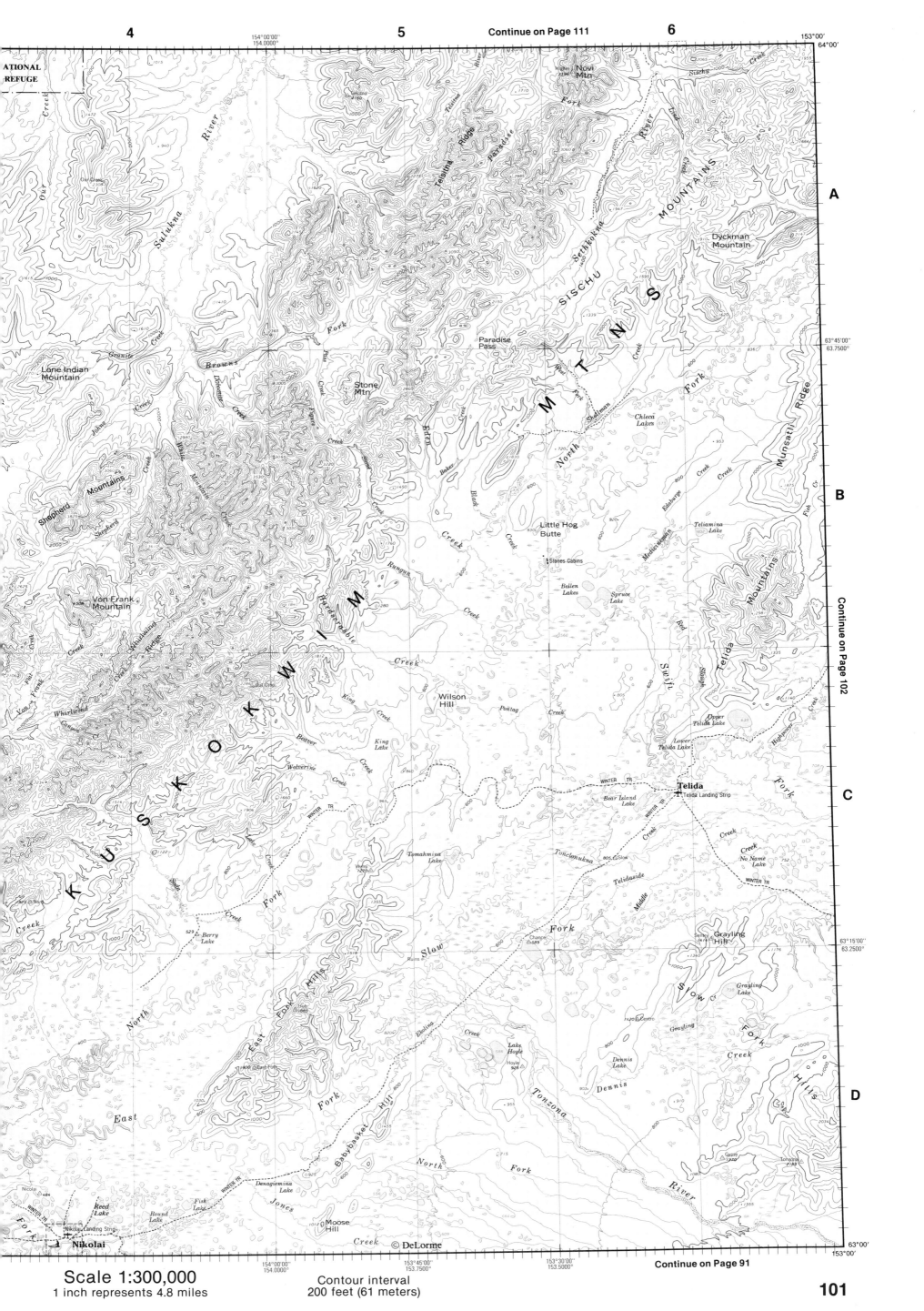

Continue on Page 102

Continue on Page 91

Scale 1:300,000
1 inch represents 4.8 miles

Contour interval
200 feet (61 meters)

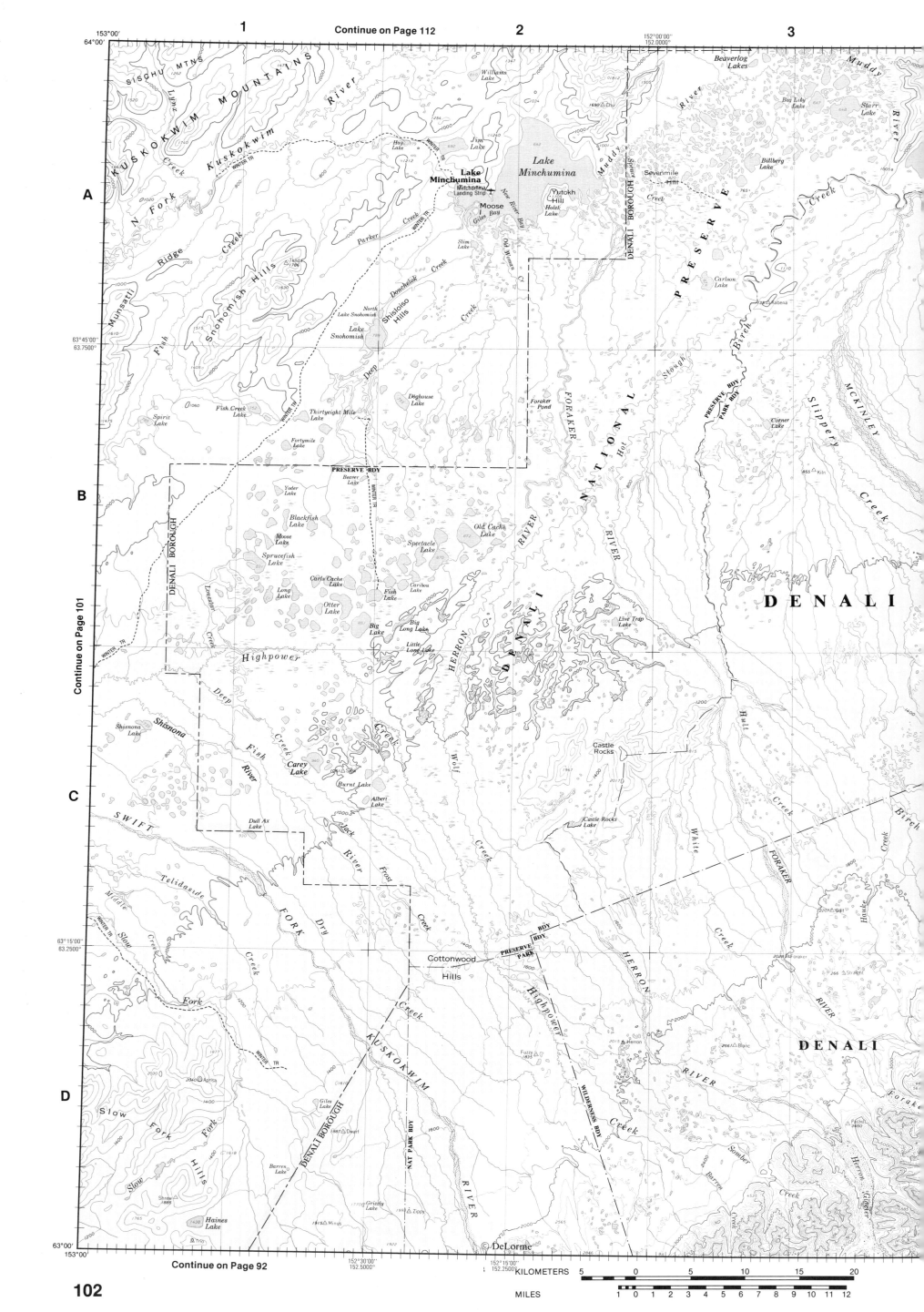

Continue on Page 101

Continue on Page 92

© DeLorme

102

KILOMETERS 5 0 5 10 15 20

MILES

DENALI NATIONAL PRESERVE

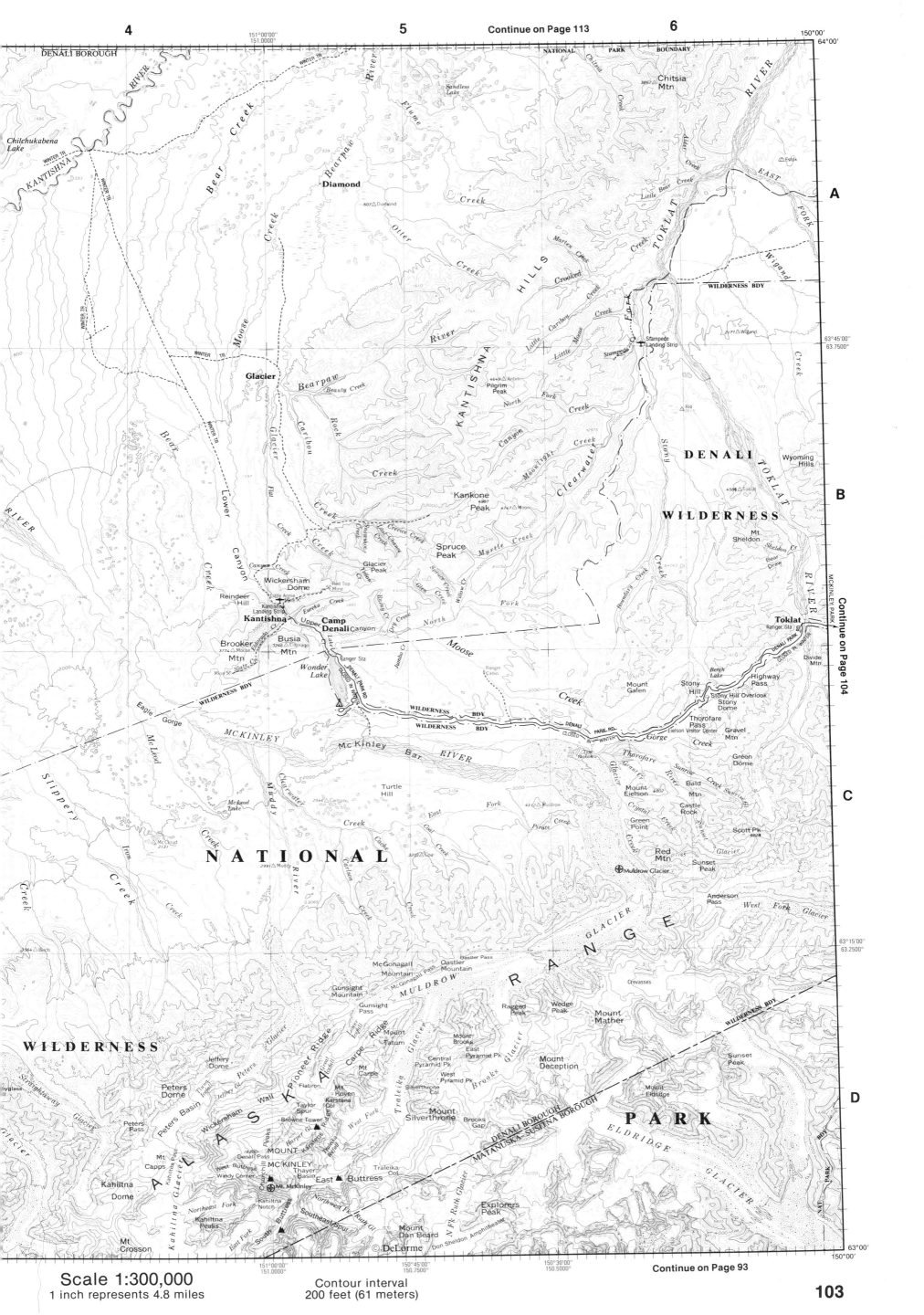

151°00'00"
151.0000°

150°00'
64°00'

DENALI BOROUGH

Chilchukabena Lake

KANTISHNA

RIVER

Bear Creek

Bearpaw Creek

Otter Creek

Diamond

607 △ Diamond

Sandless Lake

Flume

River

NATIONAL PARK BOUNDARY

3862 △ Chitsia Mtn

EAST FORK

RIVER

△ Esdox

TOKLAT

Little Bear Creek

A

Martin Creek

Crooked Creek

Caribou Creek

WILDERNESS BDY

2171 △ Wigand

Wigand

Glacier

Bearpaw

Beauty Creek

Rock Creek

Caribou Creek

Moose Creek

Lower

Glacier

Flat

WINTER TR

Bear Creek

Canyon

Pilgrim Peak

North Fork

Moonlight Creek

Clearwater

Creek

Stony

Fork

Little Caribou Moose Creek

Stampede Landing Strip

Stampede

63°45'00"
63.7500°

DENALI TOKLAT

B

Wyoming Hills

4987 Kankone Peak

4747 △ Moon

△ Toklat

WILDERNESS

Mt Sheldon

Sheldon Cr

Bear Draw

Crevice Creek

Spruce Peak

Myrtle Creek

Spring Creek

Glacier Peak

Glen Creek

Willow Cr

North Fork

River

RIVER

MCKINLEY PARK

Wickersham Dome

Red Top Mine

Kantishna Landing Strip

Eureka Creek

Kantishna

Upper

Camp Denali Canyon

Boyd Cr

Jumbo Cr

Moose Creek

Toklat
Ranger Sta

Reindeer Hill

Brooker Mtn

3774 △ Moose

Busia Mtn

3246 △ Elspraqo

Ranger Sta

Ranger Cabin

DENALI PARK

Divide Mtn

Continue on Page 104

Slate Cr

Wonder Lake

DENALI PARK RD

CLOSED IN WINTER

Creek

Bergh Lake

Mount Galen

Stony Hill

Highway Pass

WILDERNESS BDY

Eagle Gorge

McLeod

MCKINLEY

WILDERNESS BDY

WILDERNESS BDY

Stony Hill Overlook
Stony Dome

Thorofare Pass

Eielson Visitor Center

DENALI PARK RD CLOSED IN WINTER

Gorge

Gravel Mtn

Green Dome

C

Slippery

McLeod

Muddy

Clearwater Creek

McKinley Bar RIVER

2544 △ Caribou

Turtle Hill

East Fork

Pirate Creek

Thorofare River

Grant Creek

Bald Mtn

Castle Rock

Sunrise Creek

Sunset

Scott Pk
6828

Iron Creek

2131 △ McCloud

2997 △ Muddy

Cache Creek

Carlson

Creek

Coal Creek

1202 △ Coal

434 △ Muldrow

Mount Eielson
3802

Crystal Creek

Green Point

Red Mtn

Muldrow Glacier

Sunset Peak

Creek

△ Birch

Carlson Creek

GLACIER

RANGE

Anderson Pass

West Fork Glacier

63°15'00"
63.2500°

NATIONAL

McGonagall Mountain

Oastler Mountain

McGonagall Pass

MULDROW

Gunsight Mountain

Gunsight Pass

Baster Pass

Crevasses

Ragged Peak

Wedge Peak

Mount Mather

WILDERNESS BDY

Sunset Peak

D

WILDERNESS

Jeffery Dome

Peters Glacier

Pioneer Ridge

Lindley Ridge

Mt Carpe

Carpe Ridge

Karstens

Brooks Glacier

Mount Tatum

Mount Brooks

East Pyramid Pk

Central Pyramid Pk

West Pyramid Pk

Traleika Glacier

Brooks Gap

Mount Deception

DENALI BOROUGH

MATANUSKA-SUSITNA BOROUGH

Mount Eldridge

PARK

ELDRIDGE

Peters Dome

Peters Basin

Wickersham Wall

Jeffery Gl

ALASKA

Taylor Spur

Flatiron

Mt Koven

Browne Tower

Karstens Col

Harper Gl

Silverthrone Col

Mount Silverthrone

GLACIER

Straightaway Gl

Glass Gl

Peters Pass

Mt Capps

Denali Pass

West Buttress

MOUNT

McKINLEY

Thayer Basin

Traleika Col

Kahiltna Dome

Kahiltna Pass

Windy Corner

△ Mt McKinley

Kahiltna Peaks

Kahiltna Notch

Northeast Fork

East Buttress

Northwest Fk Ruth Gl

Mount Dan Beard

Explorers Peak

Mt Crosson

East Fork

Southeast Spur

South Buttress

Don Sheldon Amphitheater

© DeLorme

63°00'
150°00'

Continue on Page 93

Scale 1:300,000
1 inch represents 4.8 miles

151°00'00"
151.0000°

150°45'00"
150.7500°

150°30'00"
150.5000°

Contour interval
200 feet (61 meters)

103

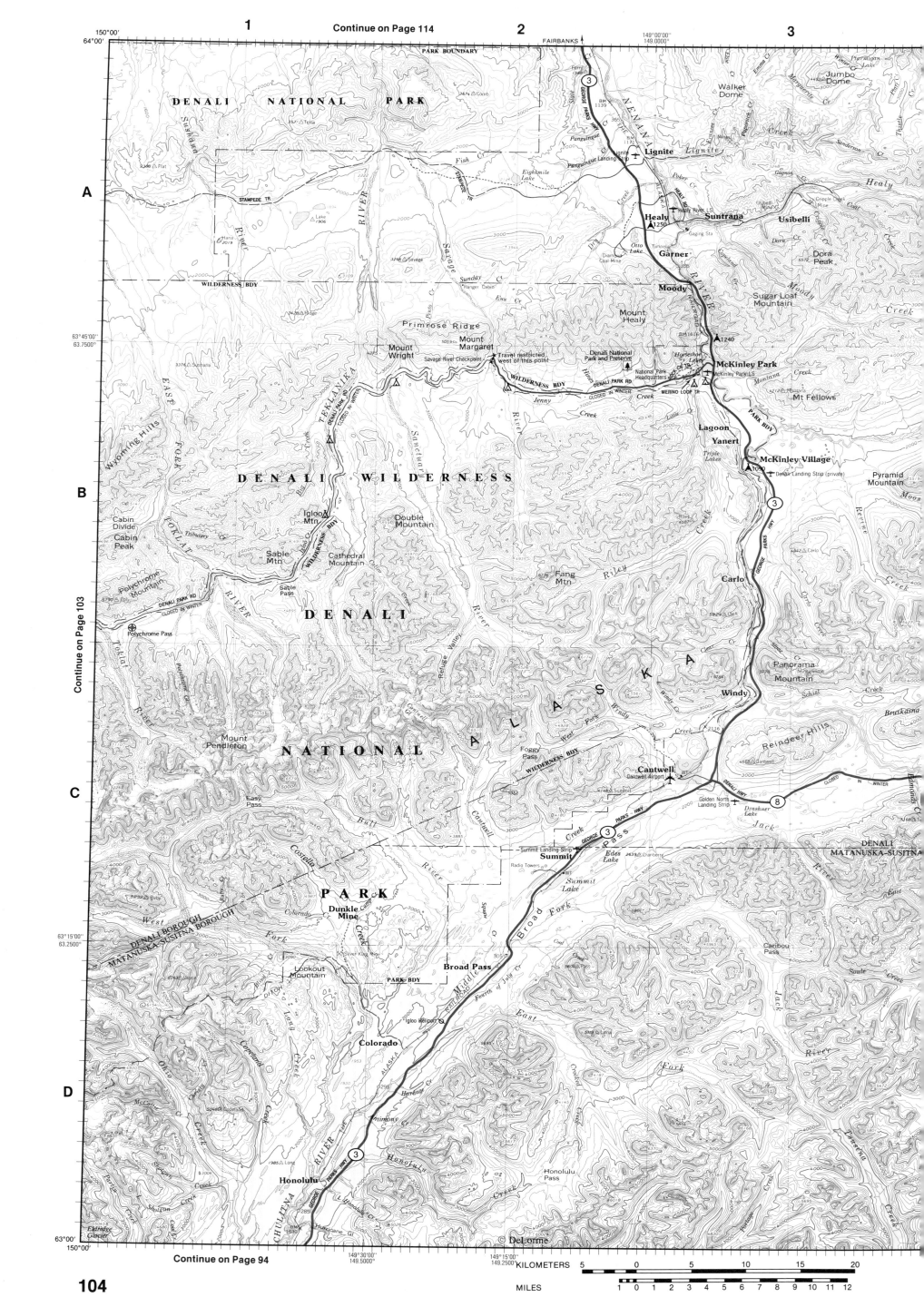

150°00'
64°00'

FAIRBANKS

149°00'00"
149.0000'

DENALI NATIONAL PARK

PARK BOUNDARY

A

Lignite

Walker Dome

Jumbo Dome

Healy

Suntrana

Usibelli

Garner

Dora Peak

Moody

Sugar Loaf Mountain

63°45'00"
63.7500'

Primrose Ridge

Mount Wright

Mount Margaret

Travel restricted west of this point

Savage River Checkpoint

Denali National Park and Preserve

National Park Headquarters

McKinley Park

WILDERNESS BDY

DENALI PARK RD

CLOSED IN WINTER

MERINO LOOP TR

Mount Healy

Lagoon

Yanert

McKinley Village

Denali Landing Strip (private)

Pyramid Mountain

B

DENALI WILDERNESS

Cabin Divide

Cabin Peak

Igloo Mtn

Double Mountain

Sable Mtn

Cathedral Mountain

Sable Pass

Fang Mtn

Carlo

Polychrome Mountain

DENALI PARK RD

CLOSED IN WINTER

DENALI

Polychrome Pass

Panorama Mountain

Windy

Reindeer Hills

Bruskasna

C

Mount Pendleton

NATIONAL

Foggy Pass

West Fork

WILDERNESS BDY

Cantwell

Cantwell Airport

Golden North Landing Strip

Drashner Lake

DENALI HWY

CLOSED IN WINTER

8

**DENALI
MATANUSKA-SUSITNA**

Easy Pass

Summit Landing Strip

Summit

Edes Lake

Cranberry

63°15'00"
63.2500'

PARK

Dunkle Mine

DENALI BOROUGH
MATANUSKA-SUSITNA BOROUGH

Colorado

Silver King Mine

Lookout Mountain

PARK BDY

Summit Lake

Broad Pass

Broad Fork

Caribou Pass

Igloo Heliport

Colorado

D

63°00'
150°00'

Honolulu

Honolulu Pass

© DeLorme

Continue on Page 103

Continue on Page 94

149°30'00"
149.5000'

149°15'00"
149.2500'

KILOMETERS   5   0   5   10   15   20

MILES   1 0 1 2 3 4 5 6 7 8 9 10 11 12

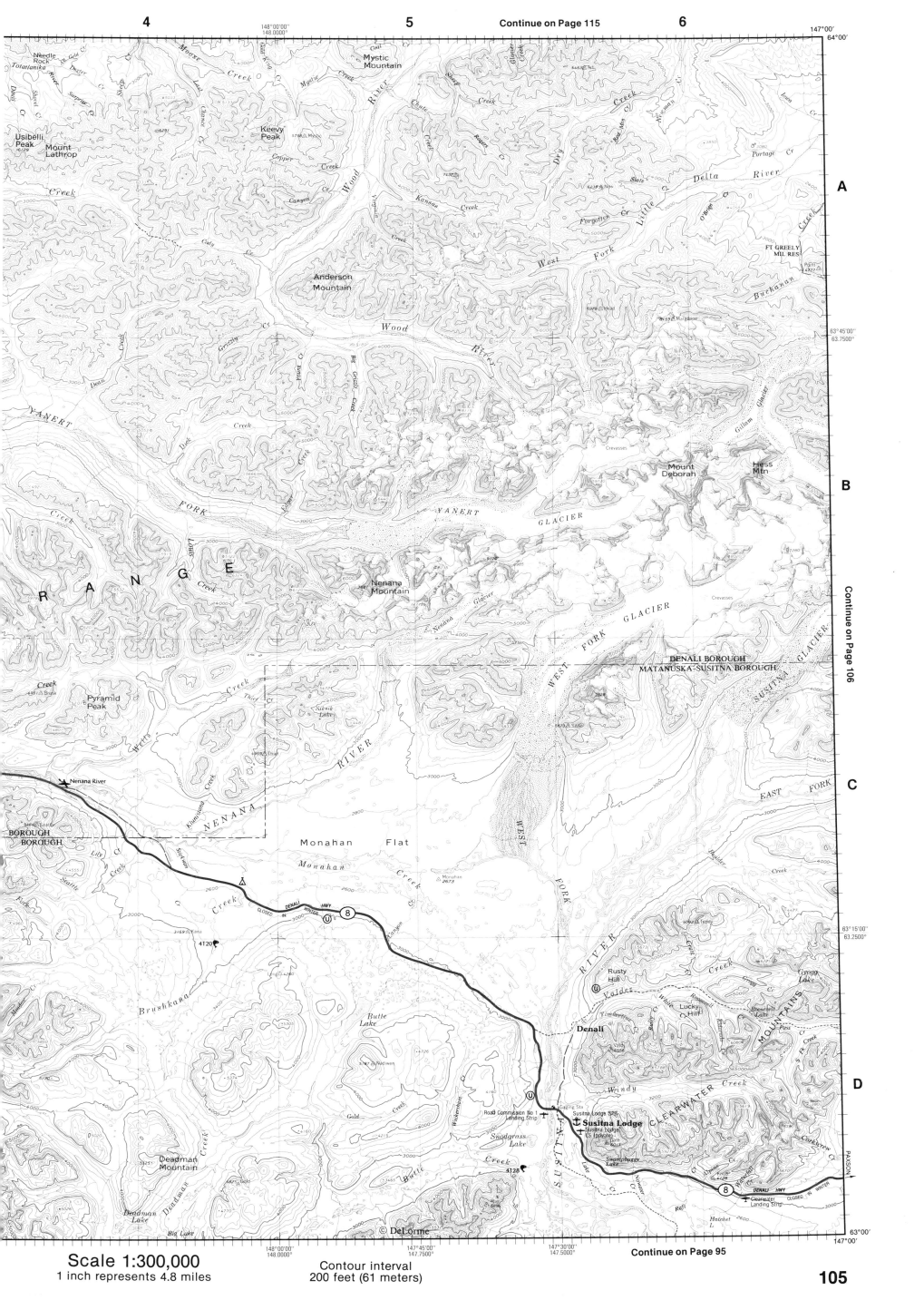

Continue on Page 106

Continue on Page 95

Scale 1:300,000
1 inch represents 4.8 miles

Contour interval
200 feet (61 meters)

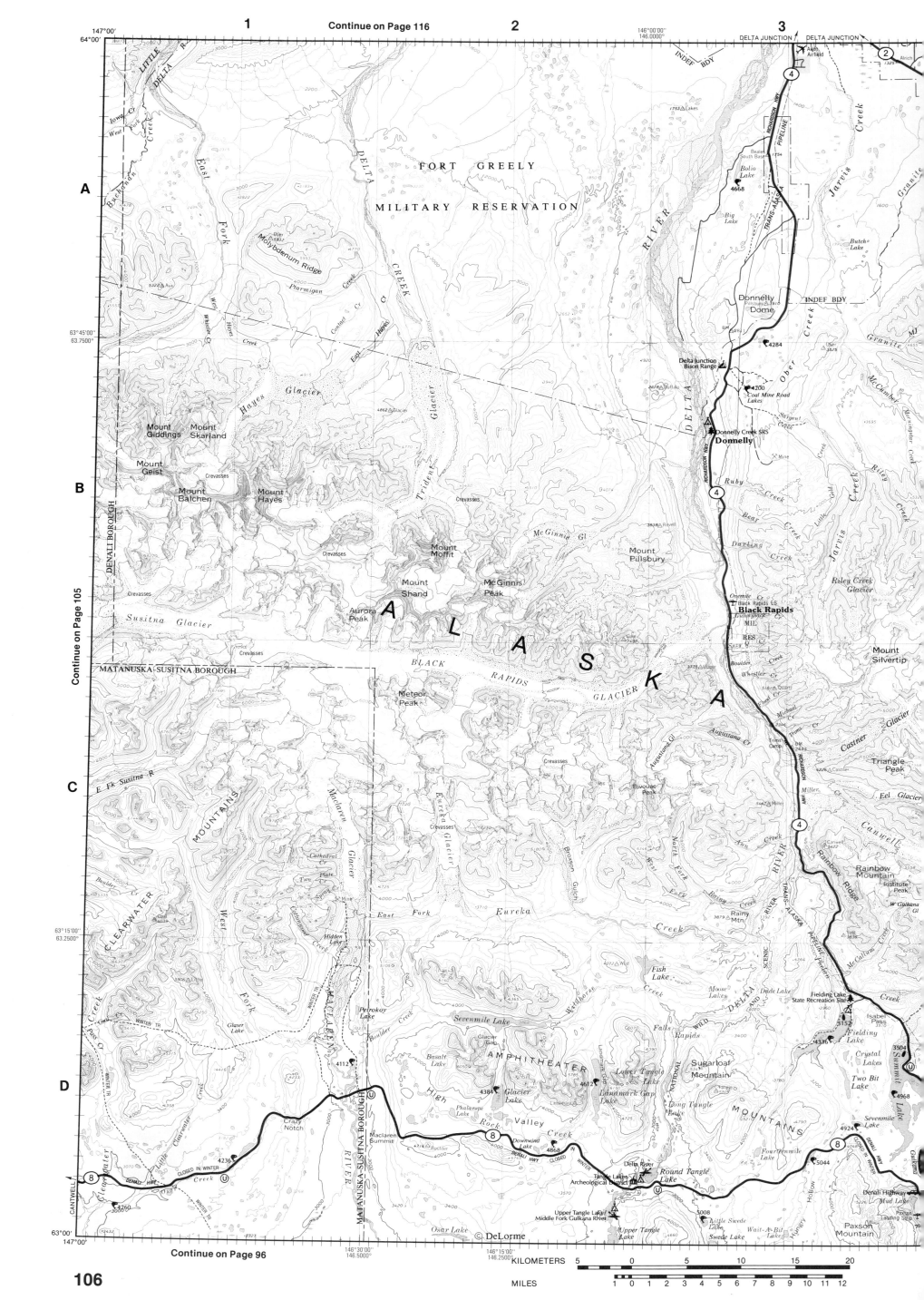

FORT GREELY

MILITARY RESERVATION

Molybdenum Ridge

Ptarmigan

Delta Junction
Bison Range

Coal Mine Road
Lakes

Donnelly Creek SRS
Donnelly

Hayes Glacier

Trident Glacier

Mount Giddings

Mount Skarland

Mount Geist

Mount Balchen

Mount Hayes

Crevasses

Mount Moffit

Mount Pilsbury

McGinnie Gl

Mount Shand

McGinnis Peak

Aurora Peak

Black Rapids LS
Black Rapids

Onemile

MIL
RES

A L A S K A

Susitna Glacier

Crevasses

Mount Silvertip

Continue on Page 105

DENALI BOROUGH

MATANUSKA-SUSITNA BOROUGH

BLACK RAPIDS GLACIER

Meteor Peak

Bivouac Peak

Augustana Gl

Augustana Cr

Triangle Peak

Castner Glacier

Eel Glacier

Canwell

MOUNTAINS

E Fk Susitna R

Maclaren Glacier

Eureka Glacier

Crevasses

Bronson Gulch

Rainbow Mountain

Rainbow Ridge

Institute Peak

Cathedral Mtn

Tiro

Plate Cr

Spruce Cr

Mine

West Fork

East Fork

Eureka

North Fork

West Fork

Rainy Cr

Rainy Mtn

W Gulkana Gl

Hidden Lake

Fish Lake

Moose Lakes

Dade Lake

Fielding Lake
State Recreation Site

Isabel Pass

Fielding Lake

Crystal Lakes

Summit

CLEARWATER

Petrokoy Lake

Glaser Lake

Sevenmile Lake

Glacier Lake

AMPHITHEATER

Sugarloaf Mountain

Two Bit Lake

Sevenmile Lake

Basalt Lake

Glacier Lake

Phalarope Lake

High Rock Valley

Lower Tangle Lake

Landmark Gap Lake

Long Tangle Lake

M O U N T A I N S

Fourmile Lake

Crazy Notch

Maclaren Summit

Downwind Lake

Delta River

Round Tangle Lake

Denali Highway
Mud Lake

WINTER TR

DENALI HWY

MACLAREN RIVER

MATANUSKA-SUSITNA BOROUGH

Tangle Lakes
Archeological District

Upper Tangle Lake
Middle Fork Gulkana River

Upper Tangle Lake

Little Swede Lake

Swede Lake

Wait-A-Bit Lake

Paxson Mountain

Osar Lake

© DeLorme

Hungry Hollow

Landing Strip

KILOMETERS   5   0   5   10   15   20

MILES   1 0 1 2 3 4 5 6 7 8 9 10 11 12

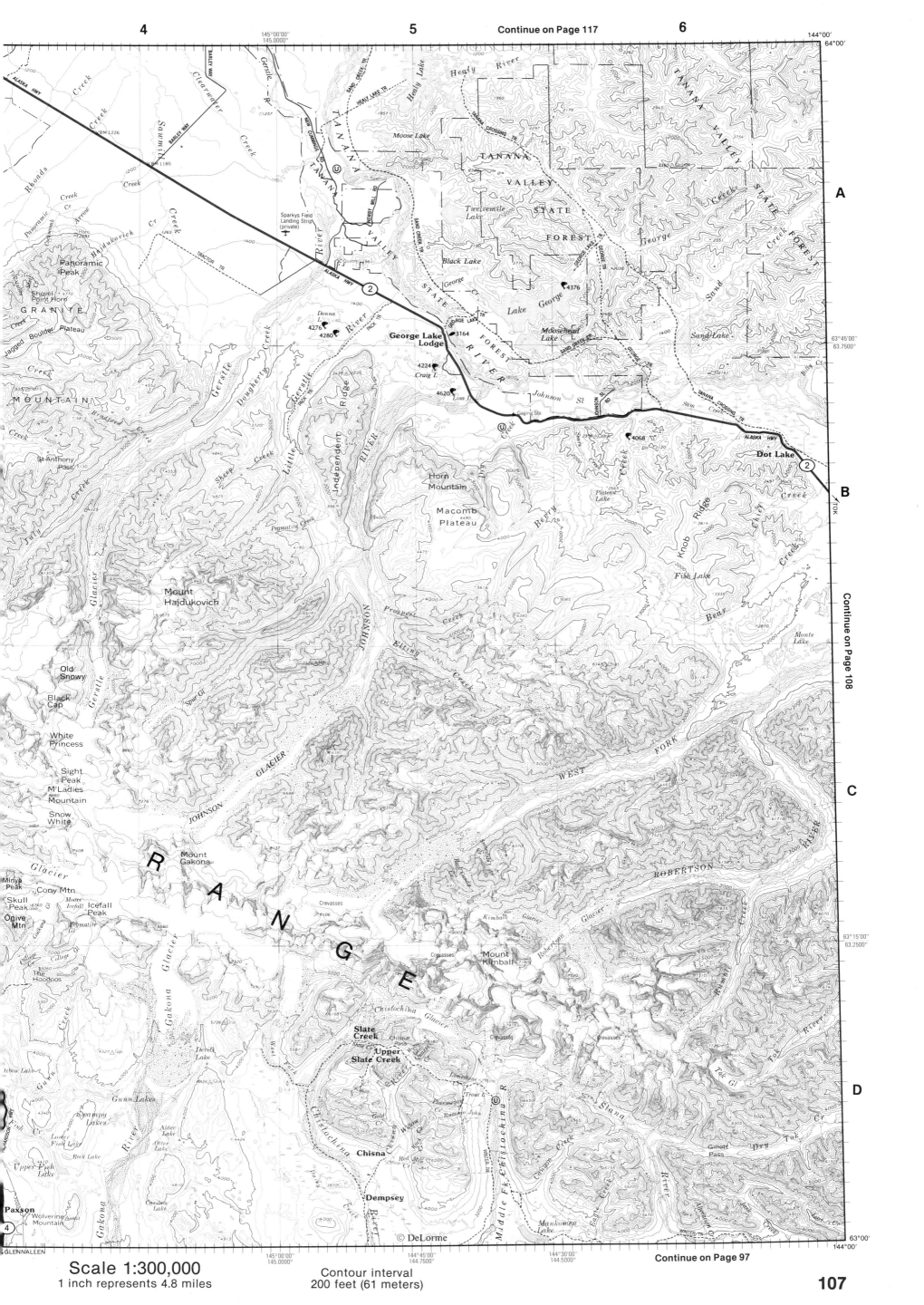

Scale 1:300,000
1 inch represents 4.8 miles

Contour interval
200 feet (61 meters)

Continue on Page 108

Continue on Page 97

107

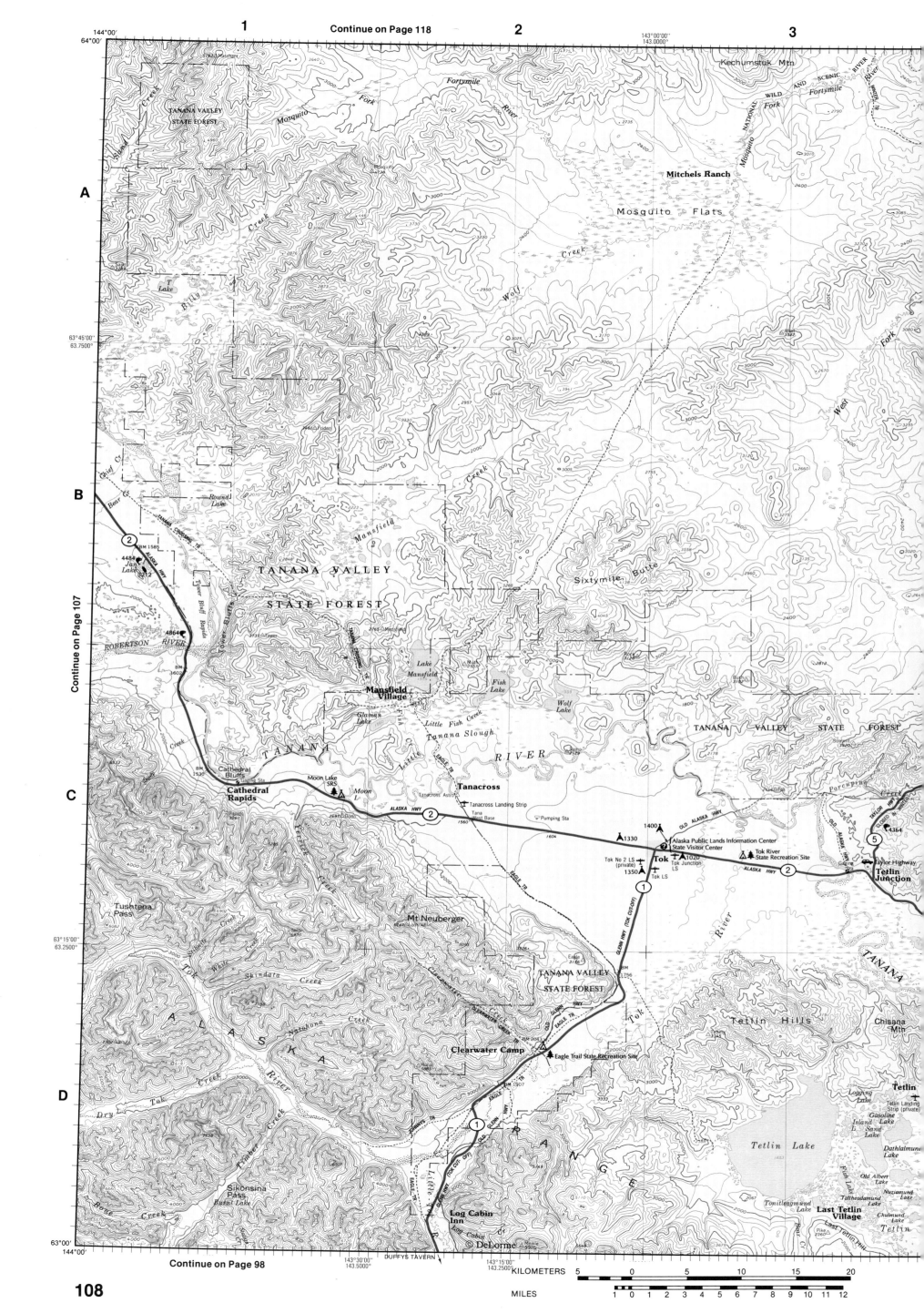

144°00'
64°00'

A

63°45'00'
63.7500°

Continue on Page 107

B

Kechumstuk Mtn

Mitchels Ranch

Mosquito Flats

Fortymile

Mosquito

Fork

Wolf

Creek

TANANA VALLEY STATE FOREST

T Lake

Billy

Creek

Chief Cr

Bear Cr

Round Lake

TANANA CROSSING TR

ALASKA HWY

BM 1585

2

4484 Jan Lake

ROBERTSON RIVER

4864

BM 1602

Tower Bluff Rapids

TANANA VALLEY

STATE FOREST

Mansfield

Mansfield Village

Lake Mansfield

Gilman Lake

Mud L

Fish Lake

Wolf Lake

Sixtymile Butte

TANANA VALLEY STATE FOREST

West Fork

C

BM 1520

Cathedral Bluffs

Cathedral Rapids

TANANA

Creek

Moon Lake SRS

Moon L

Little Tanana Slough

EAGLE TR

Tanacross

Tanacross Aston

Tanacross Landing Strip

Tana West Base

2

ALASKA HWY

Pumping Sta

RIVER

1400

1330

Alaska Public Lands Information Center
State Visitor Center

OLD ALASKA HWY

Tok River State Recreation Site

4364

5

Taylor Highway

Tetlin Junction

Tok No 2 LS (private)

1350

1020

Tok

Tok LS

Tok Junction LS

1

ALASKA HWY

2

Porcupine

Creek

TAYLOR HWY

63°15'00'
63.2500°

Tushtena Pass

Tok

White

Skindata Creek

Creek

Mt Neuberger

EAGLE TR

Eagle

GLENN HWY (TOK CUTOFF)

BM 1756

TANANA VALLEY STATE FOREST

Tok

River

Tetlin Hills

Chisana Mtn

TANANA

ALASKA

River

Natahona

Creek

CLEARWATER LAKES

OLD GLENN HWY

Clearwater Camp

Eagle Trail State Recreation Site

R

A

N

Tetlin Lake

Tetlin

Logging Lake

Tetlin Landing Strip (private)

Gasoline Lake

Sand Lake

Dathlalmund Lake

D

Dry Tok Cr

Timber Creek

Sikonsina Pass

Burnt Lake

Bone Creek

BM 1907

G

E

OLD GLENN HWY

EAGLE TR

TOK CUT OFF

Log Cabin Inn

© DeLorme

Last Tetlin Village

Tonitleagmund Lake

Old Albert Lake

Nuciamund Lake

Chumund Lake

Fish Lake

Last Tetlin Hill

Tetlin

1

63°00'
144°00'

Continue on Page 98

143°30'00'
143.5000°

DUFFYS TAVERN

143°15'00'
143.2500°

KILOMETERS   5   0   5   10   15   20

143°00'00''
143.0000°

108

MILES   1 0 1 2 3 4 5 6 7 8 9 10 11 12

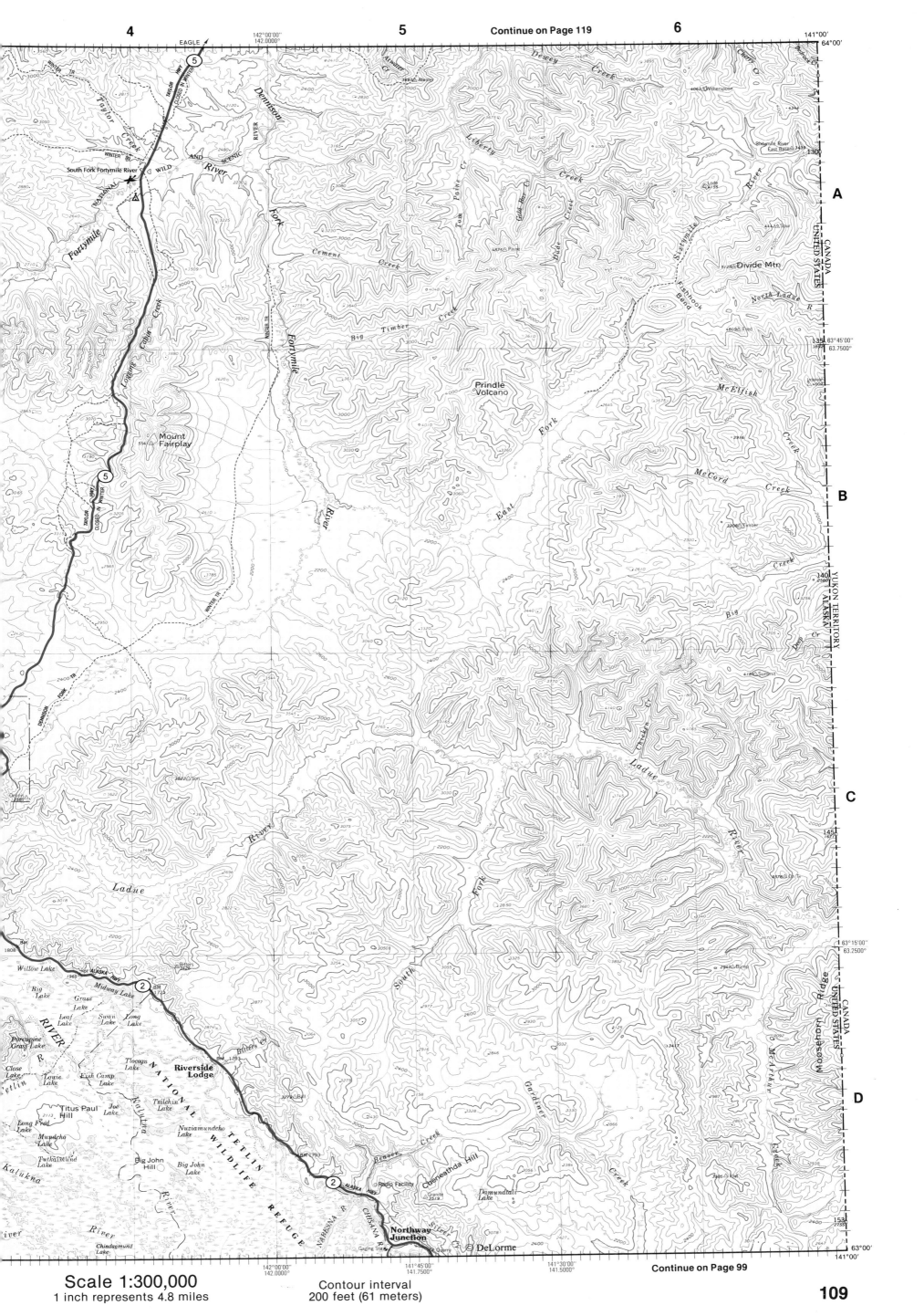

142°00'00''
142.0000'
64°00'

EAGLE

A

CANADA
UNITED STATES

135 63°45'00''
63.7500'

B

YUKON TERRITORY
ALASKA

140

C

145

63°15'00''
63.2500'

CANADA
UNITED STATES

D

153

63°00'
141°00'

141°00'

142°00'00''
142.0000'

141°45'00''
141.7500'

141°30'00''
141.5000'

© DeLorme

Continue on Page 99

Scale 1:300,000
1 inch represents 4.8 miles

Contour interval
200 feet (61 meters)

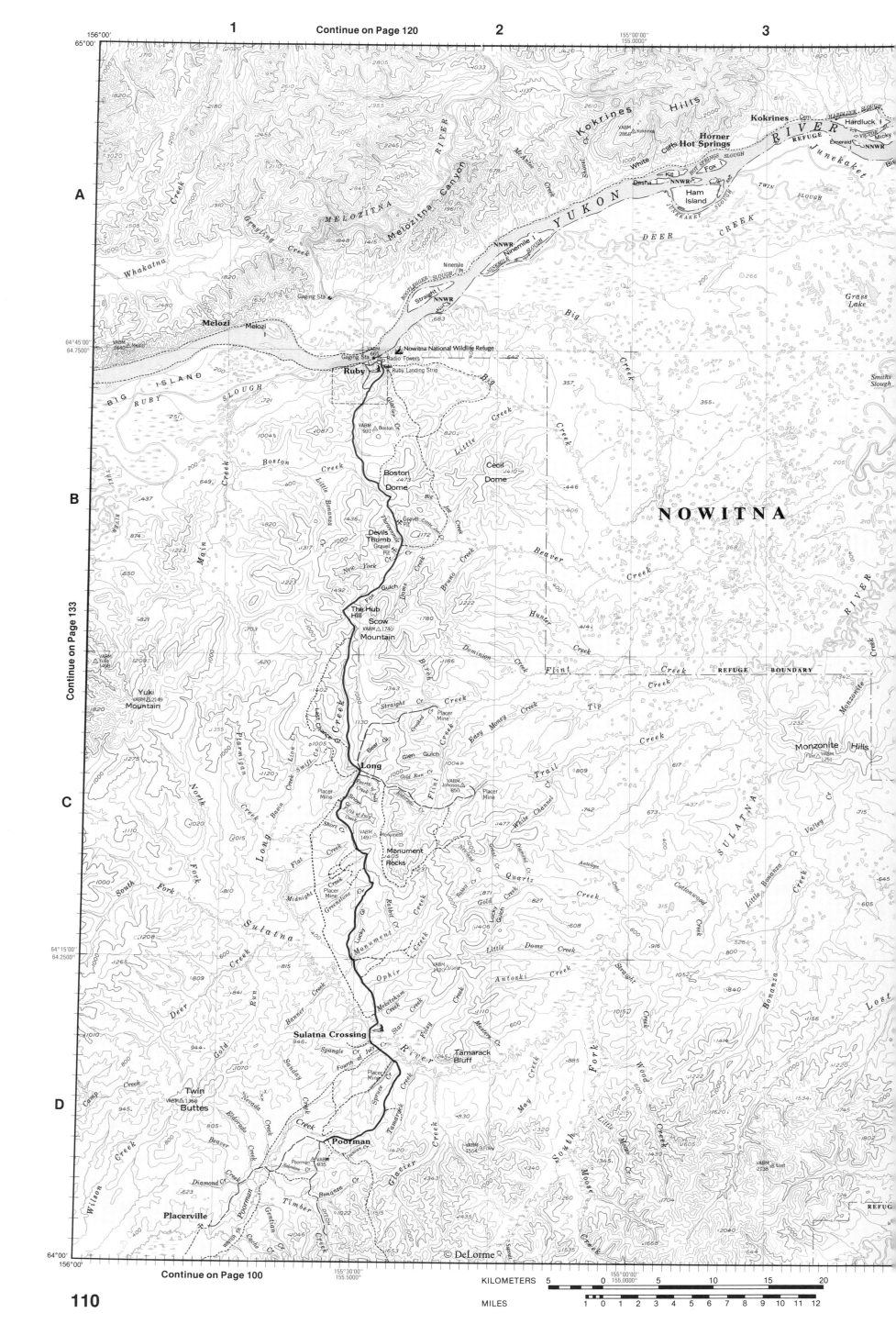

156°00'
65°00'

64°45'00"
64.7500°

64°15'00"
64.2500°

64°00'
156°00'

155°00'00"
155.0000°

155°30'00"
155.5000°

Continue on Page 133

Kokrines Hills

Kokrines

Horner
Cliffs Hot Springs
Hardluck

YUKON
RIVER

NOWITNA

MELOZITNA
RIVER

Melozitna Canyon

Whakatna Creek

Grayling Creek

Melozi

Nowitna National Wildlife Refuge
Ruby
Radio Towers
Ruby Landing Strip

BIG RUBY ISLAND SLOUGH

Boston Creek

Boston Dome

Cecil Dome

Little Creek

Big Creek

Devils Thumb

New York Gulch

The Hub Hill
Scow Mountain

Beaver Creek

Hunter Creek

Flint Creek
REFUGE BOUNDARY

Yuki Mountain

Long

Long Creek

Monument Rocks

Sulatna

Monzonite Hills

SULATNA

Deer Creek

Gold Run

Sulatna Crossing

Tamarack Bluff

River

Twin Buttes

Poorman

Placerville

SOUTH FORK

Wood Creek

Lost

© DeLorme

KILOMETERS   5   0   5   10   15   20

MILES   1 0 1 2 3 4 5 6 7 8 9 10 11 12

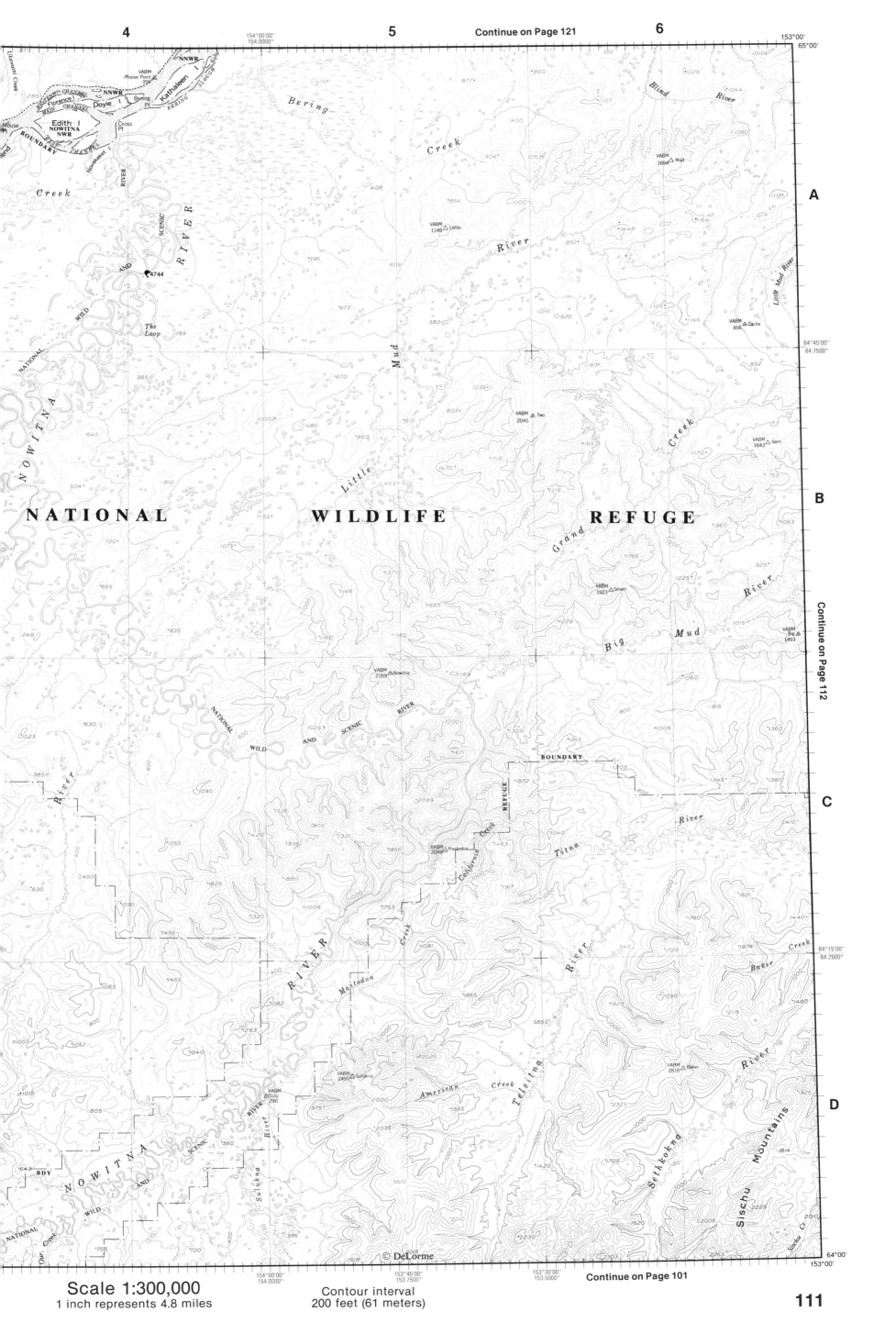

Continue on Page 112

Scale 1:300,000
1 inch represents 4.8 miles

Contour interval
200 feet (61 meters)

© DeLorme

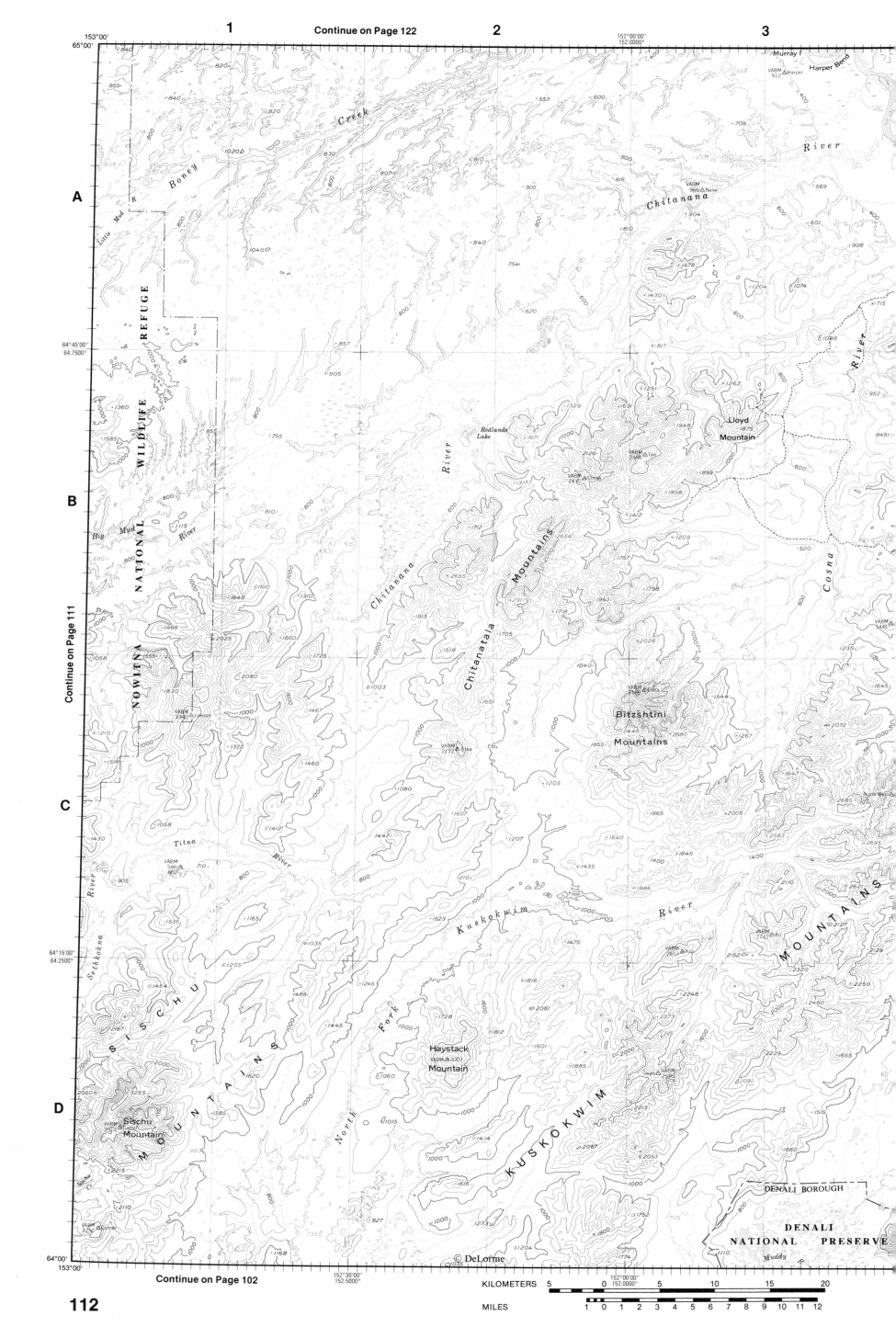

153°00'
65°00'

A

64°45'00"
64.7500°

B

Continue on Page 111

C

64°15'00"
64.2500°

D

64°00'
153°00'

152°30'00"
152.5000°

© DeLorme

152°00'00"
152.0000°

KILOMETERS   5   0 152.0000°   5   10   15   20

MILES   1 0 1 2 3 4 5 6 7 8 9 10 11 12

Murray I
Harper Bend
VABM 512 △ Harper
River
Chitanana
VABM 966 △ Naoa
Chitanana
Cosna
River
Redlands Lake
River
Lloyd Mountain
Chitanana Mountains
Chitanatala Mountains
Bitzshtini Mountains
Kuskokwim River
Titna River
Sethkokna River
North Fork
Kuskokwim
Haystack Mountain
SISCHU MOUNTAINS
Sischu Mountain
KUSKOKWIM MOUNTAINS
DENALI BOROUGH
DENALI NATIONAL PRESERVE
Muddy R
NOWITNA NATIONAL WILDLIFE REFUGE
Big Mud River
Little Mud R
Boney Creek

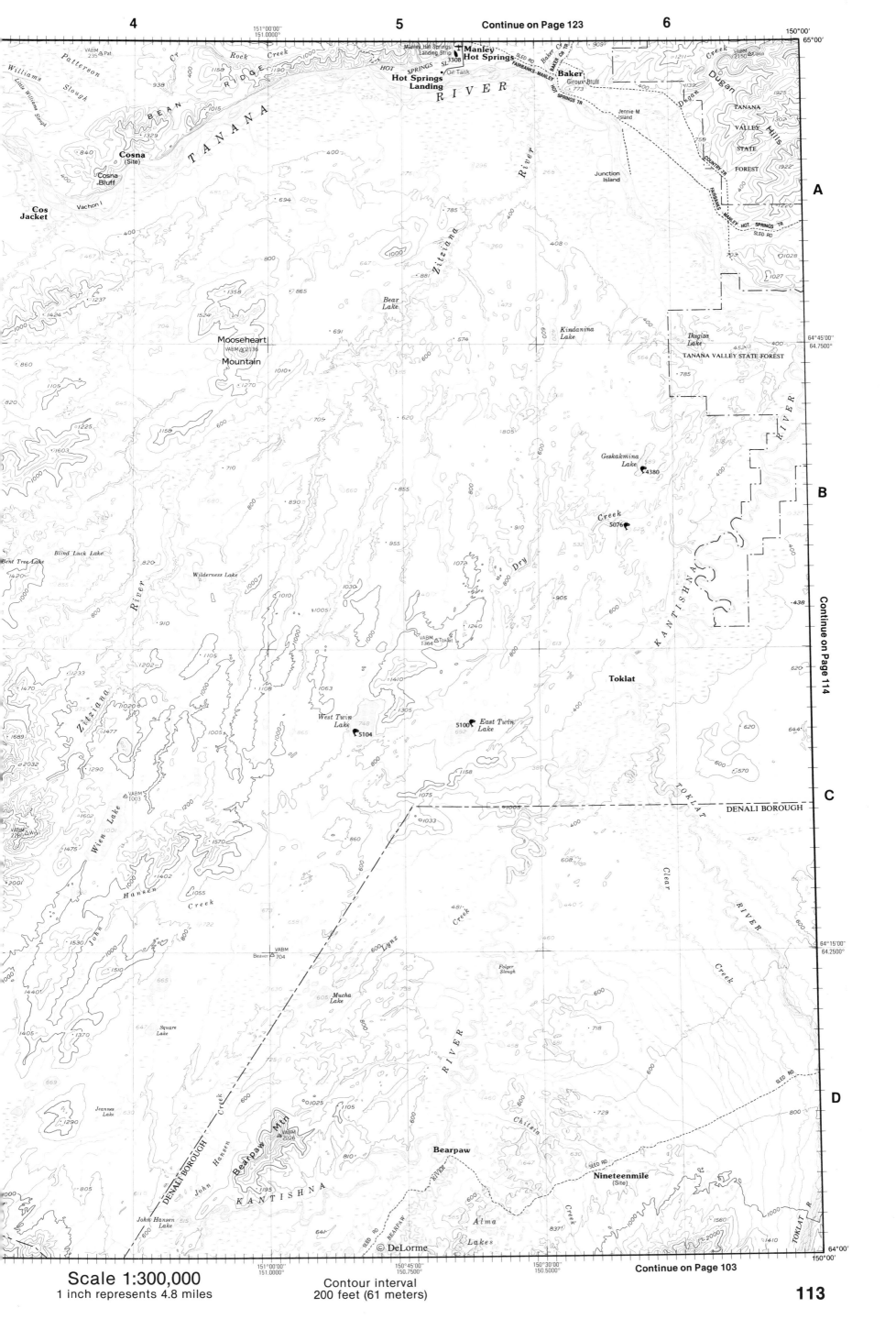

Continue on Page 114

Continue on Page 103

Scale 1:300,000
1 inch represents 4.8 miles

Contour interval
200 feet (61 meters)

© DeLorme

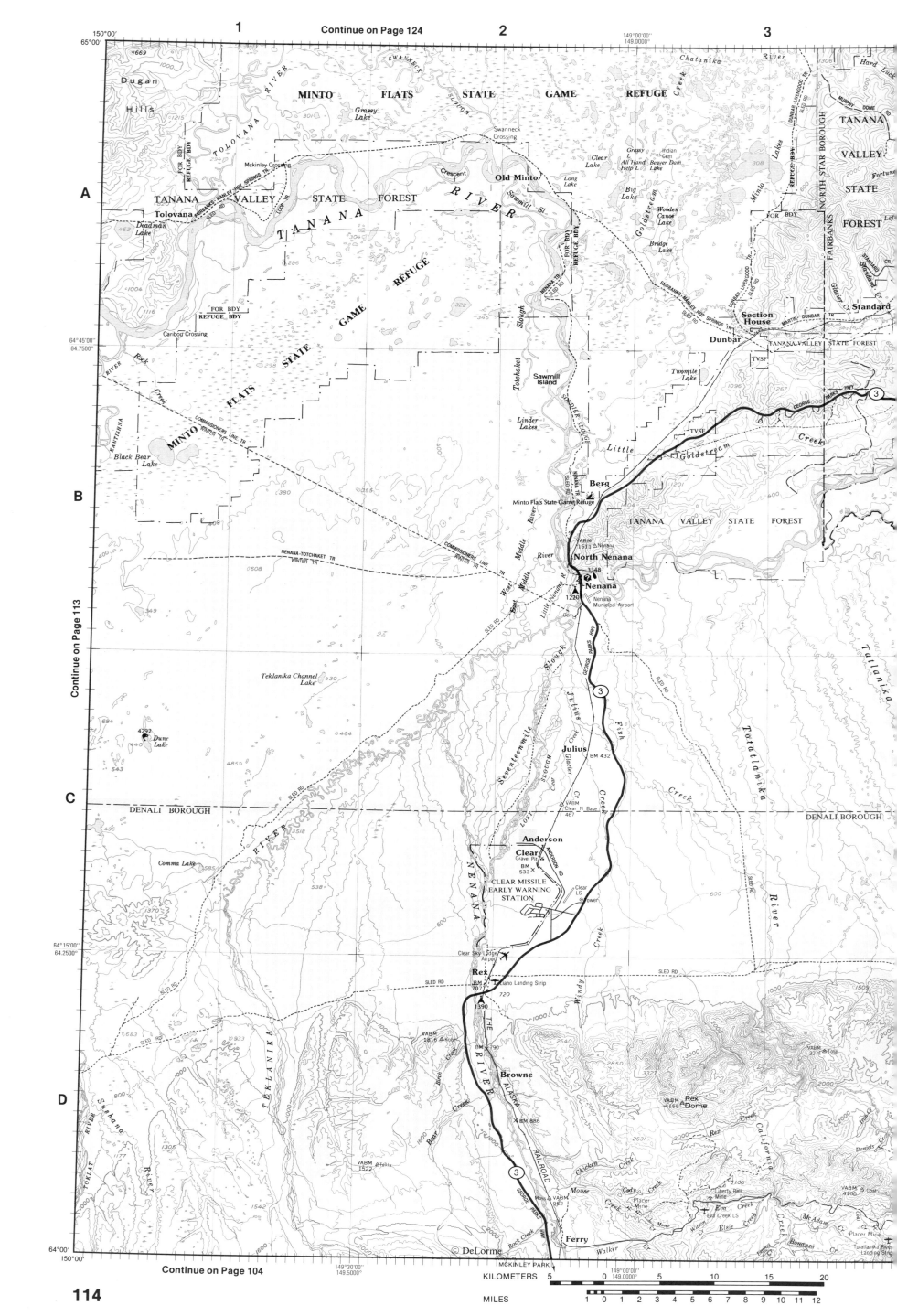

150°00'
65°00'

149°00'00"
149.0000'

A

64°45'00"
64.7500'

Continue on Page 113

B

C

DENALI BOROUGH   DENALI BOROUGH

64°15'00"
64.2500'

D

64°00'
150°00'

149°30'00"
149.5000'

Continue on Page 104

MCKINLEY PARK

149°00'00"
149.0000'

KILOMETERS   5   0   5   10   15   20

MILES   1   0   1   2   3   4   5   6   7   8   9   10   11   12

© DeLorme

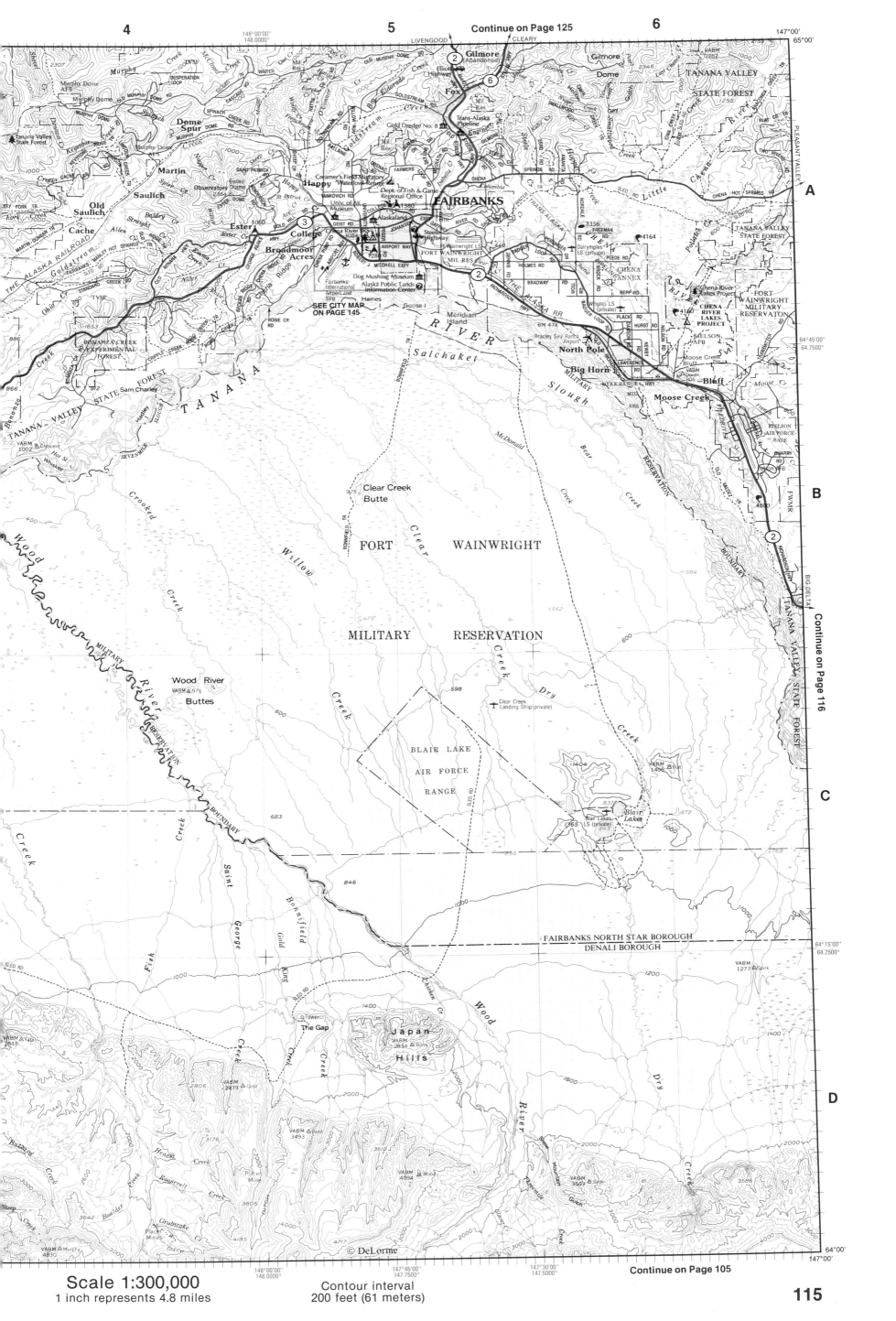

Continue on Page 125

148°00'00"
148.0000°

147°00'
65°00'

A

64°45'00"
64.7500°

B

Continue on Page 116

C

FAIRBANKS NORTH STAR BOROUGH
DENALI BOROUGH

64°15'00"
64.2500°

D

© DeLorme

64°00'
147°00'

148°00'00"
148.0000°

147°45'00"
147.7500°

147°30'00"
147.5000°

Continue on Page 105

Scale 1:300,000
1 inch represents 4.8 miles

Contour interval
200 feet (61 meters)

FORT WAINWRIGHT

MILITARY RESERVATION

BLAIR LAKE
AIR FORCE
RANGE

TANANA VALLEY STATE FOREST

TANANA

RIVER

SEE CITY MAP
ON PAGE 145

Japan Hills

Wood River Buttes

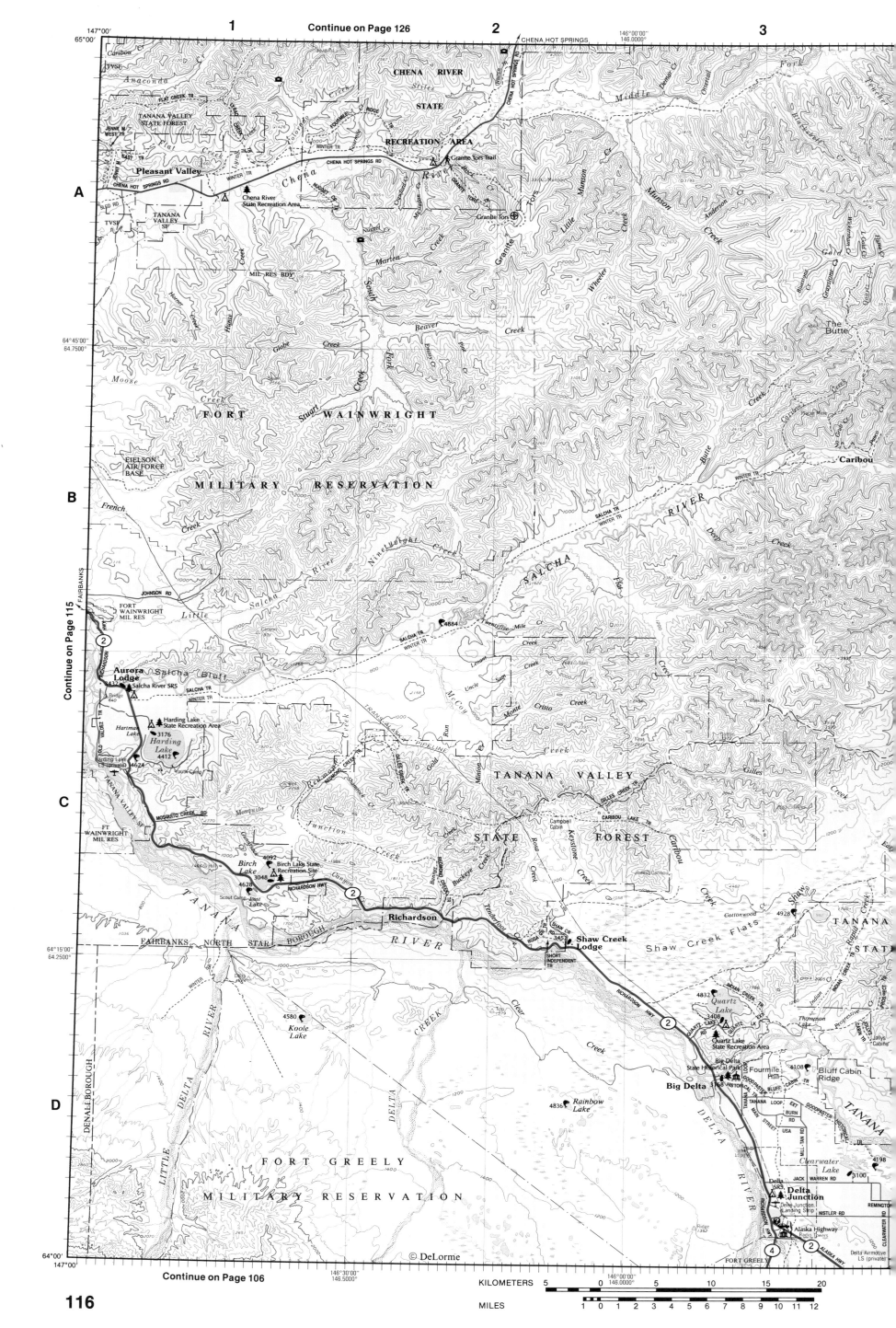

Continue on Page 115

KILOMETERS

MILES

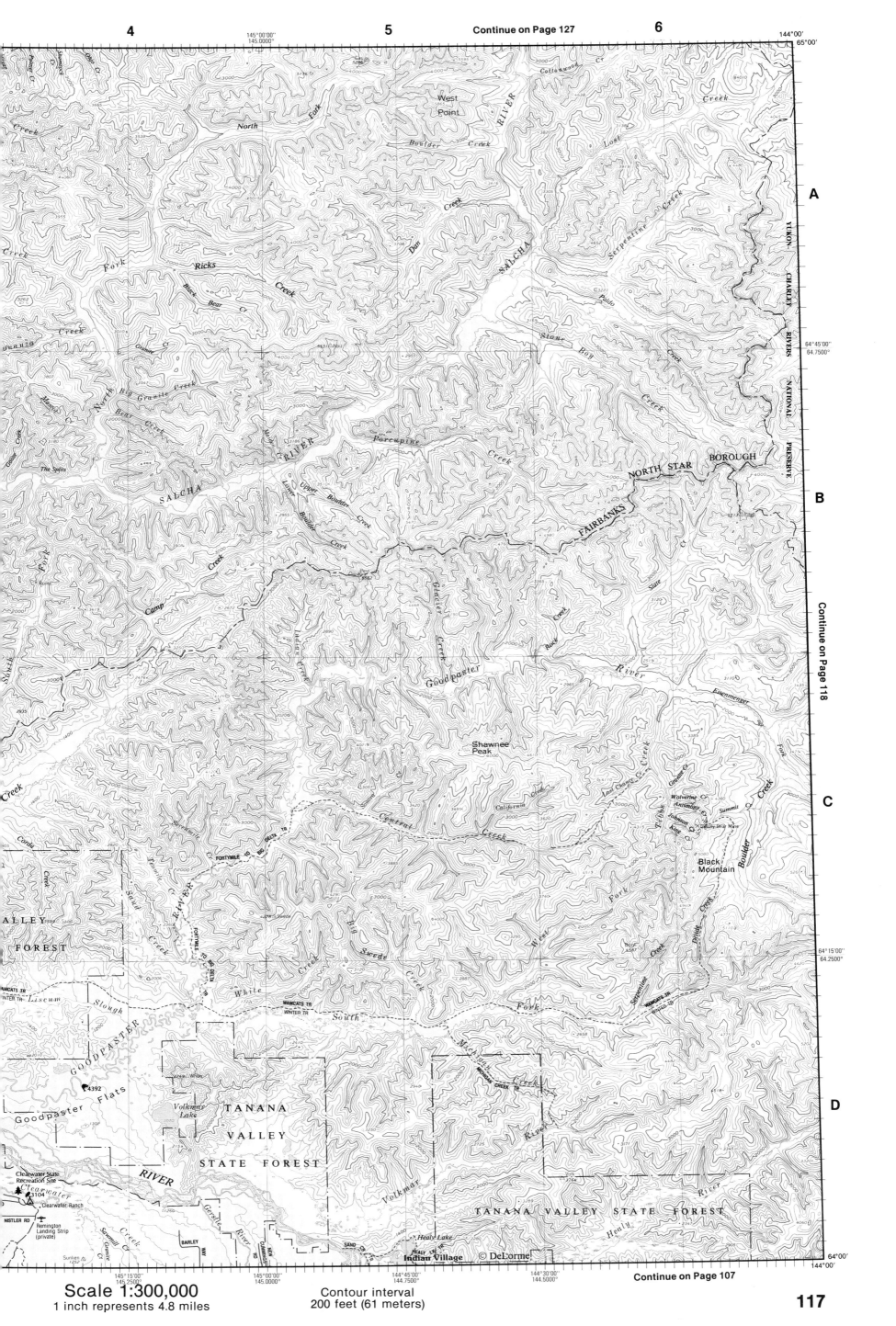

145°00'00"
145.0000°

65°00'

144°00'
65°00'

A

YUKON-CHARLEY RIVERS NATIONAL PRESERVE

64°45'00"
64.7500°

NORTH STAR BOROUGH

FAIRBANKS

B

Continue on Page 118

SALCHA RIVER

Goodpaster River

Shawnee Peak

C

Black Mountain

FORTYMILE TO BIG DELTA TR

FORTYMILE TO BIG DELTA TR

64°15'00"
64.2500°

WAMCATS TR
WINTER TR

WAMCATS TR
WINTER TR

WAMCATS TR
WINTER TR

Liscum

Slough

South Fork

Michigan Creek

White

Big Swede Creek

GOODPASTER

Goodpaster Flats

4392

Volkmar Lake

TANANA VALLEY STATE FOREST

D

Volkmar River

RIVER

TANANA VALLEY STATE FOREST

Healy River

Clearwater State Recreation Site
Clearwater Ranch
NISTLER RD
Remington Landing Strip (private)

BARLEY WAY

Gerstle River

NEW CUMMINGS RD

SAND CR

HEALY LN

Healy Lake

Indian Village
© DeLorme

Sunken

Continue on Page 107

64°00'

Scale 1:300,000
1 inch represents 4.8 miles

Contour interval
200 feet (61 meters)

145°15'00"
145.2500°

145°00'00"
145.0000°

144°45'00"
144.7500°

144°30'00"
144.5000°

144°00'

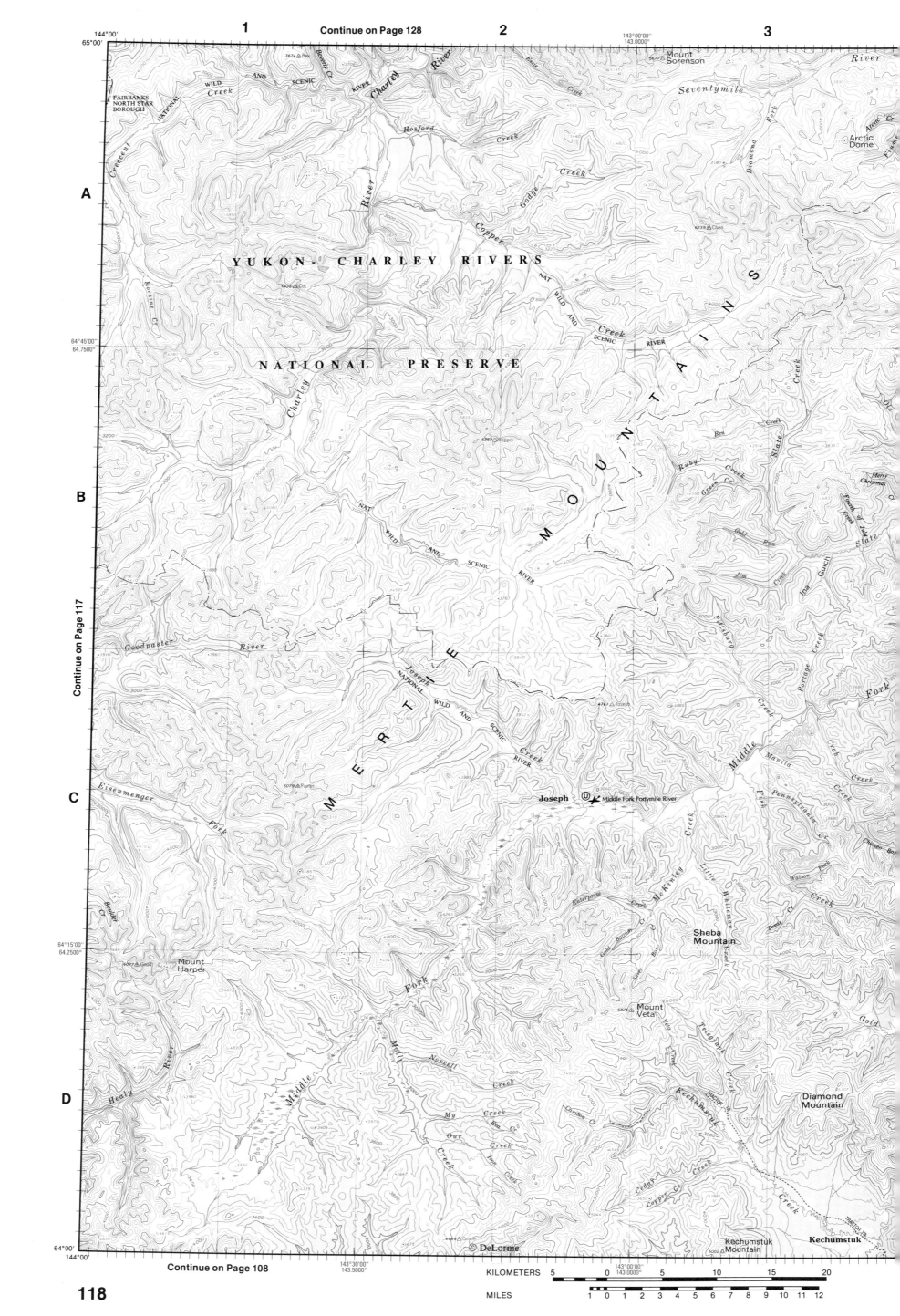

Continue on Page 117

FAIRBANKS
NORTH STAR
BOROUGH

YUKON - CHARLEY RIVERS

NATIONAL   PRESERVE

M O U N T A I N S

Mount
Sorenson

Seventymile

Arctic
Dome

Merry
Christmas

Goodpaster   River

Joseph
NATIONAL   WILD   AND   SCENIC   River

Eisenmenger

Joseph

M E R T I E

Joseph   Middle Fork Fortymile River

Sheba
Mountain

Mount
Harper

Mount
Veta

Diamond
Mountain

Kechumstuk
Mountain

Kechumstuk

© DeLorme

Continue on Page 108

KILOMETERS   5   0   5   10   15   20

MILES   1 0 1 2 3 4 5 6 7 8 9 10 11 12

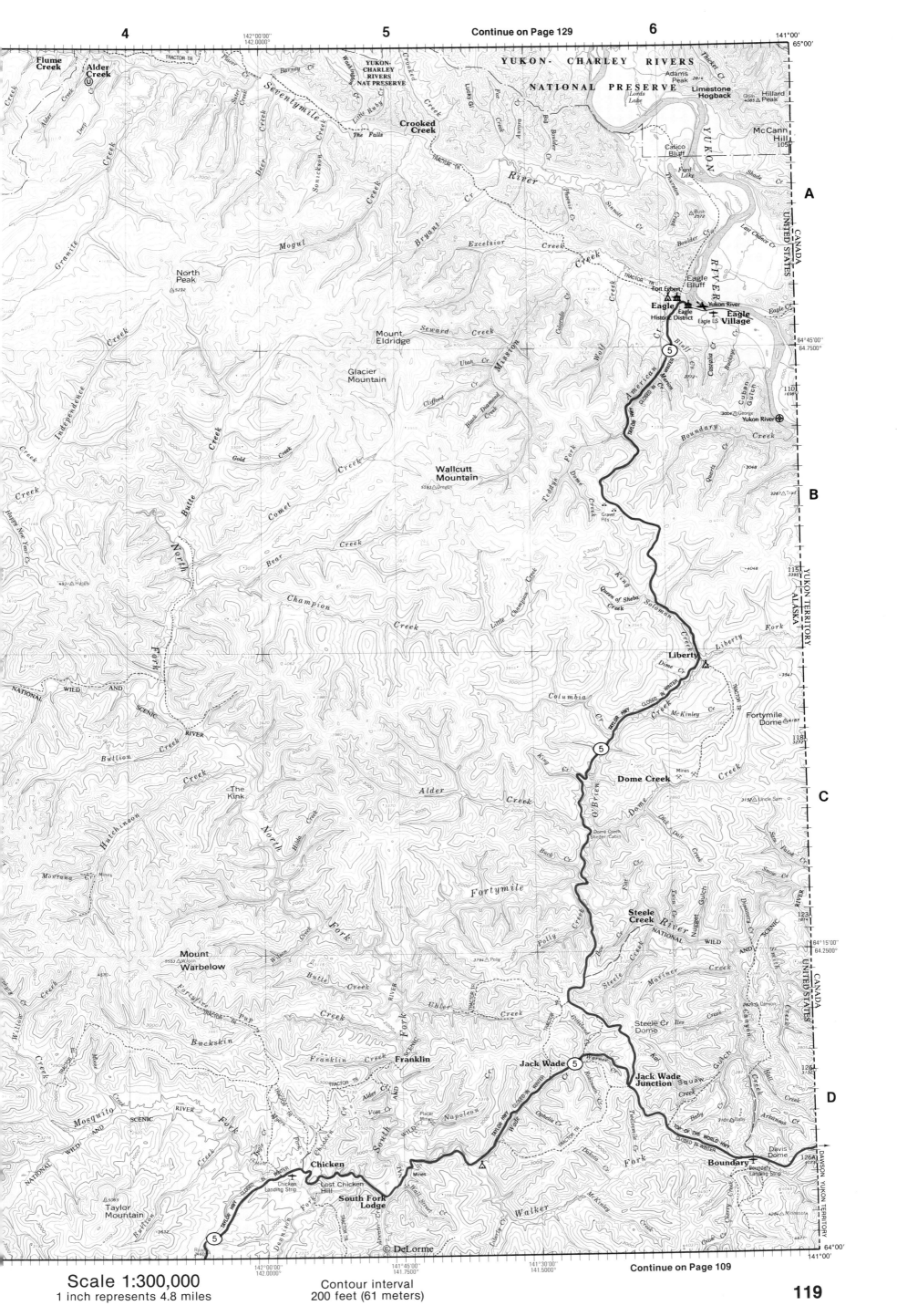

Continue on Page 109

Scale 1:300,000
1 inch represents 4.8 miles

Contour interval
200 feet (61 meters)

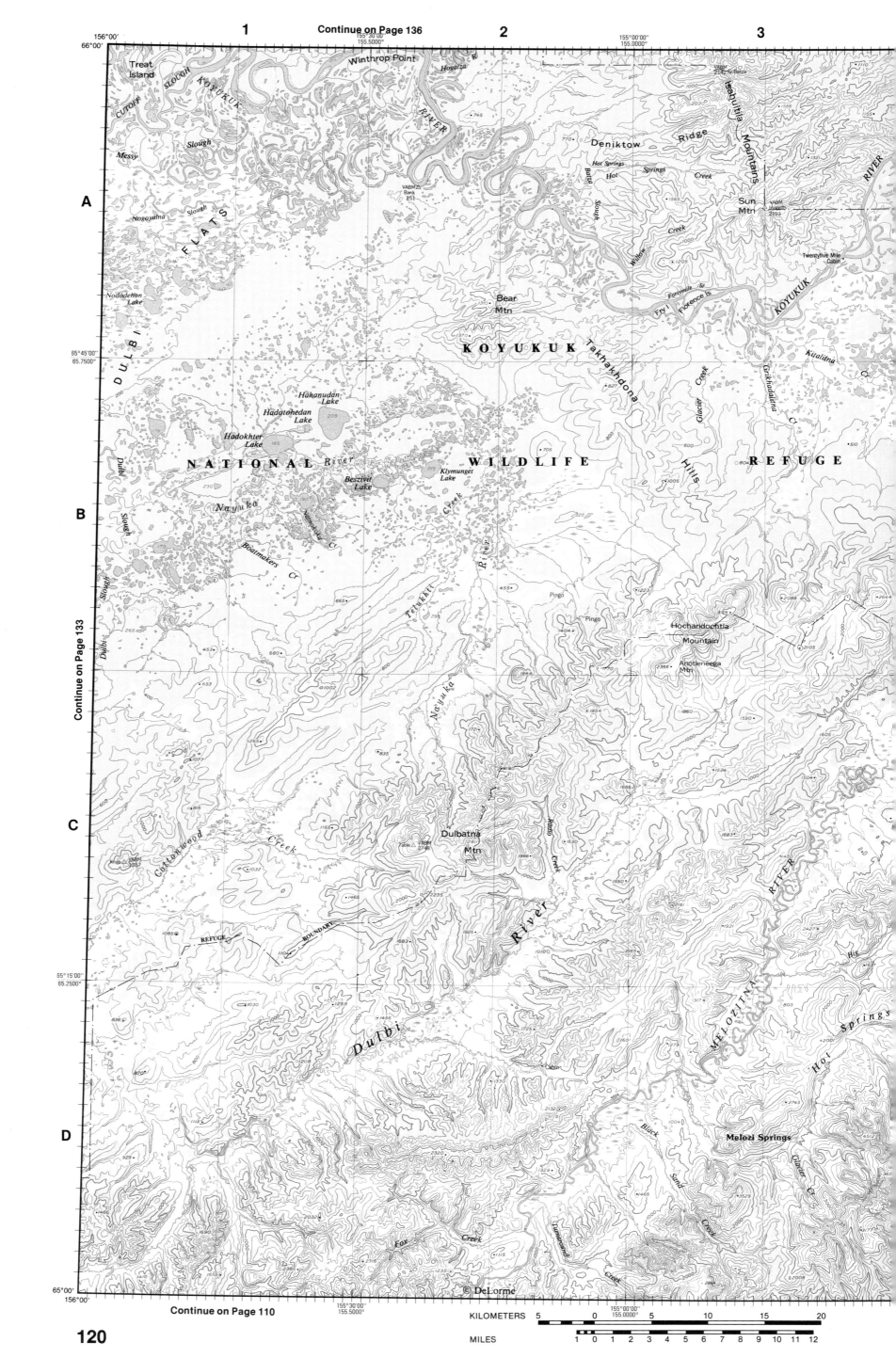

156°00'
66°00'

156°00'
155°30'00''
155.5000°

155°00'00''
155.0000°

Treat
Island

Winthrop Point

Hogatza R.

CUTOFF SLOUGH

KOYUKUK

RIVER

745

Isabultla Mountains

Deniktow   Ridge

770

RIVER

Messy   Slough

Slough

Hot Springs   Springs   Creek

Bargo   Hot
Slough

Nogoyalna   Slough

VABM
Bank
251

Willow   Creek

1000

1205

Sun
Mtn

VABM
2193

A

Twentyfive Mile
Cabin

Nodadehon
Lake

810

Bear
Mtn
1370

1370

265

Fryl   Florence Is

Fortymile Sl

KOYUKUK

65°45'00''
65.7500°

266

705

KOYUKUK

Takhakhdona

820

Kitalitna

D U L B I   F L A T S

Hahanudan
Lake

Hadotohedan
Lake   208

190

Besivil
Lake   230

Klymunget
Lake

Grikhadalitna Cr

Glacier Creek

Kitalitna
Cr

600

510

NATIONAL   River   WILDLIFE   REFUGE

Dulbi

B

Nayuka   Slough

Namudhot Cr

1223

1088

Hochandochtla
Mountain   1851

2108

Boatmakers   Cr

325

Pingo

Telukhti   River   Creek

Pingo

1404

2356   Anotleneega
Mtn

655

455

1860

1590

Slough

265

453

680

800

1854

1605

653

1002

Nayuka

1524

Dulbi

1265

835   1983

1666

1504

1077

1855

1683

C

815

1000

1000

1032

Table   VABM
2748

Dulbatna
2811   Mtn

Radio   Creek

1630

RIVER

Cottonwood   Creek

1468

2000   3235

1966

1550

MELOZITNA

1921

1382

1085

REFUGE   BOUNDARY

1100

1683

1925

1000

10 00

Big

65°15'00''
65.2500°

1030

1258

Dulbi

1451

725

917

803

Hot   Springs

1258

1200

Melozi Springs

Black

929   1103

2032

2320

2329   1465

Sand   Creek

Glacier Cr

D

836

970

1466

2318

2385

1235

2132

Cabin

Fox   Creek

1115

© DeLorme

Tamaroond   Creek

65°00'
156°00'

155°30'00''
155.5000°

155°00'00''
155.0000°

Continue on Page 133

65°45'00''
65.7500°

65°00'

KILOMETERS   5   0   5   10   15   20

MILES   1 0 1 2 3 4 5 6 7 8 9 10 11 12

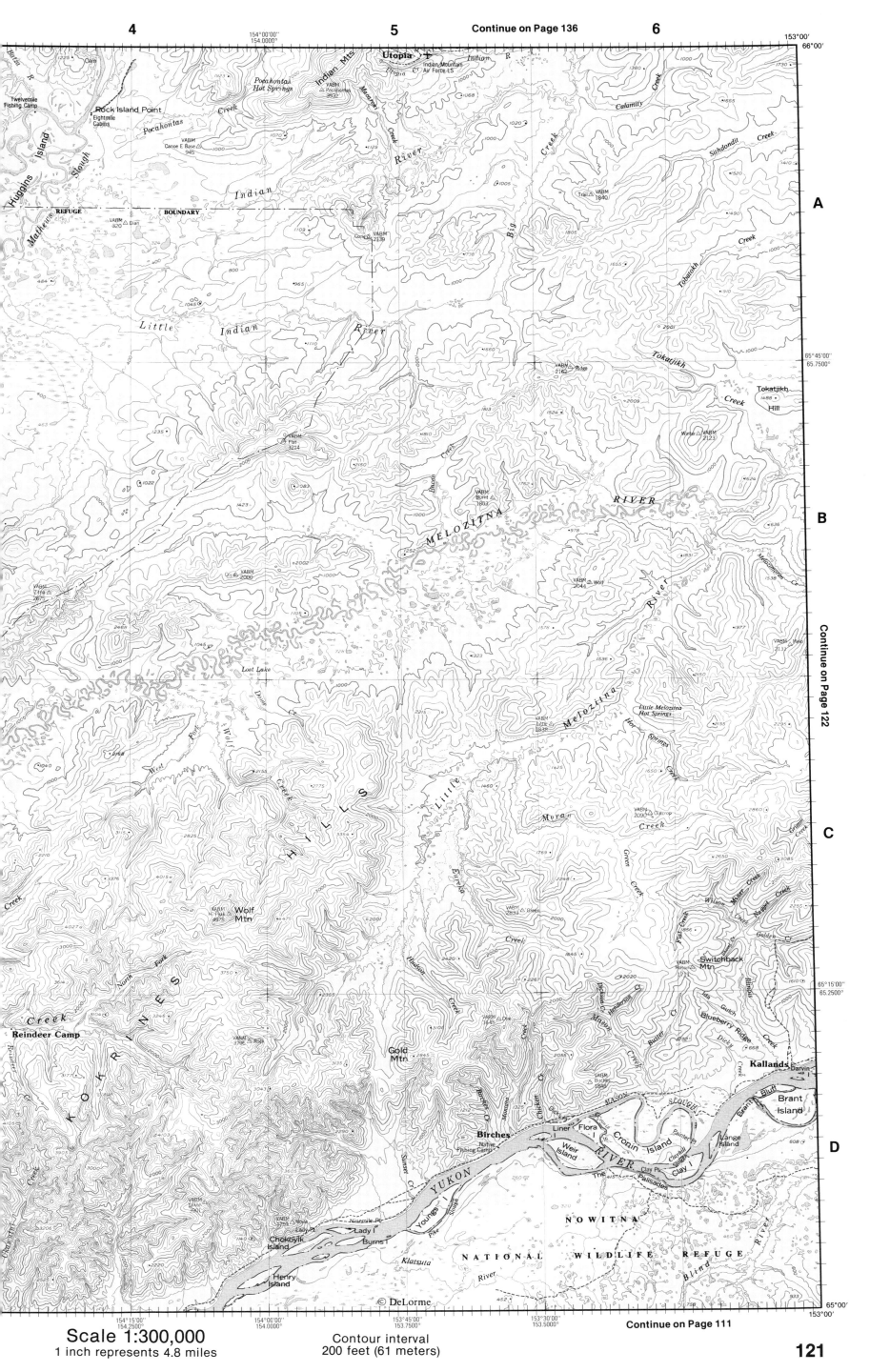

Continue on Page 122

Continue on Page 111

Scale 1:300,000
1 inch represents 4.8 miles

Contour interval
200 feet (61 meters)

© DeLorme

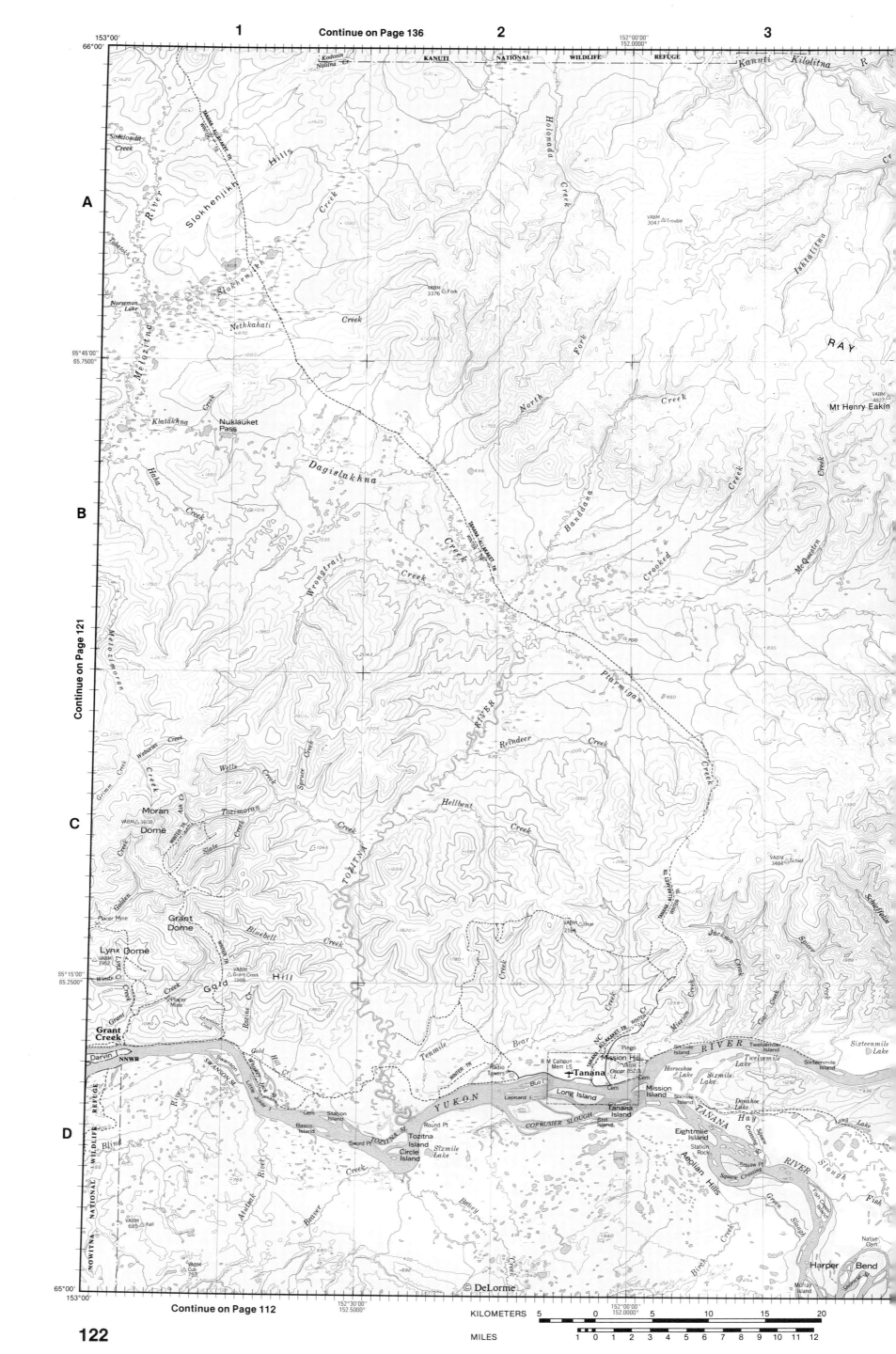

153°00'
66°00'

A

65°45'00"
65.7500°

B

Continue on Page 121

C

65°15'00"
65.2500°

D

65°00'
153°00'

© DeLorme

KILOMETERS 5   0   5   10   15   20

MILES   1 0 1 2 3 4 5 6 7 8 9 10 11 12

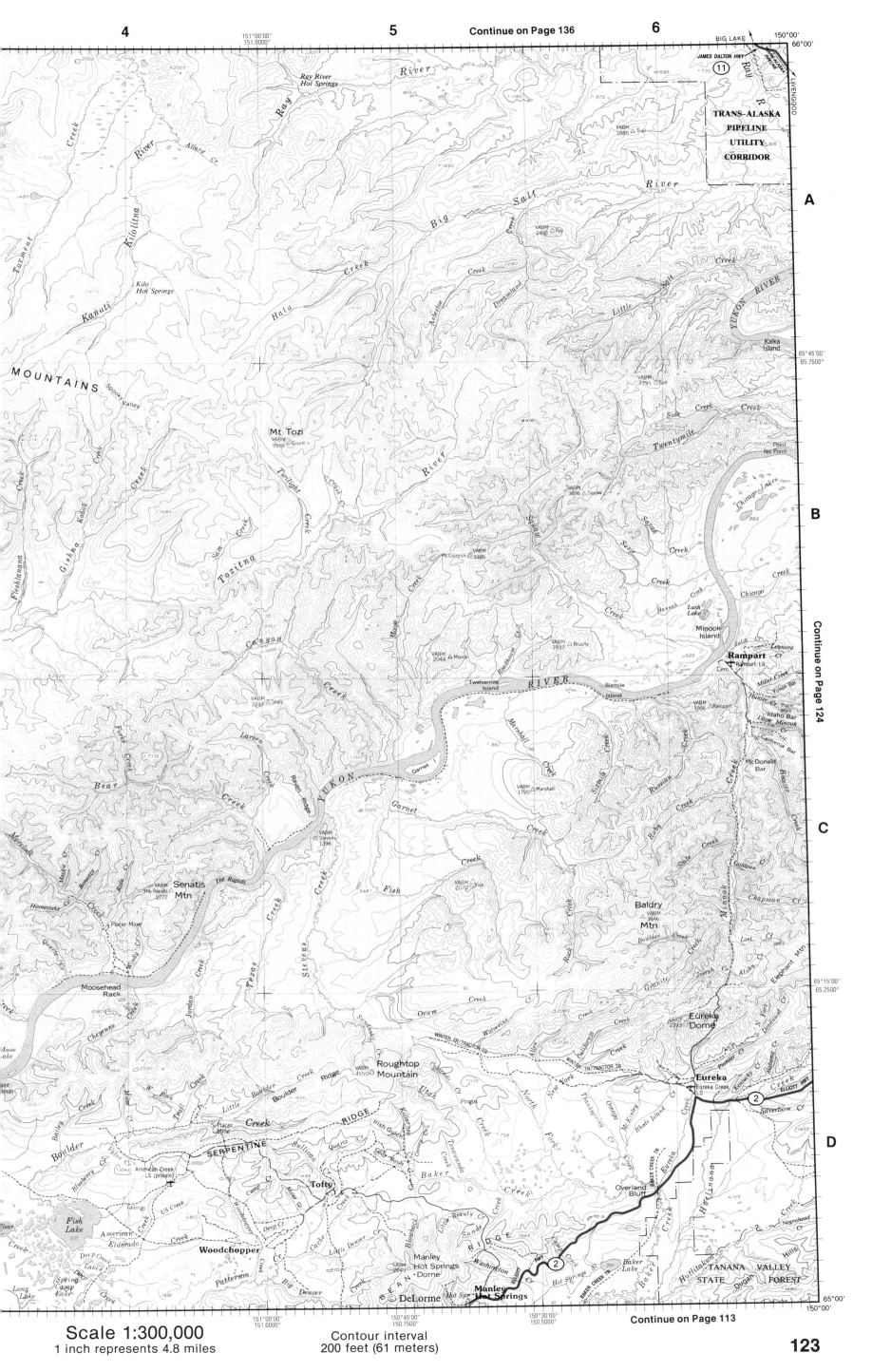

Continue on Page 124

66°00'
150°00'

BIG LAKE

JAMES DALTON HWY
(11)

LIVENGOOD

**TRANS–ALASKA
PIPELINE
UTILITY
CORRIDOR**

A

65°45'00''
65.7500°

B

C

65°15'00''
65.2500°

D

65°00'
150°00'

MOUNTAINS

Mt. Tozi

Senatis
Mtn

Baldry
Mtn

Eureka
Dome

Eureka
Eureka Creek
LS

(2) ELLIOTT HWY

Roughtop
Mountain

SERPENTINE
RIDGE

Tofty

Woodchopper

Manley
Hot Springs
Dome

© DeLorme

**Manley
Hot Springs**

(2)

TANANA VALLEY
STATE FOREST

Rampart

Minook
Island

Chicago Lake

Continue on Page 113

Scale 1:300,000
1 inch represents 4.8 miles

Contour interval
200 feet (61 meters)

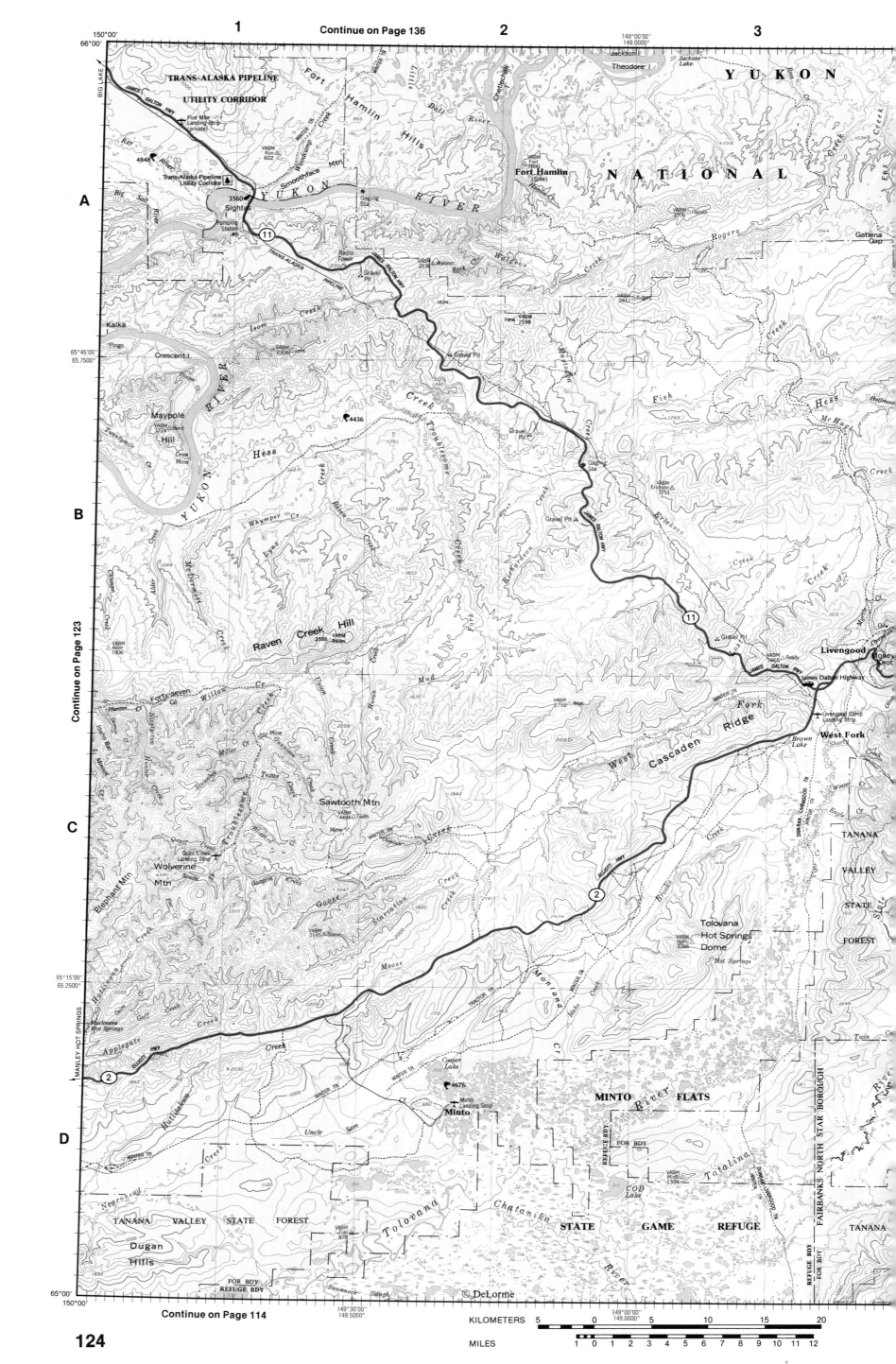

Continue on Page 123

© DeLorme

KILOMETERS   5   0   5   10   15   20

MILES   1 0 1 2 3 4 5 6 7 8 9 10 11 12

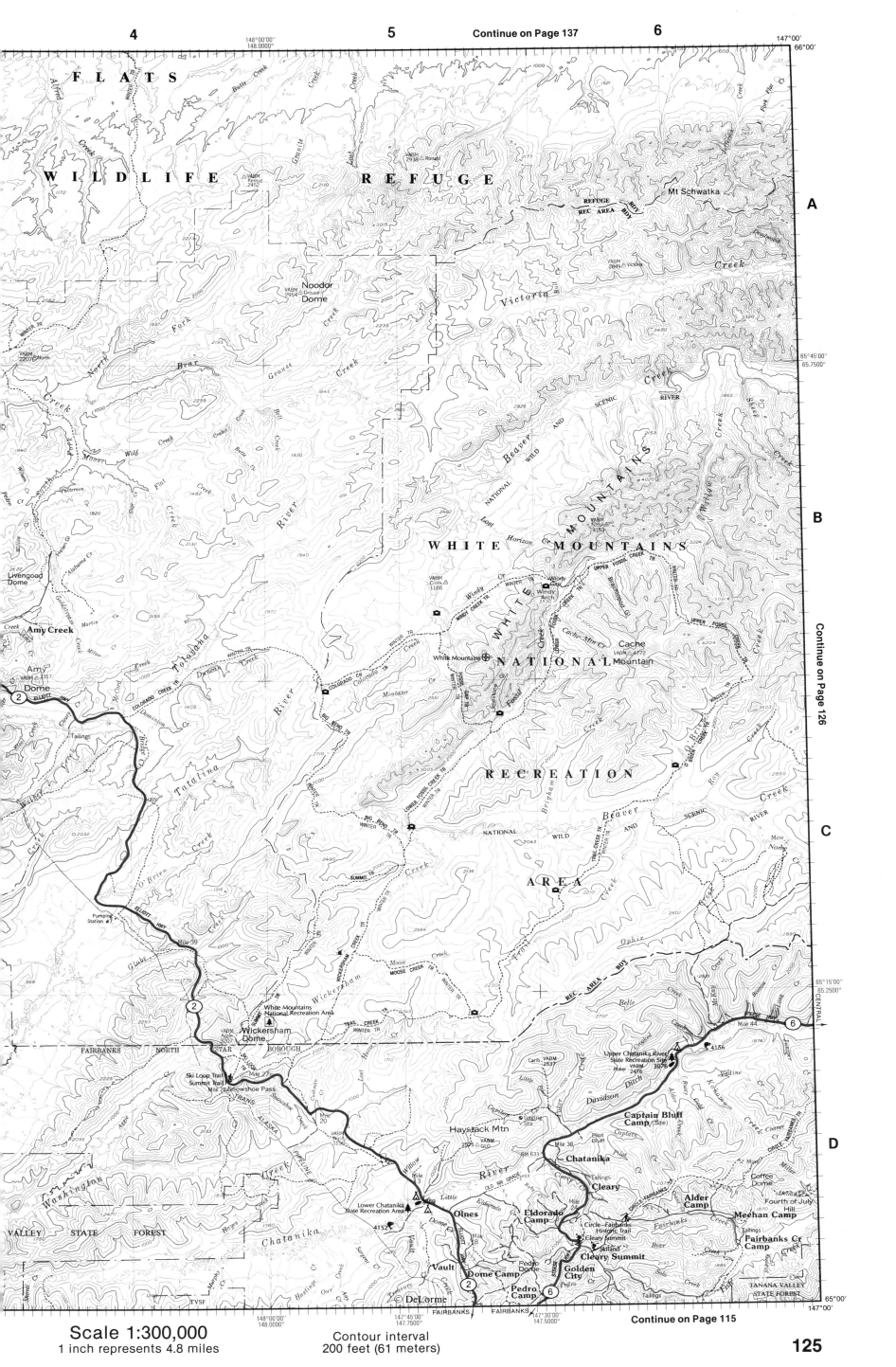

Continue on Page 126

Continue on Page 115

Scale 1:300,000
1 inch represents 4.8 miles

Contour interval
200 feet (61 meters)

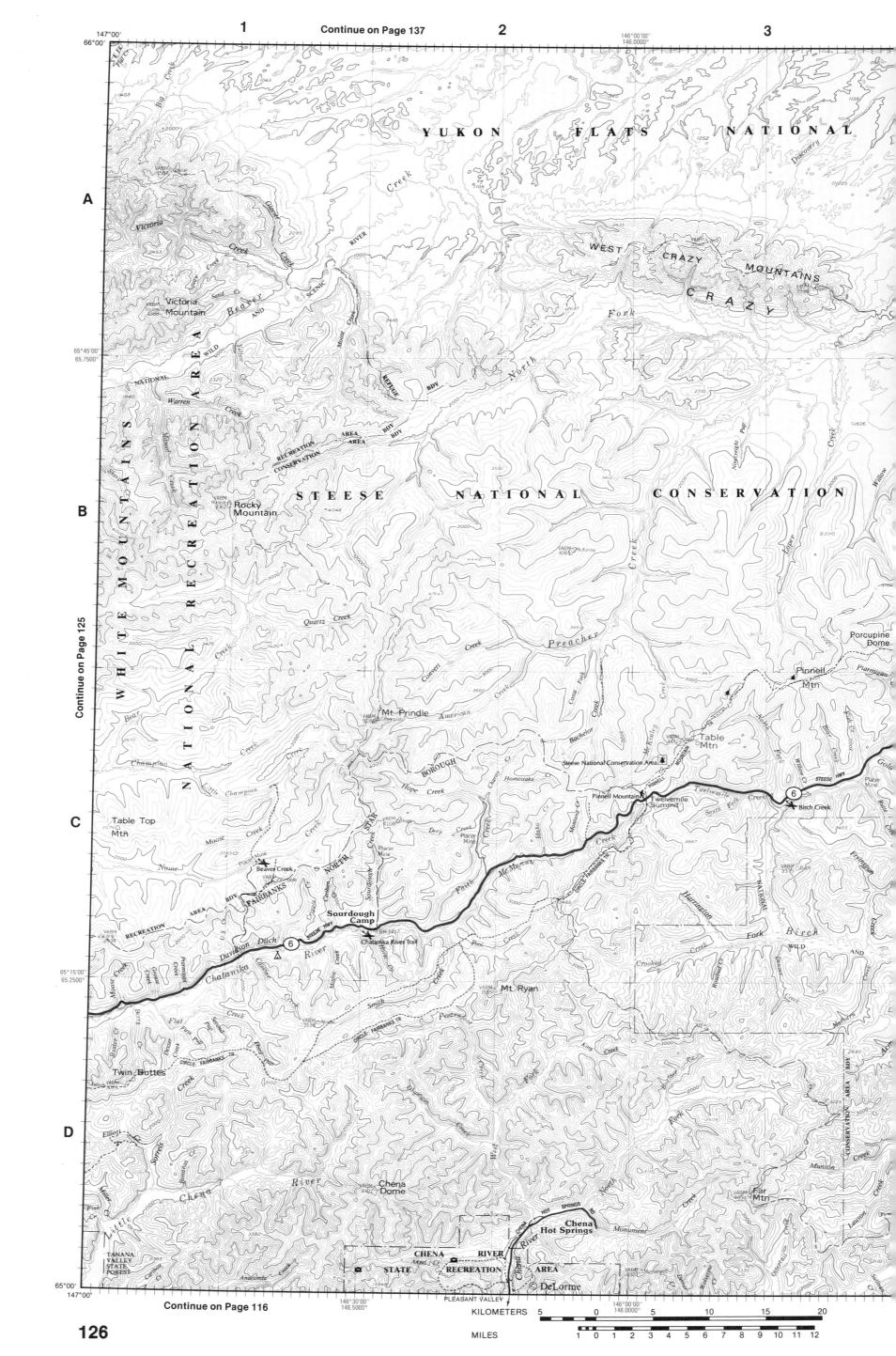

147°00'
66°00'

A

YUKON   FLATS   NATIONAL

Victoria
Creek

Victoria
Mountain

WEST   CRAZY
MOUNTAINS
CRAZY

Fork

65°45'00'
65.7500°

REFUGE   BDY

North

Continue on Page 125

NATIONAL   RECREATION   AREA

WHITE MOUNTAINS

Warren

RECREATION   AREA
AREA   BDY
CONSERVATION

STEESE   NATIONAL   CONSERVATION

Rocky
Mountain

B

McKinley

Quartz   Creek

Preacher

Creek

Porcupine
Dome

Pinnell
Mtn

Mt Prindle

American

Bachelor

Table
Mtn

BOROUGH

Hope   Creek

Homestake

Steese National Conservation Area

Table Top
Mtn

Churry

Pinnell Mountain

Twelvemile
Summit

STEESE HWY

6

Birch Creek

C

Beaver Creek

Sourdough
Creek

NORTH STAR

Deep   Creek

Faith

Placer Mine

McManus

CIRCLE-FAIRBANKS TR

South Fork

National

FAIRBANKS

RECREATION

Sourdough
Camp

BM 1417

Chatanika River Trail

Ditch

6

Chatanika   River

Pool   Creek

Crooked   Creek

WILD   AND

65°15'00'
65.2500°

Moose   Creek

Davidson   Ditch

Smith   Creek

Mt Ryan

CIRCLE- FAIRBANKS TR

Birch

Twin Buttes

CIRCLE-FAIRBANKS TR

King   Creek

West   Fork

D

Elliott

Chena

River

Chena
Dome

North   Fork

Far
Mtn

CONSERVATION AREA

Little

HOT SPRINGS RD

Chena
Hot Springs

Monument

TANANA
VALLEY STATE
FOREST

CHENA   RIVER
STATE   RECREATION   AREA

Chena River

© DeLorme

65°00'
147°00'

146°30'00'
146.5000°

PLEASANT VALLEY

146°00'00'
146.0000°

KILOMETERS   5   0   5   10   15   20

MILES   1   0   1   2   3   4   5   6   7   8   9   10   11   12

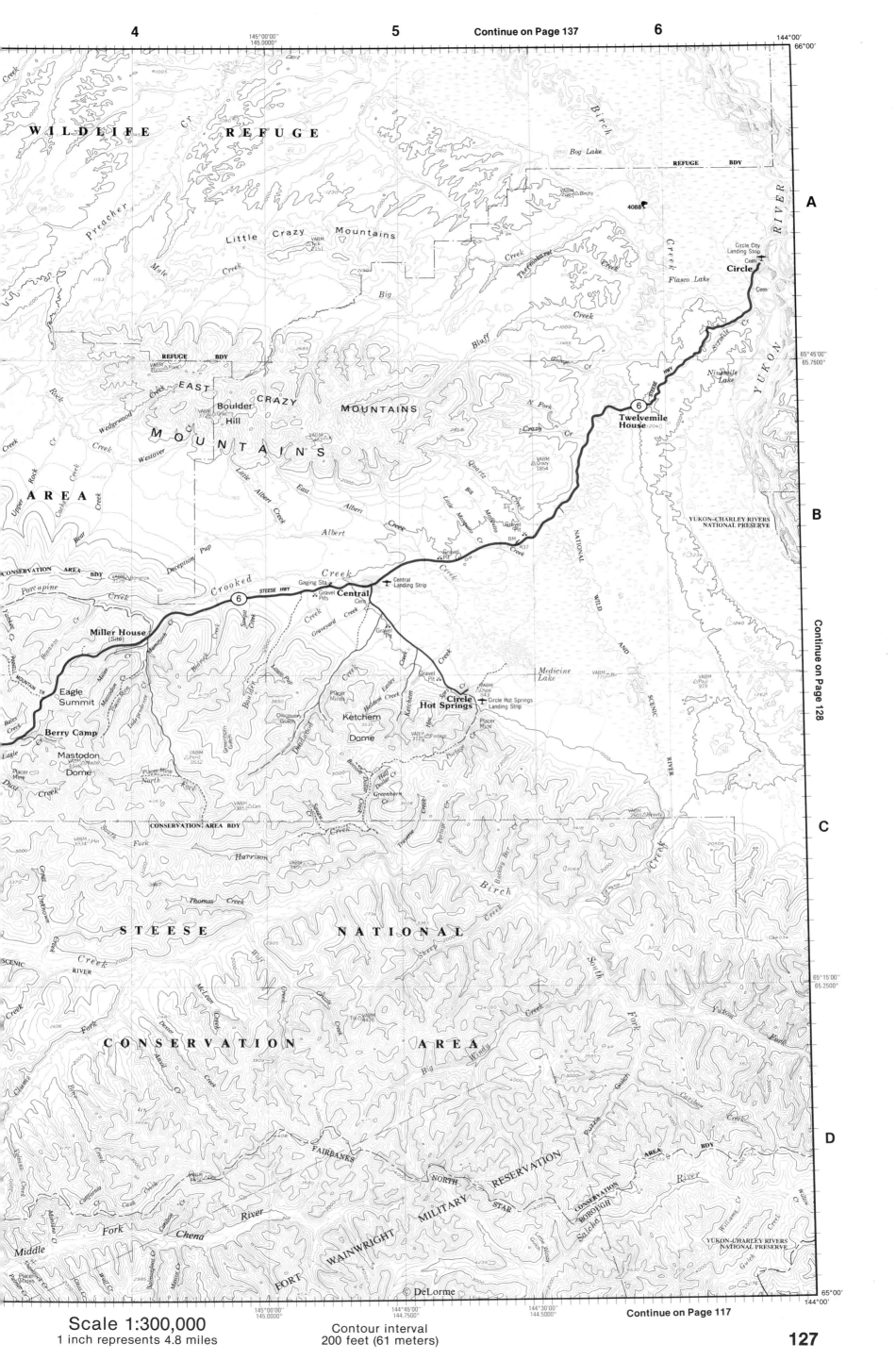

145°00'00''
145.0000°

144°00'
66°00'

W I L D L I F E   R E F U G E

Preacher

Little Crazy Mountains

REFUGE   BDY

Bog Lake

VABM
2981 Birchy

4088

Circle City
Landing Strip

Circle

Cem

A

YUKON

RIVER

Fiasco Lake

Big

Creek

Bluff

Creek

REFUGE   BDY

EAST   CRAZY

Boulder
Hill

M O U N T A I N S

C R A Z Y   M O U N T A I N S

N. Fork

Crazy   Cr.

VABM
Crazy
1854

Twelvemile
House

STEESE   HWY

6

Ninemile
Lake

65°45'00''
65.7500°

A R E A

Porcupine

CONSERVATION   AREA   BDY

VABM
Bonanza

Crooked

Creek

STEESE   HWY

6

Gaging Sta
Gravel
Pits

Central

Cem

Central
Landing Strip

B

YUKON–CHARLEY RIVERS
NATIONAL PRESERVE

N A T I O N A L

W I L D

Continue on Page 128

Miller House
(Site)

Sawpit   Creek

Graveyard   Creek

Gravel
Pit

Medicine
Lake

VABM
775

VABM
919

Eagle
Summit

Placer
Mine

Discovery
Gulch

Ketchem
Dome

Gravel
Pit

Circle
Hot Springs

VABM
843

Circle Hot Springs
Landing Strip

Berry Camp

Eagle

Mastodon
Dome

VABM
Pend
3832

North   Fork

Placer Mine

Placer
Mine

VABM
385 Cem

Half Dollar   Cr

Greenhorn

CONSERVATION   AREA   BDY

Birch

A N D

S C E N I C

C

S T E E S E

VABM
3034

Harrison

VABM
346 Tom

Thomas   Creek

N A T I O N A L

Wolf   Creek

South   Fork

Yukon   Fork

65°15'00''
65.2500°

SCENIC

RIVER

McLean   Creek

Gilles   Creek

C O N S E R V A T I O N

Big

Windy

VABM
4416

A R E A

Salcha

Gulch

Caribou   Creek

D

Middle

Fork

Chena

River

FAIRBANKS

NORTH

F O R T   WAINWRIGHT   MILITARY   RESERVATION

STAR

CONSERVATION
BOROUGH

AREA
BDY

Williams   Creek

YUKON–CHARLEY RIVERS
NATIONAL PRESERVE

© DeLorme

65°00'
144°00'

145°00'00''
145.0000°

144°45'00''
144.7500°

144°30'00''
144.5000°

Scale 1:300,000
1 inch represents 4.8 miles

Contour interval
200 feet (61 meters)

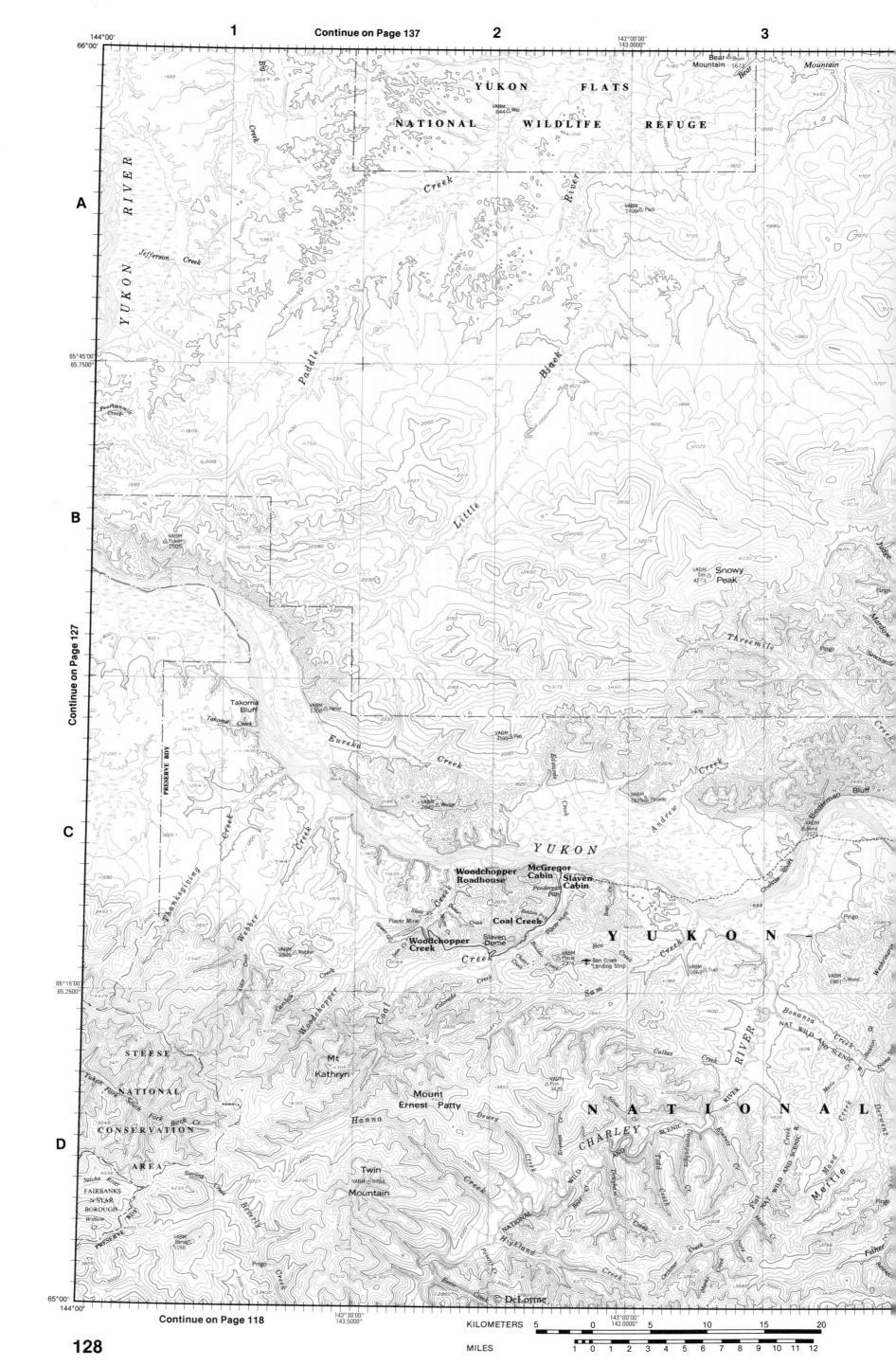

144°00'
66°00'

A

65°45'00"
65.7500°

B

Continue on Page 127

C

65°15'00"
65.2500°

D

65°00'00"
144°00'

143°00'00"
143.0000°

YUKON FLATS

NATIONAL WILDLIFE REFUGE

YUKON RIVER

Jefferson Creek

Paddle Creek

Pourtermill Creek

Takoma Bluff

Takoma Creek

Eureka Creek

Little Creek

Black River

Snowy Peak

Threemile

Andrew Creek

Edwards Creek

Biederman Bluff

YUKON

Woodchopper Roadhouse

McGregor Cabin

Slaven Cabin

Pendergast Pup

Coal Creek

Placer Mine

Woodchopper Creek

Slaven Dome

Ben Creek Landing Strip

Thanksgiving Creek

Webber Creek

PRESERVE BDY

STEESE NATIONAL CONSERVATION AREA

Woodchopper Creek

Mt Kathryn

Mount Ernest Patty

Hanna Creek

Coal Creek

Colorado Creek

Cultas Creek

Dewey Creek

YUKON - CHARLEY

NATIONAL

WILD AND SCENIC R.

NATIONAL HIGHLAND

Bonanza Creek

NAT WILD AND SCENIC R.

RIVER

Twin Mountain

FAIRBANKS NORTH STAR BOROUGH

Salcha River

Birch Cr

Yukon Fork South Fork

Sterling Creek

Bluefish Creek

PRESERVE BDY

Willow

Pingo

Mertie

© DeLorme

143°30'00"
143.5000°

143°00'00"
143.0000°

KILOMETERS   5   0   5   10   15   20

MILES   1 0 1 2 3 4 5 6 7 8 9 10 11 12

142°00'00''
142.0000°

141°00'
66°00'

Fanny Mtn

Black River

Van Hatten Creek

Wood River

Bull Creek

Midnight Surveyor Creek

VABM Bench 2411

VABM 2223 Fire

Pingo

VABM 2465 Fire

A

65°45'00''
65.7500°

CANADA
UNITED STATES

Big Sitdown Creek

VABM Charlie 2965

VABM 3414 Twd

B

Indian Grave Creek

RIVER

VABM Union 4240

Indian Grave Mtn

YUKON TERRITORY
ALASKA

Pingos
Pingo

KANDIK

Johnson Gorge

Black River

VABM Kan 2985

Step Mountains

VABM Nat 3977

Jungle Creek

Ettrain Creek

VABM Yellow 2673

Tindir RIVER

VABM 3606

Kathul Mtn

VABM 952

RIVER

Waterfall Creek

VABM Calico 4874

C

65°15'00''
65.2500°

CHARLEY RIVER

Washington Mountains

Glenn Creek

Kernin Creek

Dewey Creek

Butte Creek

Logan Creek

VABM 2452 Glenn

NATION

Hard

VABM 2931 Hard

Luck Creek

Three Castle Mtn

Calico Creek

VABM 374

Nation Reef

Nation

VABM 2976 Nation

VABM 4120 Pack

Mountains

PRESERVE BDY

Strawberry Dome

Eagle Creek

Placer Mine

Independence Creek

Fourth of July Creek

Lucky Gulch

Gold Gulch

Michigan Creek

Montauk Bluff

VABM 2643 Mity

Jones Ridge

Harrington Cr

Nimrod Peak

Squaw Mtn

D

PRESERVE

VABM Mich 2661

Dome Creek

Placer Cr

Trout Creek

Montauk Creek

Yukon—Charley Rivers National Preserve ▲

Windfall Mtn

VABM 2581

Gilliam Creek

VABM Cha 2980

VABM 2634

VABM Trout 3346

Millers Camp

TATONDUK RIVER

CANADA
UNITED STATES

65°00'
141°00'

© DeLorme

142°00'00''
142.0000°

141°45'00''
141.7500°

141°30'00''
141.5000°

Continue on Page 119

Scale 1:300,000
1 inch represents 4.8 miles

Contour interval
200 feet (61 meters)

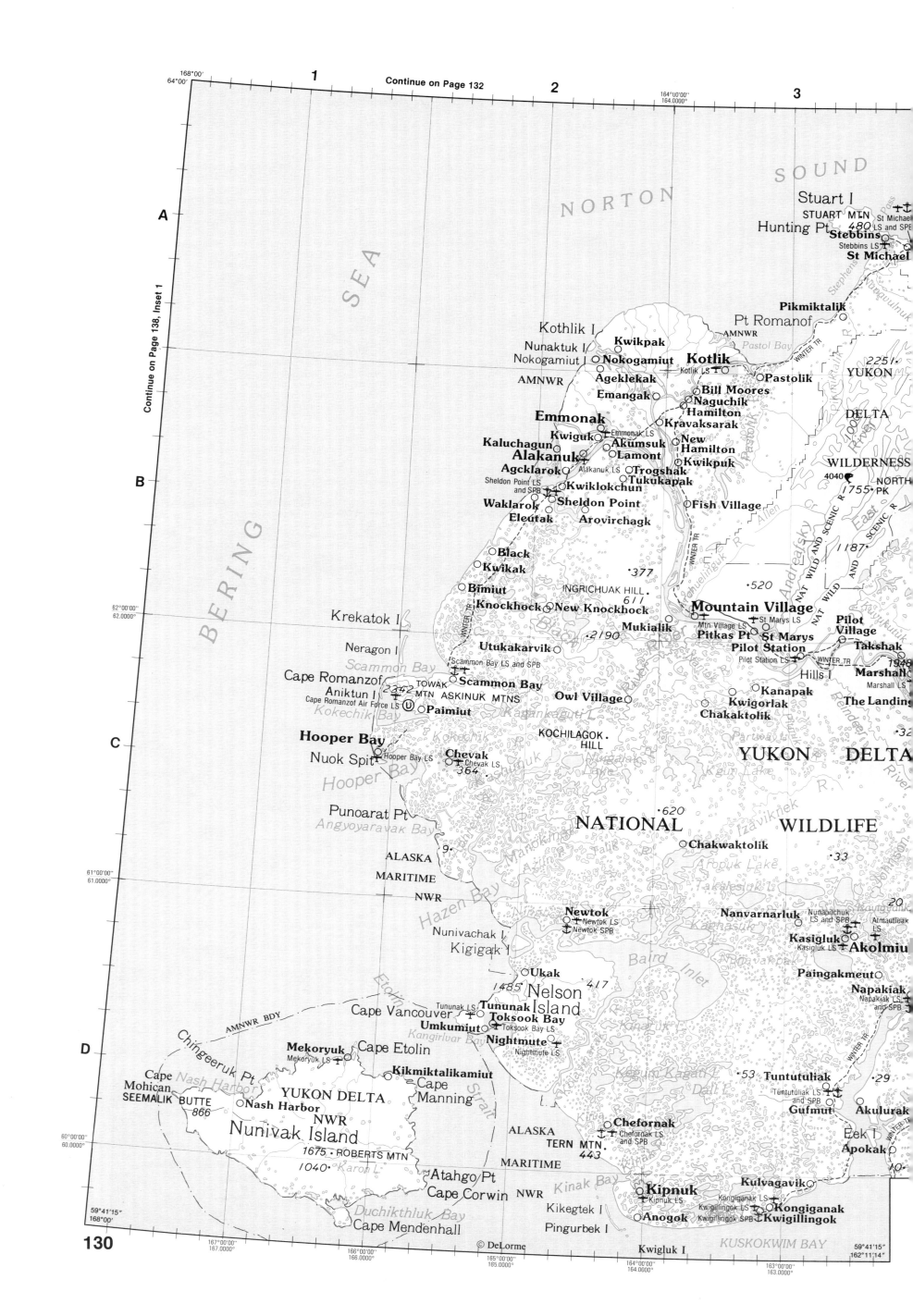

168°00'
64°00'

164°00'00"
164.0000°

A

N O R T O N   S O U N D

S E A

Stuart I
STUART MTN   St Michael
Hunting Pt   **480** LS and SPB
Stebbins
Stebbins LS
St Michael

Pikmiktalik
Pt Romanof

Continue on Page 138, Inset 1

Kothlik I
Nunaktuk I   **Kwikpak**
Nokogamiut I   **Nokogamiut**
AMNWR
AMNWR   **Ageklekak**
Kotlik LS   **Kotlik**
Pastolik
Pastol Bay
2251
YUKON

Bill Moores
Emangak   **Naguchik**
Hamilton
Kravaksarak
DELTA

Emmonak   Emmonak LS
Kwiguk   **New**
Kaluchagun   **Akumsuk**   **Hamilton**
Lamont
Alakanuk   **Kwikpuk**
Agcklarok   Alakanuk LS   **Trogshak**
Sheldon Point LS   **Kwiklokchun**   **Tukukapak**
and SPB
Waklarok   **Sheldon Point**   **Fish Village**
Eleutak   **Arovirchagk**
WILDERNESS
4040
1755 PK
NORTH
1187

B

62°00'00"
62.0000°

Black
Kwikak
Bimiut
Knockhock   **New Knockhock**
Krekatok I
INGRICHUAK HILL
611
·377
·520

Neragon I
·2190
Mukialik
Mountain Village
Mtn Village LS   St Marys LS
Pitkas Pt   **St Marys**
Pilot
Village

Scammon Bay
Cape Romanzof   TOWAK
Scammon Bay LS and SPB
Utukakarvik
Pilot Station
Pilot Station LS
WINTER TR
Takshak
1949
Marshall
Marshall LS

Aniktun I   2342 MTN   **Scammon Bay**
Cape Romanzof Air Force LS   ASKINUK MTNS
Kokechik Bay   **Paimiut**
Owl Village
Kanapak
Kwigorlak
Chakaktolik
The Landing
·32

C

61°00'00"
61.0000°

Hooper Bay
Nuok Spit   Hooper Bay LS
Chevak
Chevak LS
·364
KOCHILAGOK.
HILL
YUKON   DELTA

Punoarat Pt
Angyoyaravak Bay
·620
NATIONAL   WILDLIFE
Chakwaktolik
·33

ALASKA
9·
MARITIME
NWR
Newtok
Newtok LS
Newtok SPB
Nanvarnarluk
Nunapitchuk
LS and SPB
20
Almautluak
Kasigluk
Kasigluk LS   **Akolmiu**

Nunivachak I
Kigigak I
Paingakmeut

Hazen Bay
Ukak
1485
Nelson
417
Napakiak
Napakiak LS
and SPB

D

Cape Vancouver
Tunak LS   **Tununak**
Toksook Bay
Toksook Bay LS
Umkumiut
Nightmute
Nightmute LS
AMNWR BDY
Mekoryuk LS
Mekoryuk   Cape Etolin
Kangirlvar Bay

Cape
Mohican   Nash Harbor
SEEMALIK BUTTE
866
Kikmiktalikamiut
Cape
Manning
·53   **Tuntutuliak**
Tuntutuliak LS
and SPB
·29
Gufmut   **Akulurak**

Nash Harbor
YUKON DELTA
NWR
ALASKA
TERN MTN.
443
Eek I
Cheformak
Cheformak LS
and SPB
Apokak

60°00'00"
60.0000°
Nunivak Island
1675 ·ROBERTS MTN
MARITIME
1040·
Karon L
NWR
Atahgo Pt
Cape Corwin
Kipnuk
Kulvagavik
Kipnuk LS
Kongiganak LS   **Kongiganak**
Kwigillingok SPB   **Kwigillingok**
Anogok   Kwigillingok LS

59°41'15"
168°00'
Duchikthluk Bay
Cape Mendenhall
Kikegtek I
Pingurbek I
Kwigluk I
KUSKOKWIM BAY
59°41'15"
162°11'14"

167°00'00"
167.0000°
166°00'00"
166.0000°
© DeLorme
165°00'00"
165.0000°
164°00'00"
164.0000°
163°00'00"
163.0000°

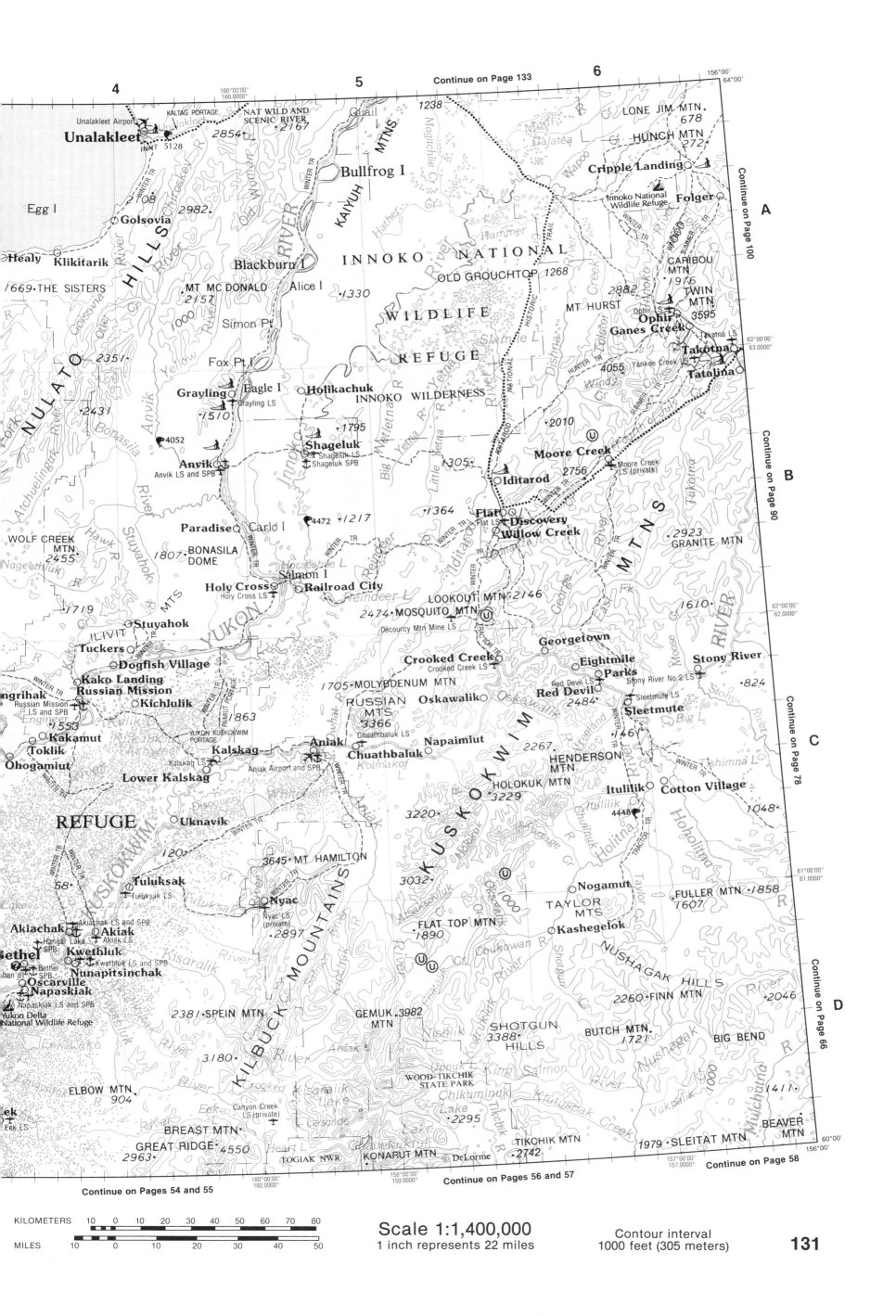

160°00'00"
160.0000'
156°00'
64°00'

Continue on Page 100

A

Continue on Page 90

B

63°00'00"
63.0000'

Continue on Page 78

C

62°00'00"
62.0000'

Continue on Page 66

D

61°00'00"
61.0000'

60°00'

157°00'00"
157.0000'

Continue on Page 58

156°00'

KALTAG PORTAGE
NAT WILD AND SCENIC RIVER
Unalakleet Airport
Unalakleet
INNT 5128
2854
Quail
1238
LONE JIM MTN. 678
HUNCH MTN 272
Galatea

Bullfrog I
KAIYUH MTNS
Cripple Landing
Innoko National Wildlife Refuge
Folger

Egg I
2708
2982
HILLS
INNOKO NATIONAL
CARIBOU MTN 1976
TWIN MTN 3595
Ophir
Ganes Creek

Healy
Klikitarik
Blackburn I
MT MC DONALD 2157
Alice I
1330
WILDLIFE
OLD GROUCHTOP 1268
MT HURST
2882
Takotna
Takotna
Tatalina

1669 · THE SISTERS
NULATO
2351
Simon Pt
Fox Pt I
REFUGE
4055
Yankee Creek
63°00'00"
63.0000'

Grayling
Eagle I
Grayling LS
1510
Holikachuk
INNOKO WILDERNESS
2010
Moore Creek
Moore Creek LS (private)

4052
1795
Shageluk
Shageluk LS
Shageluk SPB
1305
Iditarod
2756

Anvik
Anvik LS and SPB
2431
1364
Flat
Flat LS
Discovery
Willow Creek
2923
GRANITE MTN

Paradise
Carlo I
4472 · 1217

WOLF CREEK MTN 2455
BONASILA DOME
1807
Salmon I
Holy Cross
Holy Cross LS
Railroad City
Reindeer L
LOOKOUT MTN · 2146
2474 · MOSQUITO MTN
1610

1719
Stuyahok
Decourcy Mtn Mine LS

ILIVIT
Tuckers
Dogfish Village
Crooked Creek
Crooked Creek LS
Georgetown
Stony River

Kako Landing
Russian Mission
Kichlulik
1705 · MOLYBDENUM MTN
Eightmile
Parks
Stony River No 2 LS
824

grihak
Russian Mission LS and SPB
1553
1863
RUSSIAN MTS 3366
Oskawaliko
Red Devil
2484
Sleetmute LS
Sleetmute

Kakamut
Toklik
Kalskag
Chuathbaluk LS
Aniak
Chuathbaluk
Napaimiut
2267
1461

Ohogamiut
YUKON KUSKOKWIM PORTAGE
Kalskag LS
Aniak Airport and SPB
Kolmakof
HENDERSON MTN

REFUGE
Lower Kalskag
HOLOKUK MTN 3229
Itulilik
Cotton Village
1048

Uknavik
3220
4448

1205
Tuluksak
Tuluksak LS
3645 MT HAMILTON
3032
Nogamut
FULLER MTN · 1858
1607

58
Nyac
Nyac LS (private)
FLAT TOP MTN 1890
TAYLOR MTS
Kashegelok

Akiachak
Akiachak LS and SPB
Akiak
Akiak LS
2897
NUSHAGAK HILLS

Bethel
Hangar Lake
Kwethluk
Kwethluk LS and SPB
2260 · FINN MTN
2046

ban d)
Bethel SPB
Nunapitsinchak
SPEIN MTN
GEMUK MTN 3982
SHOTGUN HILLS 3388
BUTCH MTN 1721
BIG BEND

Oscarville
Napaskiak
2381
1411

Napaskiak LS and SPB
Yukon Delta National Wildlife Refuge
3180
WOOD-TIKCHIK STATE PARK
Chikuminuk Lake
2295
1979 · SLEITAT MTN
BEAVER MTN

ELBOW MTN 904

ek
Eek LS
Canyon Creek LS (private)
BREAST MTN
GREAT RIDGE 4550
2963
TOGIAK NWR
KONARUT MTN
DeLorme
TIKCHIK MTN · 2742

Continue on Pages 54 and 55

160°00'00"
160.0000'

Continue on Pages 56 and 57

159°00'00"
159.0000'

KILOMETERS   10   0   10   20   30   40   50   60   70   80

MILES   10   0   10   20   30   40   50

Scale 1:1,400,000
1 inch represents 22 miles

Contour interval
1000 feet (305 meters)

131

Continue on Page 134

CHUKCHI SEA

RUSSIAN FEDERATION
UNITED STATES

Cape Seppings

1281 ·2195

Kivalina
Kivalina LS

5180

Wulik River

Imikruk Lagoon

MULGRAVE HILLS

Noatak
Noatak LS

Rabbit R

1155

Kotlik Lagoon

CAPE KRUSENSTERN NATIONAL MONUMENT

Nauyoaruk

IGICHUK

Cape Krusenstern

Krusenstern Lagoon

Cape Krusenstern National Monument

Sheshalik
Sheshalik Spit

KOTZEBUE

ARCTIC CIRCLE

Espenberg

Kividlo Singeak

Cape Espenberg

Devil Mtn Lakes Killeak Lakes

AMWR BDY

WINTER TR

Shishmaref LS

Bering Land Bridge National Preserve

Shishmaref

Shishmaref LS (new)

Cape Lowenstern

DEVIL MTN ·798

BERING LAND BRIDGE NAT PRESERVE

Nugnugaluktuk R

Goodhope Bay

Deering L (new)

Shishmaref Inlet

Ikpek Lagoon

AMNWR BDY

WINTER TR

Penthe

Goodhope R

Fish R

Utica Creek LS

Fink Creek

Cottonwood
·2073

Cloud L

Imuruk Lake

EAR MTN ·2325

Arctic

1672

American R

Serpentine Hot Springs

2640

Trinity LS (private)

Big Diomede I

INTERNATIONAL DATELINE

BERING STRAIT

Little Diomede I

Mitletukeruk

Mugisitokiwik

Inalik

Cape Prince of Wales

Lopp Lagoon

Buck Creek LS (private)

Mint River

Pinguk River

Nuluk Shelter
·1571

2870

Taylor
Taylor LS (private)

Nukwuk River

Lava L

Wales
Wales LS

Tin City
Tin City AFLS

York

YORK MTS

BROOKS MTN ·2898

CONTINENTAL DIVIDE

SEWARD

4598

N W ARCTIC

Kuzitrin

Kuzitrin R

Cape York

York No 2 LS

Lost River

Brevig

Igloo

Dahl

BENDELEBEN MTNS

Lost River No 1 LS (private)

Agiapuk R

Quartz Creek
Kougarok LS

Brakes Bottom

Kougarok

Brevig Mission
Brevig Mission LS

Grantley Harbor

TRACTOR TR

Bunker Hill
3730·MT BENDELEBEN

Pt Spencer

Port Clarence

Davidsons Landing

Port Clarence CGLS (emergency only)

Teller
Teller LS

New Igloo

Kougarok R

Niukluk R

Kuzitrin R

WINTER TR

Port Clarence

Imuruk Basin

4804

Pilgrim Springs

1000

Bargon

King I

Ukivok

Cape Douglas

WINTER TR

Sullivan Camp

KIGLUAIK MOUNTAINS 4714·MT OSBORN

3870

4732

Iron Creek

Council (Pedersen) LS (private)

Council
Council LS

AMNWR

WOOLLEY LAGOON RD

Feather River

Salmon Lake LS

TAYLOR HWY

4892 2069

2089

Singigyak

Glacial

NOME-TELLER HWY

Jensens Camp

Solomon R

Ruby Roadhouse

Cape Rodney

1781

Oregon

4740

Casadepaga

WINTER TR

Sinuk R

Basin Creek LS

East Fork

White Mtn

BERING SEA

Sinuk

4944

Summit

Sunset

Solomon State LS (private)

White Mountain LS

Topkok

Tonok

Bluff

Golovin LS (new)

Golovin

Nome-Airport

Nome City LS

Eldorado

Solomon

NOME-COUNCIL HWY

Dickson

AMNWR

Golovin

Sledge I

Nome Gold

Iditarod National Historic Trail

Carrie McLain Memorial Museum

Nome Fort Davis

Cape Nome Port Safety

IKNUTAK MTN 1688·

Rocky Pt Golovin Mission

Golovnin Bay

AMNWR

NORTON

Continue on Page 138, Inset 1

© DeLorme

Continue on Page 130

KILOMETERS	10	0	10	20	30	40	50	60	70	80

MILES	10	0	10	20	30	40	50

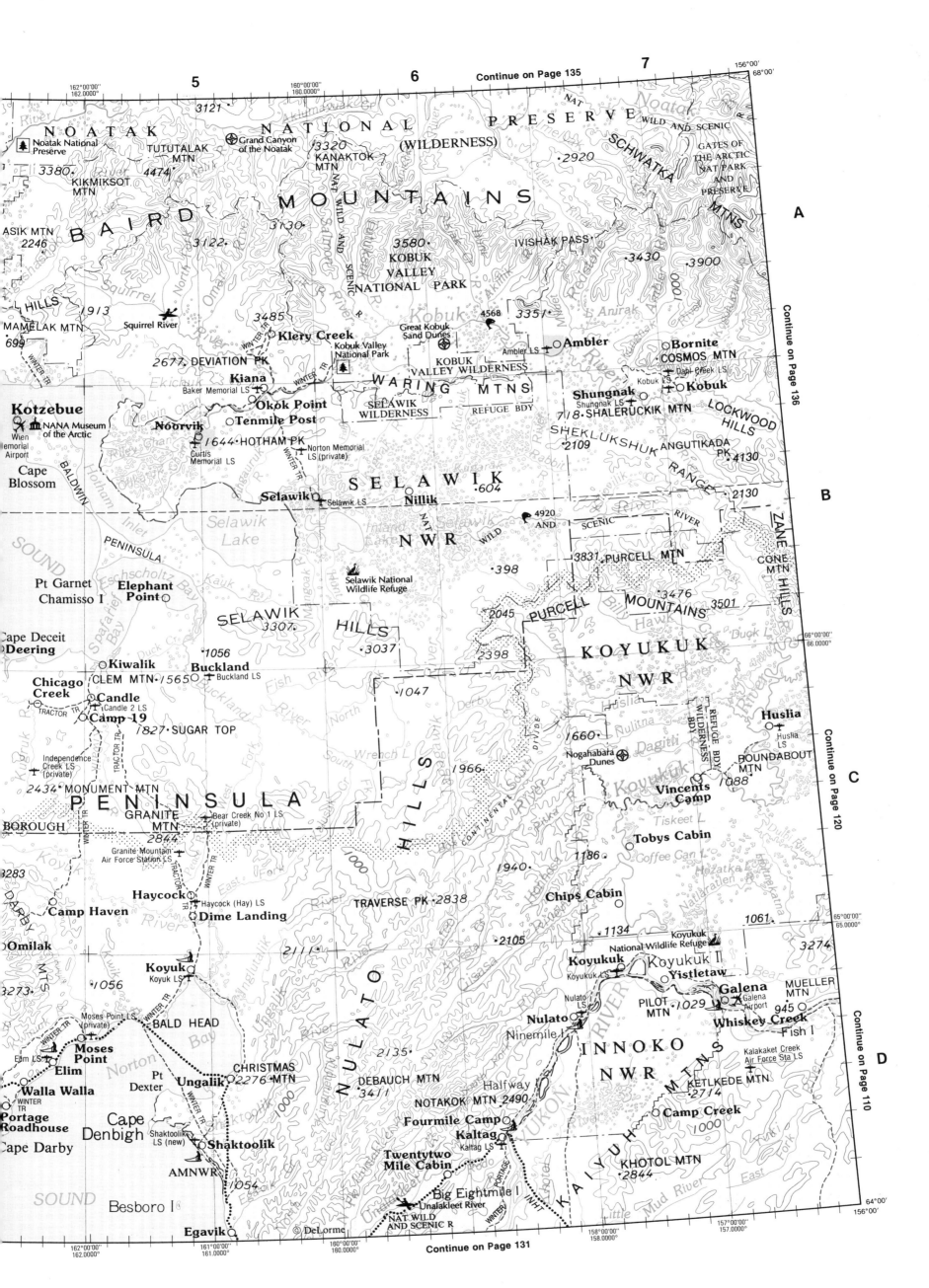

Continue on Page 136
Continue on Page 120
Continue on Page 110

Scale 1:1,400,000
1 inch represents 22 miles

Contour interval
1000 feet (305 meters)

Continue on Page 132

Continue on Page 133

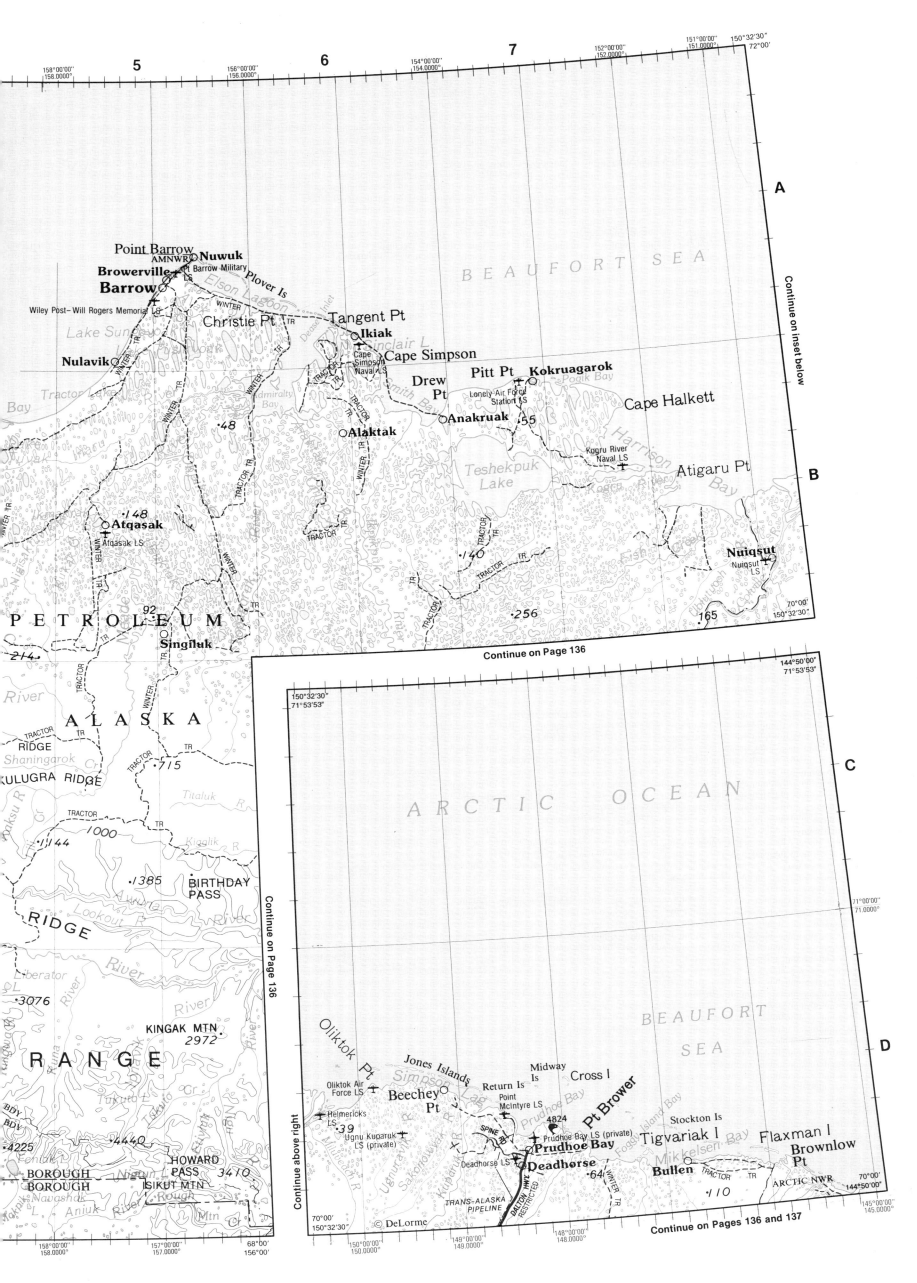

5   6   7

158°00'00" 156°00'00" 154°00'00" 152°00'00" 151°00'00" 150°32'30" 72°00'
158.0000°   156.0000°   154.0000°   152.0000°   151.0000°   150°32'30"

A

Continue on inset below

BEAUFORT SEA

Point Barrow
AMNWR Nuwuk
Pt Barrow Military
Browerville
Barrow Plover Is
Wiley Post–Will Rogers Memorial LS
Christie Pt Tangent Pt
Ikiak
Cape Simpson
Cape Simpson Naval LS
Nulavik Pitt Pt Kokruagarok
Drew Pt Lonely Air Force Station LS Cape Halkett
Anakruak ·55
·48 Alaktak
Atigaru Pt
Kogru River Naval LS
B
·148 Teshekpuk Lake
Atqasak
Atqasak LS
·140
Nuiqsut
Nuiqsut LS
PETROLEUM 92 ·256 ·165 70°00'
Singiluk 150°32'30"
·214

Continue on Page 136

ALASKA
150°32'30" 144°50'00"
71°53'53" 71°53'53"

RIDGE
Shaningarok Cr
KULUGRA RIDGE ·715
C
ARCTIC OCEAN

1000
·1144
·1385 BIRTHDAY PASS

Continue on Page 136
Continue above right

71°00'00"
71.0000°

·3076
KINGAK MTN
2972
RANGE

BEAUFORT SEA

Oliktok Pt
Jones Islands Midway Is Cross I
D
Oliktok Air Force LS Return Is
Beechey Pt Point McIntyre LS
Helmericks LS Pt Brower
·39 4824
Ugnu Kuparuk LS (private) SPINE Prudhoe Bay LS (private) Stockton Is
Prudhoe Bay Tigvariak I Flaxman I
BDY Deadhorse LS Brownlow Pt
BDY Deadhorse
·4225 ·4440 ·64 Bullen ·110 ARCTIC NWR
BOROUGH HOWARD PASS 3410 70°00'
BOROUGH ISIKUT MTN TRANS-ALASKA PIPELINE DALTON HWY RESTRICTED 144°50'00"
© DeLorme 145.0000°

68°00' 70°00' Continue on Pages 136 and 137
156°00' 150°32'30"
149°00'00" 148°00'00"
149.0000° 148.0000°

Scale 1:1,400,000
1 inch represents 22 miles

Contour interval
1000 feet (305 meters)

135

Continue on Page 135

Continue on Page 135

Continue on Page 133

Continue on Pages 120 and 121

Continue on Pages 122 and 123

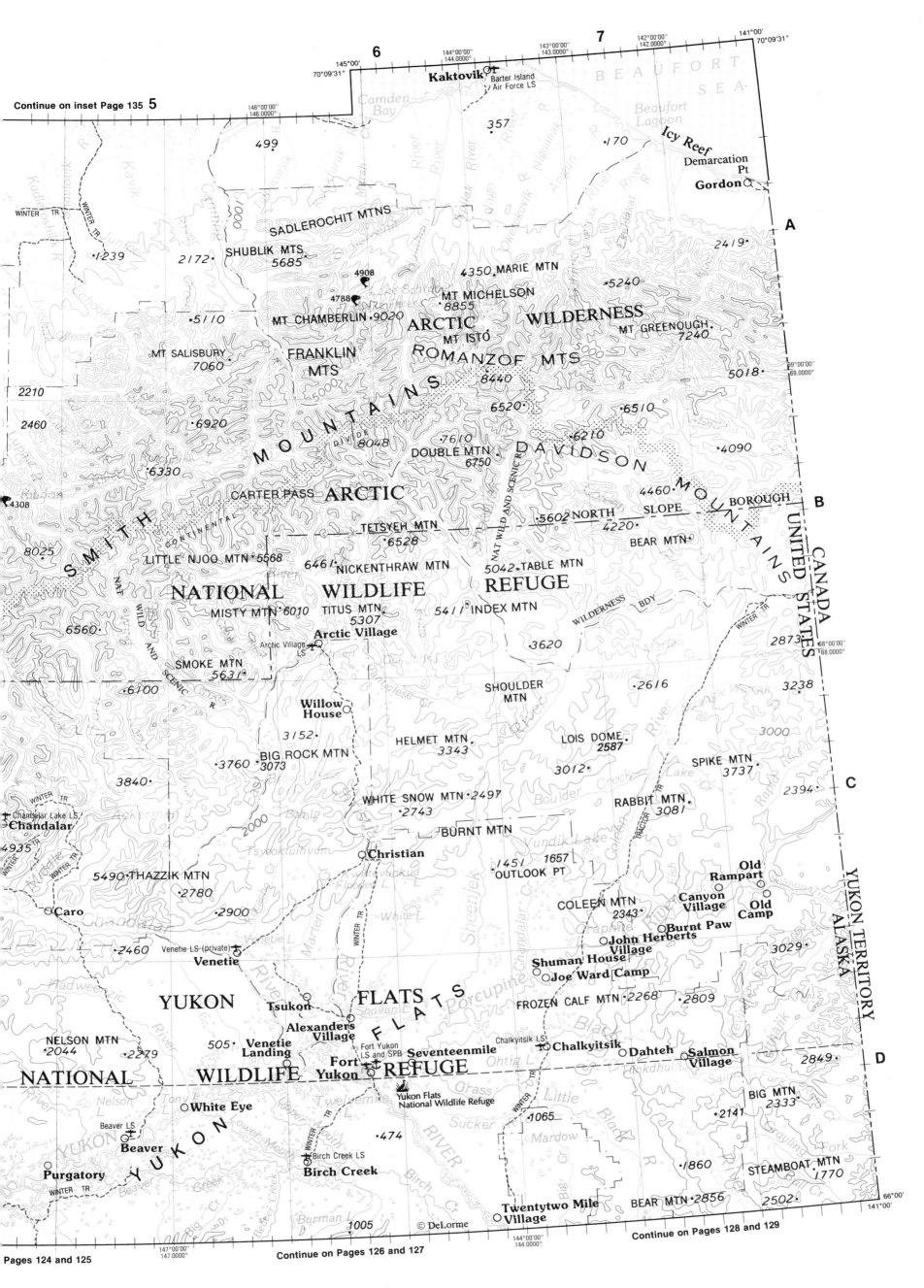

Continue on inset Page 135 **5**

6

7

145°00' 70°09'31"
146°00'00" 146.0000°
144°00'00" 144.0000°
143°00'00" 143.0000°
142°00'00" 142.0000°
141°00' 70°09'31"

Kaktovik Barter Island Air Force LS

B E A U F O R T   S E A

Camden Bay

Beaufort Lagoon

357 ·170 Icy Reef

Demarcation Pt

Gordon

499

·1239 2172· SADLEROCHIT MTNS

SHUBLIK MTS 5685

4908

4788·

·5110 MT CHAMBERLIN ·9020

MT MICHELSON 8855

4350 ·MARIE MTN

·5240

·2419

A

MT ISTÓ

ARCTIC   WILDERNESS

MT GREENOUGH 7240

MT SALISBURY 7060

FRANKLIN MTS

ROMANZOF MTS

·5018

2210 ·6920

8440

6520·

·6510

69°00'00" 69.0000°

2460

M O U N T A I N S

DIVIDE 8048

·7610

DOUBLE MTN 6750

·6210

D A V I D S O N

·4090

·6330

·4460

M O U N T A I N S

BOROUGH

B

·4308

CARTER PASS   ARCTIC

CONTINENTAL

8025

S M I T H

TETSYEH MTN ·6528

·5602 NORTH   SLOPE

4220·

BEAR MTN·

NAT WILD AND SCENIC R

LITTLE NJOO MTN ·5568

646· NICKENTHRAW MTN

5042 ·TABLE MTN

N A T I O N A L   W I L D L I F E   R E F U G E

MISTY MTN· ·6010

TITUS MTN 5307

5411· INDEX MTN

WILDERNESS   BDY

WINTER TR

2873·

6560·

·3620

68°00'00" 68.0000°

SMOKE MTN 5631·

Arctic Village LS **Arctic Village**

·6100

WILD AND SCENIC R

·2616

3238

SHOULDER MTN

C

Willow House

3152·

HELMET MTN 3343

LOIS DOME 2587

3000

SPIKE MTN 3737

·3760 BIG ROCK MTN 3073

3012·

2394·

3840·

WHITE SNOW MTN ·2497

Boulder   Creek

RABBIT MTN· 3081

·Chandalar Lake LS **Chandalar**

·2743

BURNT MTN

4935·

Christian

1451 1657

OUTLOOK PT

Old Rampart

5490·THAZZIK MTN

·2780

COLEEN MTN 2343

Canyon Village

Old Camp

Caro

·2900

John Herberts Village

Burnt Paw

·2460

Venetie LS (private)

Shuman House

3029·

Venetie

Joe Ward Camp

Tsukon

YUKON

FLATS

F L A T S

FROZEN CALF MTN ·2268 ·2809

NELSON MTN ·2044 ·2279

Alexanders Village

505·

Porcupine

ALASKA

Chalkyitsik LS **Chalkyitsik**

Dahteh

Salmon Village

2849·

D

Venetie Landing

Fort Yukon LS and SPB

Seventeenmile

Fort Yukon

WILDLIFE   **REFUGE**

Yukon Flats National Wildlife Refuge

3029·

N A T I O N A L

White Eye

·1065

·2141

BIG MTN 2333·

Beaver LS

Y U K O N

·474

·1860

STEAMBOAT MTN 1770

Beaver

Birch Creek LS

Purgatory

WINTER TR

Birch Creek

© DeLorme

1005

Twentytwo Mile Village

BEAR MTN ·2856

2502·

66°00'

141°00'

CANADA   UNITED STATES

YUKON TERRITORY

Pages 124 and 125

147°00'00" 147.0000°

Continue on Pages 126 and 127

144°00'00" 144.0000°

Continue on Pages 128 and 129

Scale 1:1,400,000
1 inch represents 22 miles

Contour interval
1000 feet (305 meters)

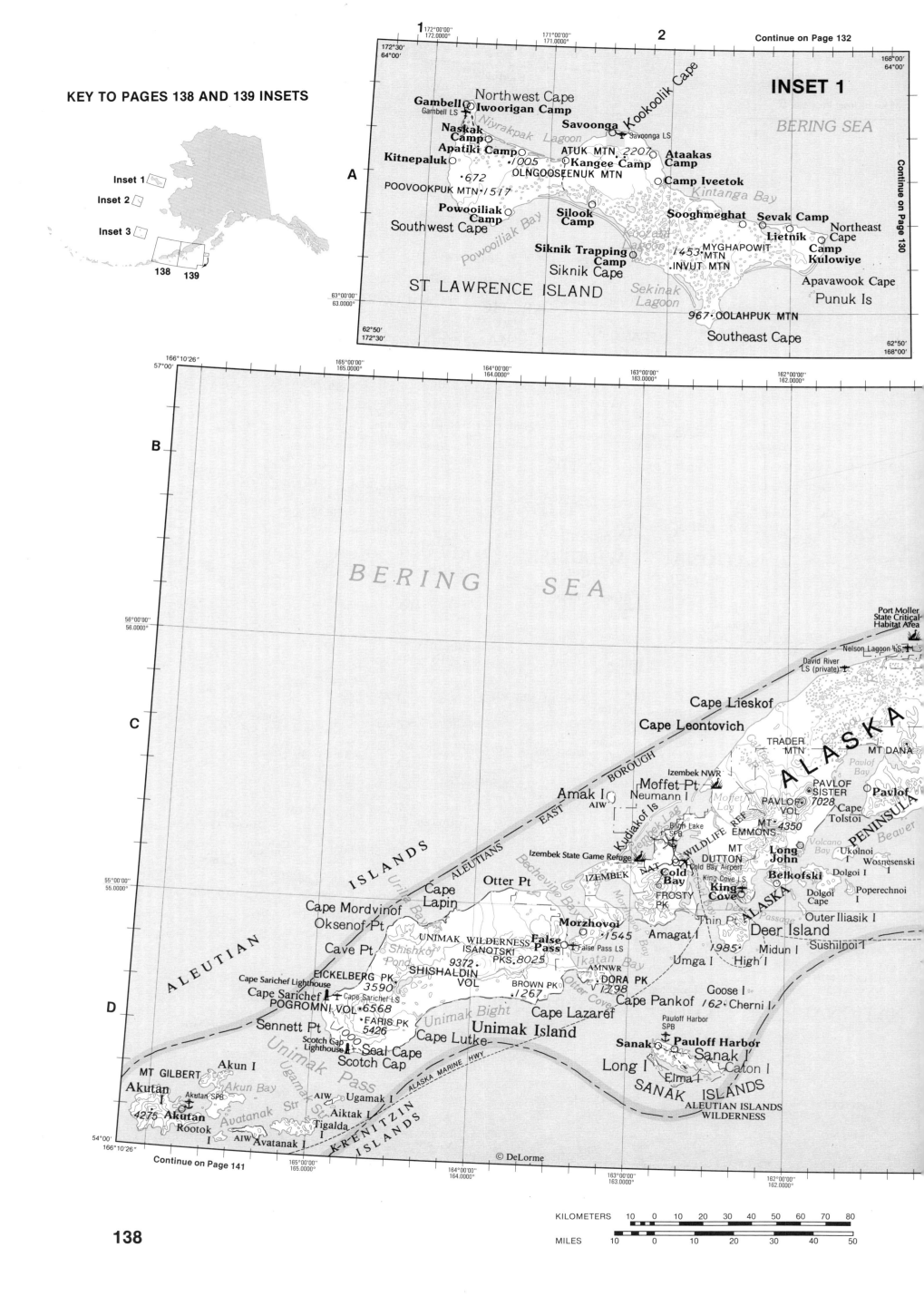

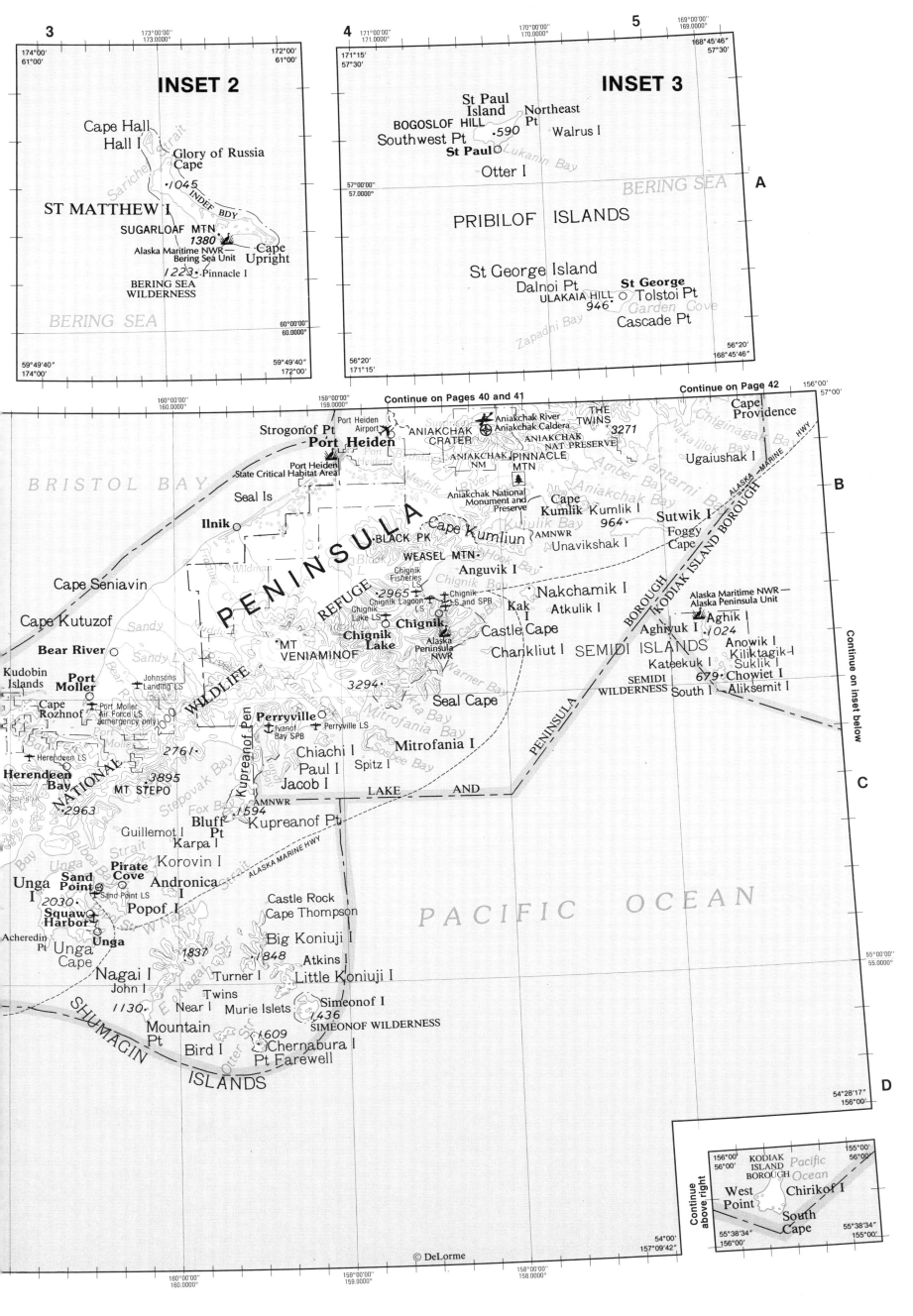

INSET 2

3

174°00'
61°00'
173°00'00"
173.0000°
172°00'
61°00'

Cape Hall
Hall I

Sariche f Strait
Glory of Russia
Cape
·1045

ST MATTHEW I
SUGARLOAF MTN
1380
Alaska Maritime NWR—
Bering Sea Unit
1223· Pinnacle I

INDEF BDY
Cape
Upright

BERING SEA
WILDERNESS

BERING SEA
60°00'00"
60.0000°

59°49'40"
174°00'
59°49'40"
172°00'

INSET 3

4
171°15'
57°30'
171°00'00"
171.0000°
170°00'00"
170.0000°
5
169°00'00"
169.0000°
168°45'46"
57°30'

St Paul
Island
Northeast
Pt
BOGOSLOF HILL
Southwest Pt   ·590   Walrus I
St Paul

Lukanin Bay

57°00'00"
57.0000°
Otter I

BERING SEA

A

PRIBILOF ISLANDS

St George Island
Dalnoi Pt   St George
ULAKAIA HILL ○ Tolstoi Pt
946·   Garden Cove
Cascade Pt

Zapadni Bay
56°20'
168°45'46"

56°20'
171°15'

Continue on Pages 40 and 41   Continue on Page 42
156°00'
57°00'

160°00'00"
160.0000°
159°00'00"
159.0000°

Strogonof Pt
Port Heiden
Airport

Port Heiden

ANIAKCHAK
CRATER
Aniakchak River
Aniakchak Caldera
THE
TWINS
·3271
Cape
Providence

Chiginagak Bay

BRISTOL BAY

Port Heiden
State Critical Habitat Area

ANIAKCHAK
NM
ANIAKCHAK PINNACLE
NAT PRESERVE MTN

Nakalilok Bay
Alaska Marine HWY
Ugaiushak I

B

Seal Is

Meshik River

Aniakchak National
Monument and
Preserve

Amber Bay

Ilnik

BLACK PK
Cape Kumlik
Cape
Kumlik
Kumlik I
964·

AMNWR

Yantarni Bay
Aniakchak Bay

Sutwik I
Foggy
Cape

Kodiak Island Borough

PENINSULA
WEASEL MTN
Kiuilik Bay
Unavikshak I

Anguvik I

BOROUGH

Cape Seniavin

Chignik
Fisheries
·2965
Chignik Lagoon

Chignik Bay
Nakchamik I
Atkulik I

Alaska Maritime NWR—
Alaska Peninsula Unit

Cape Kutuzof

REFUGE
Chignik
Lake LS
Chignik
LS and SPB
Kak
I

Aghiyuk I
Aghik I
·1024

Bear River

WILDLIFE
MT
VENIAMINOF
Chignik
Chignik
Lake
Chignik
Lake

Castle Cape
Castle Bay
Chankliut I
SEMIDI ISLANDS
Anowik I
Kiliktagik I
Suklik I

Kudobin
Islands
Port
Moller
Johnsons
Landing LS
Alaska
Peninsula
NWR
SEMIDI
WILDERNESS
South I
Kateekuk I
679· Chowiet I
Aliksemit I

Cape
Rozhnof
Port Moller
Air Force LS
(emergency only)

3294·

Warner Bay
Seal Cape

Herendeen LS
Kupreanof Pen
Perryville
Ivanof
Bay SPB
Perryville LS

Mitrofania Bay
Kujulik Bay
PENINSULA

C

HEREENDEEN
BAY
2761·
NATIONAL
3895
MT STEPO
·2963

Mitrofania I
LAKE   AND

Chiachi I
Paul I
Jacob I
Spitz I

Sosbee Bay

AMNWR
·1594
Bluff
Pt
Kupreanof Pt

Guillemot I
Karpa I
ALASKA MARINE HWY

PACIFIC   OCEAN

Korovin I

Stepovak Bay

Pirate
Cove

Fox Bay
Castle Rock
Cape Thompson

Sand
Point
Andronica
I

Unga
I
2030·
Sand Point LS
Popof I

Big Koniuji I
55°00'00"
55.0000°

Squaw
Harbor
Unga
W Nagai I

1837·
·1848
Atkins I

Acheredin
Pt
Unga
Cape
Turner I
Little Koniuji I

Nagai I
John I

Twins
Near I
Murie Islets
Simeonof I
1436·

1130·
Mountain
Pt
Bird I
·1609
Chernabura I
SIMEONOF WILDERNESS

SHUMAGIN
Pt Farewell

ISLANDS

D

54°28'17"
156°00'

160°00'00"
160.0000°
159°00'00"
159.0000°
158°00'00"
158.0000°
157°09'42"
54°00'

© DeLorme

Continue above right / Continue on inset below

156°00'
56°00'
KODIAK
ISLAND
BOROUGH
Pacific
Ocean
155°00'
56°00'

West
Point
Chirikof I

South
Cape
55°38'34"
156°00'
55°38'34"
155°00'

Scale 1:1,400,000
1 inch represents 22 miles

Contour interval
1000 feet (305 meters)

139

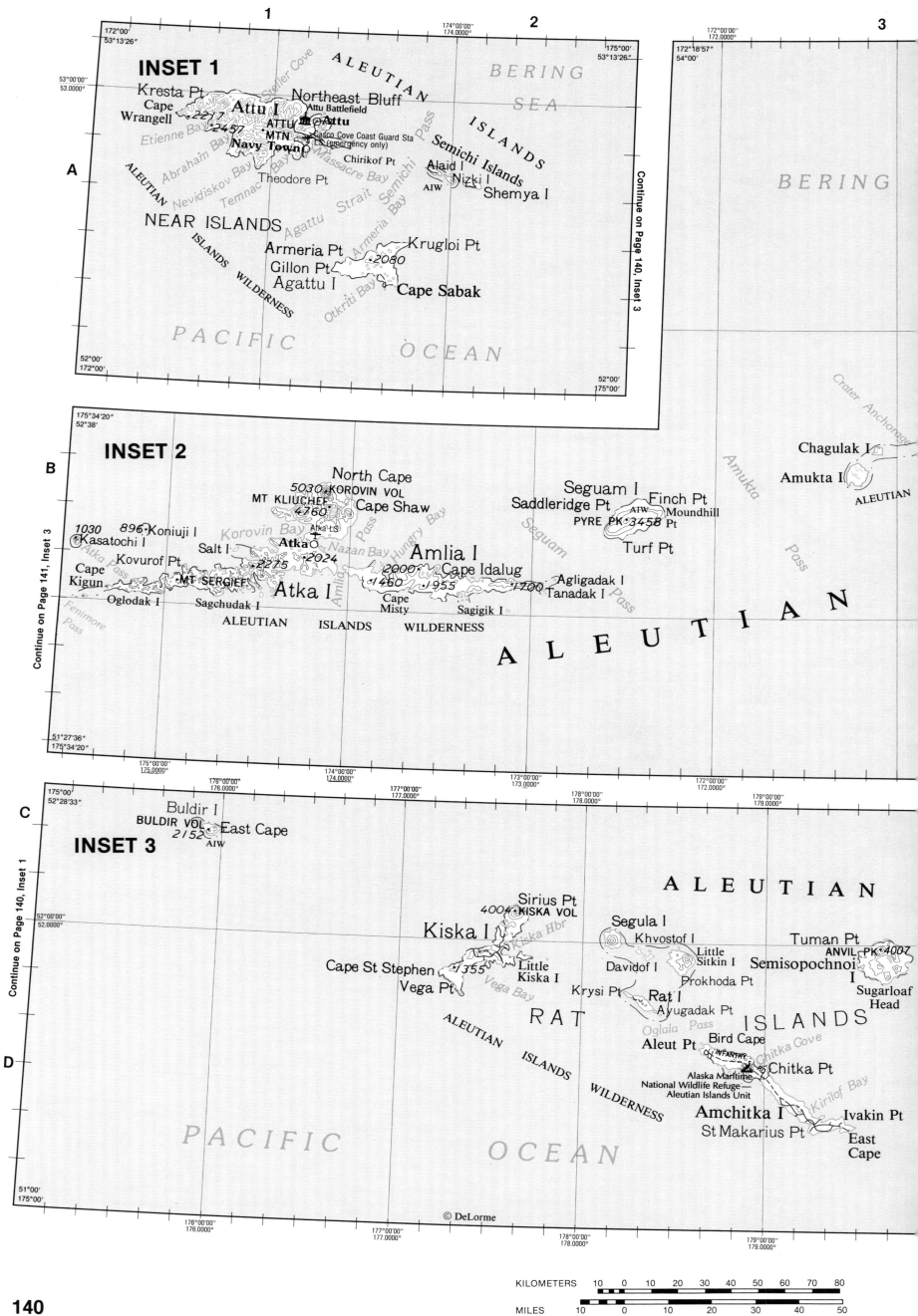

INSET 1

1   174°00'00''   2
174.0000°

172°00'   175°00'
53°13'26''   53°13'26''

53°00'00''
53.0000°

ALEUTIAN   *BERING*
ISLANDS   *SEA*

Kresta Pt   *Steller Cove*
Cape   Northeast Bluff
Wrangell   Attu I   Attu Battlefield
·2217   ATTU
·2457   ATTU   Attu
MTN   Casco Cove Coast Guard Sta
Navy Town   LS (emergency only)

A   Chirikof Pt   Semichi Islands
Alaid I
Theodore Pt   Nizki I   Shemya I
AIW

Nevidiskov Bay   *Semichi*
Abraham Bay   *Massacre Bay*   *Bay*

ALEUTIAN
Temnac Bay   *Agattu*   *Strait*

NEAR ISLANDS

Armeria Pt   Krugloi Pt
Armeria Bay   ·2080
ISLANDS   Gillon Pt
WILDERNESS   Agattu I   **Cape Sabak**
Otkriti Bay

52°00'   *PACIFIC*   *OCEAN*   52°00'
172°00'   175°00'

Continue on Page 140, Inset 3

172°00'00''
172.0000°

3

172°18'57''
54°00'

BERING

INSET 2

175°34'20''
52°38'

B

Crater Anchorage

Chagulak I
Amukta I

North Cape
5030 KOROVIN VOL
MT KLIUCHEF   Cape Shaw   Seguam I   Finch Pt
·4760   Saddleridge Pt   AIW   Moundhill
1030   896·Koniuji I   Atka LS   PYRE PK·3458 Pt
Kasatochi I   *Korovin Bay*   Turf Pt
Salt I   **Atka**   *Hungry Bay*
Kovurof Pt   ·2275   ·2024   Amlia I
Cape   **MT SERGIEF**   2000·   Cape Idalug
Kigun   *Nazan Bay*   ·1460   ·955   Agligadak I
Oglodak I   Sagchudak I   Atka I   Cape   ·1100   Tanadak I
Misty   Sagigik I
ALEUTIAN   **ISLANDS**   **WILDERNESS**

Atka Pass   *Amlia Pass*   *Seguam Pass*   *Amukta Pass*   **ALEUTIAN**

Fenimore
Pass

Continue on Page 141, Inset 3

51°27'36''
175°34'20''

A L E U T I A N

175°00'00''   174°00'00''   173°00'00''   172°00'00''
175.0000°   174.0000°   173.0000°   172.0000°

INSET 3

175°00'
52°28'33''

C

Buldir I
BULDIR VOL   East Cape
2152   AIW

A L E U T I A N

Sirius Pt
400·KISKA VOL   Segula I
Kiska I   *Kiska Hbr*   Khvostof I   Tuman Pt
Little   ANVIL PK·4007
Cape St Stephen   ·1355   Little   Sitkin I   Semisopochnoi
Kiska I   Davidof I   I
Vega Pt   Prokhoda Pt   Sugarloaf
Vega Bay   Krysi Pt   Rat I   Head
RAT
Ayugadak Pt
Oglala Pass

Continue on Page 140, Inset 1

52°00'00''
52.0000°

D

ALEUTIAN   **ISLANDS**
Aleut Pt   Bird Cape
Chitka Cove
WILDERNESS   Alaska Maritime   Chitka Pt
National Wildlife Refuge—
Aleutian Islands Unit
Amchitka I   Ivakin Pt
St Makarius Pt   East
Cape
Kirilof Bay

51°00'   *PACIFIC*   *OCEAN*
175°00'

© DeLorme

176°00'00''   177°00'00''   178°00'00''   179°00'00''
176.0000°   177.0000°   178.0000°   179.0000°

KILOMETERS   10   0   10   20   30   40   50   60   70   80

MILES   10   0   10   20   30   40   50

Continue on Page 138

4

5

54°03'26"

167°00'   166°00'   54°03'26"

170°00'00"
170.0000°

168°00'00"
168.0000°

Cape Cheerful

MARINE HWY

Driftwood LS (private)

Unalga I

Bogoslof I. 1.43

Dutch
Harbor
Unalaska   Unalaska
Airport

BOGOSLOF
WILDERNESS

MAKUSHIN VOL

Cape Kovrizhka

Makushin

Biorka

Makushin Bay

2340

Sedanka
I

SEA

Cape Tanak

Skan Bay

Spray Cape

Pumicestone Bay

Unalaska
I

Kayak Cape

Camp

Aguliuk Pt

OKMOK
CALDERA

1000

Cape Idak

Chernofski SPB

Kashega

Whalebone Cape

A

TULIK VOL

Fort
Glenn

MT KIMBLE

Usof Bay

4111

LONE PK

Cape Aiak

Lance Pt

Cape Ilmalianuk

Umnak Island

Thumb Pt

Cape Izigan

MT VSEVIDOF

MT RECHESHNOI
6510

53°00'00"
53.0000°

2915   Uliaga I

Kigul I

Ogchul I

FOX   ISLANDS

Kagamil Pass

2930

Adugak I

Vsevidof I

Nikolski LS

Carlisle I

Chuginadak I   5675

Nikolski

Cape Udak

Driftwood Bay

ISLANDS

Herbert I

Cape Sagak

Samalga I

East Cove

ISLANDS OF FOUR MTNS

Samalga Pass

Chuginadak Pass

Nikolski Bay

Yunaska I   WILDERNESS

ISLANDS

ISLANDS

52°00'00"
52.0000°

PACIFIC   OCEAN

51°27'36"

166°00'

Scale 1:1,400,000
1 inch represents 22 miles

Contour interval
1000 feet (305 meters)

175°34'20"
52°28'33"

C

Continue on Page 140, Inset 2

BERING   SEA

ISLANDS

Great Sitkin I

Ulak

Fenimore Pass

Cape Akuyan

5710

Cape Adagdak

Igitkin I

Tanaklak I

Tanaga I

Bumpy Pt

Bobrof I   KANAGA VOL

MT MOFFETT

Kanu I

Chugul

TANAGA VOL   5197

2421

4287

Adak

Umak I

Cape Sajaka

1585

Cape Sudak

2495

Amchitka   Pass

Gareloi I   MT GARELOI

Kanaga I

Adak Naval Air Sta LS
(Mitchell Field)

Little Tanaga I

5160

410

Adak I

Kagalaska

Tanaga Bay

Kanaga Pass

Kuluk Bay

1935

Elf I

Cape Amagalik

Chunu Bay

Adak Strait

Crone I

Little Tanaga Strait

Unalga I

Ogliuga I   Skagul I

Cape
Tusik

Turret Pt

Beaver Bay

Dinkum Rocks

Tag Is

Cape
Chunu

Cape Yakak

WILDERNESS

ISLANDS

Kavalga I

Gramp Rock   Ilak I

South Bay

Cape
Sasmik

Bay of Waterfalls

D

ALEUTIAN ISLANDS
WILDERNESS

ALEUTIAN   ISLANDS

Tanadak I   Ulak I

ANDREANOF

1690

Hasgox Pt

Amatignak I   Knob Pt

Nitrof Pt

© DeLorme

180°00'00"
180.0000°

179°00'00"
179.0000°

178°00'00"
178.0000°

177°00'00"
177.0000°

176°00'00"
176.0000°

175°34'20"

51°00'

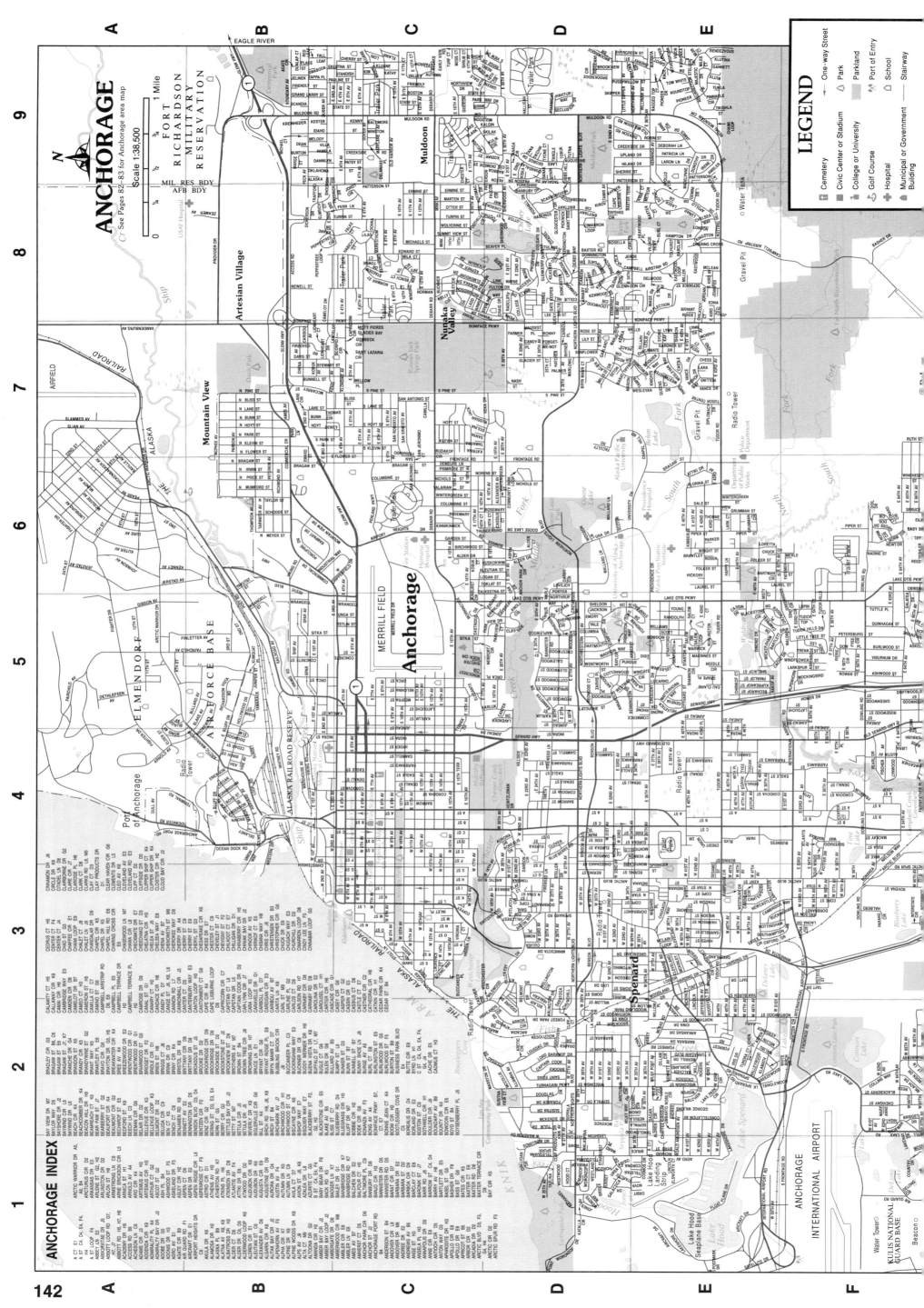

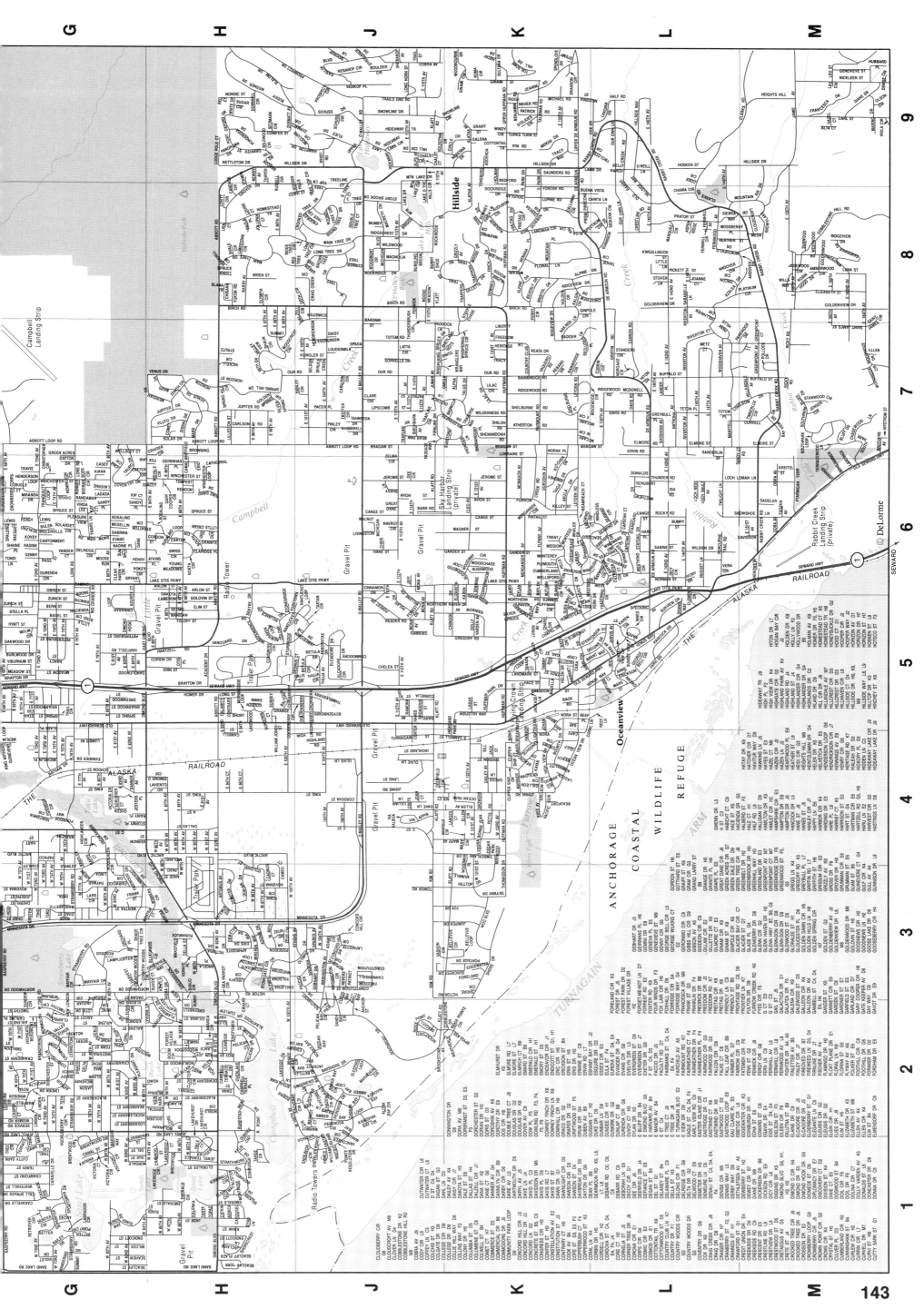

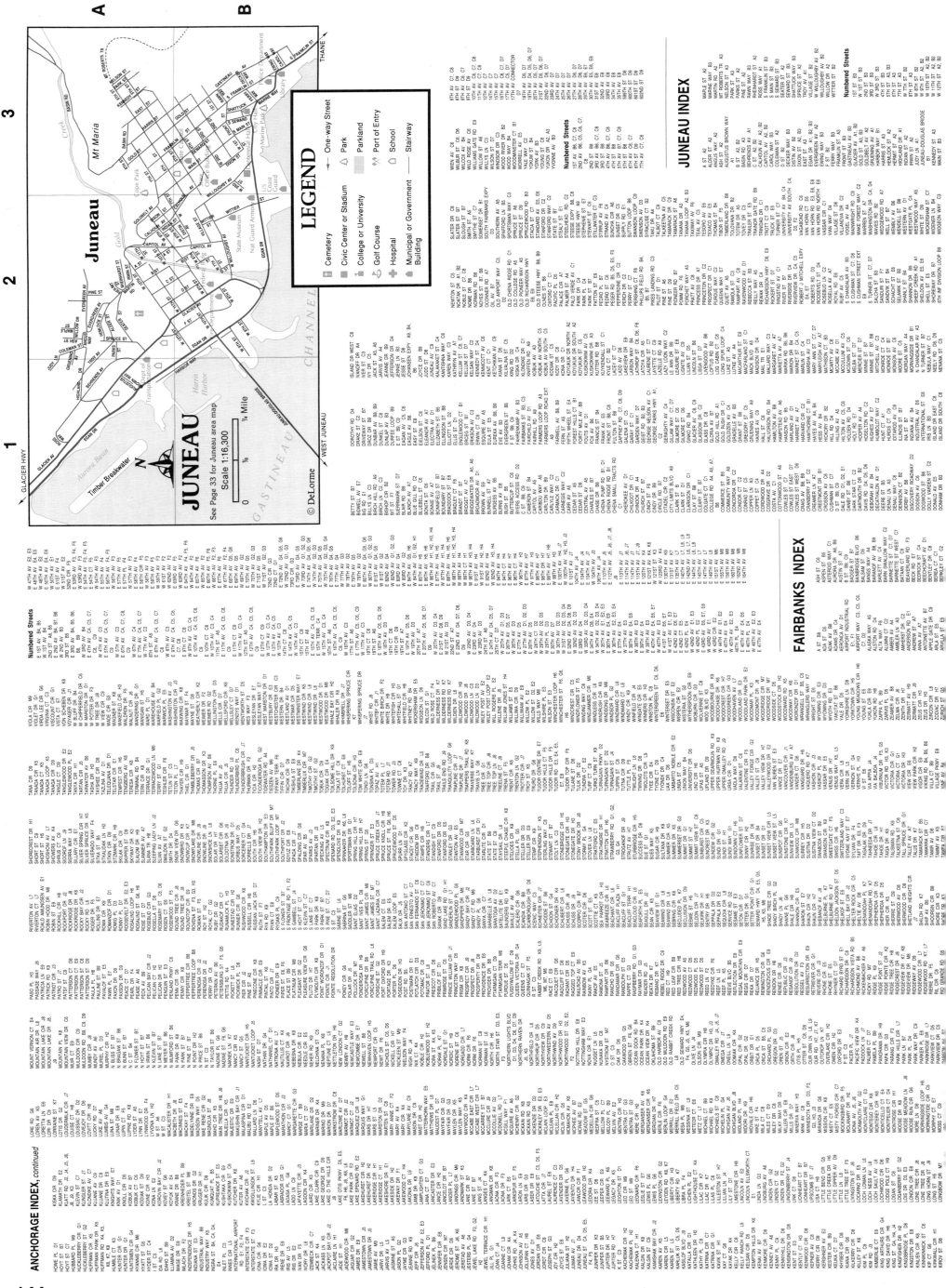

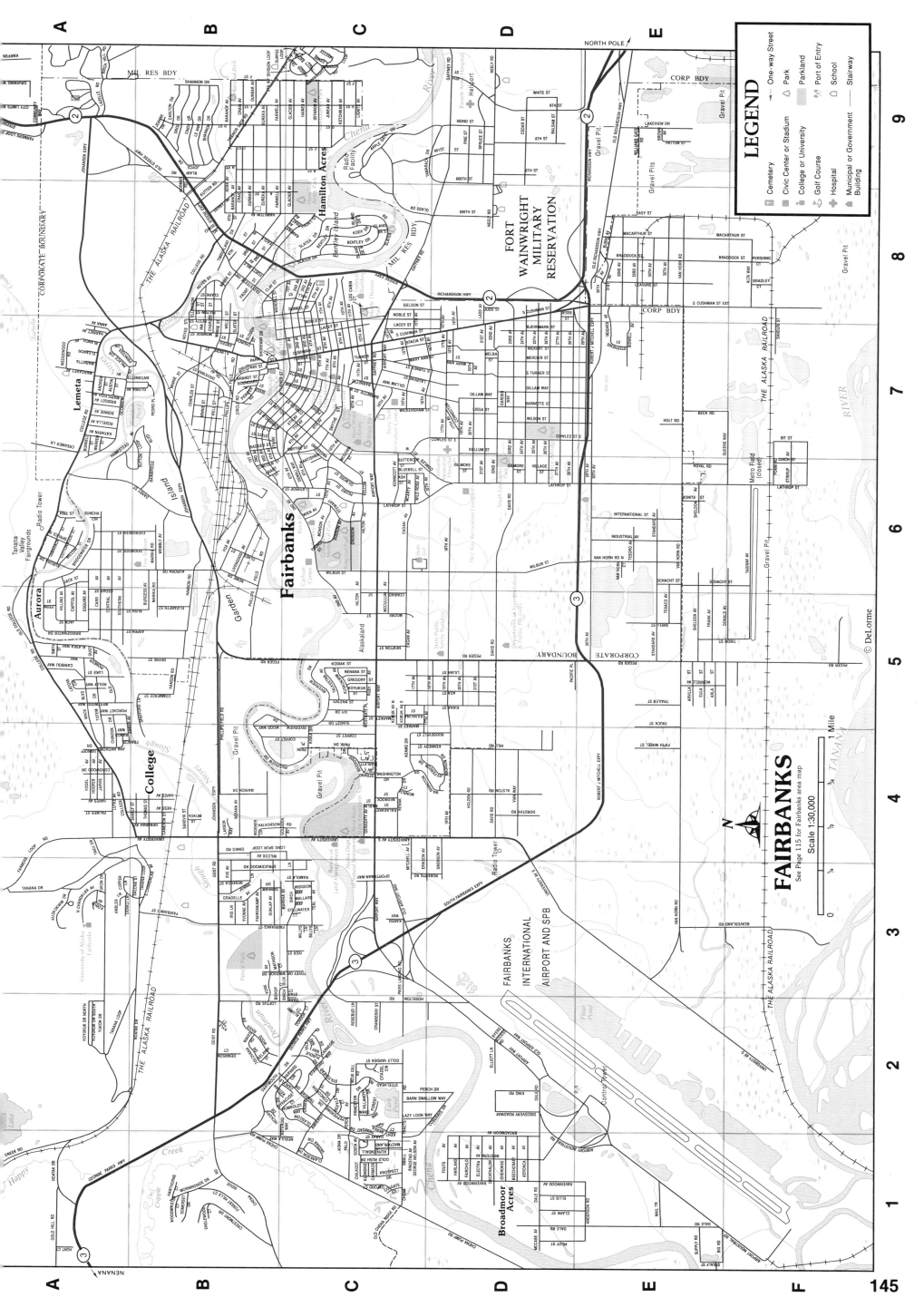

FAIRBANKS

See Page 115 for Fairbanks area map

Scale 1:30,000

Index of Placenames and Physical Features

ABOUT THE INDEX

This index contains more than 16,000 features shown on the maps on pages 16–141. Names are listed alphabetically, followed by their respective map page(s) and grid coordinates to help locate them.

Guidelines for using this index:

- boldface type is used for placenames (cities, towns, crossroads etc.); example: **Fairbanks** 115 A5;
- italic type is used for drainage names (lakes, rivers, creeks, harbors, glaciers, icefields, fiords, canals, lagoons, springs, etc.); example: *Yukon River* 110 A2;
- roman type is used for all other features (mountains, islands, rocks, points, capes, peninsulas, parks, forests, wildlife refuges, lighthouses, major highways, airports, landing strips and seaplane bases, etc.); example: Admiralty Island 27 B4;
- different features having the same name are listed separately;
- grid coordinates are given for each occurrence of a feature name;
- names beginning with Cape, Lake, Mount, Point, Port and The have been indexed by the primary part of the name; example: McKinley, Mount 103 D4;
- rivers and creeks are listed by the main tributary name, followed by the fork where applicable; example: *Blue River, West Fork* 25 C4;
- features found in Canada are followed by asterisks; example: **Bennett*** 38 A3.

Abbreviations used in the index:
AF–Air Force CG–Coast Guard LS–Landing Strip SPB–Seaplane Base

A

A B Mountain 38 B2
Aaron Creek 25 B3
Aaron Island 32 C3
Aats Bay 18 A1
Aats Point 18 A1
Abalone Island 17 A3
Abbe, Mount 31 A3
Abbess Island 19 B3
Abdallah, Mount 31 A4
Abercrombie Gulch 85 D5
Abercrombie Mountain 85 C5
Abernathy Creek 70 B3
Abraham Bay 140 A1
Abraham Islands 24 D1
Abyss Lake 31 B4
Ac Point 60 B2
Ace Creek 115 A5
Acheredin Point 139 C3
Achilles Mountain 20 C1
Ackerman Lake 137 C5
Acme Creek 76 D3
Acme Creek 126 D3
Acorn Peak 48 A2
Ada, Mount 22 B2
Adagdak, Cape 141 C5
Adair, Mount 71 C4
Adak 141 D5
Adak Island 141 D5
Adak Naval Air Station LS (Mitchell Field) 141 D5
Adak Strait 141 D5
Adam Mountains 21 B3
Adams Glacier 32 A1
Adams Inlet 31 A5; 32 A1
Adams Peak 119 A6
Adams Point 19 B4
Adams Point 20 D1
Addington, Cape 18 C2
Addison Glacier 63 A5
Admiralty Bay 135 B6
Admiralty Cove 33 D3
Admiralty Creek 33 D3
Admiralty Island 27 B4; 28 A1; 33 D3
Admiralty Island National Monument-Kootznoowoo Wilderness 27 B4
Adolph Knopf, Mount 33 B3
Adolphus, Point 32 C1
Adugak Island 141 B4
Aello Peak 89 C4
Aeolian Hills 122 D3
Aeolus Mountain 47 A3
Afanasa Creek 70 B3
Affleck Canal 23 D3
Afognak 53 D4
Afognak Bay 53 D4
Afognak Island 45 A4; 53 C4
Afognak Lake 53 D4
Afognak Mountain 53 D4
Afognak Point 45 A4
Afognak River 53 D4
Afognak Strait 45 A4
Afonasi Lake 70 B2
Agashashok River 133 A4
Agassiz Glacier 36 A1
Agassiz Lakes 36 A1; 77 D5
Agassiz Mountain 20 D2
Agassiz Peak 29 D4
Agattu Island 140 A1
Agattu Strait 140 A1
Agcklarok 130 B2
Ageklekak 130 B2
Agenuk Mountain 56 A3
Aggie Creek 125 D4
Aghik Island 139 B5
Aghiyuk Island 139 B5
Agiak Lake 136 B2
Agiapuk River 132 C2
Agligadak Island 140 B2
Agnes Cove 63 A5
Agripina Bay 42 D2
Agripina River 42 D1
Aguchik Island 52 C1
Aguirre Bay 18 B3
Aguirre, Point 18 B3
Aguliak Islands 72 C2
Aguligik Island 52 C1
Aguliuk Point 141 A4
Agulowak River 56 C2
Agulukpak River 56 B2
Ahduck Bay 35 B3
Ahklun Mountains 54 D2
Aho Glacier 68 A2
Aho Lake 81 B4
Ahrnklin River 35 C4
Ahtell Creek 97 A6
Ahtell Creek 98 B1
Ahtell Creek, West Fork 97 A6
Aiak, Cape 141 A5
Aiaktalik 64 C2
Aiaktalik Cove 64 C3
Aiaktalik Island 64 C3
Aialik Bay 63 A5
Aialik Cape 63 B5
Aialik Glacier 63 A5
Aialik Peninsula 63 A5
Aiautak Lagoon 134 D1
Aichilik River 137 A7
Aiken Cove 20 D1
Aiken Creek 20 D1
Aiken Lake 20 D1
Aiktak Island 138 D1
Airs Hill 99 B6
Ajax Reef 20 D2
Akalura Creek 44 D1
Akalura Lake 44 D1
Akamunuk Creek 55 A4
Akeku Point 17 C3
Akhiok 64 B2
Akhiok Bay 64 B2
Akhiok Island 64 B2
Akhiok LS 64 B2
Akhiok Reef 64 B2
Akiachak 131 D4
Akiachak LS 131 D4
Akiachak SPB 131 D4
Akiak 131 D4
Akiak Creek 133 A6
Akiak LS 131 D4
Akillik River 133 A6
Akjemguiga Cove 60 D1
Aklek, Cape 43 B3
Aklumayuak Creek 133 A5
Akoliakatat Pass 134 B2
Akolmiut 130 D3
Akula Lake 69 B5
Akulikutak River 131 D4
Akuluktok Peak 56 B2
Akulurak 130 D3
Akumsuk 130 B2
Akumwarvik Bay 60 D1
Akun Bay 138 D1
Akun Island 138 D1
Akunik Pass 134 C2
Akusha Island 28 C2
Akutan 138 D1
Akutan Island 138 D1
Akutan SPB 138 D1
Akuyan, Cape 141 C5
Akwe Lake 35 C5
Akwe River 35 C5
Alabama Creek 123 D6
Alabama Creek 125 B4
Alaganik 74 C2
Alaganik Slough 74 C2
Alagnak River 58 D1, D3
Alagogshak Creek 51 D4
Alai Creek 42 C1
Alai, Mount 42 C1
Alaid Island 140 A2
Alakanuk 130 B2
Alakanuk LS 130 B2
Alaktak 135 B6
Alaktak River 135 B6
Alargate Rocks 18 B3
Alaska Chilkat Bald Eagle Preserve 38 C1
Alaska Highway 99 A5, B6; 107 A4, A5, B6; 108 B1, C2, C3; 109 D4, D5; 116 D3
Alaska Maritime National Wildlife Refuge—Alaska Peninsula Unit 139 B5
Alaska Maritime National Wildlife Refuge—Aleutian Islands Unit 140 D3
Alaska Maritime National Wildlife Refuge—Bering Sea Unit 139 A4
Alaska Maritime National Wildlife Refuge—Chukchi Sea Unit 134 D1
Alaska Maritime National Wildlife Refuge—Gulf of Alaska Unit 53 A4
Alaska Peak 28 D3
Alaska Peninsula 42 C1; 49 C5; 50 C1; 52 B1; 138 D2
Alaska Peninsula National Wildlife Refuge 139 B4
Alaska Range 80 D1; 91 D6; 92 B1; 103 D4; 104 C2; 108 D1
Alatna 136 D2
Alatna Hills 136 D2
Alatna River 136 C2
Alava Bay 20 D2
Alava Ridge 20 C2
Alava, Point 20 D2
Albert Channel 49 A5
Albert Creek 43 A3
Albert Creek 95 D6
Albert Creek 127 B5
Albert Lake 102 C2
Albert Ridge 25 C4
Alberto Islands 19 B3
Alder Camp 125 D6
Alder Creek 23 C4
Alder Creek 44 C2
Alder Creek 71 A4
Alder Creek 81 B4
Alder Creek 93 A5
Alder Creek 99 C4
Alder Creek 103 A6
Alder Creek 115 A4
Alder Creek 119 A4
Alder Creek 119 A4
Alder Creek 119 C5
Alder Creek 119 D5
Alder Creek 124 B1
Alder Creek 125 D6
Alder Creek 128 D1
Alder Lake 107 D4
Alder Rock 31 C4
Alder Stream 34 B2
Alecks Creek 23 B3
Alecks Lake 23 B3
Aleknagik 56 C2
Aleknagik LS (New) 56 C2
Aleknagik Mission LS (Private) 56 C2
Aleknagik SPB 56 C2
Aleknagik, Lake 56 C2
Aleut Point 140 D2
Aleut Village 53 D4
Aleutian Islands 138 D1; 140 A1, C2
Aleutian Range 60 C1; 67 D5; 68 C1
Aleutian Rock 44 C2
Aleutkina Bay 22 A1; 27 D3
Alexander 82 C1
Alexander Creek 82 B1
Alexander Glacier 35 A4
Alexander Island 53 D4
Alexander Lake 82 A1
Alexander, Lake 28 B1
Alexander, Mount 35 A4
Alexander, Point 24 B1
Alexander, Port 22 D2
Alexanders Village 137 D6
Alexcy Lake 59 A5
Alf Island 44 C2
Alfred Creek 84 A2
Alfred Creek 125 A4
Alger Peak 80 A2
Alice Island 131 A5
Alice Lake 28 C3
Alice Peak 24 D1
Alice Peak 87 B4
Alice Rock 18 A2
Alice, Mount 71 D4
Alice, Port 18 A2
Aligo Point 63 B5
Aliksemit Island 139 C5
Alikula Bay 18 A1
Alinchak Bay 43 A4
Alitak Bay 64 C2
Alitak Lagoon 64 B2
Alitak Shoal 64 C2
Alitak SPB 64 B2
Alitak, Cape 64 C2
Aliulik Peninsula 65 B3
All Gold Creek 105 A4
All Hand Help Lake 114 A2
Allah Creek 56 C2
Allakaket 136 D2
Allakaket LS 136 D2
Allan Point 27 D3
Allard Creek 123 A4
Allen Airfield 106 A3
Allen Creek 115 A4
Allen Creek 123 D5
Allen Creek 130 B3
Allen River 75 A3
Allen River 136 C3
Allen, Mount 99 D4
Alligator Island 53 C4
Allison Creek 85 D5
Alma Lakes 113 D5
Aloha Creek 123 C6
Alpenglow, Mount 71 A4
Alphabet Hills 96 A1
Alpine Cove 44 D2
Alpine Creek 105 D6
Alpine Lake 70 C2
Alsek Glacier 36 D1
Alsek Ranges* 36 B3
Alsek River 35 D5; 36 D1
Alsek River LS 36 D1
Alteration Creek 107 D6
Althorp Peninsula 31 D5
Althorp, Mount 31 D5
Althorp, Port 31 D5
Aluklik Bay 72 D1
Alverstone Glacier 37 A5
Alverstone, Mount 37 A5
Alvin Bay 23 C4
Alyeska 71 A4
Alyeska, Mount 71 A4
Amagalik, Cape 141 D4
Amagat Island 138 D2
Amak Island 138 C2
Amakatatee Creek 55 A4
Amakdedori (Site) 60 C1
Amakdedori Creek 60 C1
Amakdedulia Cove 60 D1
Amalik Bay 51 D5
Amanka Lake 56 D1
Amargura, Point 19 C3
Amarilla Point 18 C2
Amatignak Island 141 D3
Amatusuk Hills 134 C2
Amber Bay 139 B5
Amber Lake 93 D5
Ambler 133 A7
Ambler LS 133 A6
Ambler Peak 23 A4
Ambler River 133 A7
Amchitka Island 140 D2
Amchitka Pass 141 D3
Amee Bay 45 D3
Amee Island 45 D3
Amelia, Point 26 D2
Amelius Island 23 D4
Amelius, Point 23 D4
American Bay 17 A3
American Creek 51 A3
American Creek 70 B3
American Creek 111 D5
American Creek 119 B6
American Creek 123 D4
American Creek 126 C2
American Creek LS 123 D4
American Pass 70 B3
American River 45 B4
American River 132 C3
Amherst Glacier 84 D2
Amherst Peak 33 B4
Amik Island 64 B2
Amiloyak Lake 136 B2
Amlia Island 140 B2
Amlia Pass 140 B1
Amook Bay 44 B2
Amook Bay SPB 44 C2
Amook Island 44 B2
Amos Lakes 92 A1
Amphitheater Knob 34 A3
Amphitheater Mountains 106 D2
Amphitheatre Creek 88 B2
Amukta Island 140 B3
Amukta Pass 140 B3
Amy Creek 75 A5; 87 D5
Amy Creek 125 B4
Amy Creek 125 B4
Amy Dome 125 B4
Anaconda Creek 99 D6
Anaconda Creek 116 A1; 126 D1
Anakruak 135 B7
Anaktuvuk Pass 136 B3
Anaktuvuk Pass LS 136 B2
Anaktuvuk River 136 B3
Anan Bay 25 D3
Anan Creek 25 D3
Anan Creek, East Fork 25 D3
Anan Creek, East Fork 25 D3
Anan Lake 25 D3
Anchor Cove 44 D1
Anchor Cove 64 A1
Anchor Island 17 A4
Anchor Pass 20 A2
Anchor Point 47 A4
Anchor Point 62 A1
Anchor Point 62 A1
Anchor River 62 B1
Anchor River and Fritz Creek State Critical Habitat Area 62 B1
Anchor River State Recreation Area 62 A1
Anchor River State Recreation Site 62 B1
Anchor River, North Fork 62 A1
Anchorage 83 D3
Anchorage Coastal Wildlife Refuge 82 D3
Anchorage International Airport 82 D2
Anchorage Point 38 D1
Ancon Rock 32 C1
Ancon, Point 24 C1
Andersen Creek 19 B4
Anderson 114 C2
Anderson Bay 73 C4
Anderson Bay 85 D4
Anderson Creek 73 C4
Anderson Creek 82 B1
Anderson Creek 116 A3
Anderson Glacier 85 D4
Anderson Glacier 89 D5
Anderson Mountain 105 A5
Anderson Pass 85 D4
Anderson Pass 103 C6
Anderson Peak 71 B4
Anderson Point 20 C1
Anderson, Mount 33 C3
Anderson, Mount 33 C4
Anderson, Mount 89 D5
Andreafsky River 130 B3
Andreafsky River, East Fork 130 B3
Andrean Bay 53 B5
Andreanof Islands 141 D4
Andrew Creek 24 B2
Andrew Creek 41 B5
Andrew Creek 128 C3
Andrew Creek, South Fork 24 B2
Andrew Island 24 B2
Andrew Slough 24 B2
Andrew, Mount 19 B4
Andronica Island 139 C3
Andrus Peak 88 C3
Andy Simons Mountain 71 C4
Aneskett Point 23 D4
Angel Creek 126 D2
Angel Lake 19 B4
Angel, The 79 B4
Angle Creek 50 D3
Angoon 27 B4
Angoon SPB 27 B4
Angoyakik Pass 136 A1
Anguilla Bay 18 B2
Anguilla Island 18 B2
Anguk Island 44 B2
Angun River 137 A7
Angutikada Peak 133 B7
Anguvik Island 139 B4
Angyoyaravak Bay 130 C1
Aniak 131 C5
Aniak Airport and SPB 131 C4
Aniak Lake 131 D5
Aniak River 131 C5
Aniakchak Bay 139 B5
Aniakchak Caldera 139 B5
Aniakchak Crater 139 B4
Aniakchak National Monument and Preserve 139 B5
Aniakchak River 139 B4
Aniktun Island 130 C1
Animas Island 18 B3
Anirak, Lake 133 A7
Anisak River 134 D4
Anisom Point 62 B2
Anita Bay 24 D2
Anita Point 24 D2
Aniuk River 135 D5
Anman Creek 38 C1
Anmer Creek 28 A2
Anmer, Point 28 A2
Ann Creek 106 C3
Anna, Lake 26 B1
Annahootz Mountain 27 C3
Annette Bay 20 C1
Annette Island 20 D1
Annette Island Airport 20 D1
Annette Point 20 D2
Annex Creek 33 C4
Annex Lakes 33 C4
Annin Glacier 85 D4
Anogok 130 D3
Another River 80 D1
Anotleneega Mountain 120 B3
Anowik Island 139 C5
Ansley Island 32 D2
Answer Creek 93 D6; 94 D1
Antelope Creek 110 C2
Anthracite Ridge 84 A1
Antimony Creek 104 D2
Antimony Creek 117 C6
Antipatr Lake 22 C2
Antitonnie Creek 60 A3
Antlen River 35 C4
Antler Creek 99 C4
Antler Glacier 33 A3
Antler Lake 32 A3
Antler Lake 70 A2
Antler Peaks 33 B5
Antler River 32 A3
Anton Larsen Bay 45 A4
Antoski Creek 110 D2
Anvik 131 B4
Anvik LS 131 B4
Anvik River 131 B4
Anvik SPB 131 B4
Anvil Bay 56 B2
Anvil Creek 127 D4
Anvil Mountain 43 C5
Anvil Peak 140 D3
Any Creek 115 A5; 125 D5
Anyaka Island 38 D2
Apatiki Camp 138 A1
Apavawook Cape 138 A3
Ape Point 21 D2
Apex Mountain 26 A1
Aphrewn River 130 C2
Apocalypse, The 79 B4
Apokak 130 D3
Appel Mountain 100 D2
Applegate Creek 124 D1
Applegate Glacier 71 C5
Applegate Island 72 B1
Applegate Rock 72 C3
Appleton Cove 27 C3
Approach Point 20 C1
April Creek 136 C1
Aquada Cove 18 C3
Aquadulce Creek 35 A3
Aqueda Point 19 C3
Arboleda, Point 18 C3
Arcada Rock 18 C2
Arcana Creek 56 D2
Arch Rock 62 D3
Archimandritof Shoals 62 B2
Archuelinguk River 130 B3
Arctic Circle 132 B2; 136 D3
Arctic Creek 118 A3
Arctic Dome 118 A3
Arctic Lagoon 132 B2
Arctic Lake 70 D2
Arctic National Wildlife Refuge 136 B4
Arctic Ocean 134 A1; 135 C6
Arctic River 132 C2
Arctic Village 137 B6
Arctic Village LS 137 B5
Arden, Point 33 D4
Arena Cove 18 D3
Arhymot Lake 131 C4
Ariadne Cove 63 C4
Ariadne Island 63 C3
Arkansas Creek 119 D6
Arkose Peak 83 A4
Arkose Ridge 83 B4
Arm Mountain 17 C3
Armeria Bay 140 A1
Armeria Point 140 A1
Armour, Mount 35 A5
Armstrong Point 22 C2
Armstrong, Port 22 C2
Army Heliport 83 C3
Arness Lake LS 69 B5
Arness Lake SPB 69 B5
Arnkil Island 53 D4
Arolik 54 B1
Arolik Gap 54 B2
Arolik Lake 54 C2
Arolik River 54 B1
Arolik River, East Fork 54 B2
Arolik River, North Mouth 54 B1
Arolik River, South Fork 54 C2
Arolik River, South Mouth 54 B1
Aropuk Lake 130 C3
Arovirchagk 130 B2
Arrandale* 17 C4
Arrecife Point 18 C3
Arriaga Passage 18 B2
Arrow Creek 107 A4
Arrowhead Peak 27 D3
Art Lewis Glacier 35 A5
Arthur Peak 33 D5
Arvesta Creek 133 D6
Asbestos Creek 123 A5
Ascension, Mount 71 C4
Ash Creek 122 C1
Ashiiak Island 42 D2
Ashington Range* 21 D4
Ashivak (Site) 60 D1
Ashmun, Mount* 37 B5
Asigyukpak Spit 46 B2
Asik Mountain 133 A4
Askinuk Mountains 130 C2
Aspen Creek 95 C4
Aspen Lake 70 A2
Aspero Peak 84 C3
Aspid Cape 22 B1
Astley, Point 28 B2
Aston Island 17 A3
Astrolabe Bay 31 C4
Astrolabe Peninsula 31 C4
Astrolabe Point 31 C4
Astrolabe Rocks 31 C4
Astronomical Point 21 D4
Asumcion, Port 18 C2
Ata-ai-ach Mountain 55 A4
Ataakas Camp 138 A2
Atahgo Point 130 D2
Ataku Island 22 A1
Atamautsitlguar Mountain 54 C2
Atayak Mountain 55 A5
Atchuelinguk River 131 B4
Atigaru Point 135 B7
Atigun Pass 136 B4
Atigun River 136 B4
Atka 140 B1
Atka Island 140 B1
Atka LS 140 B1
Atka Pass 140 B1
Atkins Island 139 C4
Atkulik Island 139 B5
Atlakumtsitak Mountain 54 C2
*Atlin Lake** 39 C5
Atmautluak LS 130 D3
Atmo Mountain 43 A4
Atmugiak Creek 55 A4
Atna Peaks 88 A1
Atqasak 135 B5
Atqasak LS 135 B5
Atrevida Glacier 34 A3; 37 B3
Atsaksovluk Creek 131 D5
Atshichlut Mountain 55 B5
Attu 140 A1
Attu Island 140 A1
Attu Mountain 140 A1
Atuk Mountain 138 A2
Atushagvik, Cape 52 D1
Atutsak River 122 D1
Atwater Creek 109 A5; 119 D5
Audrey, Port 72 C2
Audubon Mountain 85 C4
August Hill 68 D2
Augusta Glacier 36 A2
Augusta, Mount 36 A2
Augusta, Point 32 D3
Augustana Creek 106 C3
Augustana Glacier 106 C3
Augustin Peak 92 C1
Augustine Bay 16 A2
Augustine Island 60 C2
Augustine Volcano 60 C3
Augustine, Cape 16 A2
Auk Bay 72 D1
Auke Bay 33 C3
Auke Bay 33 C3
Auke Lake 33 C3
Auke Mountain 33 C3
Aurel, Lake 45 B4
Aurora Creek 119 A5
Aurora Glacier 31 B4
Aurora Lagoon 62 B2
Aurora Lodge 116 C1
Aurora Peak 106 B1
Aurora Point 17 B3
Aurora Spit 62 B2
Automatic Creek 91 C6
Avak Creek 135 A5
Avak River 134 B3
Avalanche Canyon 33 A4
Avalanche Mountain 83 D3
Avalik River 134 B4
Avalitkok Creek 134 B4
Avatanak Island 138 D1
Avatanak Strait 138 D1
Avery River 72 A2
Avingak Creek 134 C3
Avnulu Creek 44 D2
Avon Island 19 A4
Avoss Lake 22 B2
Awayak Creek 55 C3
Awayak Lake 55 B3
Awuna River 135 C5; 136 A1
Axel Lind Island 72 A2
Ayakulik 43 D6
Ayakulik Island 43 D6
Ayakulik River 43 C5; 44 C1
Ayiyak River 136 B2
Aylesworth, Mount 35 A5
Ayugadak Point 140 C2
Azimuth Point 21 C4
Azimuth Point 45 A5
Azun River 130 C2

B

Babbler Point 24 C2
Babe Island 20 D1
Babel River 79 B3
Babel Tower 79 B4
Baby Creek 119 D6
Baby Glacier 84 D2
Babybasket Hill 101 D5
Bachatna Creek 69 A3
Bachatna Creek, West Fork 69 A4
Bachatna Flats 69 A3
Bachelor Creek 126 C2
Back Bay 53 D4
Back Island 20 B1
Back Range 60 B3
Backbone Mountain 21 D3
Bacon Creek 33 B5
Bacon Creek 121 B5
Bacon Glacier 33 B5
Bactrian Point 21 D3
Badger Bay 21 D3
Badger Hill 62 D1
Badger Lake 21 D3
Bagley Ice Field 76 B2
Bagot, Mount 38 C2
Bahovec Peak 27 D4
Baht Harbor 24 C1
Bailey Bay 20 A1
Bailey Creek 123 D4
Bailey Rock 20 C1
Bainbridge Glacier 72 D1
Bainbridge Island 72 D1
Bainbridge Passage 72 D1
Bainbridge Point 72 D1
Bainbridge, Port 64 A3; 72 D1
Bains Cove 24 B1
Baird Canyon 75 B3
Baird Glacier 29 D4
Baird Inlet 130 D2
Baird Island 26 B1
Baird Lake 83 B4
Baird Mountains 133 A4
Baird Peak 19 A4
Baked Mountain 51 C4
Baker 113 A6
Baker Creek 101 B5
Baker Creek 111 D6
Baker Creek 113 A6; 123 D5, D6
Baker Creek, North Fork 123 D5
Baker Glacier 84 D1
Baker Island 18 C2
Baker Lake 123 D6
Baker Memorial LS 133 B5
Baker Point 19 B4
Baker, Mount 26 A1
Bakewell Arm 21 C3
Bakewell Lake 21 D3
Balandra Island 19 C3
Balboa Bay 139 C3
Balchen, Mount 106 B1
Bald Head 133 D5
Bald Head Chris Island 72 A2
Bald Hill 61 B3
Bald Mountain 18 B2
Bald Mountain 20 A1
Bald Mountain 30 B3
Bald Mountain 62 A2
Bald Mountain 94 C1
Bald Mountain 103 C6
Bald Mountain Ridge 83 B4
Bald Peak 18 A2
Bald Ridge 20 D1
Baldry Creek 115 A4
Baldry Mountain 123 C6
Baldwin Glacier 77 B5
Baldwin Peninsula 133 B4
Baldwin, Mount 89 B3
Baldy Bay 19 D4
Baldy Lake 94 D1
Baldy Mountain 77 A3
Baleful Peak 83 C5
Balika Basin 45 A5
Ballena Islands 19 C3
Baltimore Glacier 84 C2
Ban Island 53 C4
Bancas Point 35 A3
Band Cove 23 A3
Banddana Creek 122 B2
Banded Mountain 25 B4
Banks, Point 53 B5
Banks, Port 22 B1
Banner Creek 110 D1
Banner Creek 116 C2
Banner Lake 22 B2
Barabara Cove 45 A4
Barabara Creek 62 C1
Barabara Lake 70 A2
Barabara Point 62 C1
Baranof 27 D4
Baranof Island 22 A2; 27 C3
Baranof Lake 27 D4
Baranof River 27 D3
Barbara Point 44 C1
Barbara, Lake 83 C4
Barber, Point 73 C4
Bard Peak 71 B5
Bare Island 45 A3
Barkley Lake 76 B2
Barkley Ridge 76 C2
Barling Bay 44 D3
Barlow Cove 32 C3
Barlow Islands 32 C3
Barlow Point 32 C3
Barnabas Rock 45 D4
Barnabas, Cape 45 D4
Barnacle Rock 24 D1
Barnard Glacier 84 D2
Barnard Glacier 89 D4
Barnard, Mount 37 D4
Barnes Cove 72 C2
Barnes Lake 24 D1
Barnes Lake 25 B3
Barnes, Point 24 D1
Barness, Mount 26 A1
Barnette Creek 85 A4
Barney Creek 119 A5
Barnhart LS 97 B5
Barnum 54 C2
Barnum Creek 54 C2
Barometer Mountain 45 A4
Barrel Island 82 C1
Barren Creek 102 D3
Barren Island 16 D2
Barren Islands 53 A5
Barren Lake 102 D1
Barren Mountain 19 C4
Barrett Creek 75 D4
Barrie Lake 23 C4
Barrie, Point 23 C4
Barrier Creek 21 A3
Barrier Glacier 80 D3
Barrier Islands 17 A4
Barrier Islands 23 D4
Barrier Range 51 D5
Barrille, Mount 93 A5
Barrow 135 A5
Barrow, Point 135 A5
Barry Glacier 84 D1
Barry Lagoon 45 C5
Bart Lake 33 D4
Bartell Creek 98 A1
Barter Island AF LS 137 A7
Bartholf Creek 83 A4
Bartholomew Creek 21 C3
Bartlett Cove 32 C1
Bartlett Cove SPB 32 C1
Bartlett Glacier 71 B4
Bartlett Hills 94 C1
Bartlett Lake 32 B1
Bartlett Point 27 D4
Bartlett Point 28 D2
Bartlett River 32 B1
Bartolome, Cape 18 D2
Barwell Island 64 A1
Basalt Lake 106 D2
Basargin, Mount 24 B2
Basco Island 122 D1
Bashful Peak 83 C5
Basin Creek 75 C4
Basin Creek 92 A2
Basin Creek 110 C1
Basin Creek LS 132 D3
Basin Lake 20 C2
Basin, The 27 C4
Basket Bay 27 B4
Basket Creek 27 B3
Basket Lake 27 B4
Bass Harbor 72 B3
Bass Point 20 D2
Bassie, Mount 27 D3
Bat Point 20 B2
Bates Creek 81 A5
Bates Creek 127 C4
Battery Islets 24 B1
Battery Point 38 D2
Battle Creek 62 A3
Battle Glacier 33 B3
Battle Lake 59 D5
Baturin Lake 22 C2
Batza River 121 A4
Batza Slough 120 A2
Batzulnetas 98 B1
Baultoff Creek 99 D6
Baultoff Lakes 88 C2
Bautista Peak 19 C3
Bay Creek 71 A3
Bay Lake 69 C5
Bay of Islands 51 B3
Bay of Isles 72 C2
Bay of Isles, Short Arm 72 C2
Bay of Isles, South Arm 72 C2
Bay of Isles, West Arm 72 C2
Bay of Pillars 23 B3
Bay of Waterfalls 141 D5
Bay Point 24 C1
Bay Point 28 D3
Bay Point Knoll 28 D3
Bayard, Mount 25 A4
Bazan, Point 17 A3
Bazan, Port 17 A3
Bazil, Point 65 A4
Beach Creek 84 A2
Beach Lake 83 C3
Beach River 72 D3
Beacon Island 23 A4
Beak Point 16 A2
Bean Creek 70 C3
Bean Island 17 B4
Bean Lake 98 B3
Bean Ridge 113 A4
Bean Ridge 123 D5
Bear Bay 43 A4
Bear Canyon 62 B2
Bear Cape 73 C4
Bear Cove 62 B2
Bear Cove 63 A5
Bear Cove Farm LS (Private) 62 B2
Bear Creek 24 B1
Bear Creek 28 B1
Bear Creek 32 C3
Bear Creek 42 B3
Bear Creek 45 A4
Bear Creek 54 C2
Bear Creek 56 C2
Bear Creek 56 C2
Bear Creek 57 D5
Bear Creek 59 A5
Bear Creek 68 D2
Bear Creek 70 D1
Bear Creek 71 A3
Bear Creek 73 C4
Bear Creek 81 B5; 82 B1
Bear Creek 86 C2
Bear Creek 88 C1
Bear Creek 91 A4
Bear Creek 91 C6
Bear Creek 93 B5
Bear Creek 93 C5
Bear Creek 97 C4
Bear Creek 98 A3
Bear Creek 103 A4, B4
Bear Creek 103 B4
Bear Creek 106 B3
Bear Creek 107 B6; 108 B1
Bear Creek 108 D3
Bear Creek 114 D2
Bear Creek 115 B6
Bear Creek 117 B4
Bear Creek 119 B5
Bear Creek 122 D2
Bear Creek 123 C4
Bear Creek 124 C1
Bear Creek 125 A4
Bear Creek 125 D6
Bear Creek 126 C1
Bear Creek 126 C3
Bear Creek 127 B4
Bear Creek 127 D4
Bear Creek 128 C2
Bear Creek 128 D2
Bear Creek 133 D7
Bear Creek No 1 LS 133 C5
Bear Draw 103 B6
Bear Glacier 63 A5; 71 D3
Bear Glacier Point 63 A5
Bear Gulch 110 C2
Bear Harbor 23 C3
Bear Island 27 C2
Bear Island 36 D1
Bear Island 44 B1
Bear Island 53 C4
Bear Island 59 D4
Bear Island 62 B2
Bear Island 88 D3
Bear Island Lake 101 C6
Bear Lake 20 B1
Bear Lake 27 D3
Bear Lake 63 A5
Bear Lake 68 C3
Bear Lake 70 B2
Bear Lake 71 D4
Bear Lake 96 D1
Bear Lake 98 B3
Bear Lake 113 A5
Bear Lake 139 C3
Bear Mountain 19 D3
Bear Mountain 27 D3
Bear Mountain 70 C2
Bear Mountain 71 D4
Bear Mountain 120 A2
Bear Mountain 128 A3
Bear Mountain 137 B7
Bear Mountain 137 D7
Bear Mountain Creek 128 A3
Bear Pass Mountain 28 C1
Bear Point 44 C1
Bear Point 63 B4
Bear River 139 B3
Bear River 139 C3
Bear Rock 44 D2
Bear Valley 71 A5
Bear, Mount 89 C5
Beardslee Entrance 31 C5; 32 B1
Beardslee Islands 32 B1
Beare Glacier 77 D4
Bearhole Creek 88 D3
Bearpaw 113 D5
Bearpaw Mountain 113 D4
Bearpaw River 103 A5, B5; 113 D5
Beartrack Cove 32 B1
Beartrack Island 32 B1
Beartrack River 32 B1
Beartrap Bay 73 A5
Beasley Creek 35 B4
Beaton Pup 128 C2
Beatson, Mount 72 D2
Beauchamp Island 22 B1
Beauclerc Island 23 C4
Beauclerc Peak 23 C4
Beauclerc, Port 23 C4
Beaufort Lagoon 137 A7
Beaufort Sea 135 A7, D7; 137 A7
Beaufort, Cape 134 C1
Beautiful Island 63 B3
Beauty Bay 63 B3
Beauty Creek 103 B5
Beaver 137 D5
Beaver Bay 138 C3
Beaver Creek 19 C4
Beaver Creek 20 A2
Beaver Creek 20 D2
Beaver Creek 56 B2
Beaver Creek 61 A3
Beaver Creek 62 B2
Beaver Creek 69 B5
Beaver Creek 71 A4
Beaver Creek 89 A5; 99 D5
Beaver Creek 90 B1
Beaver Creek 93 D5
Beaver Creek 99 D6
Beaver Creek 101 C5
Beaver Creek 109 D5
Beaver Creek 110 B2
Beaver Creek 110 D1
Beaver Creek 116 A2
Beaver Creek 122 D1
Beaver Creek 125 B5, C6; 126 A1
Beaver Creek 136 C1
Beaver Creek 137 D5
Beaver Dam Lake 114 A3
Beaver Inlet 141 A5
Beaver Lake 20 C2
Beaver Lake 28 B1
Beaver Lake 45 A5
Beaver Lake 59 C5
Beaver Lake 70 B1
Beaver Lake 82 C2
Beaver Lake 99 D5
Beaver Lake 102 B1
Beaver Lakes 82 B3
Beaver LS 137 D5
Beaver Mountain 19 C4
Beaver Mountain 131 D6
Beaver Peak 89 A4
Beaver Point 26 D2
Beaverlog Lakes 102 A3
Becharof Creek 42 A3
Becharof Lake 42 A2; 50 D1
Becharof National Wildlife Refuge 50 B2
Becharof, Mount 42 B2
Bechevin Bay 138 C2
Beck Island 24 D1
Bede, Mount 62 C1
Bede, Point 62 C1
Bedlam Creek 70 A2
Bedrock Creek 71 A3
Bedrock Creek 109 A6
Bedrock Creek 127 B4
Bee Rocks 16 C1
Beecher Pass 24 B1
Beecher Pass State Marine Park 24 B1
Beechey Point 135 D6
Beehive Island 63 B5
Beehive, The 22 A1
Begich Peak 71 A5
Behm Canal 20 A2, B1; 21 D2
Behm Mountain 21 D2
Behm Narrows 20 A1
Belanger Pass 84 A3
Belcher, Point 134 B3
Belinda Creek 59 C4
Belkofski 138 C2
Bell Arm 20 A1; 25 D4
Bell Island 20 A1
Bell Island 23 C4
Bell Island 26 A2
Bell Island 82 C1
Bell Island Hot Springs 20 A1
Bell Island Hot Springs SPB (Private) 20 A1
Bell Island Lakes 20 A1
Bell Lake 96 C2
Belle Creek 125 D6
Bellen Lakes 101 B6
Bellicose Peak 83 D4
Bellim Bay 42 B2
Bells Butte 73 A4
Beloit Glacier 71 B5
Below the Rock Lake 100 D3
Belt Creek 56 D2
Belt Creek 125 B5
Beluga 81 D5
Beluga Hill 54 D1
Beluga Lake 81 C4
Beluga LS (Private) 81 D5
Beluga Mountain 81 B5
Beluga River 81 C5
Beluga Shoal 82 D1
Beluga Slough 82 C1
Ben Courtny Creek 58 C2
Ben Creek 118 B3
Ben Creek 128 C2
Ben Creek LS 128 C2
Ben Stewart, Mount 33 C3
Ben-My-Chree* 39 C3
Bence Mountain 86 B1
Bench Creek 71 B4
Bench Creek 86 D1
Bench Glacier 86 D1
Bench Lake 71 B4
Bench Lake 83 B3
Bench Lake 84 A2
Bench Peak 71 B4
Bendel, Cape 28 D1
Bendeleben Mountains 132 C4
Bendeleben, Mount 132 C3
Benham, Point 27 C3
Benign Peak 83 C4
Benjamin Creek 70 C2
Benjamin Island 32 B3
Benka Lake 93 D6; 94 D1
Bennett* 38 A3
Benson, Mount 71 D3
Bent Tree Lake 113 B4
Bentinck, Point 73 C5
Benzeman Lake 22 A2
Berg 114 B2
Berg Bay 24 C2
Berg Bay 31 B5
Berg Creek 24 C2
Berg Creek 32 A1
Berg Creek 87 B5
Berg Lake 69 C5
Berg Lakes 75 C5
Berg Mountain 24 C2
Berg Mountain 32 A1
Berger Bay 63 C3
Bergh Lake 103 C6
Bering Creek 111 A5
Bering Glacier 75 D5; 76 C1
Bering Lake 75 C4
Bering Land Bridge National Preserve 132 B3
Bering Point 111 A4
Bering River 75 D4
Bering Sea 47 D3; 54 C1; 130 C1; 132 D1; 138 A2, B1; 139 A3, A5; 140 A2, A3; 141 C3
Bering Slough 111 A4
Bering Strait 132 C1
Bernard Creek 86 B2
Berners Bay 32 B3
Berners Peaks 33 B4
Berners River 32 A2
Bernice Lake 69 B5
Bernice Lake State Recreation Site 69 B5
Berry Camp 127 C4
Berry Creek 107 B5
Berry Creek 126 D1
Berry Island 19 B4
Berry Island 23 A4
Berry Lake 70 A1
Berry Lake 101 C4
Bert Millar Cutoff 17 B4
Bert Point 65 B3
Bertha Bay 26 A1
Bertha Creek 71 A4
Bertha Glacier 38 D1
Bertha, Mount 31 B3
Besboro Island 133 D5
Beshta Bay 81 D5
Bess, Lake 20 A1
Bessie Creek 54 B1
Bessie Peak 24 C2
Beszivit Lake 120 B1
Beth, Lake 82 C3
Bethel 131 D4
Bethel SPB 131 D4
Bettles 136 D2
Bettles Bay 72 A1
Bettles Bay State Marine Park 72 A1
Bettles Glacier 72 A1
Bettles Island 72 D2
Bettles LS 136 D3
Bettles SPB 136 D3
Betton Head 20 B1
Betton Island 20 B1
Betton Point 20 B1
Betty Lake 22 C2
Beverley, Lake 56 B2
Beverley, Lake—Silver Horn 56 B2
Beverly Creek 118 A1; 128 D1
Beyer Bay 141 D5
Biali Rock 22 B1
Bidarka Point 73 A4
Biederman Bluff 128 C3
Bieli Rocks 27 D2
Big Alinchak Bay 43 A4
Big Alinchak Creek 43 A4
Big Bay 22 A1
Big Bay 53 B4
Big Bay 70 D1
Big Bear/Baby Bear Bays State Marine Park 27 B2
Big Bend 110 A3
Big Bend 131 D6
Big Bend Lakes 88 D3
Big Bonanza Creek 66 B2
Big Bones Ridge 95 C6
Big Boulder Creek 37 B5
Big Boulder Creek 119 A6
Big Branch Bay 22 C2
Big Branch Rock 22 C2
Big Castle Island 24 B1
Big Chief Mountain 26 A1
Big Chutes 60 A1
Big Creek 19 D4
Big Creek 23 A4; 28 D2
Big Creek 23 C4
Big Creek 42 B2
Big Creek 49 C5
Big Creek 93 C5
Big Creek 104 B1
Big Creek 109 B6
Big Creek 110 A2, B2
Big Creek 120 C3
Big Creek 121 A5
Big Creek 126 A1; 137 D5
Big Creek 127 A5
Big Creek 128 A1; 137 D7
Big Creek 136 C4
Big Delta 116 D3
Big Delta State Historical Park 116 D3
Big Denver Creek 123 D5
Big Diomede Island (Russia) 132 C1
Big Eightmile Island 133 D6
Big Eldorado Creek 115 A5
Big Flat 49 B5
Big Fort Channel 53 C5
Big Fort Island 53 C5
Big Goat Lake 21 B3
Big Granite Creek 117 B4
Big Grayling Lake 98 B2
Big Grizzly Creek 105 B5
Big Hazy Islet 18 D1
Big Hill 60 C1
Big Horn 115 B6
Big Indian Creek 70 A3
Big Island 26 C2
Big Island 59 C4
Big Island 82 C1
Big Island 110 B1
Big Joe Creek 110 B2
Big John Bay 23 A4
Big John Creek 23 A4
Big John Hill 109 D4
Big John Lake 109 D4
Big Kitoi Lake 53 D5
Big Koniuji Island 139 C4
Big Lake 19 A4
Big Lake 20 C2
Big Lake 82 B3
Big Lake 82 B3
Big Lake 95 A4; 105 D4
Big Lake 102 B1
Big Lake 106 A3
Big Lake 109 D4
Big Lake 114 A2
Big Lake 131 C6
Big Lake 136 C4
Big Lake LS 82 B3
Big Lake North State Recreation Site 82 B3
Big Lake South State Recreation Site 82 B3
Big Lily Lake 102 A3
Big Long Lake 102 B2
Big Mosquito Creek 127 B5
Big Mountain 59 C4
Big Mountain 137 D7
Big Mountain LS (Private) 59 C4
Big Mud River 111 B6; 112 B1
Big Point 74 C1
Big Port Walter 22 C2
Big River 34 D1
Big River 52 B1, B2
Big River 69 A3
Big River 79 A4; 90 B3, C3
Big River Lakes 68 A3
Big River Roadhouse 90 A2
Big River, Lyman Fork 79 A4
Big River, North Fork 68 A3
Big River, North Fork 79 A3; 91 D4
Big River, South Fork 68 B3
Big Rock 53 D4
Big Rock 60 B3

Index continues on next page

Index continues on next page

152

Index continues on next page

Index continues on next page